Poetry in Fragments

Trends in Classics –
Supplementary Volumes

Edited by
Franco Montanari and Antonios Rengakos

Scientific Committee
Alberto Bernabé · Margarethe Billerbeck
Claude Calame · Jonas Grethlein · Philip R. Hardie
Stephen J. Harrison · Stephen Hinds · Richard Hunter
Christina Kraus · Giuseppe Mastromarco · Gregory Nagy
Theodore D. Papanghelis · Giusto Picone · Kurt Raaflaub
Tim Whitmarsh · Bernhard Zimmermann

Volume 50

Poetry in Fragments

Studies on the Hesiodic Corpus and its Afterlife

Edited by
Christos Tsagalis

DE GRUYTER

ISBN 978-3-11-065857-6
e-ISBN (PDF) 978-3-11-053758-1
e-ISBN (EPUB) 978-3-11-053680-5
ISSN 1868-4785

Library of Congress Cataloging-in-Publication Data
A CIP catalog record for this book has been applied for at the Library of Congress.

Bibliographic information published by the Deutsche Nationalbibliothek
The Deutsche Nationalbibliothek lists this publication in the Deutsche Nationalbibliografie; detailed bibliographic data are available in the Internet at http://dnb.dnb.de.

© 2019 Walter de Gruyter GmbH, Berlin/Boston
This volume is text- and page-identical with the hardback published in 2017.
Logo: Christopher Schneider, Laufen
Printing: CPI books GmbH, Leck
♾ Printed on acid-free paper
Printed in Germany

www.degruyter.com

To the three women of my life:
Anna, Alexia, and Konstantina

Acknowledgments

I would like to thank all contributors for their professionalism, diligence, and cooperation. As editor I owe special thanks to the Classics and Ancient History Library of the Aristotle University of Thessaloniki, the staff of which was always eager to help me. Jonathan Ready, my fellow co-editor of the *Yearbook of Ancient Greek Epic*, has also assisted me by providing material that I was unable to find in Thessaloniki. Franco Montanari and Antonios Rengakos are equally to be commended not only for accepting this volume in the series they are directing with admirable results but also for solving any problem that came up. De Gruyter showed remarkable speed and efficiency in all matters pertaining to the production of this volume.

The last word is always personal. It belongs to the three women of my life: Άννα, Αλεξία, and Κωνσταντίνα, whose love and care are a true blessing.

Table of Contents

Note on Transliteration —— XI

Introduction —— XIII

Part I: Genre and Context

†Antonio Aloni
Hesiod Between Performance and Written Record —— 3

Andrea Ercolani
Fragments of Wisdom, Wisdom in Fragments —— 29

Deborah Steiner
Choruses and Catalogues: the Performative and Generic Context of the Asopids in the Hesiodic *Catalogue of Women* —— 47

Malcolm Davies
The Origin of Things: A Study in Contrasts —— 83

Part II: The *Catalogue of Women*

Hugo Koning
Helen, Herakles, and the End of the Heroes —— 99

Kirk Ormand
Helen's Phantom in Fragments —— 115

Irini Kyriakou
Female Ancestors in the Hesiodic *Catalogue of Women* —— 135

Benjamin Sammons
The Hesiodic *Catalogue of Women*: A Competition of Forms —— 163

Christos Tsagalis
Sound-Play in the Hesiodic *Catalogue of Women* —— 191

Part III: Hesiod's Fragments in Rome and Byzantium

Andreas N. Michalopoulos
Hesiodic Traces in Ovid's *Heroides* —— 219

Marta Cardin and Filippomaria Pontani
Hesiod's Fragments in Byzantium —— 245

List of Contributors —— 289

General Index —— 291

Note on Transliteration

With respect to the spelling of Greek proper names and toponyms, I have opted for transliteration instead of offering the latinized form, although in the case of names of ancient authors (Byzantine scholiasts and commentators excluded) I have kept their familiar anglicized or latinized form (e.g. Pindar, not Pindaros; Ibycus, not Ibykos). The same is the case with a handful of names pertaining to historical figures (e.g. Cyrus, not Kyros). I have not followed this practice in Michalopoulos' chapter, in which I have kept the Latin spelling of Greek proper names, since the author is referring to their use in Roman poetry. Greek χ is rendered by ch. I have not indicated macrons over long vowels in transliterated Greek words (e.g. *pheme*, not *phēmē* for Greek φήμη).

When the *Catalogue* is mentioned in this volume, the *Ehoiai* or *Catalogue of Women* are meant. For the 'bigger' *Ehoiai*, only the transliterated form of its Greek title (*Megalai Ehoiai*) is being employed. Fragments are numbered according to the edition by Merkelbach and West, unless specified otherwise (e.g. Sammons cites Hesiodic fragments according to Most's Loeb edition). All translations of Hesiodic passages are taken from Most's Loeb edition (with spelling modifications), unless otherwise stated.

Introduction

One remarkable feature, albeit accidental, of Hesiodic poetry is that with respect to its preserved state it stands between the Homeric epics and fragmentary Greek epic of the archaic period. While the two 'major' Hesiodic works, the *Theogony* and the *Works and Days*, have come down to us in full, nearly all the other poems attributed to Hesiod survive in tattered fragments. Seen from this angle, Hesiodic poetry seems to occupy a special position within the wider matrix of archaic Greek epic: it is both intact and fragmentary.

The study of the *Catalogue*, which represents the larger and most important part of fragmentary Hesiodic epic, can be divided into three phases: the first one begins with G. Marckscheffel's *De Catalogo et Eoeis, carminibus Hesiodiis* (Breslau 1838) and ends in the early and middle 1950s with the publication of R. Merkelbach's work on Hesiodic papyri that introduces the second phase of modern scholarly research on the *Catalogue*. The third phase begins with M. L. West's synthetic monograph on the *Catalogue of Women* in 1985 and continues to the present.

G. Marckscheffel was the first to trace systematic genealogies in the much shorter version of the *Catalogue* available to him at the time. Since one of these genealogies was that of Deukalion's family, it was obvious that the poet of this epic had planned a comprehensive presentation of genealogical stemmata covering all Greece. Marckscheffel's instinct was correct, but he failed to see how the *Ehoiai* could be adapted to such a poem. Partly influenced by the general inclination for analytical arguments so characteristic of 19th-century scholarship with respect to the composition of various ancient works, Homeric epic offering the typical case study, Marckscheffel supposed that the *Ehoiai* were narratives pertaining to a different poem altogether. They were originally separate from the *Catalogue*, only to be inserted at a later stage, after being considerably shortened.[1] This 'additive' principle of interpreting the *Catalogue* as it stood at the time was directly reflected in Marckscheffel's theory concerning the poem's structure: books 1–3 formed the original *Catalogue*, while books 4–5 contained the *Ehoiai*.

This was the prevailing view until 1879, when A. Kirchoff capitalised on a rather *en passant* observation by Marckscheffel pertaining to Io. By postulating the existence of an Io-stemma, Kirchoff had, probably without realising it, set

---

1 Marckscheffel repeated his views in his 1840 edition of archaic epic fragments *Hesiodi, Eumeli, Cinaethonis, Asii et Carmini Naupactii fragmenta*, Leipzig, 119–121.

the stage for the next important step, i.e. the claim that the presentation of genealogical trees in Apollodorus' *Bibliotheke* reflected the original structure of the *Catalogue*. Theodor Bergk[2] drew attention to the correspondence between the presentation of Hellen's family in the *Catalogue* and Apollodorus' *Bibliotheke* suggesting that the later could be used as a tool for the reconstruction of the former. This was a vital observation, which was only partly taken up by C. Robert,[3] who presented a more nuanced picture of the *Catalogue-Bibliotheke* association by stressing not only similarities but differences as well.

A significant place within this first phase of scholarship on the *Catalogue* is occupied by A. Rzach, editor of Hesiod's extant works in the Bibliotheca Teubneriana. Because of the undisputed progress made by the edition of R. Merkelbach and M. L. West (see below), Rzach's edition is often neglected or passed over. This is unfair. Seen within the context of Hesiodic research of his time, and especially of what had been done before him, Rzach's edition marks a decisive step forward from G. Marckscheffel's older edition. What really made Rzach's edition outdated was an external event: the publication of multiple papyri containing extracts from the *Catalogue*. This is accurately explained by R. Merkelbach and M. L. West in the *praefatio* of their edition of *Fragmenta Hesiodea*: 'Postquam Hesiodea annis 1902–1913 edidit vir doctus atque venerabilis Alois Rzach, satis accuratum opus et quod suis temporibus omnino sufficeret, tanta papyracorum accessit copia, ut si quis hodie reliquias Hesiodeas universas vult perlegere, plures requirat libros quam facile una manu comprehendat'.[4]

The second phase in the study of Hesiodic fragmentary epic begins with the 'advent' of the papyri. What had been to that point an almost 'phantom' epic under the title Γυναικῶν Κατάλογος or Κατάλογος gradually acquired 'flesh and bones' and began to yield important data concerning our knowledge not only of Hesiodic epic but also of catalogue-poetry and early hexameter epic writ large. But as in life, so in research, change does not happen overnight. It was 1951 when R. Merkelbach argued, on the basis of new papyri, that persons genealogically connected were treated in the same part of the epic. This was to lead to a fully-fledged account of the 'link' between the *Catalogue* and Apollodorus.[5] 1962 was the *annus mirabilis* for the *Catalogue*, since volume xxviii of the *Oxyrhynchus Papyri*, wholly devoted to Hesiodic poetry, nearly doubled the previously known material. Some years later M. L. West convincingly argued that the

---

2 *Griechische Literaturgeschichte* i. 1002 n. 83, Berlin 1872–1894.
3 *De Apollodori Bibliotheca*, Diss. Berlin 1873, 71.
4 (1967) v.
5 For J. Schwartz's *Pseudo-Hesiodeia*, see below.

available evidence made it almost certain that the arrangement of the genealogies in Apollodorus reflected their much earlier arrangement in the Hesiodic *Catalogue* and that the ἤ' οἵη formula was employed (at least in some cases) as a device that would allow the poet to return 'to branches of a family that he had partly dealt with earlier and then shelved'.[6] The first fruits of the advance that 1962 presaged became evident when R. Merkelbach and M. L. West published the *Fragmenta Hesiodea*. It is no exaggeration to say that, as far as the *Catalogue* was concerned, this was now an entirely new poem laid for inspection before the scholarly community.

1985 inaugurates the third research phase in the study of Hesiodic fragments, when M. L. West published a monograph on the *Catalogue of Women* that set forth a comprehensive theory of the poem's composition, structure, and context. West was reaping the rewards of the meticulous work he and Merkelbach had done on Hesiodic fragments, especially on organizing into a coherent whole the rich papyrus findings together with the indirect tradition. West's book laid the groundwork for further study on the *Catalogue*. The epic's basic structure as exposed in the *Fragmenta Hesiodea* and the analysis of its nature and function by West were accepted *grosso modo* by most scholars of early Greek epic. This paved the way for further research on this tantalizing poem to be carried out on this new solid ground. This phase is characterised by the publication of numerous studies concerning different aspects of the *Catalogue*, such as its language, its presentation of women, its relation to the *Theogony* and the *Megalai Ehoiai*, as well as generic issues pertaining to the nature of this epic and the place it occupies within catalogue poetry at large. It is within the scope of such intense scholarly activity with respect to the *Catalogue* that I. Rutherford published an influential study concerning the thorny question of the poem's genre. According to Rutherford, at some point in the archaic period non-genealogical *ehoie* poetry employing catalogic principles of organization was subordinated to the panhellenic tendency to organize the Greek past through genealogies. The immediate result was that independent *ehoie* narratives were 'anchored' to increasingly normative genealogical superstructure. At a later stage through a process of 'automatization' the *ehoiai* narratives became a secondary concomitant instead of a primary feature defining a given subgenre. By disclosing the existence of an earlier phase in the development of *ehoie* poetry, Rutherford's analysis shed light to the *Catalogue*'s generic identity. What we have

---

[6] The Hesiodic *Catalogue of Women*, Oxford, 1985, 35.

in front of us is a hybrid, the outcome of a generic 'crossing' of *ehoie* narratives into genealogical structures organized in catalogue form.⁷

The single, and probably most important, contribution to the study of the *Catalogue* and its 'twin' epic, the *Megalai Ehoiai*, was that of M. Hirschberger who in 2004 published a detailed commentary on these two epics.⁸ This was the most apparent confirmation of the general consensus that the *Catalogue* had acquired a status comparable to that of the two 'major' Hesiodic poems that had survived intact the test of time. Hirschberger's commentary complemented the commentaries of M. L. West on the *Theogony* and the *Works and Days* and made available to the wider scholarly community all that is necessary for a systematic treatment of each and every surviving fragment. With the publication of Hirschberger's commentary, we see the surfacing of two new directions in the study of Hesiodic poetry: the first is a reconsideration of the order followed by R. Merkelbach and M. L. West with respect to the layout offered in their 1967 edition,⁹ and the second is a growing interest in the study of the *Megalai Ehoiai* alongside the *Catalogue*.

The establishment of the *Catalogue* as an indispensable part of the Hesiodic 'trilogy' was further boosted by a volume of collected essays published by R. Hunter in 2005.¹⁰ This is one of the most influential works in the final phase of the *Catalogue*'s *Forschungsgeschichte* and testifies to a significant increase in the breadth of inquiry directed to this intriguing epic. The *Catalogue* is now seen as having a 'plot' distinct from other comparable early hexameter poetry (R. Osborne), as forming a thematic triptych with the *Theogony* and *Works and Days* (J. Strauss Clay), as well as possessing strong intertextual affinities with sympotic culture and the ideology behind it (E. Irwin). Moreover, scholars now pay more attention to individual figures (Herakles: J. Haubold) and episodes (Mestra: I. Rutherford; Helen's suitors: Cingano), to the relation of the *Catalogue* to other 'Hesiodic' epics (The *Aspis*: R. Martin; the *Megalai Ehoiai*: G.-B. D'Alessio) or to lyric poetry (Pindar and Bacchylides: G.-B. D'Alessio), and to the poem's reception and adaptation in Hellenistic (R. Hunter; H. Asquith) and Roman poetry (Ph. Hardie; R. Fletcher).

---

7 'Formulas, Voice, and Death in *Ehoie*-Poetry, the Hesiodic *Gunaikon Katalogos*, and the Odyssean *Nekuia*', in: M. Depew and D. Obbink (eds.), *Matrices of Genre. Authors, Canons, and Society*, Cambridge, MA, 81–96.
8 Gynaikōn Katalogos *und* Megalai Ēhoiai. Ein Kommentar zu den Fragmenten zweier hesiodeischer Epen, Munich-Leipzig.
9 See also 1990 with a few changes.
10 *The Hesiodic* Catalogue of Women: *Constructions and Reconstructions*, Cambridge.

The tendency for re-ordering a fair amount of the *Catalogue*'s fragments features in the second volume of G. Most's new Loeb edition[11] that replaces, and clearly surpasses, H. Evelyn-White's 1914 Loeb edition. The painstaking efforts by both M. Hirshberger and G. Most to rethink the order of several fragments, while accepting the overarching framework established by R. Merkelbach and M. L. West, is one that scholars should take seriously, even if one prefers to follow the *editores primi*.

The need for a comprehensive presentation of the progress made in Hesiodic studies and the poetry of the *Catalogue* in particular was met by the publication of a *Companion to Hesiod* by F. Montanari, A. Rengakos, and C. Tsagalis in 2009.[12] Apart from a concise presentation of the *status quaestionis* with respect to Hesiodic poetry, this Companion brought to the fore some new areas where further research on the *Catalogue* is needed: poetics (C. Tsagalis), the language of the *Corpus Hesiodeum* (A. C. Cassio), the narrative of the *Catalogue* (A. Rengakos), and ancient scholarship on Hesiod (F. Montanari).

The increase of papyrus findings pertaining to the *Catalogue* resulted not only in a wealth of studies focusing on this epic but also in its partial 'independence' from and among the other fragmentary poems forming the Hesiodic corpus. Turning to these little known epics, we may single out a few scholarly works that have allowed some progress in an area where hypotheses and speculation are the norm, given the desperately fragmentary condition of the relevant material.

J. Schwartz's research (*Pseudo-Hesiodeia. Recherches sur la composition, la diffusion et la disparition ancienne d'oeuvres attribuées à Hésiode*, Leiden 1960) marked an important step in the study of Hesiodic fragments at large. This verdict is based not so much on the results of Schwartz's work as on the material he has put at our disposal. The author offered an exhaustive presentation of the indirect tradition pertaining to the poems of the Hesiodic corpus, covering the entire span of *testimonia* from mythographers, scholiasts, and grammarians, to Christian authors and Byzantine scholars. This is perhaps the best part of Schwartz's detailed monograph. The first section of the second part of his book concerns poems such as *The Marriage of Ceyx*, *The Melampodia*, *The Cheironos Hypothekai*, *The Megalai Ehoiai*, *The Idaean Dactyls*, *The Astronomy*, and *The Aigimios*.

---

11 *Hesiod: The* Shield, Catalogue of Women, *Other Fragments*, Cambridge, MA and London, England.
12 Montanari, F., A. Rengakos, and C. Tsagalis (eds.), *Brill's Companion to Hesiod*, Leiden-Boston.

Although the *Melampodia* became the focus of a monograph (I. Löffler's short yet concise *Die* Melampodie. *Versuch einer Rekonstruktion des Inhalts*, 1963), the Hesiodic poem which attracted more interest, excepting the *Catalogue*, was the *Megalai Ehoiai*. This growing attention is partially due to the number of fragments available, and partially to the poem's relation to the *Catalogue*. In 1979, A. Casanova[13] argued that the *Catalogue* is older than the *Megalai Ehoiai*, the latter having grown out of the former. According to Casanova's theory, the title *Megalai Ehoiai* was meant to designate a longer version of the *Catalogue* published at Pergamum that contained sections excised by Alexandrian scholars. I. M. Cohen[14] (1986) explained the epithet *megalai* in the poem's title as referring to the fact 'that individual *ehoiai* were available in a fuller form, or that more such episodes had been added or retained [...] The existence of two somewhat different editions of essentially the same poem, known to later commentators by name only, may have led to confusion and the belief that there were actually two poems'.[15] One may note the growing appeal of the *Megalai Ehoiai* in M. Hirschberger's detailed commentary (2004) that concerns both the *Catalogue* and the *Megalai Ehoiai*. Shortly thereafter G.-B. D'Alessio wrote one of the most influential pieces on the *Megalai Ehoiai* and their relation to the *Catalogue* ('The *Megalai Ehoiai:* A Survey of the Fragments', 2005).[16] By offering a meticulous reconsideration of the arguments of Schwartz (1960) and Cohen (1986), who both favored the existence of a single epic known by two different titles (*Gynaikon Katalogos* or *Ehoiai* and *Megalai Ehoiai*), and a detailed survey of the extant fragments, D'Alessio has forcefully maintained that the *Megalai Ehoiai* is a separate poem and should be treated in its own right. With respect to the genesis of the the *Megalai Ehoiai*, D'Alessio rightly suggests caution: the *Megalai Ehoiai* may have been a completely independent poem from its conception or it may have grown, as Casanova (1979) suggested, out of the *Catalogue*, or again it may have shared some parts with it.

The other poem of the Hesiodic corpus, again excluding the *Catalogue*, that had attracted considerable scholarly attention is the *Aspis of Herakles*. Although it has come down to us in full through medieval tradition, the *Aspis* has always been studied almost reluctantly by modern scholarship, mainly because of its poetic 'inferiority' in comparison with the genuine Hesiodic works, the *Theogony* and the *Works and Days*. Scholars have interpreted the multiple peculiarities of

---

13 'Catalogo, *Eèe* e *Grandi Eèe* nella tradizione ellenistica', *Prometheus* 5: 217–240.
14 'The Hesiodic *Catalogue of Women* and the *Megalai Ehoiai*', *Phoenix* 40: 127–142.
15 (1986) 142.
16 In: R. Hunter (ed.), *The Hesiodic* Catalogue of Women: *Constructions and Reconstructions*, Cambridge, 2005, 176–216.

this poem in the light of the unskillfull collage of its two sections and the rhapsodic interpolations that took place during the period of the poem's success in Athens,[17] as evidenced by its presence in Attic vase-painting between 565 and 480.[18]

Such criticism of the *Aspis* has solid foundations (the poem results from the clumsy juxtaposition of two separate parts of uneven length, 1–56 [the *ehoie* of Alkmene] and 57–480 [the death of Kyknos by Herakles]), though a recent study by R. P. Martin (2005)[19] has tried to show the limitations of such an approach and to open new vistas for the exploration of this poem. Martin sees the *Aspis* as an example of what he calls 'trash aesthetic' and draws an analogy with modern pulp culture. He sees episodic narration, teleological movement, a focus on outward appearances and a reluctance to dramatize action, as well as consistency of character and a simple plotline (the superhero Herakles defeating the bad Kyknos in a single combat) as defining features of the *Aspis*, the exact typical constituents of pulp aesthetic.[20] Martin also suggests that the *Aspis* was initially a part of the *Catalogue* from which it was later separated and subsequently treated as an independent poem.[21]

A well-informed and balanced presentation of the current state of affairs with respect to our knowledge of all the works of the Hesiodic corpus has been given by Cingano[22] (2009), whose analysis has also the advantage of offering a survey of both the early evidence of the Hesiodic corpus (6th–5th centuries BC) and the corpus' 'life' during the Hellenistic and Imperial age.

Having briefly sketched modern research on the Hesiodic corpus, emphasizing its directions and trends, I now turn to the present volume, which aims at bringing together a number of studies treating different aspects of this variegated material. Contributors to this volume explore questions of the three more common facets of Hesiodic research on fragmentary poems: genre, the *Catalogue*, and the afterlife (literary and scholarly alike) of parts of the corpus.

---

17 See C. F. Russo, *Hesiodi Scutum*, rev. ed. (Florence) 1965; R. Janko (1986). 'The Shield of Heracles and the Legend of Cycnus', *CQ*, New Series, 36.1: 38–59; R. Lamberton (1988). *Hesiod*. New Haven and London, 137–144; P. Toohey (1988). 'An (Hesiodic) danse macabre: The *Shield of Heracles*', *ICS* 12: 19–35.
18 See H. Shapiro (1984). 'Herakles and Kyknos', *AJA* 88: 523–539.
19 'Pulp Epic: the *Catalogue* and the *Shield*", in: R. L. Hunter (ed.), *The Hesiodic* Catalogue of Women. *Constructions and Reconstructions*, Cambridge, 153–175.
20 Martin (2005) 157.
21 Martin (2005) 173.
22 In: F. Montanari, A. Rengakos, and C. Tsagalis (eds.), *Brill's Companion to Hesiod*, Leiden-Boston, 91–130.

The first part of the volume is dedicated to generic considerations pertaining to the Hesiodic corpus, especially the fragmentary poems. Contributors discuss such topics as the boundaries between oral and written record and the generic classification of various Hesiodic epics, the subgenre of wisdom poetry within the larger Hesiodic framework, the *Catalogue*'s relevance to choral *partheneia* that may also function as an indicator of this epic's performative contexts, as well as the theme of the 'origins' as a tool for evaluating generic affinities.

Antonio Aloni ('Hesiod Between Performance and Written Record') argues that *Works and Days* is a poem entirely different from the other poems ascribed to Hesiod and for this reason the possible object of an independent transmission. He claims that the *Works and Days* constitute a *sylloge* in the manner of the *Theognidea*, which was created by a Hesiodic bard. This accumulation of different parts observable in the text of the *Works and Days* reflects generic adaptability aiming to cater to the needs of different situations by having at its disposal a song for every occasion. Aloni takes issue with an influential view expressed by Irwin, according to which the *Catalogue* is much more suited to sympotic performance than to public festivals. He counters that, although participants in a banquet interacted with songs encomiazing a hero's lineage of the size found in various entries of the *Catalogue*, the extended form of the *Catalogue* is a *sylloge* of multiple songs of a particular Hesiodic bard who decided 'to put down in writing his now Panhellenic competence'.

Andrea Ercolani ('Fragments of Wisdom, Wisdom in Fragments') begins from the premise that 'early Greek epic poetry can be regarded as a 'tribal encyclopedia' ... embrac[ing] all relevant knowledge and value-systems of the society which produced it' and in that sense it is 'not simply a literary phenomenon but a social one in a broader sense'. He looks at Hesiodic poetry within the larger context of the social (sub)genre of traditional wisdom that has inundated the entire Hesiodic corpus. Ercolani's approach is based on a carefully delineated methodological framework that goes hand in hand with his analysis of a group of fragments from the *Keykos Gamos, Melampodia, Cheironos Hypothekai, Megala Erga*, and *Astronomia*. He argues that the content and themes of these poems should be examined against the backdrop of the *Works and Days*, the content of which they either supplement or correspond to. The emerging picture from this analysis is that fragmentary Hesiodic epic belongs to a larger supergenre of wisdom poetry in hexametric form. Seen from this vantage point, the issue of the generic classification of the *Works and Days* acquires a new dimension, the more so since it reflects a wider social phenomenon: practical and ethical wisdom. Ercolani's approach is in certain ways complementary to that of Aloni, who has equally suggested an analogy between the *Works and Days* and fragmentary Hesiodic epic.

Deborah Steiner ('Choruses and Catalogues: the Performative and Generic Context of the Asopids in the Hesiodic *Catalogue of Women*') compares the *Catalogue of Women* with the parthenic *choreia* as depicted in the sources of the archaic and early classical period. Going beyond the age-old suggestion that the 'Hesiodic' *Catalogue* recalls the structure, content and diction of certain *partheneia*, Steiner explores the full range of shared affinities both in the choice of the physical and moral attributes which typify the groups of *parthenoi* and in the often elliptical narratives of courtship and marriage/abduction. By extending her study to the artistic representations of maiden choral ensembles during the archaic period, Steiner shows that artists highlight the same features of the dancers (feet, dress, ornaments, beautiful locks) that are privileged in the *Catalogue*. The same conclusion applies to the nobility and fertility of the *Catalogue*'s heroines 'so as to position them as declarations of familial status and wealth ... and to turn them into objects of desire', as well as to the themes of wooing and abduction. In light of this entire range of associations between choral poetry, artistic representations of *choreia*, and the *Catalogue*, Steiner determines their value for proposed performance scenarios and possible contexts for the *Catalogue*. She argues that the *Catalogue* may have been shaped, at least in part, under the influence of poems 'sung and danced by *parthenoi* in the context of civic and extra-urban rituals, chiefly those grounded in the coming-of-age festivals in which young girls participated as nubile members of the community now ripe for courtship and marriage'. It is in such contexts that it would make sense for them to 'rehearse their future roles as citizens' wives and mothers'.

Taking his cue from Guthrie's claim that 'Homer was not interested in the origins of things' in contrast to poets who dealt with 'early cosmogonical and theogonical myths', Malcolm Davies ('The Origin of Things: A Study in Contrasts') tests this claim against Hesiodic fragments. These fragments garner a keen interest in 'first beginnings', which testifies to a completely different narrative framework from the one given in Homeric poetry. The first race of men (frr. 4 [Deukalion], 5 [Graikos-Greeks], 9 [Hellen-Hellenes], 40 (Crete and Europa], 207 [Aigina and ants], the origin of civilisation and culture heroes (frr. 238–239 [Dionysos], 297 [Palamedes]), and the origins of the Trojan War (frr. 196–204), are some of the specific manifestations of an interest in 'the origin of things' attested in the fragments. The interest in the topos of *primus inventor* or πρῶτος εὑρετής, which falls under the umbrella of 'the origin of things', is equally absent from the Homeric poems, in contrast to antiquarian and genealogical epic of the archaic period (e.g. *Danais*, *Phoronis*). Davies thus concludes that 'Hesiodic' poetry displayed a keen interest in aetiological narrative.

The second part of this volume focuses on the best preserved fragmentary 'Hesiodic' epic, the *Catalogue*. Studies included in this section cover a wide range of topics relevant to the *Catalogue:* Helen and Herakles, two of the most instrumental figures of this epic (but also of the standard Hesiodic works, the *Theogony* and the *Works and Days*); the *Catalogue's* 'femininity', i.e. its highlighting of female ancestors by adopting a female-oriented procreation mechanism; the exploration of a range of functions of the *ehoie*; and last, a hitherto neglected aspect of Hesiodic style: sound-play in the *Catalogue*.

Hugo Koning ('Helen, Herakles, and the End of the Heroes') argues that although Hesiod's 'Big Three' (*Theogony, Works and Days* and *Catalogue*) should not be understood as a single coherent narrative, they present the same view of history and agree on the relative chronology of gods, heroes and men. By zooming in on Helen and Herakles, Koning shows how these two famous mythical figures become instrumental in bestowing cohesion and continuity to the Big Three. Helen and Herakles also give the *Catalogue* 'a teleological thrust that has often been denied to the poem'. Helen is crucial for Zeus' cosmic planning: a metaphorical descendant and ultimate manifestation of Pandora who features in both *Theogony* and *Works and Days*, she embodies the *telos* sought by all beautiful heroines of the *Catalogue*. At the same time, Helen is a powerful agent of destruction. Pandora begins the life cycle, Helen brings it to an end. Herakles, another child of Zeus, is a weapon of sheer force who destroys different kinds of half-breeds, monsters in the *Theogony* and shape-shifters in the *Catalogue*. Herakles is both similar to and different from Helen. He brings the heroic era to an end but in contrast to Helen's near-barrenness he is extremely fertile, producing abundant offspring. Helen and Herakles emblematize the *Catalogue's* middle position between the world of the *Theogony* and that of the *Works and Days*. They may have different models, Pandora and Zeus respectively, but they are both children of Zeus and it is together that they become instruments in his cosmic plan to bring the era of heroes to an end.

Kirk Ormand ('Helen's Phantom in Fragments') argues that recent studies have favored an 'intertextual' understanding of archaic hexameter poetry, demonstrating that extant poems (especially those of Homer) interact in a highly allusive, literary way with the oral 'texts' of other poems within the Greek mythic tradition. Ormand maintains that the Hesiodic *Catalogue of Women* uses this technique even more explicitly, interacting intertextually with the poems of Stesichorus. In particular, he suggests that fr. 23a refers deliberately to Stesichorus' innovation of an *eidolon* that replaces Helen in the stories of the Trojan war.

Irini Kyriakou ('Female Ancestors in the Hesiodic *Catalogue of Women*') asks how and why the fragmentary Hesiodic poem known as the *Catalogue of Women* is a woman-centered composition in which it is mainly female, not male, protagonists who are recognized as ancestors. By exploiting the expression ἤ' οἵη, Kyriakou maintains that this verbiage allow the reader to see the gendered characteristics of a poem structured around women. Previous research has stressed the fact that, in tune with the programmatic declaration in the proem of the female-centered subject of the *Catalogue*, the discursive and narrative function of the epic's genealogical references evince a novel way of referencing female ancestors by means of, e.g., beauty, sexual encounters with both mortals and immortals, and marriage. Kyriakou goes beyond this observation and claims that the *Catalogue* offers a characteristic way of reading genealogies, where female ancestors are placed at the center of genealogical presentation. Beyond the recognition typically linked to maternal-ancestral status, the heroines in the *Catalogue* are praised as the ancestors on whom depends the continuation of lineage. Kyriakou proposes to rethink kinship in Greek epic poetry according to gender.

Benjamin Sammons ('The Hesiodic *Catalogue of Women:* A Competition of Forms') argues that within the Aiolid stemma the poet of the *Catalogue* stages an evolution of poetic forms: the genealogical blueprint gives way to a narrative thrust, with or without the use of the *ehoia* formula. When the poet leaves the Aiolid stemma, he employs free narrative elaboration as the principal poetic form (the stories of Salmoneus and Kretheus). Calling attention to the fact that several *ehoiai* refer to groups of daughters and not to individual female figures, Sammons suggests that the *ehoie*-formula is employed as a device that allows the placement of short catalogues within larger genealogical contexts. The *ehoie* thus has a range of functions that go beyond the standard use of introducing entries in women catalogues. It could also be employed to incorporate stories of various heroes whom genealogical narrative could hardly include, 'as in the case of the sons of Aiolos who are left far behind by the extended genealogical lines descending from his daughters'. The *ehoie*-formula seems in places to be in a state of competitive symbiosis with the genealogical superstructure of the poem, the more so since genealogy proper could not have given to women narratives whose colorful features make them stand out. After all, this is a poem about women, and the *ehoie* proper seems to be the means through which women rise above simple genealogies with their built-in catalogic framework.

The artistic qualities of the *Catalogue* are rarely studied and are therefore rarely appreciated, mainly because the lion's share of scholarly interest has fallen to questions of genre or of interpretation of individual fragments. In 'Sound-Play in the Hesiodic *Catalogue of Women*', Christos Tsagalis explores how sound-patterns, ranging from simple alliteration to vocalic, syllabic, and near-syllabic repetition in both word-initial and word-terminal position are deftly employed so as to facilitate interpretation. Sound-play operates both on and beyond the verse-level. In the latter case aural associations function to underscore part of the narrative in a given episode or an *ehoie*. Tsagalis shows that aural links also draw the audience's attention to a point or interpretation not explicitly stated in the text. The range, variety, and sophistication of sound-play explored in this chapter has important implications not only for a more positive evaluation of the *Catalogue* as poetry but also for the poem's generic classification. If indeed the *Catalogue* represents an amalgam of *ehoie*-poetry and catalogue-poetry, poetic sophistication of the sort explored in this chapter may signal an attempt by this generic hybrid to develop strong artistic qualities that would give it a distinct poetic character. Trying to make space for itself amidst a collection of epic poems that had successfully dealt with both the world of gods and the world of heroes, the *Catalogue* had to invent itself as an innovative blend of narrative- and catalogue-poetry without a single thematic thread. The 'jigsaw' for cutting out this slot is style, elaborate sound-play being one of its aspects.

The third part of this volume ('Hesiod's Fragments in Rome and Byzantium') devotes itself to the Roman and Byzantine afterlife of minor works attributed to Hesiod. In contrast to various studies focusing on the use and reuse of Hesiod's major works (*Theogony, Works and Days*) in Rome and Byzantium, here the stress is on the *Catalogue*'s literary reception and influence and on scholarly questions pertaining to the study of the Hesiodic corpus.

Andreas Michalopoulos ('Hesiod in Ovid's *Heroides*') investigates the influence of the *Catalogue of Women* on Ovid's *Heroides*. By tracing thematic affinities, common motifs, markers of allusion, and similarities in diction which witness the interrelation between these two works, Michalopoulos argues that Ovid had direct access to the *Catalogue*. It was with this work in hand that the famous Latin poet engaged in a dialogue with the Greek genealogic-catalogic tradition. Michalopoulos uses Deianeira's letter to Hercules (*Her.* 9) as a case-study in order to explore how several features of the *Catalogue* (concern for the *oikos*, sexual unions of gods with mortal women, struggles for the sake of a woman, interest in ancestors and genealogy) are shared by the *Heroides* and, more striking, within the shared context of a Hercules-based story: a story whose protagonist is a figure of cardinal importance for the *Catalogue* and Hesiodic poetry at large.

Marta Cardin and Filippomaria Pontani ('Hesiod's Fragments in Byzantium') study the two main Byzantine sources citing fragments from minor works of the Hesiodic corpus: Ioannes Tzetzes and Eusthathios of Thessalonica. In a meticulously detailed study of remarkable precision, Cardin and Pontani draw attention to certain significant quotations from the *Catalogue* or other lost works in Eustathius' commentaries on the *Iliad* and *Odyssey*, and in Tzetzes' commentaries on Homer. Their aim is not only to place stress on fragments known exclusively from these two Comnenian era scholars, but also to bring into the limelight the point of view from which they study Hesiodic fragments. Grammatical and erudite considerations aside, these two Byzantine scholars display different attitudes with respect to titles and attributions. Eustathios' philological precision contrasts with Tzetzes' looser method which even assumes the existence of unknown, lost works by the poet from Askra.

Part I: **Genre and Context**

†Antonio Aloni
Hesiod Between Performance and Written Record

The visit that Pausanias made to Askra and the Valley of the Muses in the foothills of Mt. Helikon held many surprises for him (Paus. 9.29–31). It was, as Calame has said, a real journey through the poetic and mythical past of the region.[1] The first and fundamental problem that faces Pausanias in the Valley of the Muses seems to be the need to harmonize a local tradition about the Muses – three Muses on Helikon – with the better known and more widespread nine Muses, daughters of Zeus and resident in Pieria at the foot of Olympos (Paus. 9.29.1–4). Two of the founders of Askra, the brothers Otos and Ephialtes, the sons Aloeus, established a cult to the three Muses of Helikon. They gave the Muses the names Melete, Mneme and Aoide. The nine Panhellenic Muses were imported by the Macedonian Pieros, who introduced their cult in Thespiai, establishing the names by which they came to be known. It is not clear if this duplication of the Muses should be understood as a chronological sequence or a geographical distinction. Does the cult at Thespiai replace the one at Askra, or join it? It is clear, however, that Thespiai and Askra are the two poles around which this dual designation of the Muses revolves.

Most of the monuments that Pausanias saw and describes refer in various ways to the Muses: Eupheme is nurse of the Muses, Linos is recipient of an annual sacrifice that precedes the one offered to the Muses, and the monuments dedicated to poets and musicians of Panhellenic fame, from Thamyris to Arion to Sakadas, and even to Orpheus, also bear affinity to the Muses.

Set between the statue of Sakadas and the monumental group dedicated to Orpheus, there is the description of a statue of Hesiod.[2] In Pausanias' itinerary Hesiod in fact plays an important role as a local poet of Panhellenic renown, equally devoted to the ancient Muses of Helikon and those of Olympus. However, this Hesiod functions primarily to serve Pausanias' point of view or the horizon

---

Translated by L. Edmonds.

1 See Calame (1996b) 43–44.
2 The name Hesiod is ambiguous in this work. It refers, in different contexts, either to an individual, who lived perhaps between the eighth and sixth centuries, or to a poetic tradition formed around this name. Hesiod is a much less common name than Homer (see West 1999, 374–376; contra, Nagy 2004, 58–59 n. 31), but stills refers to the poetic profession. In Most (2006, 176–177) see a review of opinions and an attempt at a conclusion (pp. XIV–XVI).

of expectations within which Pausanias believes he can inscribe the poet. It must be said that in reality the Hesiod that Pausanias finds in Askra and its environs is a particular Hesiod, somewhat different from the one he knows, and this is exactly what causes surprise and some embarrassment.

The *Works and Days* as a *Sylloge*

The three monuments in particular that Pausanias sees and describes are the signs of a hero cult dedicated to the poet:[3] a statue of the poet sitting with a kithara on his knees (Paus. 9.30.3), the tripod won by the poet in the contest at Chalkis and dedicated to the Helikonian Muses (Paus. 9.31.3), and finally, at the fountain Hippokrene, the tablet (or more likely the tablets) of lead with *Works and Days* inscribed upon them (Paus. 9.31.4–5). Twice Pausanias intervenes directly in his own account of these monuments to compare and correct what he sees and is told with what he knows and what is commonly known about the poet.

The description of the statue with a kithara is followed by a sort of exclamation: οὐδέν τι οἰκεῖον Ἡσιόδωι φόρημα ('not at all an ornament that suits Hesiod'). The Hesiod of Helikon is one who sings, a poet similar to the ancient *aoidoi* (like Thamyris) or a lyric poet. For Pausanias it is evident that the sculptor, and/or those who commissioned the statue, did not know the *Theogony* well, where the object symbolizing Hesiod's poetic activity is the laurel staff. Continuing, Pausanias can see the tripod, of venerable antiquity, that Hesiod won at the contest in Chalkis and then devoted to the Helikonian Muses, according to the account in *Works and Days* (658–659).

The perplexity of Pausanias increases when he is shown the copy of *Works and Days* which, on one hand, lacks the proem and, on the other, is presented to him as the only authentic work of Hesiod. This forces Pausanias into a short digression that does justice to the poet of Askra, attributing to him, contrary to his countrymen's opinion, many other poems, from the *Catalogue* to the *Theogony* to the *Melampodia* to the *Cheironos Hypothekai* (Paus. 9.31.5).[4]

In short, the Hesiod of Helikon is a poet different from the one known in the rest of Greece: a Hesiod who wields not the laurel staff but the kithara and is reduced to a single work – one that is docked of the preface dedicated to the Muses

---

[3] See Calame (1996b) 51–54. Doubts about the cult but not about the heroic statue are expressed by Koning (2010) 97.
[4] On the *Melampodia* and the *Cheironos Hypothekai*, see Ercolani 33–38 (this volume).

of Pieria, the nine Panhellenic Muses. Both of these features should be examined carefully, beginning with the absence of the proem.

The absence of the prooemial verses on the tablets of Helikon is not in itself extraordinary given the nature and characteristics of proems. Proems serve to contextualize the ensuing song and to assure the audience of the song's divine provenance and thus its truth and pragmatic effectiveness. In the context of glorifying a poet now heroized and thus semi-divine, the proem loses its necessity and meaning. In other words, visitors to the Valley of the Muses had no need to be reassured concerning the divine inspiration of the hero-poet whom they worshiped.[5]

This means, however, that the text seen by Pausanias was not a simple copy of the text recorded as part of the work of Hesiod the Panhellenic poet. Instead he had to rely on a local tradition, to some extent independent of the other one.[6] It is a pity that the tablets were so damaged (Paus. 9.31.4: τὰ πολλὰ ὑπὸ τοῦ χρόνου λελυμασμένον, 'largely ruined by time') that Pausanias probably could not read the poem and compare it with the one he knew. The fact remains that, with Hesiod thus reduced, the only mention of the Muses in *Works and Days* is limited to verses 658–659: τὸν μὲν ἐγὼ Μούσῃσ' Ἑλικωνιάδεσσ' ἀνέθηκα / ἔνθα με τὸ πρῶτον λιγυρῆς ἐπέβησαν ἀοιδῆς ('This I dedicated to the Helikonian Muses, where they first set me upon the path of clear-sounding song'),[7] in partial contradiction to what is proclaimed in verses 22–25 of the *Theogony*.[8]

There exists therefore a Panhellenic tradition, depending on the revelation of the Olympian Muses, attaching to Hesiod and recording in writing a multiplicity of poems under his name. There exists, however, a different tradition, recognized in a single poem, highly localized in its context and in its characters, which affirms the origin of the song in the Muses of Helikon. One possible reason for this could be that *Works and Days* refers to events and characters who were, at least in origin (see below), rooted in those places. But even such local chauvinism does not seem enough for the radical excision of a single poem from the rest of the Hesiodic poetic corpus. This would, moreover, be a decidedly self-harming chauvinism, which would deprive the poet of a large part of his fame. The real reason must be sought elsewhere. The hypothesis that I will pursue is that *Works and Days* is a poem entirely different from the rest of the poems of

---

5 See Calame (1996b) 53–54.
6 (1996a) 53, too, speaks of a 'local preservation'.
7 The translations of Hesiod are those of Most (2006 and 2007).
8 To speak of contradiction is obviously only a simplification. Would it be better to speak of variation?

Hesiod that have been (at least partially) preserved and for this reason the possible object of an independent transmission.

We can start from the statue that so surprised Pausanias. A Hesiod with his kithara indicates a poet who sings, but for Pausanias Hesiod has nothing to do with song: the 'instrument' that defines him is the staff of the rhapsode, given him by the Olympian Muses. But what Pausanias sees is not the statue of the rhapsode of Panhellenic fame but the monument to a poet revered on Helikon, author of a single poem. It is this poem, *Works and Days*, that defines a poet who sings.

In a previous study I have argued at length for the original sympotic function of *Works and Days*, emphasizing the particular *performance arena* and intentions halfway between iambic aggression and the sententiousness of elegy. I presuppose the conclusions of that work here.[9]

The poem, in its Panhellenic version,[10] opens with a cletic proem, unusual in epic, where a generic assistance is requested of the Muses. The Muses are not the source of the truth that the poetic 'I' intends to proclaim, and the relationship between poet and Muse is not one of total dependence, as it is in epic that narrates distant events. Rather, here it is based on a request for generic assistance independent of the contents of the current song.[11] At the end of the proem the Muses almost seem destined to do nothing. Zeus is asked to straighten justice, and it is for the 'I' to say things that are ἐτήτυμα to Perses.[12]

The whole system of enunciation that underlies the proem is articulated around this relationship between 'I' and 'you'. [13] The relationship between two

---

9 See Aloni (2010). The performance of Hesiodic poetry in a sympotic context has been affirmed recently also by other scholars, notably by Irwin (2005) and Koning (2010). Later I will discuss some of the assertions of these scholars. For now I will only observe that Koning (2010, 48–49) seems to assume – without distinction for the whole Hesiodic corpus – initially festivals and competition amongst singers and only later symposia and competition among symposiasts. As will be seen, this path is likely for the *Catalogue*, while it is different for *Works and Days*, which, in my opinion, has a sympotic origin and and was later reused in festival contexts.
10 The Panhellenic proem depends in fact on the Panhellenic audience of this version of *Works and Days*, but its characteristics are determined, it seems to me, by the nature of the song that follows.
11 Pucci (1996) 192–193.
12 A relation of this kind with the Muses is analogous to that of an elegiac text like fr. 1 W. of Archilochus or to the definition of the Muse as ἐπίκουρος in the Plataia elegy of Simonides (frr. 10–18 W); see Aloni and Iannucci (2007) 102–105. In *Theogony* however, only and exclusively the Muses (sometimes) speak true things (ἐτήτυμα). But the subject-matter and the intended audience of *Theogony* are completely different from those of *Works and Days*.
13 V. 10 is transmitted mainly in the form τύνη· ἐγὼ δέ κε Πέρσηι ἐτήτυμα μυθησαίμην. In my view, the form τύνη, ἐγὼ δέ κε, Πέρσηι, ἐτήτυμα μυθησαίμην, is preferable, even if transmitted

people is understood as unidirectional, without, that is, there being any dialogical space available for an inversion of roles between sender and receiver. It is a relationship analogous, or at least comparable, to the one found in Ibycus vis à vis Polykrates, in Sappho vis à vis Attis, in Theognis vis à vis Kyrnos.[14]

The features attributed to this 'you' in the course of the poem are also an indication of the stratified nature of *Works and Days*. The poem appears so changeable and contradictory that it makes of Perses a character not real but generic, capable, that is, of reflecting the different circumstances and needs of the same kind of performance. For this reason also the parallel with Kyrnos is apposite, since in Theognidean poetry he seems sometimes a model boy and sometimes good for nothing.[15] West, in his analysis of the character of Perses,[16] concludes that *Works and Days* cannot be explained from a single personal situation and that the 'failings' that characterize him are not only different in different contexts but are determined by the contexts themselves at any given time, and in some cases invented on the basis of context.[17]

But in the deictic system of the poem there are not only the poetic 'I' and 'you', but also an interlocutor of ambiguous nature: the King, sometimes designated by 'you' (plural), sometimes by the third person ('they'). We will see how these deictics of the second and third person are of a phantasmal kind. A deixis thus articulated and extended, with the poetic *ego* as point of origin, seems extraneous to the performance circumstances of epic, whether heroic and narrative or catalogic and genealogical. Such distinctiveness may be a further indication of a different purpose and a different context of transmission.[18]

---

by only a minority of manuscripts. The placement of τύνη in enjambement in line-initial position has no parallel (the τύνη of *Th*. 36 seems to me completely different, and it is not in enjambement). Even on the usual reading, v. 10 immediately establishes a relationship with the one who, just after the digression on the two Erides, at v. 27 appears explicitly as the recipient, or rather the target, of the song.

14 See Calame (1996a) especially 174–175.
15 This parallel is found already in the *Prolegomena* to F. G. Welcker's edition of Theognis: see Welcker (1826) LXXVII–LXXVIII.
16 See West (1978) 33–40.
17 See West (1978) 35–36. It should not be forgotten that there is a vast literature that aims at highlighting the deep (indeed very deep) consistency of the figure of Perses, as well as that of the poem as a whole. I mention, recently, Clay (1993) and (2003) 34. On the other hand, the inconsistencies and contradictions related to the figure of Perses were in the nineteenth century the subject of reflection by analytical criticism, including the extreme cases of Schoemann (1869) and Kirchhoff (1889), who imagined a variety of poems put together by an editor.
18 Pucci (1996, 201) has also thought of interlocutors who are 'wholly or in part the product of fiction', but sees in this a sign of writing in the text of *Works and Days*, intended from the start to be for written distribution.

The whole poem is also characterized by the assertion of values and non-values, linked to the polar functions of praise and blame. As Calame has shown,[19] praise and blame are present in the *pheme* dispensed by Zeus, but the two Erides are especially objects of praise and blame respectively (*Op.* 12–13). At the same time Perseus hangs suspended between actual blame and possible praise.

The same concept (the reasons for the difficulty of existence) is described by two different juxtaposed exempla that *eventually* become alternatives. First there is the story of Pandora,[20] which helps explain why men must struggle to get enough to survive (*Op.* 47–105).[21] There follows the myth of the human races (*Op.* 107–201). This bears a closer look, beginning with the two verses that introduce it:

> Εἰ δ' ἐθέλεις, ἕτερόν τοι ἐγὼ λόγον ἐκκορυφώσω
> εὖ καὶ ἐπισταμένως· σὺ δ' ἐνὶ φρεσὶ βάλλεο σῇισιν.
>
> If you wish, I shall recapitulate another story
> correctly and skillfully, and you lay it up in your spirit.
>
> Hes. *Op.* 106–107

We find a similar transition in the performances of heroic words by Glaukos (*Il.* 6.150, after the comparison between men and leaves) and Aineias (*Il.* 20.213, after having proclaimed his divine descent, he goes on to tell also the Dardanid genealogy as a whole):

> εἰ δ' ἐθέλεις καὶ ταῦτα δαήμεναι ὄφρ' ἐῢ εἰδῇς
> ἡμετέρην γενεήν, πολλοὶ δέ μιν ἄνδρες ἴσασιν·
>
> Yet if you wish to learn all this and be certain
> of my genealogy: there are plenty of men who know it.[22]
>
> *Il.* 6.150–151 = 20.213–214

With respect to epic usage, the transitional link seems to be employed differently. While the words of Glaukos and of Aineias respond to an actual request by the interlocutor, the use of the same transitional formula in *Works and Days*, through the address to the generic addressee, aims openly to engage the real recipient – in short, the audience – in such a way that the further (ἕτερον) exemplum that

---

19 See Calame (1996a) 171 and 177–178 with n. 23.
20 On Pandora, see Davies 87 (this volume); Koning 105–108 (this volume); Tsagalis 200 (this volume); Cardin and Pontani 274–277 (this volume).
21 Calame (1996a, 186 n. 46) observes how common the mention of Elpis is in elegiac and sympotic poetry.
22 Trans. by Lattimore (1951) 157.

he is going to furnish is presented as requested by the latter. On further consideration, however, the exemplum following such a *heteron* is not an exemplum, since it merely expresses, with a different story, the concept just outlined by the myth of Pandora, i.e. the hardness of life. The existence of two myths, different yet identical in their basic meaning, is a fact that it will be necessary to keep in mind, because it does not depend solely on the generic characteristics of the poem that we are investigating.

Besides Perses, the object of the poetic 'I' is the kings. They also have need of instruction even if they are defined as wise,[23] and therefore he tells them the story of the hawk and the nightingale (*Op.* 202–212). The verse that introduces the story is telling:

Νῦν δ' αἶνον βασιλεῦσιν ἐρέω φρονέουσι καὶ αὐτοῖς

And now I will tell a fable (*ainos*) to kings who themselves too have understanding.

Hes. *Op.* 202

It shows an indubitable similarity to the initial verses of an epode of Archilochus:[24]

ἐρ<έω> τιν' ὕμιν αἶνον, ὦ Κηρυκίδη,
ἀχνυμένηι σκυτάληι

I'll tell you people a fable, Kerykides, with a grieving message stick.[25]

Archil. fr. 185.1 W.

The appeal to the *ainos*, to the animal fable, with the specification that it is a matter of *ainos*, seems to be a characteristic trait of the iambic genre (Archil. frr. 174–181 and 185–187 W).[26] The co-presence of mythical narrative and *ainos* points

---

23 The text of *Op.* 202 is not without problems; the sense is, however, in any case positive. See further below.
24 It is not by chance that the similarity has to do with the initial verse of the epode. In many cases in *Works and Days* one has the impression that the song repeats, after reaching a fixed point.
25 West (1993, 2) gives the fragment the title 'To a Member of the College of Heralds' and translates the first two lines: 'I want to tell you folk a tale, your Honour, / – oh, it's a mournful dispatch'.
26 For a thorough discussion of *ainos* in archaic poetry, see Lasserre (1984) with the important 'Discussion' following Lasserre's own paper (97–103). Nagy (1990, 146–148) states that *ainos* is extraneous to epic. About *ainos* in *Works and Days* he observes (48 n. 11): 'In any case, I see no compelling reason to assume that Hesiodic poetry is epic', which is what, limited to *Works and Days*, is here maintained.

decisively to a sympotic context: compare the new elegy of Archilochus, in which a part of the story of Telephos[27] is told (and re-told). The *ainoi*, again those of Archilochus, were intended for the same sympotic ambience.

The predominantly aggressive and iambic function of *ainos* is clear not only from Archilochus' usage but also from most of the cases where *ainos* appears in archaic and classical literature. I mention only the *ainos* narrated by Kyros to the ambassadors of the Aiolians and the Ionians in rejecting their demands (Herod. 1.141) and those that appear in the comic scene between Bdelykleon and the Woman in Aristophanes' *Wasps* (1399 ff.). [28]

It should also be noted that the Hesiodic *ainos* manifests very particular characteristics that allow a multiplicity of decodings, depending on whom (the kings, Perses, the poetic 'I') at any given time we want to identify with the animal protagonists of the *ainos*.[29] The *ainos* thus presents itself in enigmatic form; but the riddle, of course, arises for us and for those who, like us, are not *sophoi* like the poet and his audience. These are the *basileis* (202) and those involved in the performance, in solidarity with the poet and therefore able immediately and correctly to decode the meaning of the story. The riddle, as Gentili showed, is an integral part of the relationship between the aristocratic poet – like Pindar and Theognis – and the small circle of those who are able to understand and interpret the veiled and allusive words of the poet. [30] The riddle, then, refers to an addressee who had been in some way chosen.

There is still a non-epic trait to keep in mind within the paradigm of sympotic traits that we are constructing: the use, in a fairly circumscribed section of *Works and Days*, of kenning of a descriptive type.[31]

Absent in Homer and in the *Homeric Hymns*, these kennings – of the type ἀνόστεος (524) for the octopus or τρίπους βροτός (527) for the old man with the stick – occur with high frequency (6x) between *Op.* 524 and 605, with a further recurrence at *Op.* 742. As Waern noted,[32] kennings of this type occur only in Theog-

---

27 *POxy* 4708; for an interpretation and bibliography: Aloni and Iannucci (2007) 205–237.
28 Cyrus tells the ainos ὀργῆι ἐχόμενος, 'possessed by anger' (Herod. 1.141.4). On *ainos* in epic poetry, see Davies (2001). On the presence and function of *ainos* in comedy, see Zanetto (2001).
29 See van Dijk (1997) 127–134; in particular the very numerous interpretations that have been formulated and the vast pertinent literature are summarized in pp. 129–131.
30 See Gentili (1995) 57–59; see also Collins (2004) 127–129 and Yatromanolakis (2009). See further Aloni and Iannucci (2007) 63–66.
31 Waern (1951) 38 ff. The term originally designated a particular means of expression in medieval Norse literature. A kenning is a poetic phrase that is substituted for the name of a person or of a thing, replacing it with an often enigmatic metaphor (e.g., 'the bones of the earth' are 'stones').
32 See Waern (1951) 40–41.

nis, Timocreon, Pindar and later in Aeschylus, to stay within the classical period. The first two refer clearly to a sympotic ambience. Generally in lyric (and also later) these kennings are used in reporting or alluding to a folktale or an oral story. In short, the kennings combine perfectly with the use of *ainos*, in a sympotic context, halfway between elegy and iambic.

On the whole, such evidence is not reflected in the hexameter epic known to us,[33] and it brings *Works and Days* close to poetic forms such as the elegy and iambus, even unites this poem with them. In particular, the pervasive analogy of the basic characteristics of *Works and Days* with those found in the Theognidean *sylloge* appears extraordinarily significant.

We proceed with the hypothesis that we advanced at the outset: *Works and Days*, not unlike the Theognidean poem, is a *sylloge* into which a singer, deeply rooted in the Hesiodic tradition, has poured his expertise on a specific topic. We might call this poem 'admonitions to Perses', where 'Perses' is understood as a generic feature. This means that in the text we read there exists an accumulation of different parts belonging to a genre that adapted itself to a variety of situations by applying a suitable song to every occasion. At the moment of registration in writing, the singer has poured his expertise into a single text without caring whether or not a total coherence of the parts resulted. In any case he did not read the text, and it is rather questionable whether the text was written to be read: at most, it could be a help (but not a script) for performance. But the choice of which episodes to include – to wit, of what to say – was once again up to the present singer, exactly as in a situation of total orality (the audience had no *libretto* before its eyes in which to follow the song of the poet). In this context, the solution proposed by Martin[34] for the so-called dittographies present in *Aspis* is important. They are part of the compositional habit of the poet, for whom 'no expansion is too bad to venture' (2005, 169). However, I would attribute the phenomenon to the process of recording in writing (see further below) rather than to re-composition amidst performance.

---

33 Except perhaps in the works of Xenophanes, Parmenides and Empedocles. This point is one that for now I do not intend to take up, for the reason that it would be necessary to define the modality of performance presupposed by these poems.
34 Martin (2005) 166–169.

The Socio-Political Context of the *Works and Days*

In common with the Theognidean *sylloge* there is also the socio-political context that forms the backdrop to Hesiod's poem, and it is this context that produces the double tradition of *Works and Days*.

The contents help us to understand the nature and disposition (in other words, the social and political status) of the poem's intended audience. This audience is generic: it stands for different real audiences across time and space.

The poem itself imbues the events it describes with a precise geographical framework for the poetic 'I' and Perses: Askra. This village has been the object of careful studies from various perspectives: archaeological, topographical, historical and sociological.[35] The fact that Askra is defined as a village is not only the result of a quantitative reality. The village is an element of a political and anthropological process that takes shape in the course of the archaic period, say from the eighth century. It is the process leading to the formation of the city-state and its control of the territory that surrounds it, including smaller communities, like villages, which were until that point autonomous. In this case, the city is Thespiai, located about ten kilometers to the southeast of the Valley of the Muses and Askra. The opposition, noted at the outset, between two different traditions relating to the Muses seems to repeat itself at the political level. In this case too the limited and retrograde horizon is Askra's, the broader and more innovative is Thespiai's.

Within the process of synoechism (but also later, when the process was completed: think of the monologue of Dikaiopolis that opens Aristophanes' *Acharnians*)[36] the relationship between the city and the village is normally antagonistic.[37] In the specific case of Askra and Thespiai their rivalry is confirmed both by the fact that at some point Askra was destroyed by the Thespians, according to a statement from a gloss to the *Works and Days* (633–640, pp. 201–202 Pertusi = Aristot. fr. 565 Rose [= fr. 580 Gigon] = Plut. fr. 82 Sandbach),[38] and by the fact that the target of the polemic of the poetic 'I' of *Works and Days* – firmly rooted in Askra – are the *basileis* of Thespiai, as affirmed by almost all scholars.[39] The

---

35 In Edwards (2004) there is a practically complete bibliography.
36 See in particular vv. 33–36.
37 See in Carter (1986) ch. 4, 'The Peasant Farmer', 76–98.
38 On the dating of this event see below.
39 Lardinois (2003, 2), however, thinks that they are the kings of Askra. In this regard, the text does not allow a definitive answer. I personally think that the kings who are 'eaters of gifts' are

reasons for and the nature of the conflict that drives the whole poem, namely the conflict between the poetic 'I' and Perses, must therefore be analyzed within the more complex picture of the antagonism between Thespiai and Askra as it is reflected in the poem (through the mention of the *basileis*). Much scholarship has emerged dealing with Askra and also with the nature of the conflicts that animate the *Works and Days*. The fine book by Edwards (2004) is a useful starting point because it sums up many of the strengths and weaknesses of the literature on this subject.

Edwards argues rightly that the conflicts at the center of *Works* and *Days* are two: one between Hesiod (or rather the poetic 'I', since he never says his name, which would moreover be useless to his audience) and Perses, and one between polis (Thespiai) and village (Askra). In short, after the division of the inheritance, instead of devoting his energies to agricultural production, Perses begins to attend the *basileis* and to offer them gifts, counting on obtaining benefits from them. That they then issue some ruling on the conflict between the poetic 'I' and Perses, or at least are occupied with the matter, is unclear and depends above all on how the passage consisting of verses 34–41 is interpreted.[40]

More precisely, it is the interpretation of *Op.* 34–35 which makes it possible to outline the state of the conflict between the poetic 'I' and Perses, and the role played by the *basileis* up to that point.

σοὶ δ' οὐκέτι δεύτερον ἔσται
ὧδ' ἔρδειν· ἀλλ' αὖθι διακρινώμεθα νεῖκος

But you will not have a second chance to act this way, – no, let us divide up our allotment right here.

Hes. *Op.* 34–35

With good logical and grammatical arguments Edwards maintains that the expression σοὶ δ' οὐκέτι δεύτερον ἔσται ὧδ' ἔρδειν cannot refer to the foregoing fact that only those who have abundant stocks in their warehouses can embark on legal proceedings aimed at seizing others' property. ὧδε in ὧδ' ἔρδειν has rather a proleptic function in relation to action that is described a few verses later:

---

to be distinguished from those 'wise men' (*Op.* 202) to whom the *ainos* of the hawk and the nightingale is addressed. The simplest solution (for reasons to be adduced shortly) seems to me to be that the former, the corrupt ones, are those of the distant city, and the latter are closer and probably sympathetic to the poetic 'I', even if not involved in the performance. Thespiai and Askra are, in short, two useful names for indicating the varying disposition of the poetic 'I' toward them.

40 See the detailed analysis of Edwards (2004) 41–44.

ἤδη μὲν γὰρ κλῆρον ἐδασσάμεθ', ἄλλα τε πολλὰ
ἁρπάζων ἐφόρεις μέγα κυδαίνων βασιλῆας
δωροφάγους, οἳ τήνδε δίκην ἐθέλουσι δικάσσαι.

For already we had divided up our allotment, but you snatched much more besides and went carrying it off, greatly honoring the kings, those gift-eaters, who want to pass this judgement.

Hes. *Op.* 37–39

What cannot be repeated a second time is the division of the inheritance, which Perses has largely depleted to support and subsidize (so the poetic 'I' sees it) the *basileis*, those 'eaters of gifts'. The *neikos* between the brothers, which could lead to a new division of their inheritance,[41] has not yet been submitted, still less has it been judged by the kings of Thespiai; this eventuality is what the whole poem wants to avoid.

Edwards then tends to overestimate the first conflict, and to consider the one between *polis* and village as a side effect of the clash between successful farmer and failed farmer. But his entire sequence of reasoning here is undermined by the fact that he starts from the assumption that the poem reflects a particular moment in the history of Askra and Thespiai, and in particular that Askra is, 'at the time of Hesiod', still independent of Thespiai.[42] This assumption is based on two seemingly historical data: 1) the date of the submission of Askra to Thespiai, and 2) the date of the death of Hesiod or, if we want to be less controversial, the dating of Hesiod, which Edwards sets between the end of the eighth and the beginning of the seventh century.[43] Right here, in my opinion, the reasoning of Edwards, and also of many other scholars, shows its limits.

First of all, a problem exists regarding the possible historical existence of Hesiod and the contents of the poems attributed to him. Because of the traditional nature of archaic poetry it is unlikely for the physical death of a poet – indeed, of a poet who is the putative forefather of a poetic tradition – to cut off the evolution and constant updating of poems deemed part of his or her tradition.

Next, as regards the submission of Askra to Thespiai, the opinions of scholars are divided, although the opinion of those who place the annexation of Askra in a period prior to Hesiod prevails.[44] Then there are those who, like Buck,[45] hypothesize a situation intermediate between the total autonomy and the total sub-

---

41 See Edwards (2004) 44.
42 See Edwards (2004) 166–173.
43 See Edwards (2004) 26–28.
44 For example, Snodgrass (1985) 94 and (1990) 130–135; Bintliff (1996) 197; Tandy (1997) 205.
45 See Buck (1979) 97–99.

mission of Askra to Thespiai. But even here there are many things that do not add up.

The reading of the sources and analysis of the archaeological data (all thoroughly set out by Edwards) show that the annexation of the village of Askra to the city of Thespiai was a process that took place over time, rather than a traumatic, one-time event. The violent destruction of Askra at the hands of the Thespians mentioned above occurred probably very late, perhaps as late as the fourth century.⁴⁶

The submission of Askra to Thespiai is, in short, an event certainly to be set in the archaic era – say between the eighth and sixth centuries – of which, however, we cannot fix the date, except through recourse to Hesiod, or rather by combining a possible interpretation of the *Works and Days* (the *basileis* of Thespiai exercise justice in the affairs of Askra) with the dating of Hesiod.

All of this would make sense if *Works and Days* had been composed directly in writing, and thus constituted the record of a unique and unrepeatable event. This is basically what Tandy says, who sees in it the expression of a minority, anti-aristocratic faction of Askra.⁴⁷ But this view accords poorly with what we know of ancient Greek culture and of its poetry in particular.

Works and Days, in fact, is certainly not a testamentary record for future memory, nor witness of a single moment of conflict between Thespiai and Askra, nor of a unique incident, involving assets, that put Hesiod at odds with Perses. On the contrary, these things should be considered parts of a paradigmatic story that poetic performance realizes, with full pragmatic effect, whenever the poem is repeated, even far from Askra and in different socio-political contexts.

In addition, the survival of a poetic text cannot depend only on the existence of a (theoretical) written registration from a point in time when there was still no circulation of books, not even a readership.⁴⁸ A text lives – that is, is handed down – for as long as it is repeated in successive performances in different times and places, by different singers, with continual updating, so as always to be pragmatically effective with respect to the actual situation present at any given time.⁴⁹ That is why it is handed down. Recording in writing, when it occurs,

---

46 See Snodgrass (1985) 94.
47 See Tandy (1997) 198–201. It is a political framing of the matter that persists also in other recent studies, for example in Koning (2010) 187–188.
48 As for the possibility that a large poetic text might be recorded in writing in the archaic period see Aloni (2006) 93–108.
49 It is the process of composition in performance, for which see Lord (1960) and in particular 13 and 60–65. A synthetic formulation in Nagy (1996a) 17; Nagy (1996b) is fundamental. An example by way of clarification: there is no doubt that we owe the survival of the work of Hesiod – not

does not stop this constant updating of the text relative to the circumstantial exigencies of timebound performances.

For all these reasons it does not make sense to try to make *Works and Days* say what it cannot say. From the perspective of oral traditional poetry *Works and Days* contains an attack by a poetic 'I' located in a village called Askra upon a twofold target, two implicit listeners: a 'you' who is nearby, but not for this reason present at the performance, and 'kings', who may be those of Thespiai or of any other place that, like Thespiai vis-à-vis Askra, advances claims of dominion or at least of synoechism and political centralization. To this we must limit ourselves. But this is not insignificant. We have before us a song of Hesiod, a poetic tradition that goes back to a great and influential poet, which over time repeats the opposition of a village (Askra, but not only Askra) and its agricultural class to a city and its claims of imperializing interference. It does this through its own institutions, in the forms of power and the relationships typical of the village. All this belongs to the normal contrast between the politics of the city and the 'pre-political' forms of land management by aristocratic clans, observable in Athens and elsewhere in the sixth and fifth centuries.[50] This situation also endured the passage of time, making the song always fresh in each of its subsequent permutations.

Despite these limitations relating to the nature of the conflicts that animate *Works and Days*, the economic model which, according to Edwards, is dominant in the Hesiodic poem seems to me correct. We are faced with a sharing-based system based upon the obligation of reciprocity. In other words, each household lives from its own production; in the case of a failed or poor harvest, the victim may appeal to someone (a neighbor, for example: we remember how important neighbors are in Hesiodic precepts)[51] to borrow what he needs, with the under-

---

a towering poet and from a city only slightly represented in the Greek literary panorama – above all to oligarchic groups' and Athenian conservatives' reuse of this work in the sixth and fifth centuries. In the verses of Theognis they discovered and in part projected their own political and existential points of view, on which see Vetta (2000) and Bowie (2012).

50 An analysis of the modalities of state formation and of the relationship between state and villages, understood as pre-political communities, can be found in Morris (1994). For a brief analysis of the different degrees of political cohesion of citizens and territory around civic foundations, see Aloni (2012).

51 For the importance of neighbors, see *Op.* 23, where the good *eris* consists in the ζῆλος of neighbor towards his industrious neighbor. *Op.* 342–351, apparently a sort of etiquette for the good neighbor, is in essence a summary of the principles that govern the sharing system we are talking about. The same concepts, but expressed in a negative form through the invitation to Perses to work so that he can avoid recourse to neighbors, return in *Op.* 397–400. Finally, in the matrimonial precepts in *Op.* 694–705 the neighbors are present in two ways: the good

standing that not only is the return mandatory but that any future surpluses should be primarily available for loan to those who have need of it. Hence the reluctance in *Works and Days* as regards trade and navigation, which are based on the exchange of surpluses outside the community.

Hesiod's reproach to the kings of Thespiai (*Op.* 38–39) is literally to charge them with 'eating gifts'; that is, their being in a position in which they do not have to practice reciprocity. Leaving aside the personal greed of a single *basileus*, there is the implication of what in a centralized system will be called taxation: to provide a portion of one's own income to the *polis*, which provides certain services (for example, justice, but not only justice). That this is represented as a form of gift (even today, however, many, if and when they pay taxes, are convinced that they are giving money to the state) is nothing but a matter of perspective.[52] Conversely, Thucydides (6.54.5) and Aristotle (*Ath. Pol.* 16.4) refer to the 'taxation' of Peisistratos with the terminology of taxation of their own times (πράττεσθαι + τῶν γιγνομένων / ἀπὸ τῶν γιγνομένων + δεκάτην / εἰκοστήν).

Contrary to Edwards,[53] it is necessary to say that the *basileis* of Thespiai will hardly have been only judges. This for the simple reason that at such an early date it seems difficult to hypothesize a distinction between different functions and different powers. Among other things, if there are judges with broad jurisdiction, there will be laws (and someone who will have made them) and there will be bodies that will cause the decisions of the judges to be respected. The *basileis* – one of the generic traits of *Works and Days* – are, in short, nothing but the magistrates of the city that is slowly forming, in the face of the complete parcelization and autonomy of rural communities.

This also explains the oscillation of the values associated with the *basileis*. In the *Theogony* (80 ff.) they are something completely different from what appears in *Works and Days*. Further, *Works and Days* is ambiguous in its evaluation of the *basileis*. Although they are almost always 'eaters of gifts', or otherwise subject to criticism and attacks by the poetic 'I', they are called wise in the introduction to the *ainos* of the hawk and the nightingale (*Op.* 202 cited above). The reason (or the possible reason) is that the kings of the *Theogony* seem almost

---

wife must come from the neighborhood, and the selection should also be careful, so that the ubiquitous neighbors will not laugh and speak of an unfortunate choice.

52 There is perhaps also the difficulty of giving verbal and poetic expression to an event – the justice exercised by magistrates *coram populo* – that is relatively new. Similarly, the judicial episode represented on the Shield of Achilleus is not very clear (*Il.* 18.498–508): in this case the compensation for the judges is presented as if it were the reward in a competition; cf. Edwards (1991) 217–218 on *Il.* 18.507–508, see also Collins (2004) 71–72.
53 Edwards (2004) 42 ff.

to be thaumaturgic leaders of the communities they serve (the model of Ithaca and neighboring islands with many kings seems applicable here). In *Works and Days* they are mainly the heads of a *polis* that claims to exercise power over an entire territory that includes other communities, which in turn could have kings, precisely those 'wise men' mentioned above.

This resistance to synoechism is not so much a matter of more or less wealth as between Thespiai and Askra, which is in any case difficult to imagine for adjacent agricultural territories. The reality is that between the seventh and sixth centuries the farming households see reluctantly that the city is replacing them in exercising power over the territory. Synoechisms, civic magistracies and courts put into question the autonomy of the clans that make their own self-sufficiency the basis for political autonomy and a kind of regime based on egalitarianism among the well-born.[54]

If this is the situation in which the performance and the performances over time of *Works and Days* are located, we must conclude that the main reason for the poem, and especially the tradition that lies behind it, is political, in the sense that it is a sort of *plaidoyer* against changes that have occurred in what one had hoped would be an immutable situation (the *hesychia* so beloved of all the aristocrats),[55] where the poetic 'I' has a polemical target, represented by a 'you' who for his part adheres to the new situation. The venue for such plaintive speeches, both in their origin and in their tradition up to their codification in writing, is not, it has to be said, usually the square or the public holiday, but the symposium, as the fragments of the poetic oeuvre of Solon and the Theognidean *sylloge* well demonstrate.[56]

The 'political' contents of *Works and Days* explain the different traditions identifiable, for example, between the Panhellenic poem and the diminished Hesiod of Helikon. On the one hand, in fact, we have the transmission in time (through re-composition in performance) of a poem strongly rooted in the symposia of aristocratic conservative groups, both in and outside of Boiotia, when

---

[54] It is a conception, and also a way of life, that continues in time and that we encounter again in the figure of Ischomachos, the exemplary protagonist of the *Economicus* of Xenophon, a conservative and phil-oligarch if ever there was one.

[55] For a discussion of the motif of *hesychia* in Pindar, Thucydides and Plato, especially in the second half of the fifth century, see Carter (1986) 42–48. It is significant that in *Works and Days* the only race that lives in perfect *hesychia* is the golden one (*Op.* 118–120).

[56] Above all when, as in the case of Theognis, the lament comes from the losing side. In that corner of Boiotia, too, the process of synoechism and politicization went forward, despite the words of Hesiod. As for the use of the hexameter in sympotic settings see Irwin (2005) 58–59, Collins (2004) 129–134 and Aloni (2010) 141–142.

there existed socio-political conditions similar to those that are at the base of the Hesiodic poem: conditions that make the performance contemporary, even far from the narrow confines of Askra and Thespiai.

The *Works and Days* in the Context of Hesiodic Poetry

On the other hand, *Works and Days* is part of a wider number of hexameter epics traditionally attributed to a great poet named Hesiod. Meter and 'authoriality' are the elements that it has in common with the rest of the tradition and that allow the survival of *Works and Days* together with various other poems attributed to Hesiod. It is a matter of a poetic tradition that diffuses outside of Boiotia and acquires a strong Panhellenic character, both through the proems to individual poems and through contents (catalogues, genealogies, theogonies) that look not only to the mythical past of Boiotia but to all of Greece. The Hesiodic poems are, in short, available for recitation at festivals and in contests, together and in competition with those of other traditions, especially the Homeric.[57]

As for the circulation of the Hesiodic poetic tradition outside of Boiotia, an important hub is surely Athens. West had already supported an elaboration of the *Catalogue* in an Athenian ambience, and Irwin's essay goes in the same direction. Congruity between *Works and Days* and other poetic traditions (especially Solon, but also Theognis) circulating in Athens is identified by Koning.[58] It is a matter of the existence in Athens of an aristocratic milieu in which the ideological contents of different poetic traditions were accepted, elaborated and remembered over time. This does not necessarily imply that Athens is the sole path for the Panhellenic diffusion of the poetry of Hesiod, nor that the setting down in writing of the Panhellenic Hesiod took place in Athens. Nevertheless, it is indubitable that once again Athens plays a key role in the definition of a poetic tradition.

The silence of Pausanias about the text (beyond the proem) of *Works and Days* recorded on Helikon prevents us from comparing the text engraved on the lead tablet with that of the Panhellenic tradition. Nevertheless, we can try to use the features of *Works and Days* that we have highlighted to come to a better understanding both of the original modality of the performances of the Hes-

---

[57] The tradition of the *Certamen* is not a matter of chance.
[58] See West (1985), Irwin (2005) 65–83, Koning (2010) 172–175 (in an intertextual perspective unrelated to the present discussion). For the Athenian elaboration of Theognis see above n. 49.

iodic corpus as a whole and of the various processes of scribal recording that our texts assume.

I confine analysis here to the best preserved poems, the *Theogony*, the *Aspis* and the *Catalogue*. As I have just said, the three poems belong to the Panhellenic phase of the poetry of Hesiod. This is clear both from their subject matter, which is open to a broad and internally diverse public, and from the fact that they were preserved down to the Hellenistic period and in part down to modern times.[59] A countercheck is that the 'Helikonian' version of *Works and Days* remained confined to the lead tablet of the Valley of the Muses.

Let us start with the *Catalogue*. It is a genealogical poem that narrated the heroic lineages descending from the union of various women with gods.[60] The poem is divided into five books and has come down to us in fragments. It opens with a proem only partially preserved (fr. 1). The proem is followed by numerous micronarratives of various sizes, not always consistent with the theme proposed in the proem. Such is the case, for example, of the large section devoted to the narrative of the suitors of Helen (frr. 196–204).[61] As regards the performance of the poem, execution of the text in its entirety does not seem conceivable, first of all because of its size. For this and other reasons, Irwin (2005) has argued for a sympotic origin of the *Catalogue*, in which the different entries could represent the performances of individual symposiasts. She would be quite right if we considered the text of the *Catalogue* that has reached us to be an exact reflection (in short, the written record) of the performance of the Hesiodic genealogical and catalogic tradition. There are, however, clear signs that things did not stand thus. This will become clear from my analysis of the *Aspis*.

The *Aspis* is a poem of some 500 verses. From a quantitative point of view it is perfectly compatible with performance by a singer. Its peculiar structure and articulation of different themes help one to understand its technique of compo-

---

59 See the summary of the Days in Nagy (1989) 273–274, where a lucid definition of pan-Hellenism can also be found: 'To be pan-Hellenic, a given composition must highlight those aspects of Greek tradition that are shared by most locales, while all along shading over those aspects that vary from locale to locale'.

60 The theme is clearly announced in vv. 1–4 of fr. 1: Νῦν δὲ γυναικῶν [φῦλον ἀείσατε, ἡδυέπειαι / Μοῦσαι Ὀλυμπιάδε[ς, κοῦραι Διὸς αἰγιόχοιο, / αἳ τότ' ἄρισται ἔσαγ[καὶ κάλλισται κατὰ γαῖαν / μίτρας τ' ἀλλύσαντο δ[ιὰ χρυσέην τ' Ἀφροδίτην / μισγόμεναι θεοῖσ[ιν ('And now sing the tribe of women, sweet voiced / Olympian Muses, daughters of aegis-holding Zeus, / those who were the best at that time [and most beautiful on the earth / and they loosened their girdles [and because of golden Aphrodite / mingling with gods').

61 The catalogue of the suitors, according to the reconstruction proposed by Merkelbach and West (frr. 23a-24), was at the beginning of Book 5, while the genealogy of Hellen, as a descendant of Aiolos, was in Book 2; cf. Cingano (2005) 118–121.

sition.⁶² By composition I mean re-composition in performance, and also in writing, itself a form of performance and thus of re-composition.

The poem opens with an *ehoie* of Alkmene that continues until verse 56. That it is an *ehoie* is confirmed by the fact that the same verses appear in Book 4 of the *Catalogue*, in the section devoted to the offspring of the daughters of Pelops (frr. 193–195). The first three verses set out the subject of the *ehoie*:

Ἤ οἵη προλιποῦσα δόμους καὶ πατρίδα γαῖαν
ἤλυθεν ἐς Θήβας μετ' ἀρήιον Ἀμφιτρύωνα
Ἀλκμήνη, θυγάτηρ λαοσσόου Ἠλεκτρύωνος·

... Or like her: leaving behind her houses and her father's land, she came to Thebes following warlike Amphitryon – Alkmene, the daughter of host-rousing Elektryon.

The announcement of the subject precedes an expansion on the beauty of Alkmene (vv. 3–8).⁶³ This is a traditional theme that returns in frr. 180.10 and 251a.9 of the *Catalogue*. From v. 9 to v. 47 of the *Aspis* we have a further expansion on the story of Amphitryon and Zeus. The same formula, πολυχρύσου Ἀφροδίτης, in line-final position precedes (v. 8) and ends (v. 47) the sequence. This repetition shows the seam between the different parts and the return to the main theme.⁶⁴ From v. 48 to v. 56 the *ehoie* of Alkmene continues (and concludes) with the births of Herakles and Iphikles. At v. 57 the story abandons Alkmene and focuses on Herakles, in fact on a specific adventure: the struggle with Kyknos. The expansion opens with a connective expression (ὅς καὶ) that in the context seems a little enigmatic.⁶⁵ This kind of connection is quite rare in archaic hexameter poetry, where it is used, usually at the beginning of the verse, to in-

---

62 On the *Aspis* there has always weighed the stain of 'pseudo-someone'. From the point of view of traditional oral poetry I think it is a pseudo-problem. An annotated list of different opinions on the subject can be found, however, in Martin (2005, 153–157), who is a firm believer that the *Aspis* belongs to the Hesiodic tradition. The pseudo-problem is, nevertheless, a trace that is significant, for our purposes, for thinking about the transition from oral traditions (linked to the authority of a traditional name that is the guarantor of the truth of the contents of the poem, see Aloni 2013) to the formation of a written corpus that is gradually defined starting from the poetic tradition and therefore a long-term process, hardly tied to a single 'author'.
63 *Aspis* 4–5: ἥ ῥα γυναικῶν φῦλον ἐκαίνυτο θηλυτεράων / εἴδεΐ τε μεγέθει τε ... ('She surpassed the tribe of female women in form and size'); *Cat.* fr. 180.10: ...]εΐνεκ' ἄρ' εἴδει ἐκαίνυτο [φῦλα γυναικῶν ('because in beauty she surpassed the [tribe of women]'). *Cat.* fr. 251a.9: Εὐαίχμην, ἣ εἴδε[ι ἐκαίνυτο φῦλα γυναικῶν ('Euaechme, who in beauty [surpassed the tribe of female women').
64 See Thalmann (1984) 36–38.
65 So enigmatic that in his translation Most feels the need of inserting a footnote in which he explains that Herakles is being spoken of.

troduce an expansion limited to a few verses or even just one.[66] In fact, the whole story to follow – that is, the fight against Kyknos – is already summarized in a transitional verse, followed in the next verse by a new start with an explanatory γάρ.

The struggle between Herakles and Kyknos occupies the poem until the end, which is not marked by any feature that indicates the end of the story. The expansion is structured in three typical and traditional moments. Vv. 58–121 present the two contenders and the reasons for their dispute. In this section there is another expansion, in which Herakles tells Iolaos of the different fates that befell him and his brother Iphikles (the father of Iolaos).

There follows the arming, divided into two different sections: the first is a typical scene (vv. 122–140), which stops at the moment of taking up the shield, itself the subject of an expansive digression in descriptive style (vv. 141–324). It is a piece of bravura that should be part of the baggage of every good singer.[67] Finally the deadly clash of Kyknos with the prowess of Herakles is narrated, the death of the son of Ares and, in a crescendo of Heraklean heroism, even the wounding of Ares, in a sequence to some extent comparable to the wounding of Aphrodite by Diomedes. Only at the end do we understand the reason for such violence: the desire for Apollo to rid the road leading to Delphi of the presence of Kyknos, who is obviously harmful to the interests of the sanctuary.

Compared to the *ehoie* of Alkmene in the *Catalogue*, the *Aspis* looks like an expansion that transforms that segment of the *Catalogue* into a poem adequate, in quantity and content, to a performance. The relation between the two poems is similar, though not identical, to the one we observe in the *Homeric Hymns*: the large- and medium-sized ones can be seen as expansions of a core that we can observe in the shorter *Hymns*, consisting of a prayer, a statement of the qualities and characteristics of the god, and a farewell. A narrative linked to the god who is the addressee expands this basic scheme to larger dimensions, indeed adequate to a performance.

We can conclude that the *Catalogue*, too, like *Works and Days*, presents the features characteristic of a *sylloge*, thematically oriented to the collection of erotic stories of women who united with a god and with him begat a race of heroes.

---

[66] See for example *Il.* 2.872–875, 5.52–54, 16.154.
[67] The perfect example is the Shield of Achilleus described in the *Iliad*, but examples are not lacking in other poetic forms, from the *Seven Against Thebes* to the *Phoenician Women*. I agree with Martin (2005, 170–173) on the fact that the description of a shield was part of the repertory of every rhapsode, and that the *Aspis* and the *Catalogue* belong to the same poetic tradition. I am less in agreement, as will soon be seen, with the solution that he proposes for the relation between the two poems.

The *Aspis*, in turn, reflects a performance based on an entry in the *Catalogue*. This is my point of disagreement with the conclusions of Martin mentioned above. The *Aspis* is part of the same poetic tradition as the *Catalogue*, but it is not a part extracted from it, at least as it now stands. The very nature of *sylloge*, an aid to performance but not the recording of a performance, which belongs to the *Catalogue*, distinguishes the two poems. My disagreement with Irwin (2005) is analogous. She has rightly shown that the *Catalogue*, as we read it, is much more suitable to a sympotic performance than to a public festival occasion. It cannot be excluded, indeed it is likely, that individual participants in the symposium challenged one another with shorter or longer songs exalting the lineage of this or that hero. The size of the individual entries in the *Catalogue* that has reached us is easily suitable to such songs. But this poem is not the recording of sympotic performances in Athens or some other place, but (to repeat) the *sylloge* comprising the competence of a singer, who – probably in Athens or, less probably, elsewhere – has decided or was induced to put in writing his now Panhellenic competence.

We come now to the *Theogony*. It is a genealogical narrative poem of 1022 verses, with parts almost completely catalogic, especially towards the end, and parts where the genealogical chain stops to give place to more or less extensive narrative expansions. But the most notable feature of the poem is that it opens with at least three proems simply juxtaposed to one another. The first is dedicated to the Helikonian Muses (1–34) and contains the story of the initiation of Hesiod by the Olympian Muses. The second is dedicated to the Olympian Muses (36–103) and has all the traits of an independent hymn on the scale of the Homeric Hymns of intermediate size, with a conclusion (104) that forms the transition to the third and final proem, dedicated again to the same Olympian Muses (105–115).[68] The conclusion is not entirely linear or finished: in 963–964 the poem gives a first farewell (ὑμεῖς μὲν νῦν χαίρετ', Ὀλύμπια δώματ' ἔχοντες, / νῆσοί τ' ἤπειροί τε καὶ ἁλμυρὸς ἔνδοθι πόντος 'Farewell now to you who dwell in mansions Olympian, and you islands and continents and the salty sea within'), followed by a thematically different reprise of the song (there is a switch from divine to heroic races born to a female deity)[69] and finally in 1019 ff. there is an

---

[68] On the three proems of the *Theogony*, see Aloni (2010).
[69] *Th.* 965–968: νῦν δὲ θεάων φῦλον ἀείσατε, ἡδυέπειαι / Μοῦσαι Ὀλυμπιάδες, κοῦραι Διὸς αἰγιόχοιο, / ὅσσαι δὴ θνητοῖσι παρ' ἀνδράσιν εὐνηθεῖσαι / ἀθάναται γείναντο θεοῖς ἐπιείκελα τέκνα ('And now, sweet-voiced Olympian Muses, daughters of aegis-holding Zeus, sing of the tribe of the goddesses, all those who bedded beside mortal men, and, immortal themselves, gave birth to children equal to the gods').

additional leave-taking, where the intention to sing the heroes, who are sons of gods and human women, is expressed.

The conclusion of the *Theogony* (1019–1022) seems to close the circle with the *Catalogue:*

αὗται μὲν θνητοῖσι παρ' ἀνδράσιν εὐνηθεῖσαι
ἀθάναται γείναντο θεοῖς ἐπιείκελα τέκνα.
νῦν δὲ γυναικῶν φῦλον ἀείσατε, ἡδυέπειαι
Μοῦσαι Ὀλυμπιάδες, κοῦραι Διὸς αἰγιόχοιο.

These are the goddesses who bedded beside mortal men and, immortal themselves, gave birth to children equal to the gods. And now sing of the tribe of women, sweet-voiced Olympian Muses, daughters of aegis-holding Zeus.

After the leave-taking there follows immediately a transition (1021–1022) to another narrative, with a formulation identical to the one that opens the proem to the *Catalogue*.[70]

Apropos of the proems it should be noted that both transitions, at *Th.* 34 and *Th.* 104, are traditional[71] and similar to the leave-takings in the Homeric Hymns. They signal the end of the proem and how the leave-takings lead the way to the next song. What can be inferred? The *Theogony* presents an entirely open structure, not locked in a definitive textuality. The proems testify to the use and reuse of the song in different contexts, for which one of the proems is by turns more suitable than the others. The repeated leave-takings that introduce a new, different song point in the same direction. The *Theogony*, too, reveals therefore a multiple nature: on the one hand it is the establishment in writing of a poem that could be the subject of a single performance; on the other it is also the recording of a competence that at any given time can generate, through re-composition in performance, different songs.

This description fits, in different ways, but only from a quantitative point of view, all the Hesiodic poems. The basic modality of the written record is the syl-

---

70 On the proem of the *Catalogue*, see Kyriakou 139–142; Sammons 164–165 (this volume).
71 For v. 34 compare: *Hom. Hymn to Apollo* (21) 4–5: ... σὲ δ' ἀοιδὸς ἔχων φόρμιγγα λίγειαν / ἡδυεπὴς πρῶτόν τε καὶ ὕστατον αἰὲν ἀείδει ('and of you the bard with his clear-toned lyre and sweet verse ever sings in first place and last', trans. West); Theogn. 3–4: ἀλλ' αἰεὶ πρῶτόν τε καὶ ὕστατον ἔν τε μέσοισιν / ἀείσω· σὺ δέ μοι κλῦθι καὶ ἐσθλὰ δίδου ('but I will ever sing of you first, last, and in between; and you give ear to me and grant me success', trans. Gerber); Arat. *Phaen.* 14: τῶι μιν ἀεὶ πρῶτόν τε καὶ ὕστατον ἱλάσκονται ('wherefore him do men ever worship first and last', trans. Mair). For the theme based on the connection between the imperatives of χαίρω and δίδωμι see for example: *Hom. Hymn to Aphrodite* (6) 19–20; *Hom. Hymn to Aphrodite* (10) 4–5; *Hom. Hymn to Herakles* (15) 9.

loge of the traditional competence of a singer in traditional themes: the divine and the heroic generations, the contrast between two different ways of governing. In one case, that of the *Aspis*, this is something created for a performance of traditional thematic material accumulated in the *sylloge* of the *Catalogue*. But even in this case we should not think either of the exact recording of a performance, or of the *libretto* of a song to be repeated exactly in performance. In each case it is a matter of open texts, which can be the base of or, as Nagy says, an aid to, performance.

This description also explains the thematic dispersion and aesthetic discontinuity that seems to characterize all of Hesiodic poetry. Beyond the greater or lesser poetic genius of the singer who recorded the text, what we possess is not, except partially, the song or the songs of that singer. The *sylloge* must, in every performance, be deconstructed and born anew.[72]

Bibliography

Adrados F. R. and O. Reverdin (1984). *La Fable*, Entretiens Hardt 30, Vandœuvres-Geneva.
Aloni, A. (2006). *Da Pilo a Sigeo. Poemi cantori e scrivani all'epoca dei Tiranni*, Alessandria.
Aloni, A. (2010). 'Esiodo a simposio. La performance delle *Opere e Giorni*', in: Cingano, 115–150.
Aloni, A. (2012). 'Epinician and Polis', *BICS* 55.2: 21–37.
Aloni, A. (2013). 'La sanzione del canto: strategie della verità (e della falsificazione) nella poesia greca arcaica', *Pallas* 91: 29–42.
Aloni, A. and A. Iannucci (2007). *L'elegia greca e l'epigramma dalle origini al V secolo. Con un'appendice sulla nuova elegia di Archiloco*, Florence.
Bintliff, J. L. (1996). 'The Archaeological Survey of the Valley of the Muses and Its Significance for Boeotian History', in: Hurst – Schachter, 193–224.
Blaise, F., P. Judet de la Combe, and Ph. Rousseau (1996). *Le métier du mythe. Lectures d'Hésiode*, Lille.
Bowie, E. (2012). 'An Early Chapter in the History of the *Theognidea*', in: Riu and Portulas 121–148.

---

[72] I must thank Hugo Koning for having made me read in a new way a Hesiodic testimonium that contains a statement attributed to Simonides (Gnom. Vat. Gr. 1144, f. 222ᵛ = T16 Most): Σιμωνίδης τὸν Ἡσίοδον κηπουρὸν ἔλεγε, τὸν δὲ Ὅμηρον στεφανηπλόκον, τὸν μὲν ὡς φυτεύσαντα τὰς περὶ θεῶν καὶ ἡρώων μυθολογίας, τὸν δὲ ὡς ἐξ αὐτῶν συμπλέξαντα τὸν Ἰλιάδος καὶ Ὀδυσσείας στέφανον ('Simonides said that Hesiod was a gardener and Homer a weaver of garlands, since the former planted the mythological stories about gods and heroes, while the latter wove together the garland of the *Iliad* and *Odyssey* out of them'). The opposition between Hesiod the gardener and Homer, whatever its meaning for Simonides, defines rather well the major part of the Hesiodic tradition, blooming with songs, which nevertheless require the voice of a singer in order to become real poetic communication.

Buck, R. J. (1979). A History of *Boeotia*, Edmonton.
Budelmann, F. (2009). *The Cambridge Companion to Greek Lyric Poetry*, Cambridge.
Calame, C. (1996a). 'Le proème des *Travaux* d'Hésiode, prélude à une poésie d'action', in: Blaise, Judet de la Combe, and Rousseau, 169–189.
Calame, C. (1996b). 'Montagne des Mouses et *Mouséia*: la consecration des *Travaux* et l'héroïsation d'Hésiode', in Hurst – Schachter, 43–56.
Calame, C. and R. Chartier (2004). *Identités d'auteur dans l'antiquité et la tradition européenne*, Grenoble.
Carter L. B. (1986). *The Quiet Athenian*, Oxford.
Cavarzere A., A. Aloni, and A. Barchiesi (2001). *Iambic Ideas. Essays on a Poetic Tradition from Archaic Greece to the Late Roman Empire*, Lanham.
Cerri, G. (2000). *La letteratura pseudoepigrafa nella cultura greca e romana*, Naples.
Cingano, E. (2005). 'A catalogue within a catalogue: Helen's suitors in the Hesiodic *Catalogue of Women* (frr. 196–204)', in: Hunter, 118–152.
Cingano, E. (2010). *Tra panellenismo e tradizioni locali: generi poetici e storiografia*, Alessandria.
Collins D. B. (2004). *Master of the Game. Competition and Performance in Greek Poetry*, Cambridge, MA.
Davies M. (2001). 'Homer and the Fable: *Odyssey* 21.293–306', *Prometheus* 27: 193–210.
Doukellis, P. N. and L. G. Mendoni (1994). *Structures rurales et sociétés antiques*, Paris.
Edwards, A. T. (2004). *Hesiod's Askra*, Berkeley-London.
Gentili, B. (1995³). *Poesia e pubblico nella Grecia antica*, Rome-Bari.
Gerber, D. E. (1999). *Greek Elegiac Poetry from the Seventh to the Fifth Centuries B.C.E.*, Cambridge, MA.
Hunter, R. (2005). *The Hesiodic* Catalogue of Women: *constructions and reconstructions*, Cambridge and New York.
Hurst, A. and A. Schachter (1996). *La montagne des Muses*, Geneva.
Irwin, E. (2005). 'Gods among men? The social and political dynamics of the Hesiodic *Catalogue of Women*', in: Hunter 35–84.
Kirchhoff A. (1889). *Hesiodos' Mahnlieder an Perses*, Berlin.
Koning, H. H. (2010). *Hesiod: The Other Poet, Ancient Reception of a Cultural Icon*, Leiden and Boston.
Lardinois, A. P. M. H. (2003). 'The Wrath of Hesiod: Angry Homeric Speeches and the Structure of Hesiod's *Works and Days*', *Arethusa* 36: 1–20.
Lasserre F. (1984). 'La fable en Grèce dans la poésie archaïque', in: Adrados and Reverdin, 61–103.
Lattimore, R. (1951). *The Iliad of Homer*. Chicago.
Lord, A. B. (1960). *The Singer of Tales*, Cambridge, MA.
Mair, A.W. and G. R. Mair (1921). *Callimachus: Hymns and Epigrams, Lycophron and Aratus*, Cambridge, MA.
Martin R. (2005). 'Pulp Epic: the *Catalogue* and the *Shield*', in: Hunter, 153–175.
Morris, I. (1994). 'Village Society and the Rise of the Greek State', in: Doukellis and Mendoni 1994, 49–53.
Most, G. (2006). *Hesiod I*. Theogony, Works and Days, *Testimonia, Edited and Translated by G. W. Most*, Cambridge, MA and London.

Most, G. (2007). *Hesiod II. The* Shield, Catalogue of Women, *other fragments, Edited and Translated by G. W. Most*, Cambridge, MA and London.
Nagy G. (1989). 'The Pan-Hellenization of the "Days" in the *Works and Days*', in: Sutton, 273–277.
Nagy G. (1990). *Pindar's Homer. The Lyric Possession of an Epic Past*, Baltimore and London.
Nagy G. (1996a). *Homeric Questions*, Austin.
Nagy G. (1996b). *Poetry as Performance. Homer and Beyond*, Cambridge, MA.
Nagy G. (2004). 'L'aède épique en auteur: la tradition des Vies d'Homère', in: Calame and Chartier, 41–67.
Pucci P. (1996). 'Auteur et destinataires dans les *Travaux* d'Hésiode', in: Blaise, Judet de la Combe, and Rousseau, 191–210
Riu, X. – Portulas, J. (2012). *Approaches to Ancient Greek Poetry*, Messina.
Roesch, P. and G. Argoud (1985). *La Béotie antique*, Paris.
Schoemann G. F. (1869). *Hesiodi quae feruntur carminum reliquiae cum commentatione critica ed. G. F. Schoemann*, Berlin.
Snodgrass, A. M. (1985). 'The Site of Askra', in: Roesch – Argoud, 87–95.
Strauss Clay J. (1993). 'The Education of Perses: from "Mega Nepios" to "Dion Genos" and Back', *MD* 31: 23–33.
Strauss Clay J. (2003). *Hesiod's Cosmos*, Cambridge.
Sutton, R. F. (1989). *Daidalikon: Studies in memory of Raymond V. Schoder*, Wauconda.
Tandy, D. W. (1997). *Warriors into Traders. The Power of the Market in Early Greece*, Berkeley, Los Angeles, and London.
Thalmann, W. G. (1984) *Conventions of Form and Thought in Early Greek Poetry*, Baltimore.
van Dijk G.-J. (1997). Ainoi, logoi, mythoi. *Fables in Archaic, Classical, and Hellenistic Greek Literature. With a Study of the Theory and Terminology of the Genre*, Leiden.
Vetta, M. (2000). 'Teognide e anonimi nella Silloge teognidea', in: Cerri, 123–141.
Waern I. (1951). ΓΗΣ ΟΣΤΕΑ. *The Kenning in Pre-Christian Greek Poetry*, Uppsala.
Welcker F. T. (1826). *Theognidis reliquiae, novo ordine disposuit, commentationem criticam et notas adiecit F. T. Welcker*, Frankfurt am Mein.
West M. L. (1978). *Hesiod*. Works and Days, *Edited with Prolegomena and Commentary by M. L. West*, Oxford.
West M. L. (1985). *The Hesiodic Catalogue of Women. Its Nature, Structure, and Origins*, Oxford.
West M. L. (1993). *Greek Lyric Poetry*, Oxford.
West M. L. (1999). 'The Invention of Homer', *CQ* 49: 364–382.
Yatromanolakis, D. (2009). 'Ancient Greek Popular Songs', in: Budelmann, 263–276.
Zanetto G. (2001). 'Iambic Patterns in Aristophanic Comedy', in: Cavarzere, Aloni, and Barchiesi, 65–76.

Andrea Ercolani
Fragments of Wisdom, Wisdom in Fragments

Early Greek epic poetry can be regarded as a 'tribal encyclopedia',[1] meaning that its content embraces all the relevant knowledge and value-systems of the society that produced it. The Greek society of the 7th century BC was still a predominantly oral culture (and remained such at least until the end of the 5th century BC), wherein epic poetry was not simply a literary phenomenon, but a social one.

This is our historical and cultural point of reference for understanding all of Hesiod's poems, including *Works and Days*. Ignoring for the moment questions of authenticity and chronology, the Hesiodic *corpus* forms a set of typical poems, each of which – even with its own specific content – represents and preserves a *summa* of shared traditional knowledge:[2] that is to say, the practical and ethical knowledge of an actual human group (at a given time and in a given place) has been collected and re-shaped in these poems. The aim of this paper is precisely to emphasize the traditional wisdom-content[3] of some Hesiodic fragments, primarily those belonging to poems which seem to have dealt, entirely and directly, with both practical and ethical wisdom.[4]

A few preliminary considerations: on the whole, the themes of the poems we take into account sometimes correspond with, and sometimes are complementary to, those of *Works and Days*. By considering the Hesiodic fragmentary poems together with *Works and Days* we can obtain a general overview of what kind of beliefs, knowledge, values, etc. were relevant for ancient Greek society (presently disregarding questions of strata and chronology of each poem or fragment). The poetic form of the texts suggests, first and foremost, that they were composed to be memorized: both the hexametric form and the rhetorical elaboration of the

---

[1] Havelock (1963).
[2] On the concept of tradition applied to epic poems in general, see Cantilena (2012). With respect to the the Hesiodic poems, I have repeatedly offered arguments supporting this view (Ercolani 2010, 39–42; Ercolani 2012; Ercolani 2016).
[3] Traditional wisdom should be considered – anthropologically – a proper ethnoscience in hexametric form.
[4] For brevity's sake I have intentionally excluded the fragments of *Catalog of Women*, as well as the *dubia* and the *incertae sedis*, despite the fact that here too we find material relevant to our question: for example, frr. 304, 309, 321 M.-W. (the latter reads ἔργα νέων, βουλαὶ δὲ μέσων, εὐχαὶ δὲ γερόντων: a typical structure in proverbial form, with nominal sentences). Fr. 338 is discussed below (p. 37).

texts seem to have served to facilitate memorization of the content. One more point must be duly emphasized: in collecting the fragments, we should take into account both formal elements and content. Among the former we may single out those elements which wisdom traditions use as expressive structures (i.e. kennings, *gnomai*, textual portions with particular rhetorical and/or rhythmical elaboration); as for the content, we may think of all the themes belonging to the so-called ethnoscience: technical knowledge, procedural norms, dietary prescriptions, astronomical lore, instructions on behaviour etc. In what follows I collect the relevant fragments under the title of the poem to which they certainly or presumably belong; in the commentary, clearly, *Works and Days* is the privileged point of reference.

Keykos gamos

The *Keykos gamos* (i.e. *Wedding of Keyx*) is a poem in hexameters attributed to Hesiod.[5] It seems to have dealt mainly with the wedding-episode in a narrative form.[6] Some of the fragments contain γνῶμαι and sentences in riddle-form, both typical of wisdom literature[7].

1. Fr. 264* (*apud* Zenob. II 19 = *CPG* I, 36–37)

   αὐτόματοι δ' ἀγαθοὶ ἀγαθῶν ἐπὶ δαῖτας ἵενται

   Of their own accord, good men hasten to the banquets of good men.

The verse, *stella notatus* by Merkelbach – West 1967 in light of its *minus certa origo*,[8] was undoubtedly perceived as a παροιμία, a 'proverb'.[9] The formal elab-

---

[5] For more information on title, content and attribution, see Schwartz (1960) 200–209; Merkelbach – West (1965). For a recent summary and synthesis, see Cingano (2009) 125–126.
[6] None the less, note the cautious considerations of Merkelbach – West 1965, p. 301 n. 4.
[7] See e.g. Ercolani (2010) 32–33 and 58 notes 68–70.
[8] See p. V in their edition. The attribution to Hesiod rests on a conjecture by Schneidewin. The text reads Ἡράκλειτος; yet 'Verum Heracliti nomen corruptum esse opinor ... Certissima emendatione reduco Hesiodum, qui herculem in Κήυκος γάμωι ista loquentem fecit' (*CPG* I, p. 37, *adnot.*).
[9] See e.g. Plat. *Symp.* 174b; Athen. 5.5; see as well the comic distortions of Eupolis (fr. 315 K.-A.) and even more so in Cratin. (fr. 182 K.-A.: οἱ δ' αὖθ' ἡμεῖς, ὡς ὁ παλαιὸς / λόγος, αὐτομάτους ἀγαθοὺς ἰέναι / κομψῶν ἐπὶ δαῖτα θεατῶν) who, regardless of the *detorsio comica*, clearly refers to this proverb as παλαιὸς λόγος. A final and definitive confirmation was its inclusion in the collection of proverbs of the *paroemiographoi*.

oration of the text is perfectly coherent with its proverbial tone: the polyptoton ἀγαθοὶ ἀγαθῶν, typical of the sententious formulations and the paroemiac *colon* (υυ – υυ – υυ – –‖) demonstrates the proverbial tone also from the rhythmic point of view.[10] The verse paradigmatically records the proclivity of equal peers to show up uninvited to each other's feast.[11] This social norm is like many others recorded in *Works and Days*. The fact that the *testimonia* attribute the παροιμία both to Heraclitus/Hesiod[12] and to Bacchylides[13] is not surprising, since it is not an isolated phenomenon: aside from the dubious case of fr. 266c discussed later, see at least fr. 273[14] and *Works and Days* 285, which corresponds to the final verse of the oracle *apud* Herod. 6.86γ, or even *Works and Days* 370, attributed to Pittheus, Theseus' grandfather, in an ancient tradition known to Aristotle (fr. 598 Rose = fr. 615 Gigon) and Plutarch (*Thes.* 3.4). In all of these cases, we are dealing with verses of wisdom-content (whether oracular or proverbial) with which, from what we can tell, many poems of various authors engaged, producing a circulation of diverse texts and contexts and resulting in a plurality of 'authors'. In these and similar cases, to think in terms of authenticity and to attempt a *reductio ad unum* of paternity risks utilizing an inappropriate methodology as well as being historically inaccurate.

---

10 On the poliptoton see. e.g. *Op.* 23 with the comment of Ercolani (2010) *ad loc.*; on the hexameters with paroemiac cadence, see Pellizer (1972); Sbardella (1995); summary and synthesis in Ercolani (2010) 70–71. In general, on sententious statements in *Works and Days*, see Ercolani (2009).
11 A similar norm is found in *Kalevala* as indicated by Merkelbach – West (1965) 303 n. 10. In any case, it is difficult fully to reconstruct the cultural data behind it. For an ancient discussion, see the passage by Plato cited above (note 9). Participation in communal meals and the expected behaviour attached thereto are considered in many areas of Greek literary production: see for example the material compiled by Athenaeus 8.66 [364a-d] cited and discussed below (p. 39–42).
12 See note 8.
13 On this, see Athenaeus 5.5, who enjoys presenting as much similar material as possible: Βακχυλίδης δὲ περὶ τοῦ Ἡρακλέους λέγων ὡς ἦλθεν ἐπὶ τὸν τοῦ Κήυκος οἶκόν φησιν (*Pae.* 4. 21–25 Maehl.) 'ἔστη δ' ἐπὶ λάινον οὐδόν, τοὶ δὲ θοίνας ἔντυον, ὧδέ τ' ἔφα· 'αὐτόματοι δ' ἀγαθῶν δαῖτας εὐόχθους ἐπέρχονται / δίκαιοι φῶτες'. αἱ δὲ παροιμίαι ἣ μέν φησιν· 'αὐτόματοι δ' ἀγαθοὶ ἀγαθῶν ἐπὶ δαῖτας ἴασιν', ἣ δέ 'αὐτόματοι ἀγαθοὶ δειλῶν ἐπὶ δαῖτας ἴασιν'.
14 See p. 34 (this volume).

2. Fr. 266c (*apud* Trypho(?) *de tropis* 23 = *Rhet. Gr.* III 224–225 Spengel = West 1965, pp. 246–247)[15]

I quote the fragment with the entire context, exactly following Merkelbach – West 1967:

> Αἴνιγμά ἐστι φράσις διάνοιαν ἀποκεκρυμμένην καὶ ἀσύνετον πειρωμένη ποιεῖν, ὡς τὰ παρ' Ἡσιόδωι περὶ τῆς κύλικος λεγόμενα·
>
> μηδέ ποτ' οἰνοχόην τιθέμεν κρητῆρος ὕπερθεν. [= *Op.* 744]
> < >
> αὐτὰρ ἐπεὶ δαιτὸς μὲν ἐίσης ἐξ ἔρον ἕντο,
> †οἷον οὔ μητέρα μητρὸς < > ἄγοντο
> <ἀζαλέην τε καὶ ὀπταλέην σφετέροισι τέκεσσι
> τεθνάναι.
>
> ... «ἀζαλέην καὶ ὀπταλέην», ἐπεὶ δοκεῖ πρῶτα μὲν ξηραίνεσθαι, εἶτα ὀπτᾶσθαι. σφετέροισι τέκεσσι, τοῖς ἑαυτοῦ τέκνοις, λέγει δὲ τοῖς ξένοις. τὸ δὲ τεθνάναι, καθὸ δοκεῖ ἐκ τῆς ὕλης ἐκκεκόφθαι.

> An enigma is an utterance which tries to make its meaning hidden and unintelligible, as for example what is said in Hesiod about the wine-cup:
>
> And do not ever put the ladle on top of the wine-bowl. [= *Op.* 744]
> < >
> but when they had put away the desire for the equal banquet
> † mother's mother [ ] they led <to the children,>
> <dry and roasted to their own children
> to die.>
>
> ... "Dry and roasted", since it seems that first they are dried, then roasted. "To their own children", to their own children, he means to their guests. "To die", since it seems to have been cut out of the wood.

It is worth noticing that the cited verses, from the point of view of the commentator, constitute an αἴνιγμα, as expressly declared in the beginning of the text. That is, they are formulated as a riddle, a pattern frequently employed in *Works and Days*.

---

[15] The fragment is also known by P.Oxy. 2495, fr. 37 (= fr. 266a, vv. 8–11; the *testimonia* also point to fragments such as fr. 266b). Cross-referencing the papyrus textual data – specifically v. 5, which reads καθ.εδρας deleted by the hand of the scribe and, *suprascriptum*, τρα]πεζας – with Athen. 2.32 [49b] (and Poll. 6.83) ὅτι Ἡσίοδος ἐν Κήυκος γάμωι ... τρίποδας τὰς τραπέζας φησί, it seems evident that we must refer the information of Athenaeus to the beginning of the papyrus, and therefore we must assign the fragment to *Keykos gamos*. It is worth mentioning, even if only in passing, that the aforementioned gloss implies that the fragmentary text relative to τρίποδας / τραπέζας should also be an αἴνιγμα.

Regarding the citation of *Works and Days* 744, West (1965), and later Merkelbach – West (1967), hypothesize an omission immediately thereafter assuming that the subject is fully a citation.[16] In any case, there is no gap in the paradosis, and the absence of explicative formulations that isolate the cited verse (as occurs systematically in the other passages discussed by Tryphon) gives weight to the hypothesis that we are dealing with an extract taken entirely from *Keykos gamos*, a poem that evidently featured the same hexameter as that of *Works and Days* 744. If this is so, we would have a further example of traditional wisdom material used in diverse contexts.[17] In whatever manner the question is posed, it is clear that in formal terms as well as in content, we are dealing with verses that we can consider fully fit to be included in a wisdom tradition.[18]

3. Fr. 268 (*apud* Σ *Il.* 7.76)

ἀπάτωροι

fatherless ones

Even without a clear context, it appears that we are dealing with a kenning that speaks of the first, or original, people (see also the note by Merkelbach and West in *app. ad loc.*).[19]

Melampodia

An epic three-book poem, according to ancient sources, concerning the seer Melampus. The figure of the seer, central to the narrative, coincides with that of the

---

16 See e.g. West (1965) 246 *ad loc.*: 'post eum [*scil. Op.* 744] excidisse existimo interpretationem nescioquam'.
17 See the above discussion on fr. 264. As a macroscopic example, regardless of the details, the relation between *Aspis* and *Catalogue* comes to mind.
18 Rather than enigma, perhaps we should speak of γρῖφος or riddle. In any case, as much as the enigma is found in other communicative contexts, for example the symposium, the point is that regardless of where it is used, its interactive function vis-à-vis the intended recipient, who is called to decode a message, implies a mental process that fits well in the didactic dynamics of the wisdom traditions. On αἴνιγμα and γρῖφος in general, see Monda (2012). On the Hesiodic material, see also Ercolani (2010) and notes in 430, 524, 533.
19 Similar formulations are found in Ercolani (2010) 32–33; for linguistically parallel formations, see ἄτριχος (Hes. fr. 204.129).

'wise man' (or medicine-man or something similar) present in many cultures.[20] For this reason the poem as a whole can be labeled as a wisdom epic.[21]

1. Fr. 273 (*apud* Clem. Alex. *Strom.* 6.2.26 [II 442. 16 Stählin], *de furtis poetarum Graecorum*)

> Ἡσίοδός τε ἐπὶ τοῦ Μελάμποδος ποιεῖ·
>> ἡδὺ δὲ καὶ τὸ πυθέσθαι, ὅσα θνητοῖσιν ἔνειμαν[22]
>> ἀθάνατοι δειλῶν τε καὶ ἐσθλῶν τέκμαρ ἐναργές
>
> καὶ τὰ ἑξῆς, παρὰ Μουσαίου λαβὼν τοῦ ποιητοῦ κατὰ λέξιν.

> and Hesiod writes about Melampus,
>> and it is sweet too to learn the clear distinguishing mark
>> of bad and good things that the immortals have assigned to mortals.
>
> And so on, taking it literally from the poet Musaios

The source, Clement of Alexandria, cites two hexameters of gnomic content from the *Melampodia* as Hesiodic (evidently reading from a larger *perikope* if not the entire work, given the formulation καὶ τὰ ἑξῆς). Clement affirms that Hesiod had taken them κατὰ λέξιν ('verbatim') from the poet Musaeus. Both the structure of the text (an impersonal formulation in the infinitive, typical of formulations of a general scope)[23] as well as its content (knowledge of divine designs) are characteristic of a wisdom tradition. The fact that the same text circulated under the name of Musaeus, that is, that of another poet with marked characteristics of a wise man, confirms the claim. For this reason I believe we should give greater

---

[20] The few certain data in this poem pertain to the figures of some wise men: Teiresias' relationship to the animal world and his changes of gender come to mind (see fr. 275 M.-W.), for Melampous, one thinks of his traits as healer (fr. 272 M.-W., that most probably refers to healing Iphiklos); in both cases the 'wise' men are seers.

[21] On the *Melampodia*, see Schwartz (1960) 210–228 and Löffler (1963); more recently Cingano (2009) 121–123, and now Cozzoli (2016). On the relationship between oracular poetry and Hesiodic epic, Fernández Delgado (1986) remains definitive.

[22] ἔνειμαν is a conjecture of Schneider; the manuscripts have ἔδειμαν; this changes little regarding our understanding of the passage. On the textual question see Bernabé (2007) 51, in the crit. app. on fr. 99, with bibliography.

[23] On the *incipit* in the first hexameter, see *Od.* 20.391 || ἡδύ τε καί. On the impersonal gnomic formations with ἡδύ, see for example Eur. *Troad.* 683, *Hel.* 665, *Or.* 1175f., *I.A.* 1218f. etc. On the structure 'neuter adjective (+ ἐστί) + infinitive', see Ercolani (2009), especially 37f.

consideration to the hypothesis that there existed a 'reservoir of wisdom', so to speak, from which the multiple and different poets were able to draw.²⁴

2. Fr. 274 (*apud* Athen. 2.13 [40f])

ἡδύ ἐστιν

    ... ἐν δαιτὶ καὶ εἰλαπίνηι τεθαλυίηι
τέρπεσθαι μύθοισιν, ἐπὴν δαιτὸς κορέσωνται

it is sweet

    ... in the feast and blooming banquet
to take pleasure in stories, when they have their fill of the feast.

Thus reads the text in Merkelbach – West 1967. Athenaeus' text (in the edition of G. Kaibel) has ἡδὺ ἐστ' ἐν δαιτὶ καὶ εἰλαπίνηι τεθαλυίηι, which does not scan as a hexameter, given that it starts with a cretic (– υ –).²⁵ The text is easily corrected using any of the proposed emendations: ἥδιστον δ' ἐν δαιτὶ (Meineke) or ἡδὺ <μέν> ἐστ' (Peppmüller). The result is a general affirmation with a common formal structure, that is, an impersonal construction in the infinitive (on this point, see above the discussion on fr. 273).²⁶ The text deals with proper social behavior, that is, to enjoyment of narratives (epics?) following a communal or shared meal, that of the δαίς. This brings to mind analogous situations described in the *Odyssey*, where singing or story-telling (for example the *apologoi* of Odysseus at the court of Phaiakians in *Od.* 9–12) follows the feast. The text of the fragment cor-

---

24 On this issue, see above 30–33 the discussion of frr. 264* and 266.
25 I do not incline to admit a trochee in the first metron, even if Wilamowitz (1928) 56–57 (on *Op.* 132) maintained that this is characteristic of the Hesiodic hexameters such as *Op.* 22, 132, 372, 550, 655, *Th.* 454 (also *Th.* 466 and 532 according to the text given by the manuscript tradition). If Wilamowitz is right, however, the transmitted text does not require correction.
26 If, as hypothesized by Meineke (Merkelbach – West 1967 *in app. ad loc.*), frr. 273 and 274 are joined, the beginning of 274 could read more plausibly ἥδιον ἐστ' ἐν, applying a slight correction to the text of Athenaeus (i.e. ἥδιον *pro* ἡδύ). We would thus have a sequence of general affirmations that covers the length of two hexameters. A strict linguistic parallel for the succession ἡδὺ ... ἥδιον is found in *A.P.* 5.169 ἡδὺ ... ἡδὺ δὲ ναύταις / ἐκ χειμῶνος ἰδεῖν εἰαρινὸν Στέφανον·/ ἥδιον κτλ. The conceptual climax is not foreign to the Hesiodic poetic tradition: for example, note the descending climax in *Op.* 293–297 (πανάριστος / ἐσθλός / ἀχρήιος), here too with conceptual unity organized in blocks of two hexameters. On the fact that the fragments constitute a single extract, see also Buttmann (1825) 128 (cited by Rzach *in app. ad* fr. 163) who, however, places them in inverted sequence, that is, frr. 274+273.

responds to well-documented anthropological practice in Greek culture, with the sequence '(communal) meal > story-telling', with the objective of *terpein*.[27]

3. Fr. 275 (*apud* Apollod. 3.6.7, Σ Hom. *Od.* 10.494, Σ Lycophr. 683 [II 226 Scheer]; see Phlegon *Mirab.* IV, pp. 73–74 Keller)

> οἵην μὲν μοῖραν δέκα μοιρέων τέρπεται ἀνήρ,
> τὰς δὲ δέκ' ἐμπίπλησι γυνὴ τέρπουσα νόημα.

> In only one portion out of ten portions a man has delight,
> but the ten a woman fills out, delighting her senses.

These verses constitute the answer given by Teiresias to the question of whether sexual relations are more pleasurable for women or for men, a question that sets off a fight between Zeus and Hera. The story, known in summary form and paraphrased by witnesses,[28] is presented as a consultation with an oracle. Oracular poetry, we should remember, absolves itself of the need to explain the past and the present, thus forming one of the qualities of wisdom traditions.[29]

4. Fr. 278 (*apud* Strab. 14.1.27)

> 'θαῦμά μ' ἔχει κατὰ θυμόν, ἐρινεὸς ὅσσον ὀλύνθων
> οὗτος ἔχει, μικρός περ ἐών· εἴποις ἂν ἀριθμόν';

> τὸν δ' ἀποκρίνασθαι·

> 'μύριοί εἰσιν ἀριθμόν, ἀτὰρ μέτρον γε μέδιμνος·
> εἷς δὲ περισσεύει, τὸν ἐπενθέμεν οὔ κε δύναιο'.
> ὣς φάτο, καί σφιν ἀριθμὸς ἐτήτυμος εἴδετο μέτρου.
> καὶ τότε δὴ Κάλχανθ' ὕπνος θανάτοιο κάλυψεν.

> 'Astonishment grips me in my spirit at how many figs
> this fig-tree holds, small though it is: could you tell the number?'

> And the other replied,

> 'Ten thousand is the number, and the measure is a bushel;
> one is left over, which you could not add to it'.

---

[27] On τέρπειν as the goal of aedic songs, see *Od.* 1.368–371 and 421–423, 4.15–18, 8.367–369 and 429, 13.26–28, 17.385; see as well 17.605–606 and 18.304–306. For a synthesis see Ercolani (2006) 136–137. The communal meal, the δαίς, is also dealt with elsewhere in Hesiodic poetry. In addition to *Op.* 722–723, see below the discussion of the *Testimonium* of the *Megala Erga*.
[28] For a detailed discussion of witnesses, see Schwartz (1960) 216–220.
[29] On oracular poetry as an integral part of a wisdom tradition, see the discussion in Ercolani (2016) on the subject of Musaeus and Hesiod. In general, on oracular poetry in ancient Greece, see Vannicelli (2014), with extensive bibliography.

So he spoke, and they saw that the number of the measure was true;
and then the sleep of death shrouded Kalchas.

This passage relates to the rivalry between two seers, Kalchas and Mopsos (the latter a descendent of Teiresias), resolved with Kalchas' loss and death (v. 6). It deals with a wisdom-duel that follows a well-documented anthropological model of competition[30] especially common in Greek culture.[31]

Cheironos Hypothekai

A poem in hexameters centered on Achilleus receiving advice from Cheiron.[32] The latter word of the title, *hypothekai* ('exhortations'), indicates a kind of generic subcategory of the more general category of 'wisdom literature'.[33]

1. Fr. 283 (*apud* Σ Pind. *Pyth.* 6.22 [II 197 Drachmann])

> Εὖ νῦν μοι τάδ' ἕκαστα μετὰ φρεσὶ πευκαλίμηισι
> φράζεσθαι· πρῶτον μέν, ὅτ' ἂν δόμον εἰσαφίκηαι,
> ἔρδειν ἱερὰ καλὰ θεοῖς αἰειγενέτηισι
>
> Now note well all these things in your prudent spirit:
> first, whenever you come home,
> make a beautiful sacrifice to the eternally living gods.

Ritual instructions of this type, specifically recommendations of a preliminary sacrifice for the gods, fall under the broader category of wisdom prescriptions. On the theme of sacrifice in Hesiodic poetry, see *Op.* 336–341, in particular

---

30 See Levi-Strauss (1958) 192–196.
31 See e.g. the agonal structure of the *Certamen* as a representation of the rhapsodic contests. On *Certamen* see Bassino (2013); regarding the contrast as a pattern (and motif) typical of wisdom texts, see Ercolani (2015) with further bibliography.
32 On this poem, see Schwartz (1960) 228–244 and Cingano (2009) 128–129 ('Its purpose can be traced to the traditional wisdom poetry of the Near East, represented in Greece by the early gnomic poetry ...' [128]).
33 See for example the various 'instructions' or 'teachings' known in the Near East (see West 1997 with bibliography). Specifically on material of Indo-European origin, see Martin (1984) and Canevaro (2014).

336 κὰδ δύναμιν δ' ἔρδειν ἱέρ' ἀθανάτοισι θεοῖσιν, with the value of the prescription clearly manifest, as here, by the jussive infinitive ἔρδειν.[34]

2. Fr. 338 (*apud* Plut. *de Stoic. repugn.* 8 [*Mor.* 1034E])

> μηδὲ δίκην δικάσῃς, πρὶν ἄμφω μῦθον ἀκούσῃς
>
> do not pass judgment before you hear the speech of both

This fragment, among the *fragmenta dubia* of Rzach 1902 (see fr. 271 of that edition) and of Merkelbach – West 1967, was assigned to the *Cheironos Hypothekai* by Schneidewin, followed by Evelyn-White (see Evelyn-White 1914, *ad loc.*). Even without accepting that it forms part of the *Cheironos Hypothekai*, it is certainly hexametric and abounds in proverbial and wisdom content (decreeing, essentially, the juridical principal of *altera pars audiatur*) as confirmed by Aristoph. *Vesp.* 725–726: ἦ που σοφὸς ἦν ὅστις ἔφασκεν, 'πρὶν ἂν ἀμφοῖν μῦθον ἀκούσῃς, / οὐκ ἂν δικάσαις'.[35]

Megala Erga

The title seems to indicate a larger version of *Works and Days*. If so, the existence of two different forms of a single poem, whose content agrees perfectly with the definition of wisdom literature, can be better explained by considering different (geographically and diachronically) kinds of addressees.[36]

1. Fr. 286 (*apud comm. in Aristot. Eth. Nicom.* 8 [*Comm. in Aristot. gr.* XX 222.22])

> εἰ κακά τις σπείραι, κακὰ κέρδεά <κ'> ἀμήσειεν·
> εἴ κε πάθοι, τά τ' ἔρεξε, δίκη κ' ἰθεῖα γένοιτο
>
> If someone sowed evils, he would reap evil profits,
> if he suffered what he committed, the judgment would be straight

This fragment is a proverb attributed to Rhadamanthys (τὸ τοῦ 'Ραδαμάνθυος in the introduction to the citation; Merkelbach – West 1967 *in app. ad loc.* speak in

---

[34] On the usage of the jussive infinitive in similar formulations see Ercolani (2009) 35 (in 2.6.2) and Ercolani (2010) 387.
[35] On this concept's diffusion in Greece, see Rzach (1902) 412 *ad loc.*
[36] On the *Megala Erga* we have scant information: see Schwartz (1960) 245–246 and Cingano (2009) 129.

terms of 'lex Rhadamanthys'). The causistic structure (following the usual logical model 'if ... then ...') is typical of prescriptive literature.[37] Regarding its meaning, the hexameters insist, from different points of view, on the idea of reciprocal compensation as found in the biblical proverb 'they have sown the wind, and they shall reap the whirlwind' (Hosea 8:7).[38] The notion that 'one reaps what one sows', or 'what goes around comes around', is common in traditional proverbs of many cultures.[39]

2. *Testimonium* to the *Megala Erga* (Merkelbach – West 1967, p. 146 = T66 Most)
This testimony deserves special attention. It deals with a passage of Athenaeus (8.66 [364a-d]) on the participation in sacrifices and related sacrificial meals.

οἱ δὲ νῦν προσποιούμενοι θεοῖς θύειν καὶ συγκαλοῦντες ἐπὶ τὴν θυσίαν τοὺς φίλους καὶ τοὺς οἰκειοτάτους καταρῶνται μὲν τοῖς τέκνοις, λοιδοροῦνται δὲ ταῖς γυναιξί, κλαυθμυρίζουσιν τοὺς οἰκέτας, ἀπειλοῦσι τοῖς πολλοῖς, μονονουχὶ τὸ τοῦ Ὁμήρου λέγοντες (*Il.* 2.381)·
  νῦν δ' ἔρχεσθ' ἐπὶ δεῖπνον, ἵνα ξυνάγωμεν Ἄρηα,
ἐπὶ νοῦν λαμβάνοντες τὰ εἰρημένα ὑπὸ τοῦ τὸν Χείρωνα πεποιηκότος, εἴτε Φερεκράτης ἐστὶν εἴτε Νικόμαχος ὁ ῥυθμικὸς ἢ ὅστις δή ποτε (Pher. fr. 162 K.-A.)·
  μηδὲ σύ γ' ἄνδρα φίλον καλέσας ἐπὶ δαῖτα θάλειαν
  ἄχθου ὁρῶν παρεόντα· κακὸς γὰρ ἀνὴρ τόδε ῥέζει·
  ἀλλὰ μάλ' εὔκηλος τέρπου φρένα τέρπε τ' ἐκεῖνον.
νῦν δὲ τούτων μὲν οὐδ' ὅλως μέμνηνται, τὰ δὲ ἐξῆς αὐτῶν ἐκμανθάνουσιν, ἅπερ πάντα ἐκ τῶν εἰς Ἡσίοδον ἀναφερομένων μεγάλων Ἠοίων καὶ μεγάλων Ἔργων πεπαρῴδηται·
  ἡμῶν δ' ἤν τινά τις καλέσηι θύων ἐπὶ δεῖπνον,
  ἀχθόμεθ' ἢν ἔλθηι καὶ ὑποβλέπομεν παρεόντα
  χὥττι τάχιστα θύραζ' ἐξελθεῖν βουλόμεθ' αὐτόν.
  εἶτα γνούς πως τοῦθ' ὑποδεῖται, κἆιτά τις εἶπε
  τῶν ξυμπινόντων 'ἤδη σύ; τί οὐχ ὑποπίνεις;
  οὐχ ὑπολύσεις αὐτόν;' ὃ δ' ἄχθεται αὐτὸς ὁ θύων
  τῶι κατακωλύοντι καὶ εὐθὺς ἔλεξ' ἐλεγεῖα (Theogn. 467)·
  'μηδένα μήτ' ἀέκοντα μένειν κατέρυκε παρ' ἡμῖν
  μήθ' εὕδοντ' ἐπέγειρε, Σιμωνίδη'. οὐ γὰρ ἐπ' οἴνοις
  τοιαυτὶ λέγομεν δειπνίζοντες φίλον ἄνδρα;
ἔτι δὲ καὶ ταῦτα προστίθεμεν (Hes. *Op.* 722–723)·
  μηδὲ πολυξείνου δαιτὸς δυσπέμφελον εἶναι
  ἐκ κοινοῦ· πλείστη τε χάρις δαπάνη τ' ὀλιγίστη.

---

37 On precepts expressed in hypothetical-conditional form, see Ercolani (2009) 34–35.
38 See e.g. *Op.* 721 εἰ δὲ κακὸν εἴποις, τάχα κ' αὐτὸς μεῖζον ἀκούσαις. See as well, with a different approach, *Op.* 265–266 οἷ αὑτῶι κακὰ τεύχει ἀνὴρ ἄλλωι κακὰ τεύχων, / ἡ δὲ κακὴ βουλὴ τῶι βουλεύσαντι κακίστη, on which see Ercolani (2010) *ad loc.*
39 A sample of similar proverbs can be found in Arthaber (1989) nr. 489.

People today, on the other hand, make a pretence of sacrificing to the gods and inviting their friends and family to the event, but then swear at their children, speak rudely to their wives, reduce their slaves to tears, threaten the group as a whole, and do everything but quote the Homeric line (*Il.* 2.381):

But now go to your dinner, so that we can join battle,

not keeping in mind the words of the author of the *Cheiron* – whether this is Pherecrates (fr. 162), or the rhythmician Nicomachus, or whoever it may be:

If you invite a friend to a large meal,
don't be upset when you see him there; this is how a bad man behaves.
Instead, enjoy yourself, entirely at your ease, and make him happy.

Whereas nowadays they forget these lines entirely, and memorize those that come immediately after them, all of which are adapted from the *Megalai Ehoiai* [and *Megala Erga*] attributed to Hesiod:

If one of us invites a guest to dinner when he's making a sacrifice,
we're upset if the fellow comes, and we give him dirty looks while he's there,
and want him to leave as soon as possible.
Then somehow he recognizes this and puts on his shoes; but one of the other guests
says 'Are you leaving already? Why don't your drink a bit?
Take off his shoes!', And the man making the sacrifice gets upset
at the one doing the detaining, and immediately quotes the elegiac lines:
'Neither hold back anyone who is unwilling to remain with us,
nor wake the man who is asleep, Simonides'. Don't we say things like this
over our wine, when we have a friend to dinner?

I also add the following passage (Hes. *Op.* 722–723):

Don't act put out if there are many guests at a feast;
when everyone contributes, there's more pleasure and considerably less expense.[40]

The underlined section of the Greek text expressly states that the hexametric citations are taken from the poems *Megalai Ehoiai* and *Megala Erga* attributed to Hesiod. The difficulty in assigning a single text to two different works led to the removal of one of the two: Kaibel (1887, 296), in the edition of Athenaeus' text, following Dindorf (see *in app. ad loc.* and also Marcksheffel 1840, 188), removed [καὶ μεγάλων Ἔργων], therefore attributing the citations to the *Megalai Eoiai*;[41] Merkelbach and West (1967, 146), even while reproducing the text of the manu-

---

[40] The translation is by S. Douglas Olson (*Athenaeus:* The Learned Banqueters, Books 8–10.420E, Cambridge, MA and London, England, 2008, 169–171) with some modifications and one addition in square brackets [ ].
[41] Similarly Olson's translation. Gulick (1969, 148) refrains from taking a position and prints the text of the manuscripts in addition to mentioning Dindorf's removal. Schwartz (1960, 30 and 245) refrains as well, even mentioning the passage from Athenaeus.

scripts, included a note of warning (2) 'verba μεγάλων Ἠοίων καὶ delenda videntur', thus making the text a witness of the *Megala Erga*.⁴² Without changing the text, the words of Athenaeus can be understood at face value, meaning that the two citations from the *Cheiron*⁴³ combine verses from two different works attributed to Hesiod.⁴⁴ Another possibility, even if less probable, is that Athenaeus' text could be indicating, vaguely and approximately, two 'Hesiodic' works from which the citations might possibly be taken.

In any case, we are not concerned with determining which 'Hesiodic' poem or poems were cited; rather, our interest is their content. Athenaeus expressly declares that he deals with parody. Yet, the distortions natural to the genre of parody seem to characterize the second hexametric extract, clearly illustrating the opposite behavior with respect to the 'positive norm' of the former. It is precisely this second extract that seems to be a comic *pastiche* combining various elements: a 'Hesiodic' portion of text that is more or less reshuffled, a few autonomous elements from Pherecrates (or whoever else), other poetic materials from Theognis.⁴⁵ Altogether, the feeling of the text is that the first hexametric extract is a genuinely 'Hesiodic' citation, while the second is a kind of comment that combines material of different origins.⁴⁶ In this regard, it is important to high-

---

42 Along these lines, Marckscheffel acutely saw (1840, 182–188) *Megala Erga* as a conglomeration of a series of Hesiodic poems ('carminum Hesiodiorum didactici generis collectionem', 188), that is, *Works and Days, Ornithomanteia, Oionoskopia, Cheironos Hypothekai*.
43 It is worth highlighting that this work (most surely a comedy; see e.g. Markscheffel 1840, 184: 'his [scil. verbis] comoediam significari Chironis nomine inscriptam patet'), at least in its title refers to Cheiron's centaur figure, Achilleus' tutor, thus recalling by implication the Hesiodic tradition of *Cheironos Hypothekai*. Marckscheffel's reasoning (1840, 188) is thus plausible: since the comic poet is dealing with a poem of gnomic content, 'itaque conienctura nostra, quam supra e comoediae nomine ductam significauimus, non improbabilis iudicabitur, Χείρωνος ὑπο- θήκας illud carmen fuisse'. That Hesiodic precept-material would be taken up by a comedy or the like dealing with Cheiron as tutor is perfectly reasonable; that it truly deals with *Cheironos Hypothekai*, even hypothetically, is likewise reasonable.
44 Most 2007 also seems to suggest this, invoking the testimony (T66) for both *Megalai Eoiai* (p. 205) and *Megala Erga* (p. 209). See also, n. 46.
45 On Theognis, the *Theognidea*, and Hesiodic poetry, see Aloni 3–27 (this volume).
46 This I believe was B. Gulick's (1969, 149 n. b) intention, regardless of the attribution of the verses, when he commented on the first extract of three hexameters: 'Assigned to the comic poet Pherecrates, but possibly copied by him verbatim from the Hesiodic Eoeae', following an interpretive line that can be traced at least to Bergk (1838, 225): 'haec non ab ipso Pherecrate sunt profecta, sed ex Hesiodo, ut uidetur ex his ipsis Achillis praeceptis, mutuo translata et huic comoediae accomodata'. For Bergk, even the successive verses reflect in large part the originals: 'uti etiam ii uersus, qui sequuntur, magna ex parte ex Hesiodi Operibus et fortasse ex magnis Eoeis et ex Theognidis Elegiis sunt petiti' (225–226).

light a few stylistic features from the first citation that are fully coherent with the formal features of the precepts; that is, the use of the imperative and the use of the term ἀνήρ.[47] Since these features adhere to both the first citation and the precepts, we should recognize these hexameters as *ipsissima verba hesiodea* and include them at least in the *fragmenta incertae sedis*. A fact that seems less uncertain is that the extract of citations assembled by Athenaeus focuses exclusively on sacrifice and the sacrificial meal (even when comparing a positive exemplary model of the past with a negative model from the present). The sacrifice and its related feast are a wisdom theme, one which appears as a locus of concern in the Hesiodic prescriptive texts, as seen in the passage from Athenaeus, and which certainly was a point of focus in *Op.* 722–723. These two verses, in the form of an *addendum* (ἔτι δὲ καὶ ταῦτα προστίθεμεν) expound behavioural norms in the occasion of a δαΐς.[48] It is exactly this minimum *datum* that I want to highlight: the presence of precepts related to the sacrificial meal in the Hesiodic poetic tradition, transmitted both directly (*Works and Days*), as well as in dispersed fragments no longer clearly assignable or identifiable to a specific poem, yet considered Hesiodic nonetheless.

Astronomia[49]

A poem (or a section of a poem?)[50] dealing with astronomical data, largely used by farmers (in order to determine seasonal times) and by mariners. Astronomical observation, that is, the observation of the celestial realm and the movement of the constellations, constitute one of the first forms of marking time, clearly functional in determining seasonal periods in which to conduct economic activities.[51] It is thus understandable that in astronomical digressions we are dealing with a central theme of many wisdom traditions, including Greek traditions found condensed in a number of poems. For example, Pleiades and Hyades constituted a

---

47 On the use of ἀνήρ in general sentences, see Fernández Delgado (1978).
48 On the interpretive questions regarding the text see Ercolani (2010) *ad* 722 and 723.
49 I consider here only fragments of certain attribution. On the possibility that other fragments should be ascribed to *Astronomia*, especially frr. 148, 149, 163, 169, 170, 394, see Merkelbach – West (1967) 150.
50 In addition to the detailed discussion in Schwartz (1960) 248–261, see as well Cingano (2009) 129–130.
51 On astronomical observation for calendar purposes, especially observation of the Pleiades for marking seasonal periods, see Ercolani (2010) 280 f. *ad* 383–384 with bibliography.

central subject in the case of Musaeus, in the Hesiodic fragments discussed below, and in the *loci* of *Works and Days*.⁵²

1. Frr. 288–290 (*apud* Athen. 11.80 [491c-d])

> καὶ ὁ τὴν εἰς Ἡσίοδον δὲ ἀναφερομένην ποιήσας Ἀστρονομίαν αἰεὶ Πελειάδας αὐτὰς λέγει (fr. 288)
> τὰς δὲ βροτοὶ καλέουσι Πελειάδας.
> καὶ πάλιν (fr. 289)
> χειμέριαι δύνουσι Πελειάδες.
> καὶ πάλιν (fr. 290)
> τῆμος ἀποκρύπτουσι Πελειάδες.

> The author of the *Astronomy* attributed to Hesiod always calls them Pleiades:
> mortals call these Pleiades.
> And again:
> The wintry Pleiades set
> And again:
> At that time the Pleiades conceal

The citations appear to have been collected from different sections of the *Astronomia*, and seem to refer to the Pleiades as seasonal indicators, that is, as different periods of the year distinguished by the varying visibility of the constellation in the sky, exactly as it happens in *Op.* 383–384 (rising and setting), 572, 615 (rising), 619–620.

2. Fr. 291 (*apud* Σ Arat. *Phaen.* 172 [pp. 369–370 Maas])

> ... νύμφαι Χαρίτεσσιν ὁμοῖαι,
> Φαισύλη ἠδὲ Κορωνὶς ἐυστέφανός τε Κλέεια
> Φαιώ θ' ἱμερόεσσα καὶ Εὐδώρη τανύπεπλος,
> ἃς Ὑάδας καλέουσιν ἐπὶ χθονὶ φῦλ' ἀνθρώπων

> ... Nymphs similar to the Graces,
> Phaisyle and Koronis and well-garlanded Kleeia
> and lovely Phaio and long-robed Eudora,
> whom the tribes of human beings on the earth call the Hyades

Fragments of catalogic type (one of the stylistic markers most evidently associated with the Hesiodic poetic tradition, recognized *ab antiquo* as a feature of the ἡσιόδειος χαρακτήρ)⁵³ dealing with the Hyades, that is, of another constella-

---

52 See the material collected under 88F Bernabé (= B18 D.-K.).
53 On this aspect, see Hunter (2014) 282ff. and especially 297–299.

tion, together with Pleiades, whose observation was used to determine seasonal periods: see most importantly *Op.* 615–617 Πληιάδες θ' Ὑάδες τε τό τε σθένος Ὠρίωνος / δύνωσιν, τότ' ἔπειτ' ἀρότου μεμνημένος εἶναι / ὡραίου etc.

Conclusions

Particular expressions such as kennings, riddles, proverbs, *gnomai* and prescriptions are a sort of trademark of the fragmentary texts discussed above. This fact (with all its necessary reservations) reveals a formal homogeneity that, in turn, highlights a substantial consistency of content, that of traditional wisdom. Those poems that are little more than individual fragments for us, and which seem to deal with (at least from their titles) disparate material, constitute, individually and as a whole, a storehouse of knowledge in poetic, epic and hexametric form: wisdom, in fact, expressed by specific traditional features and patterns.

Bibliography

Arthaber, A. (1989). *Dizionario comparato di proverbi e modi proverbiali in sette lingue,* Milan.

Bassino, P. (2013). *Certamen Homeri et Hesiodi: Introduction, Critical Edition and Commentary,* Diss. University of Durham.

Bergk, Th. (1838). *Commentationum de reliquiis comoediae atticae antiquae libri duo,* Leipzig.

Bernabé, A. (2007). *Poetae Epici Graeci*, II.3, Berlin and New York.

Buttmann, Ph. (1825). *Lexilogus,* I, Berlin.

Gulick, Ch. B. (1969). *Athenaeus. The Deipnosophists*, vol. IV, Cambridge, MA and London.

Canevaro, L. G. (2014). 'Hesiod and *Hávamál:* Transitions and the Transmission of Wisdom', *Oral Tradition* 29: 99–126. (http://journal.oraltradition.org/issues/29i/canevaro)

Cantilena, M. (2012). 'Intorno alla tradizione', *SemRom* n.s. 1: 147–163.

Cingano, E. (2009). 'The Hesiodic Corpus', in: F. Montanari, A. Rengakos, and C. Tsagalis (eds.), *Brill's Companion to Hesiod*, Leiden, 91–130.

CPG = *Corpus Paroemiographorum Graecorum,* I, edited by E. L. Leutsch and F. G. Schneidewin, Göttingen 1839.

Cozzoli, A. T. (2016). 'Un poema mantico: la *Melampodia* pseudoesiodea', in: Ercolani and Sbardella, 145–162.

Ercolani, A. (2006). *Omero. Introduzione allo studio dell'epica greca arcaica,* Rome.

Ercolani, A. (2009). 'Enunciati sentenziosi nelle *Opere e giorni* di Esiodo', in: E. Lelli (ed.), *PAROIMIAKOS. Il proverbio in Grecia e a Roma,* Rome, 31–43.

Ercolani, A. (2010). *Esiodo.* Opere e giorni, Rome.

Ercolani, A. (2012). 'Una rilettura di Esiodo, *Opere e giorni.* Contributo all'individuazione dell'epos sapienziale greco', *SemRom* n.s. 1: 235–252.

Ercolani, A. (2015). 'La contesa tra Esiodo e Perse, tra fatto storico e motivo sapienziale', *SemRom* n.s. 4: 1–13.
Ercolani, A. (2016). 'Esiodo e Museo. Secondo contributo all'individuazione dell'epos sapienziale greco', in: Ercolani and Sbardella, 129–144.
Ercolani, A. and L. Sbardella (eds.) (2016). *Esiodo e il* corpus Hesiodeum: *problemi aperti e nuove prospettive*, Rome.
Evelyn-White, H. G. (1914). *Hesiod, The Homeric Hymns and Homerica*, Cambridge, MA and London.
Fernández Delgado, J. A. (1978). 'Poesía oral gnómica en los *Trabajos y los Días*; una muestra de su dicción formular', *Emerita* 46: 141–171.
Fernández Delgado, J. A. (1982). 'La poesia sapiencial de Grecia arcaica y los origenes del hexametro', *Emerita* 50: 151–173.
Fernández Delgado, J. A. (1986). *Los oráculos y Hesíodo. Poesía oral mántica y gnómica griegas*, Cáceres.
Hunter, R. (2014). *Hesiodic Voices. Studies in the Ancient Reception of Hesiod's* Works and Days, Cambridge.
Huxley, G. (1969). *Greek Epic Poetry from Eumelos to Panyassis*, London.
Kaibel, G. (1887). *Athenaei Naucratitae Dipnosophistarum Libri* XV, vol. II, Leipzig.
Kinkel, G. (1877). *Epicorum Graecorum Fragmenta*, Leipzig.
Lévi-Strauss, C. (1958). *Anthropologie structurale*, Paris.
Löffler, A. (1963). *Die* Melampodie. *Versuch einer Rekonstruktion des Inhalts*, Meisenheim am Glan.
Marckscheffel, G. (1840). *Hesiodi, Eumeli, Cinaethonis, Asii et Carminis Naupactii Fragmenta*, Leipzig.
Martin, R. P. (1984). 'Hesiod, Odysseus, and the Instruction of Princes', *TAPA* 114: 29–48.
Merkelbach, R. and M. L. West (1965). 'The Wedding of Ceyx', *RhM* 108: 300–317.
Merkelbach, R. and M. L. West (eds.) (1967). *Fragmenta Hesiodea*, Oxford.
Monda, S. (ed.) (2012). *Ainigma e griphos. Gli antichi e l'oscurità della parola*, Pisa.
Pellizer, E. (1972). 'Metremi proverbiali nelle *Opere e i giorni* di Esiodo', *QUCC* 13: 24–37.
Rzach, A. (1902). *Hesiodi carmina*, Leipzig.
Sbardella, L. (1995). 'La struttura degli esametri in Esiodo, *Erga* 383–828', in: M. Fantuzzi, and R. Pretagostini (eds.), *Struttura e storia dell'esametro greco*, I, Rome: 121–133.
Schwartz, J. (1960). *Pseudo-Hesiodea. Recherches sur la composition, la diffusion et la disparition ancienne d'œuvres attribuées à Hésiode*, Leiden.
Vannicelli, P. (ed.) (2014). *Verbum Dei. Oracoli e tradizioni cittadine nella Grecia antica*, Rome (= *SemRom* n.s. 3.2).
West, M. L. (1965). 'Tryphon *De Tropis*', *CQ* 15: 230–248.
West, M. L. (1997). *The East Face of Helicon. West Asiatic Elements in Greek Poetry and Myth*, Oxford.
Wilamowitz-Moellendorff, U. von (1928). *Hesiodos* Erga, Berlin.

Summary Tables

Table 1: Formal Structures

Type	Fragment
Precept	283
Gnome	364, 273, 274, 286
Kenning/Riddle	266c, 268
Oracle	275

Table 2: Content

Theme	Fragment
Astronomical data (calendar information?)	288–291
Behavioural norms (vis-à-vis people)	264, 266c, 274, 286
Behavioural norms (vis-à-vis gods)	283

Table 3: Quantitative data[54]

Poem	Number of conserved fragments (M.-W.)	Wisdom fragments (for reasons of style and/or content)	Ratio of wisdom fragments to total fragments
Keykos gamos	7 (frr. 263–269)	3 (frsr. 264, 266c, 268)	3:7 (= 42,8%)[55]
Melampodia	10 (frr. 270–279)	4 (frsr. 273, 274, 275, 278)	4:10 (= 40%)[56]
Cheironos Hypothekai	3 (frr. 283–285)	1 (fr. 283)	1:3 (= 33,3%)[57]
Megala Erga	2 (frr. 286–287)	1 (fr. 286)	1:2 (= 50%)
Astronomia	6 (frr. 288–283)	4 (frr. 288, 289, 290, 291)	4:6 (= 66,6%)

---

54 I am well aware of the scarcity of the fragments and of the risk of statistics based on insufficient data. I present this table only for the purpose of providing an overview and a summary, without bestowing any proof-value on the numerical data. I leave to others to evaluate for themselves and to offer their own conclusions.

55 Fr. 269 = P.Oxy. 2495 fr. 38 is illegible, and should not be considered for statistical analysis.

56 Fr. 277 is limited to a single word, and in the absence of proper context is thus difficult to evaluate.

57 Fr. 285 is actually irrelevant for statistical purposes.

Deborah Steiner
Choruses and Catalogues: the Performative and Generic Context of the Asopids in the Hesiodic *Catalogue of Women*

Μουσάων Ἑλικωνιάδων ἀρχώμεθ' ἀείδειν,
αἵ θ' Ἑλικῶνος ἔχουσιν ὄρος μέγα τε ζάθεόν τε,
καί τε περὶ κρήνην ἰοειδέα πόσσ' ἁπαλοῖσιν
ὀρχεῦνται καὶ βωμὸν ἐρισθενέος Κρονίωνος·
καί τε λοεσσάμεναι τέρενα χρόα Περμησσοῖο
ἠ' Ἵππου κρήνης ἠ' Ὀλμειοῦ ζαθέοιο
ἀκροτάτωι Ἑλικῶνι χοροὺς ἐνεποιήσαντο,
καλοὺς ἱμερόεντας, ἐπερρώσαντο δὲ ποσσίν.
ἔνθεν ἀπορνύμεναι κεκαλυμμέναι ἠέρι πολλῶι
ἐννύχιαι στεῖχον περικαλλέα ὄσσαν ἱεῖσαι

Let us begin to sing from the Helikonian Muses, who possess the great and holy mountain of Helikon and dance with supple feet around the violet-dark spring and the altar of the Kronos' broad-strengthed son. And having washed their tender skin in Permessos or the spring of Hippokrene or holy Olmeios, they perform fair, desire-instigating choral dances on highest Helikon and ply their feet. Setting out from there, enshrouded in much mist, they process by night, emitting their very beautiful voice.[1]

Hes. *Th.* 1–11

Hesiod's *Theogony* opens in a manner that sharply differentiates it from its Homeric counterparts: in place of the singular 'goddess' or 'Muse' whom the *Iliad* and *Odyssey* proems invoke, Hesiod's divinities form a plurality. More than this, the opening vignette depicts the Muses engaged in a particularized and signature activity: they perform a ring dance around a body of water and altar with the 'tender feet' distinctive of choral maidens in archaic epic and lyric poetry.

The divinities' presentation as an archetypal chorus continues through this opening visualization: a few lines on, we meet them 'making dances', plying their feet again in the manner of Iliadic and other parthenaic choristers, and like the prototypical chorus on the shield of Achilleus and those that follow in the lyric corpus, the Muses' ensemble is both beautiful and desire-instigating.[2] Even as the performers engage in song – thereby satisfying the later Platonic definition of *choreia* as 'song-dance' – their motion changes: now, marching (στείχω

---
[1] All translations in this chapter are the author's own unless otherwise noted.
[2] *Il.* 18.590–601. For representations of the maiden choruses in the lyric and dramatic corpus, which recapitulate the terms used here, see Swift (2016).

regularly denotes orderly, ranked movement) down from the Helikonian heights, the deities process. Here poetic content and choral formation coincide. Just as the Muses perform a reverse *Theogony*, beginning at the end of the succession struggle as they descend to lower land, so they invert the regular sequence that structures choral motion: first the linear procession to the sacred site, then the ring dance, typically performed around an altar or other centre point, when it reaches its destination; the Helikonian Muses quit the 'altar of Kronos' son' and the divinely-inhabited bodies of water (so often the site of choral dancing) so as to travel down into the mortal realm. The broader question informing this chapter concerns the relation, both here and elsewhere in archaic epic and lyric poetry, between the Muses' emphatic presentation as a chorus of singing, dancing maidens, and the catalogic poetry that immediately follows this opening.

The discussion falls into four sections. Part one seeks simply to establish the premise of my argument, offering its own selective 'catalogue' of passages from texts of the archaic period that underscore the relation between individuals or items presented as a list and the plurality and chorality of its performers. In part two, I suggest some reasons for this kinship, exploring continuities between the morphology of catalogues and choruses in the poetic and visual repertoires. Part three turns more narrowly to what is perhaps the most outstanding extant example of early catalogic poetry, the 'Hesiodic' *Catalogue of Women*, and focuses on one specific instance of the overlap between choral maidens and the work's generic design: namely, the Asopids, exemplary of the intersections explored here and who, according to the broadly accepted reconstruction of West,[3] would have occupied a central place in the *Catalogue*'s fourth book. As I document, not only are the daughters of Asopos, in the view of the archaic and early classical sources, an archetypal chorus on whom mortal ensembles 'project' themselves in moments of choral self-referentiality,[4] but accounts of the Asopids in a variety of early genres also regularly take catalogic form, aligning the daughters and their histories with items audibly and visually presented as a list. The chapter's conclusion offers a necessarily speculative suggestion concerning the manner in which the *Catalogue of Women*, or portions of the piece that antedated the text as transmitted to us, might once have been performed.

---

[3] West (1985) 100–103. See too Larson (2001) 139–140.
[4] For this 'self-referentiality', see Henrichs (1994–1995) and (1996).

Catalogues Become Choruses

For early audiences, relations between the chorus and the catalogue would have been self-evident. Critics have long noted that Homer regularly invokes the Muses, sometimes in the singular, but more frequently as an ensemble, before embarking on an extended list. Such invocations aim, in their view, to enhance authority, comprehensiveness, and the mnemonic challenge posed by the enumeration as well as to emphasize its intensity or capstone quality.[5] But Carruesco, noting the seemingly unmotivated switch from the single Muse of the *Iliad* proem to the invocation of the collective goddesses in the second preface before the show-stopping Catalogue of Ships, makes a different suggestion:[6] here, by virtue of the heterogeneity and sheer number of contingents about to be recited, the poet spins out this idea of multiplicity, making it clear that the human bard must here function as an equivalent to the divine chorus, equipped with the ten voices and ten tongues that a singing group naturally enjoys to achieve this superhuman feat; so too the poet stresses his singularity in contrast to the first person plural used of the Muses and, setting himself, a lone *ego*, in opposition to the 'crowd' that he goes on to list, closes with a final declaration of multiplicity (*Il.* 2.484–493):

> Ἔσπετε νῦν μοι Μοῦσαι Ὀλύμπια δώματ' ἔχουσαι·
> ὑμεῖς γὰρ θεαί ἐστε πάρεστέ τε ἴστέ τε πάντα,
> ἡμεῖς δὲ κλέος οἶον ἀκούομεν οὐδέ τι ἴδμεν·
> οἵ τινες ἡγεμόνες Δαναῶν καὶ κοίρανοι ἦσαν·
> πληθὺν δ' οὐκ ἂν ἐγὼ μυθήσομαι οὐδ' ὀνομήνω,
> οὐδ' εἴ μοι δέκα μὲν γλῶσσαι, δέκα δὲ στόματ' εἶεν,
> φωνὴ δ' ἄρρηκτος, χάλκεον δέ μοι ἦτορ ἐνείη,
> εἰ μὴ Ὀλυμπιάδες Μοῦσαι Διὸς αἰγιόχοιο
> θυγατέρες μνησαίαθ' ὅσοι ὑπὸ Ἴλιον ἦλθον·
> ἀρχοὺς αὖ νηῶν ἐρέω νῆάς τε προπάσας.

> Narrate to me now, Muses having your home on Olympos, for you are goddesses and are present and know all things, but we hear only hearsay nor do we know anything, those who were the leaders of the Danaans and the rulers; I would not be able to speak of nor to name the throng, not even if I had ten tongues and ten mouths and a voice unbroken and a brazen heart were within me, unless the Olympian Muses, daughters of aegis-bearing Zeus, were to remember as many as came beneath Troy. I will speak the leaders of the ships and all the ships.

---

[5] See chiefly Minton (1962), Minchin (1996), Perceau (2002), Sammons (2010), these last two with other older and more recent bibliography.
[6] Carruesco (2010) 272–273.

That an individual should possess the capacity to speak or sing in multiple voices seems pure poetic fantasy, but one Homeric character displays just this skill. Witness Helen as she approaches the Trojan horse in Menelaos' damning story in *Od.* 4.277–287:

> τρὶς δὲ περίστειξας κοῖλον λόχον ἀμφαφόωσα,
> ἐκ δ' ὀνομακλήδην Δαναῶν ὀνόμαζες ἀρίστους,
> πάντων Ἀργείων φωνὴν ἴσκουσ' ἀλόχοισιν.
> αὐτὰρ ἐγὼ καὶ Τυδεΐδης καὶ δῖος Ὀδυσσεὺς
> ἥμενοι ἐν μέσσοισιν ἀκούσαμεν, ὡς ἐβόησας.
> νῶϊ μὲν ἀμφοτέρω μενεήναμεν ὁρμηθέντε
> ἢ ἐξελθέμεναι, ἢ ἔνδοθεν αἶψ' ὑπακοῦσαι·
> ἀλλ' Ὀδυσεὺς κατέρυκε καὶ ἔσχεθεν ἱεμένω περ.
> ἔνθ' ἄλλοι μὲν πάντες ἀκὴν ἔσαν υἷες Ἀχαιῶν,
> Ἄντικλος δὲ σέ γ' οἶος ἀμείψασθαι ἐπέεσσιν
> ἤθελεν·

> Three times you circled around the hollow ambush, feeling it, and you called out, naming them by name, to the best of the Danaans, and made your voice like to that of the wives of all the Argives. But I, and the son of Tydeus and brilliant Odysseus sitting in the middle heard how you cried out, and Diomedes and I both started up, both minded to go outside, or else to answer your voice from within. But Odysseus restrained us and held us for all our yearning. And all the other sons of the Achaians ɪsat in silence, but there was only one, it was Antiklos, who was ready to respond.

On several counts, the singular performer seems to become a collective chorus: three times Helen walks around the trap in what resembles a choral circumambulation about an *agalma*,[7] calling out to each hero in turn by name – in effect an enumerative catalogue such as she performs for Priam in the *Teichoskopia* of *Il.* 3, where, Muse-like in her omniscience, she lists the Achaian heroes whom she surveys. A second detail in the Odyssean scene further suggests chorality: Antiklos wishes to respond (ἀμείψασθαι, 286), the choral activity *par excellence*, as demonstrated by Hom. *Hymn to Apollo* 189 (Μοῦσαι μέν θ' ἅμα πᾶσαι / ἀμειβόμεναι ὀπὶ καλῆι), and still more appositely, *Od.* 24.58–61:

> ἀμφὶ δέ σ' ἔστησαν κοῦραι ἁλίοιο γέροντος
> οἴκτρ' ὀλοφυρόμεναι, περὶ δ' ἄμβροτα εἵματα ἕσσαν.
> Μοῦσαι δ' ἐννέα πᾶσαι ἀμειβόμεναι ὀπὶ καλῆι
> θρήνεον· ἔνθα κεν οὔ τιν' ἀδάκρυτόν γ' ἐνόησας
> Ἀργείων· τοῖον γὰρ ὑπώρορε Μοῦσα λίγεια.

---

[7] Carruesco (2012) 161. My discussion of the scene draws much from both Carruesco and Martin (2008).

> And around you stood the daughters of the old man of the sea lamenting piteously and wearing immortal clothing; and the nine Muses sang the *threnos*, all responding with beautiful voice. There you would perceive none of the Argives who was not weeping; such was the power of the shrill-voiced Muse to stir up.

As Martin, connecting these lines with the Helen episode, explains, the switch from the choral Nereids and Muses to the singular goddess at the passage's end, 'one Muse leads the group and responds to them as they respond to her and to one another ... If Helen is conceptualized as ἐξάρχουσα – a chorus leader – we might be able to imagine that she crystallizes the power of choral song, within her individual performance'.[8] As Martin notes, like that Muse soloist, Helen is lead performer in what resembles a θρῆνος; her enumeration constitutes a roll call of those about to die should the heroes heed her invitation to respond, a point to which I return.

But most uncanny in Menelaos' account is Helen's multiplication of her voice so as to counterfeit the call of each warrior's wife. Closest to this mimetic feat is the spectacle by the Delian Maidens in the *Hom. Hymn to Apollo*, featured in another passage that highlights multiplicity and sets up the play between the singular bard and choral plurality (157–163):[9]

> κοῦραι Δηλιάδες Ἑκατηβελέταο θεράπναι·
> αἵ τ' ἐπεὶ ἂρ πρῶτον μὲν Ἀπόλλων' ὑμνήσωσιν,
> αὖτις δ' αὖ Λητώ τε καὶ Ἄρτεμιν ἰοχέαιραν,
> μνησάμεναι ἀνδρῶν τε παλαιῶν ἠδὲ γυναικῶν
> ὕμνον ἀείδουσιν, θέλγουσι δὲ φῦλ' ἀνθρώπων.
> πάντων δ' ἀνθρώπων φωνὰς καὶ κρεμβαλιαστὺν
> μιμεῖσθ' ἴσασιν·

> The maidens of Delos, the handmaids of the far-shooter, who, after first hymning Apollo, and then in turn Leto and Artemis arrow-pourer, turn their thoughts to the men and women of old and sing a song that charms the race of all people. They know how to mimic all people's voices and their motions.

Here, as in the invocation in *Il.* 2, a series of terms underscores multiplicity. The heterogeneous audience forms a crowd (ἀθρόοι, 153) that collectively shares in the delight inspired by the performance (πάντων, 154 and 162; cf. πολλά, 155). A direct address to the Delian maidens follows their performance of what is effectively a mini-catalogue – 'first' Apollo, and 'then again' Leto and Artemis

---

8 Martin (2008) 121.
9 Both Martin (2008, 119–120) and Carruesco (2012, 159–160), making different arguments, cite the parallel.

(αὖτις δ' αὖ, with double use of this typical catalogue 'connective')[10] – as the poet greets the markedly multiple chorus (ὑμεῖς πᾶσαι, 166); he then bids them fulfill the mnemonic role played by the catalogue (μνήσασθ', 160, 167) before closing the passage with a contrast, reminiscent again of *Il.* 2, between his singularity and the Delians' collective voice. While they respond as a group performing in unison (171), his hymnic celebration features only one subject (Apollo) and is sung as a monody (ἐγών, 177).

The rule of thumb these examples from archaic hexameter poetry suggest – that if mourning becomes Elektra, then catalogues become choruses – finds confirmation in choral lyric. As part of their self-description, the chorus of Spartan maidens performing Alcman's first *Partheneion* includes a by-the-book catalogue, made up of items and names (64–76):

> οὔτε γάρ τι πορφύρας
> τόσσος κόρος ὥστ' ἀμύναι,
> οὔτε ποικίλος δράκων
> παγχρύσιος, οὐδὲ μίτρα
> Λυδία, νεανίδων
> ἰανογ[λ]εφάρων ἄγαλμα,
> οὐδὲ ταὶ Ναννῶς κόμαι,
> ἀλλ' οὐ[δ'] Ἀρέτα σιειδής,
> οὐδὲ Σύλακίς τε καὶ Κλεησισήρα,
> οὐδ' ἐς Αἰνησιμβρ[ό]τας ἐνθοῖσα φασεῖς·
> Ἀσταφίς [τ]έ μοι γένοιτο
> καὶ ποτιγλέποι Φίλυλλα
> Δαμαρ[έ]τα τ' ἐρατά τε ϝιανθεμίς·
> ἀλλ' Ἁγησιχόρα με τείρει.

> For a surfeit of purple does not help. Nor a chased golden snake-bracelet, nor a Lydian circlet, pride of violet-eyed maids, nor Nanno's tresses, not even godlike Areta or Thylakes and Kleesithera, nor will you go to Ainesimbrota's house and say: 'let Astaphis stand by me, and let Phillyla and Damareta and lovely Hianthemis look upon me, but Hagesichora effaces me'. (trans. after Ferrari)

What the list presents is a group of eleven maidens, introduced in the form of three adornments – metonymns for their wearers – and then eight names (excluding the extra-choral Ainesimbrota). Like Hesiod and Homer, the composer flags plurality by setting against this group of self-cataloguing girls a single Helen-like figure: Hagesichora. Here I adopt the reading and interpretation of line 99, which seemingly declares that the *choregos* has the voice of ten, pro-

---

[10] For this, see Perceau (2002) 150 and another example cited below.

posed by several commentators:¹¹ because Hagesichora sings like a decad – in accordance with the model given in the proem to the Catalogue of Ships – in her single voice, she performs 'over and above' the eleven, the number that should most likely be restored in the preceding line. Like Helen, this supremely skilled singer takes the form of an ensemble, her vocal powers outmatching that of the chorus whose performative and expressly choral skills their preceding catalogue put on show.

But the eleven-fold enumeration delivered by the chorus does not stand alone in the poem. As Robbins details,¹² it closely parallels the list with which the extant portion of the fragment opens. At the start of the papyrus' legible section is Polydeukes' name, followed by a verb signaling the nature of what comes next, ἀλέγω – a negation of and play on the cataloguing verb *par excellence*, καταλέγω –¹³ that introduces the list of Hippokoontidai. Not only do eleven members make up both catalogues, but in each a preeminent pair, both with equine associations, outperforms the ensemble, the Tyndaridai surpassing the fraternity, Agido and Hagesischora (likened to prize-winning coursers) their choristers. As for the maidenly aggregate, just as the Hippokoontidai form a band of brothers and are the Tyndaridai's cousins, so kinship links the eleven-fold group who likewise declare Hagesichora their cousin (52). Through this act of choral projection, the choristers equate themselves with the members of the opening catalogue, instantiating each of the names making up the list. Ferrari draws attention to the threnetic quality of the opening account, which she reads as an enumerative commemoration and celebration of the dead of the Spartan community.¹⁴ A heroic epithet would have accompanied each brother's name, creating that rhythmic repetition characteristic of laments that is so prominent in the Iliadic Catalogue of Ships.

It is, somewhat surprisingly, that celebrated Catalogue with which this section began that supplies my final example of the choral dimension informing lists in hexameter poetry. In the persuasive interpretation of Heiden,¹⁵ and consistent with the initial appeal to the Muses in their collective capacity as a chorus, is the structure and diction of what they inspire the bard to recite. The rhythmic repetition of the same formulaic phrases concluding many of the entries recalls the refrains more typical of formal lyric – whose strophes observe just

---

11 See Robbins (1994) 10 with earlier bibliography.
12 Robbins (1994) 13–15.
13 Perceau (2002) 16–35 analyzes the term closely.
14 Ferrari (2008) 120–121.
15 Heiden (2008).

such reiteration – than of hexameter poetry.[16] More particularly, repetition is a hallmark of the threnetic genre, a likeness that, in Heiden's argument, makes the Catalogue resemble a collective song-and-dance – under the plural Muses' leadership – which celebrates those whose death at Troy their townsmen in their homelands will commemorate and lament in choral performances executed by citizen choruses on the occasion of the burial of the war dead.

Add to this the vocabulary (much of which Heiden also notes) used to evoke the naval contingents and that invites us to view the vessels not just as soldiers advancing in their ranks but as members of choral collectives who descend in the 'stichic' formations used of the Hesiodic Muses' procession cited at this chapter's start. The expression νέες ἐστιχόωντο closes four of the entries while the στίχες assumed by the dancers on Achilleus' Shield (*Il.* 18.602) similarly characterize the Phokian troops positioned on the plane (στίχας ἵστασαν, 525). The verb used for this stationing becomes the *vox propria* for 'setting up', 'readying' or 'instituting' a chorus in a phrase visible from the late archaic period on, στῆσαι χορόν.[17] Consistent too with this choral model is the frequent deployment of terms for 'leading' and 'following', which cast each leader as chorus-commander to the maritime ensemble that follows; even so do the terms coincide in Pindar's depiction of how the *choregos*-father marshals his parthenaic troupe, while his daughter, heading the line of maidens, follows in his wake (fr. 94b.66–67 Snell-Maehler). Even the *kosmesis*, the decking out of choristers prior to their performance (see Pind. *Pyth.* 9.118), figures in the Catalogue of Ships when Menestheus is singled out for his skill in arranging/adorning his men and horses (κοσμῆσαι, 555). The accumulation of this choral terminology combined with the generically hybrid quality of the Catalogue of Ships suggests that lists such as these may offer an instance of exchanges between hexameter poetry and the choral lyric that formed no less a part of the musical landscape of the period.

Choral and Catalogue Morphologies

As argued above, archaic sources demonstrate intimate connections between the 'set-piece' catalogue and its performance by a choral group. In this second sec-

---

[16] Heiden (2008) 148.
[17] For this, see Calame (1997) 88–89, Nagy (1990) 361–362 and particularly Myers (2007); note too Kavoulaki (2011) 371–373.

tion, I take up the larger question that Carruesco poses:[18] beyond the intuitive notion that a multiplicity of items requires plural performers, do deeper relations exist between catalogue poetry and choruses, and is this association discernible within the textual and visual evidence? In attempting some answers, I propose beginning with the morphology (to borrow the term of Calame)[19] of the chorus – its make up, the relations between its different members, choreographic formations, and movements through space – and demonstrating that catalogues in archaic and epic possess exactly corresponding features.

In Sammons' definition, a catalogue, whether made up of two or multiple members, is 'a list of items which are specified in discrete entries … no explicit relation is made except for the shared suitability to the catalogue's specified rubric'. He further defines a rubric as 'a stated category or class which legitimates the involvement or exclusion of potential items'.[20] This 'rubric' can be aligned with Calame's delineation of the three most broad-based features determining membership of a chorus: ties of kinship, locality, and age (all choristers belong to one time of life).[21] These map still more closely onto the typical criteria for inclusion in a catalogue: just as so many real and mythical choruses form sororities or fraternities and have a parent or other relation by way of lead member (in addition to the Muses and Graces, we encounter the Pleiades, Nereids, Asopids, and Hyades), so kinship ties unite the members of the extended family groupings that structure the *Catalogue of Women*, or the list of ancestors in Diomedes' genealogical recitation at *Il.* 6.146–211. There are any number of examples of 'epichoric' choruses, among them the Deliades, Caryatides and the maidens on Aigina featured in Bacchylides 13, who celebrate the local (τ' ἐ[πιχω]ρί-αν, 91) festival on their island in song and dance and are also neighbours (89).[22] Analogous to these are the entries in some catalogues, or parts thereof, whose inclusion in the list depends on geographical proximity: the suitors enumerated by Telemachos at *Od.* 16.247–254 all come from nearby islands (they belong to the same age class too) while the several women clustered at the start of Odys-

---

18 His explanation remains a very generalized one; the overlap is based on 'la similitud morfológica de una unidad articulada a partir de una pluralidad de miembros, como en el más profunda de la funcíon, que es precisamente la capacidad activa de generar esa articulación' (Carruesco 2010, 272).
19 Calame (1997).
20 Sammons (2010) 9. While he goes on to draw some distinctions between catalogues and lists, the former marked by a degree of elaboration, he grants that the division is a very narrow one. I do not differentiate between the two in this discussion.
21 Calame (1997) 26–34.
22 Several of these examples receive more detailed treatment later on.

seus' list of the heroines whom he saw in the Underworld (*Od.* 11.234–329) share a common Boiotian derivation.

Beyond membership of an overarching 'rubric', studies of the catalogic form in early poetry have isolated a variety of syntactic structuring principles. Most simply, that of parataxis, sustained by bare connectives, these often repeated in a rhythmic sequence marked by the occurrence of the expressions in the same position in the hexameter line. While Dolon's list of the Trojan allies in *Il.* 10.428–434 uses the conjunctions καί and πρός to link the different contingents introduced sequentially, the expressions τε and καί, sometimes combined, coordinate the list of Nereid names at *Il.* 18.38–49. Enumerating his liaisons in *Il.* 14.313–28, Zeus introduces each conquest with the term οὐδέ, anticipating the structure of the second catalogue in Alcman's first *Partheneion*; as in the Iliadic instance, the terms οὔτε and οὐδέ prefacing each name cluster in first position in the line (cf. Tyrt. 12.1–10).

Compare to this the visual representation of choruses on Geometric and early classical vases: each member stands discrete, singularized in a fashion that serves much as the 'epithet' frequently individualizing the items in a list, and that distinguishes him or her from the adjacent chorister; only their joined hands link each performer to the next.[23] The chorus of the 'twice-seven' occupying the top band of the familiar François Vase of ca. 570,[24] and whose story bands stacked one on the other have often been compared to the catalogue of scenes on the Shield of Achilleus,[25] offers a prime example of this simple arrangement. Each chorister wears a different dress and bears a different name, while their interlinked hands and coordinated step connect each discrete member to the next dancer in the line. Reading off the names inscribed above the youths and maidens one after the other, the viewer of the vase would effectively recite a catalogue corresponding to the visual image. Much like the epithets accompanying each Hippokoontid in Alcman's first maiden song are the different shield devices that distinguish each dolphin rider in the chorus on a red-figure psykter by Oltos of ca. 520–510;[26] differentiation coexists with connections, here established by the riders' identical poses, mounts and costumes, and the refrain

---

[23] Just as parataxis is classified as what Aristotle terms εἰρομένη λέξις or the 'strung-along style' at *Rh.* 1409a27-b1, so Lucian views a chorus as the 'necklace' at *Salt.* 12, each chorister like a bead strung on a connecting string; strikingly, early vase images show chorus members tied together by a rope (for examples and discussion see Langdon 2008, 176).

[24] Florence, Museo Archeologico Nazionale 4209.

[25] Notopoulos (1949) 22 styles the work the '*locus classicus* for parataxis in vase painting'.

[26] New York, Metropolitan Museum of Art 1989.281.69.

inscribed in the same position above each chorister, which functions like the repeated elements observed in the orderly shaping of catalogues.

A second simple organizational device is a 'first to last' arrangement, frequently marked by such temporal expressions as πρῶτος, ἔπειτα, and τότε;[27] this may also coincide with another frequent feature of Homeric catalogues, the suggestion that the speaker is visually scanning a scene, whether in the mind's eye or as he or she actually performs the list. As Dolon reviews the Trojan allies at *Il.* 10.428–434, he presents the contingents according to their localization in space (the 'positioning' verb ἔλαχον is used at 430); so the placement of each scene on the surface of the Iliadic Achilleus' Shield, one after, above, or below the next, dictates the order of the poet's cataloguing narrative. The *Teichoskopia* in *Il.* 3 underscores the idea of the list as visual survey: Priam questions Helen on what he sees on the plain beneath him while she responds by enumerating the individual heroes as she conjointly views them. Different forms of εἴδω occur in lines 163, 169, 194, 225 and 226, a motif reinforced by the focus on each hero's appearance. Again choral morphology, with each chorister positioned one after the other in their lines or other formations, dovetails with this spatial or locational structure. In Alcman's parthenaic ensemble, its second catalogue may form a piece with the performers' actual choral formation; quite plausibly, the singers list their members' accessories and names in accordance with their position in the chorus-line, much as with the ordering of the inscribed names on the François Vase.[28]

Beyond these simple devices, many lists display more artful and complex patterning. Poets may introduce hierarchy and a progressive degree or diminishment of elaboration through the addition or subtraction of epithets and/or by including additional information concerning the more privileged member(s). In the terms Faraone uses of this gradual *auxesis*, and the correspondingly expanded space allotted an item that stands solo in a line or extends over more than one, such lists culminate in a 'superlative name cap' flagged by the terms πλεῖστον, μάλιστα or other superlatives.[29] There is a ranking here, a move from less significant objects, places or individuals to those of greater impressiveness, cost, status and (previous or subsequent) importance in the narrative. Often the individual singled out occupies the first or last place in the birth order, a position

---

[27] Perceau (2002) 98 with examples.
[28] Beyond the scope of this article is a point made in many discussions of the chorus, whether in its self-presentation or in the accounts of such ensembles in poetic and other descriptions: the intensely 'spectacularized' nature of a chorus whose members are both viewers and more frequently viewed. Most recently, Swift (2016). Note too Peponi (2004).
[29] Faraone (2013), from whom I draw the subsequent examples.

that coincides with his or her place in the list; so the daughters of Keleos in the *Hom. Hymn to Demeter* 109–110, where final position is reserved for the eldest, or Hesiod *Th.* 137; there Kronos is the final born of the offspring of Okeanos and Gaia and the closing entry in that catalogue. Indeed, the passage at 133–139 well illustrates the ordering devices that Faraone observes: a bare connective joins the first eight names, distributed four per line, while only two names, complete with epithets marking their greater importance, appear in line 136; allowed two lines and two superlatives is the final child, the one destined to succeed his father.

Just this hierarchy structures the choral collective where we witness divisions between one or several members and the rest; visual representations distinguish the *choregos* most simply by granting him or her the lead or last position in the line, a primacy sometimes underscored by the addition of an accessory, more elaborate clothing, or otherwise augmented stature. Hierarchy within an overall unity appears on a black-figure kylix from Argos, dated to ca. 600–550:[30] a single mantle covers the nine female choristers identically coiffed while at the line's head, the artist positions a maiden who, uniquely, carries a garland.[31] A geometric water pitcher in Munich shows a line of ten girls dressed in the same long robes;[32] while the lead figure lacks a distinguishing feature, the last one wears a crown. The 'specialness' accorded the third dancer on a late eighth-century Geometric hydria from Aigina,[33] whose skirt is chequered differently from those worn by the rest, might be a visual device for establishing leadership when the dancers form a ring, as they do so frequently when they circle around the neck or shoulder of a vase. Faraone well explains the privileging of Kalliope, introduced last and given an entire line with superlative in Hesiod's list of the nine Muses at *Th.* 76–79;[34] might the artist of a Corinthian aryballos of ca. 600 have had her primacy in that poem, which had by that time become canonical, as he painted the Muses on his pot? The vessel shows two groups, with three women in each, identified by the inscriptions *Mousia* and *Mosai*, while a further figure, named Kalliopa, is singled out from the rest; she appears separately, led by Apollo with a lyre.[35] On the François Vase, dated to a decade or two after, Kalliope likewise stands out among the representation of the nine

---

30 Berlin, Staatliche Museen zu Berlin, Antikensammlungen F 3993.
31 See D'Agostino (2016) for detailed discussion.
32 Munich, Staatliche Antikensammlungen 6228 with Calame (1997) 22.
33 Berlin, Antikensammlung 31312.
34 Faraone (2013) 300–301.
35 See Wachter (2001) 57–61 for this and other vessels where the Muses are identified by name.

Muses, each identified by name:[36] she not only leads the line, but the artist further grants her prominence by means of her frontality and syrinx.

The topmost band of the François Vase also illustrates the primacy afforded the *choregos*, the correlate to the singling out of the catalogue's first or last entry: here Theseus, positioned at the head of the line, is clearly demarcated from the rest. Whereas the other youths wear cloaks and himatia and proceed empty-handed, he has a full-length robe and carries a lyre. That he is group leader, and the most important, the diminutive figure of the nurse facing him further emphasizes; and while all the other names appear above the choristers, similarly positioned, his alone occurs beneath, its direction reversed. On a Corinthian aryballos dated to the early sixth century the prominence of the lead dancer and *choregos* is also emphatic;[37] he too occupies the start of the chorus line, where, viewing from left to right, we encounter this prize-winner before the rest. Appearing alone among his otherwise indistinguishable followers presented in pairs lined up behind him, he is named in the accompanying inscription, and where the others stand immobile as they wait to begin their dance, he commands attention by performing a tricky leap, the so-called *bibasis*.

Ring composition and internal linkages furnish other structural devices in textual catalogues. We encounter the first several times in the *Theogony*, where the poet encloses the list of Nereids by the double mention of their father Nereus, 'who bore them', at 240 and 263;[38] the name of the last listed daughter, Nemertes, prepares the way for the second mention of her also 'infallible' father by introducing the quality of 'unerringness' that he possesses. A second, smaller ring occurs in the catalogue's first half, bracketed by the repetition of Amphitrite, first and last, at 243 and 254. Two rings, a larger one enclosing a smaller, likewise structure the list of Okeanos' daughters and sons; lines 337 and 365–366 demarcate the larger circle, while 346 and 362–363 bookend the inner circuit. A similar arrangement is visible in Alcman's first *Partheneion*, where chorus line and catalogue design again coincide. Prior to its self-introduction, the chorus draws attention to its *choregoi*, first Hagesichora, then Agido; following the closure of the list of adornments and names, the singers return to their point of departure, naming Hagesichora first and Agido second. A sixth-century (?) skyphos supplies a visual parallel:[39] the two identical male figures that punctuate the extended lines of maiden dancers can be regarded as the same *choregos*, or two leaders

---

[36] Florence, Museo Archeologico Nazionale 4209.
[37] Corinth, Achaeological Museum C 54.1.
[38] See Faraone (2013) 308–309.
[39] Athens, National Archaeological Museum 874.

indistinguishable from one another, who begin and end the line and delimit the two semi-choruses; on a Geometric oinochoe from Pithekoussai in London all but identical male figures, both executing the same step, likewise 'frame' what may be a representation of the Crane Dance.[40]

Additional patterns in textual catalogues depend on verbal, acoustic and rhythmic relations between the different parts. Anadiplosis, homoioteleuton or isocolon frequently occur, creating affinities between two or more items, sometimes separated by other elements in the linear sequence. For all the apparent parataxis in the catalogue of Nereids at *Il.* 18.37–51, the poet creates internal echoes, variations and progressions through the placement of the names and their assonance and alliteration: so Κυμοδόκη τε appears at the end of 39 while Κυμοθόη τε begins 41. Picking up on the suffix of her sister's name, but introducing a new prefix, Ἀμφιθόη enters at 42, followed by the phrase καὶ Καλλιάνειρα, who is audibly paired with Καλλιάνασσα, also preceded by καὶ and in verse-final position in 46. Such subtle but distinct internal iterations and recapitulations find their match in visual representations of choral collectives, prompting viewers to perceive relations between discrete dancers sometimes adjacent, sometimes positioned at different points in the file. The painter of the chorus on the neck of a Late Geometric hydria in Rome duplicates features in some of the performers, and not in others:[41] while many carry only branches, others are additionally equipped with wreaths, establishing connections between dancers otherwise separated in the line. From the mid sixth-century comes an Attic black-figure krater-cup[42] with a choral procession of men on the outside (the dolphins on the internal rim, paradigmatic choral dancers in our sources, confirm the marchers' choral identity); different designs on the participants' gowns, as well as the alternation between those carrying staffs and those with drinking horns, construct internal patterns and variations. The artist of an early sixth-century Corinthian kotyle creates other connections between individual members through paired-off dancers;[43] on the aryballos, also from Corinth and cited above, the six chorus members are grouped in twos.

As the examples from the poetic sources already cited demonstrate, two chief structural principles are visible in catalogues from the hexameter repertoire: one linear or paratactic, which may additionally involve the progressive amplification or diminishment of the members in a ranked arrangement, the other determined by the creation of units of repetition and patterning that

---

40 London, British Museum 49.4–18.18.
41 Rome, Villa Giulia 1212.
42 Paris, Musée du Louvre CA 2998.
43 Paris, Louvre CA 3004.

turn linearity into several circles or one grand ring. These overarching arrangements not only correspond to the two principal choral formations, processional and circular, but their frequent presence within a single catalogue parallels the ways in which choral dancing so frequently involves alternations between both modes of performance. The Hesiodic presentation of the Muses' circular dance followed by a processional descent cited at this chapter's start recalls the motions of the chorus on the Shield of Achilleus in *Il.* 18; here the youths and maidens sometimes turn in circles, as the simile of the spinning potter's wheel clearly indicates, and then switch off into lines or 'ranks' (566–569):

οἳ δ' ὁτὲ μὲν θρέξασκον ἐπισταμένοισι πόδεσσι
ῥεῖα μάλ', ὡς ὅτε τις τροχὸν ἄρμενον ἐν παλάμῃσιν
ἑζόμενος κεραμεὺς πειρήσεται, αἴ κε θέῃσιν·
ἄλλοτε δ' αὖ θρέξασκον ἐπὶ στίχας ἀλλήλοισι

And at times they were running very lightly on their knowing feet, just as a potter while seated makes trial of his wheel fitted to his hands to see if it might run; and at others they were running in rows up to one another.

Visual representations suggest a further choral formation: the convergence of two discrete choral lines, sometimes fashioning a 'v'.⁴⁴ Two groups of choral dancers, one female, the other male, circle around the neck of a hydria of ca. 700 by the Analatos Painter; a phorminx player appears at the juncture between the two.⁴⁵ We might compare catalogues with gender divisions, such as that of the sons and daughters of Okeanos at Hes. *Th.* 337–370, where Tethys' role in giving birth to them (346) serves as the 'meeting point' between the genders. On a diminutive lekythos by the Amasis Painter,⁴⁶ nine women divided into two groups of three and six perform a epithalamic dance, their subdivision visually articulated by the *auletes* and lyre-player who bracket each ensemble. Lonsdale notes further distinctions: the group on the lyre player's left place their hands over the wrists of their fellow dancers, while those in the other chorus link hands.⁴⁷ As in the hexameter examples of choral dancing, linear and circular motion here coexist: the interlinked hands of the six, together with the more vigorous step three of their number perform, suggest a ring dance while the smaller, more measured motions of the trio evoke a processional formation.

---

44 For discussion of this somewhat debated formation, see Calame (1997) 37 drawing on the treatment in Crowhurst (1963) 293–298.
45 Paris, Musée du Louvre CA 2985.
46 New York, Metropolitan Museum of Art 31.11.10.
47 Lonsdale (1993) 215–217.

The musicians are the place at which the two lines converge. On the lekythos' companion piece, also in New York,[48] two choruses of eight, again each adopting a distinct manner of moving, come together at the point where Amasis places a figure seated on a throne, wearing a peplos and holding a wreath. As each girl heading the lines moves towards the centrepoint, she glances back and makes a gesture of invitation with her left hand, a fresh connection between the two choral collectives.[49]

The Asopids

So far I have suggested that, in both art and text, representations of the morphology of the chorus, its composition, arrangement, formations and motions map closely onto the characteristics of catalogues and their performance by speakers and poets in a variety of genres. But time now to turn to the Hesiodic *Catalogue of Women*, and its fourth book's inclusion of a lengthy section devoted to the daughters of Asopos. In the argument made here, representations of the Asopids in other poetic and visual sources typically take catalogue form even as they figure the maidens as an archetypal chorus. In offering an instance of the coincidence of chorality and the list, this sorority allows me to demonstrate more closely how and why the rhetorical and performative practices intersect.

We encounter our first extant extended references to the daughters of Asopos and their father in works by Pindar and Bacchylides, where the maidens' status as a parthenaic ensemble onto which the present-day performers project their identity *qua* chorus is much in evidence. Bacchylides 13, a work composed for the Aiginetan Pytheas following his victory in the pankration at Nemea, offers a complex set of associations between the paradigmatic Asopid chorus and those now lauding Pytheas' victory. After praising the youth, and narrating his return home crowned in his victory garland, the singers turn to address their native island and its eponymous Asopid heroine (77–95):

ὦ ποταμοῦ θύγατερ δι-
νᾶντος Αἴγιν' ἠπιόφρον,
ἦ τοι μεγάλαν [Κρονίδας] ἔ-
δωκε τιμάν
ἐν πάντεσσιν [υ --]
πυρσὸν ὣς Ἕλλ[ασι --]

---

48 New York, Metropolitan Museum of Art 56.11.1.
49 Calame (1997) 71.

φαίνων· τό γε σὸν [κλέος αἰ]νεῖ
καί τις ὑψαυχὴς κό[ρα -]
[- υυ - υυ]ραν πό-
δεσσι ταρφέως
ἠΰτε νεβρὸς ἀπεν[θὴς]
ἀνθεμόεντας ἐπ[' ὄχθους]
κοῦφα σὺν ἀγχιδόμ[οις] θρώισ-
κουσ' ἀγακλειτα[ῖς ἑταίρα]ις·
ταὶ δὲ στεφανωσάμε[ναι φοιν]ικέων
ἀνθέων δόνακός τ' ἐ[πιχω]ρί-
αν ἄθυρσιν
παρθένοι μέλπουσι τ[υ - υυ]ς

Daughter of the eddying river, gentle-minded Aigina, truly (the son of Kronos) has given you great honour, showing forth among all the Greeks (a new victory) like a beacon; and some high-vaunting girl sings in praise of your (power/fame), often springing lightly on (white?) feet (over your sacred soil?), as a carefree fawn towards the flowery (hills/banks) with her illustrious near-dwelling (companions); and garlanded with the local adornment of crimson flowers and reeds those maidens sing, queen of a hospitable land, of your (child) ...

As others have detailed, there is no mistaking the tight connection between the internal chorus introduced in these lines and the performers of the composition being enacted in the *hic et nunc:* both engage in song and dance (μέλπω is used of each set of singer-dancers at 94 and 190), the maiden *choragos* performs a *hymnos*, the term which describes the epinician song at 223, and both choruses praise the prowess of the objects of their celebration, the *kratos* of Aigina standing counterpart to Pytheas' 'strength' cited in 75. Even the garlands of the maidens re-visualize the (probably) wreathed performers of the ode and of their *laudandus* Pytheas, who returns with his 'crowns of all-flourishing flowers' at 36–37.[50] Bacchylides also highlights the choral character of the maidens: not only are the members of the group tied by bonds of locality and defined as *hetairai*,[51] the term used by Pindar for the maidens who sing a nuptial song for Koronis (*Pyth.* 3.17–19),[52] but the maiden chorus-fawn equivalence occurs in sources that pre- and post-date the composition (Sappho fr. 57.5–6 Voigt, Eur. *El.* 860–861, *Ba.* 866–867) and seems a (parthenaic) choral *topos*. Power's

---

[50] Power (2000) 72 details these points; as he goes on to observe, the very invocation of Aigina together with the celebration of Aigina's descendants that follows can be read as the utterance of the maiden singers now channeled through the Bacchylidean chorus; for additional discussion, see Fearn (2007) 116–118. For the garlands and flowers, cf. Pindar's own celebration of Pytheas in *Nem.* 5.53–54.
[51] This term depends on a broadly accepted textual reconstruction.
[52] Also noted by Calame (1997) 33.

acute reading considers this embedded performance an instance of choral projection, and views the celebrants of Pytheas' one-off victory as identifying their performance with that of the standing maiden chorus that regularly sang and danced in honour of the island's founding nymph and her offspring; in so doing, they aim to enhance their local status and turn their one-off performance into one of *longue durée*.[53]

While the lines contain no explicit mention of Aigina's sisters, their presence in the extended visualization would be plain to an audience attending the performance. Even as the *choregos* spotlighted by Bacchylides occupies the preeminent position afforded Aigina, so her more anonymous companions, and the corresponding present day choristers, would take on the role of the island-nymphs' sisters. The suggestion of the maiden chorus' location beside the banks of the Asopos (hence the reeds and fawn heading for the river banks) would further turn the two latter-day collectives, positioned at the same riverine site,[54] into that original family grouping headed by their father/*choregos* Asopos. The introduction of a parthenaic chorus engaged in the celebration of Aigina multiplies the levels of choral 'mapping'; even as the occasional performers of Pytheas' praise assimilate themselves to the chorus of Aiginetan *parthenoi* engaged in the repeated, ritualized celebration of Pytheas' native land, so those maidens take as their models the ever singing-dancing Asopids, these too destined to leave the group, each in turn, as brides to illustrious gods.

Material evidence confirms the presence of female choral activity on Aigina, and even in conjunction with the Asopids. The island yielded three archaic representations of choruses, of which the first appears on a late eighth- or early seventh-century hydria cited earlier (n. 33).[55] Here, nine women led by a male lyre player and aulodist circle around the neck of the vessel.[56] As though in anticipation of Bacchylides' embedding stratagem, which superimposes male and female choruses one on the other, a procession of twelve men moving to the right occupies the neck's lower zone; here too an *aulos* player leads the line. The male cho-

---

[53] Power (2010); for additional discussion, see Stehle (1997) 106.
[54] For this localization, see Fearn (2007) 102–105 who argues for the presence of a river named Asopos on Aigina. According to Fearn, some time in the sixth century the Aiginetans would have built an underground watercourse (or, in Privitera's suggestion (1988), an aqueduct) following the route of a dry riverbed on the island so as to carry water from the region of Mt. Panhellenios in the southern part of Aigina to the central town. For Aiginetan choruses dancing by the Asopos, see Pind. *Nem.* 3.4 and Steiner (forthcoming).
[55] Berlin, Antikensammlung 31312 (31573). For this and the other vases, see Calame (1997) 67–68.
[56] While the number of Asopids varies from one source to the next, in the work by Corinna treated at this section's end, they number nine.

rus differs from that of the maidens above in several respects; not only in number, but also in the more vigorous motions that two of its members perform; and where the girls carry the branches so common in depictions of parthenaic choruses, the men are empty handed, their arms bent perhaps in order to perform a clapping gesture.[57] Both separate and juxtaposed, the two choruses suggest the relations of equivalence and difference that Bacchylides' later song would stage.

The tight association between the Aiginetan Asopos (hero and river), his daughters, and chorality is equally pronounced in Pindaric song. *Paean* 6 includes an extended instance of the interweaving of the Asopids and the real and mythical parthenaic choruses cited as paradigmatic ensembles by the current performers of the piece. The song opens with a statement of the 'orphaned' state of the performance site, a condition that the arrival of the speaker with his chorus will put to rights (fr. 52f.1–11 Snell-Maehler):

πρὸς Ὀλυμπίου Διός σε, χρυσέα
κλυτόμαντι Πυθοῖ,
λίσσομαι Χαρίτεσ-
σίν τε καὶ σὺν Ἀφροδίται,
ἐν ζαθέωι με δέξαι χρόνωι
ἀοίδιμον Πιερίδων προφάταν·
ὕδατι γὰρ ἐπὶ χαλκοπύλωι
ψόφον ἄϊων Κασταλίας
ὀρφανὸν ἀνδρῶν χορεύσιος ἦλθον
ἔταις ἀμαχανίαν ἀ[λ]έξων
τεοῖσιν ἐμαῖς τε τιμ[α]ῖς·

Golden Pytho, famed for seers, I beseech you by Olympian Zeus, with the Graces and Aphrodite, receive me, the interpreter of the Pierides, famed in song, at the sacred time. For having heard, at the water of Kastalia with its gate of bronze, its sound bereft of the dancing of men, I have come to ward off helplessness from your townsmen and my privileges.

While most commentators assume that it is the sound of the fountain, its plashing waters, that lacks the accompaniment of the dance, Hardie observes that the syntax of lines 5–6 can be differently construed: reading ὕδατι with Kastalia and ψόφον with ἀνδρῶν, the phrase then means 'for having heard, at the bronze-gated water of Kastalia, a noise – bereft of males – of dancing...'. Understood this way, the sound belongs not to the fountain, but to that made by the choral dancers.[58] In Hardie's view, the ambiguity may be deliberate: drawing on the

---

57 Crowhurst (1963) 36.
58 Hardie (1996) 221; as he additionally points out, Callimachus twice uses ἄψοφος of the absence of the beat made by the feet of dancers, and other sources similarly refer to the sound of

commonplace equation between moving, audible water and dance, Pindar intends us to understand that the ψόφος heard by the speaker belongs both to the fountain and the dancers, these of an expressly non-masculine kind; hence the need for the Pindaric performers.

The identification of these unspecified Delphic choristers comes just a few lines on: in the passage announcing the poetic ego's presence at the precinct of Apollo, a chorus of maidens, the site's regular occupants, duly appears (15–18):

> τόθι Λατοΐδαν
> θαμινὰ Δελφῶν κόραι
> χθονὸς ὀμφαλὸν παρὰ σκιάεντα μελπ[ό]μεναι
> ποδὶ κροτέο[ντι γᾶν θο]ῶι
>
> where the maidens of Delphi often sing to Leto's son at the shady navel of the earth and beat the ground with rapid foot

These female dancers are the standing chorus of the Delphides who supply the more permanent celebrants of the god on whom the male performers, onetime newcomers to the space, model themselves. As Hardie details, the phrasing picks up on the opening visualization of the Kastalia: 'the action (and the verb κροτέοντι in particular) suggests the noise denoted by ψόφος. Given the association between ψόφος and χόρευσις at 8f., it is hard to believe that Pindar did not intend an internal cross-reference between the two passages and thus ... the noise of Kastalia may correlate in some positive way with the noise of the dance of women'.[59]

In what turns out to be a reprise of the *mise en scène* at the poem's start, the final epode introduces a second maiden collective dancing riverside. Here, hailing the island of Aigina in her astral identity, the performers imagine her receiving their praise and answering their choral tribute by recounting the story of her abduction from her paternal home (125–129):

> νᾶσος, [ὦ] Διὸς Ἑλ-
> λανίου φαεννὸν ἄστρον.
> οὔνεκεν οὔ σε παιηόνων
> ἄδορπον εὐνάξομεν, ἀλλ' ἀοιδᾶν
> ῥόθια δεκομένα κατερεῖς ...
>
> island, o shining star of Zeus Hellanios, therefore we will not put you to bed without a feast of paeans; rather, receiving the plashing waves of song, you will narrate ...

---

the footfall as a ψόφος; ψοφέω properly describes the sound of one thing striking against another.

59 Hardie (1996) 222.

After fresh celebration of the island, the chorus gives Aigina's back history in a narrative that refigures what was earlier a toponym into a water-based nymph (134–138):

ὑδάτ‹εσσ›ι δ' ἐπ' Ἀσ[ω-
ποῦ π[οτ' ἀ]πὸ προθύρων βαθύκολ-
πον ἀγερέψατο παρθένον
Αἴγιναν·

and by the waters of the Asopos, [Zeus] once carried off from her forecourt the deep-breasted maiden Aigina.

Typically of Pindaric ring-composition, these lines circle back to the opening of the *Paean*, reprising the prelude in imagery, diction, and syntax. As the choristers supply Aigina with the promised sustenance in the form of 'pulsing waves (ῥόθια) of song' (128–129), they select a term that re-works the combination of sound, motion and water apparent in the opening description of the noise issued by the Kastalia and the complementary beat of the Delphides' feet. ῥόθια connotes not just the seawaters, but the rushing and plashing breakers generating that noise, a counterpart to the choristers' rapid footwork as they strike the ground. And just as the *persona loquens* of the poem's start arrived so as to remedy a lack, and further presented himself at the first triad's end performing a libation of song (58–61),[60] so the chorus here declares itself giver of a liquid tribute as well as supper of paeans.[61]

It is Hardie, once again, who draws attention to dictional and syntactical parallels between the opening passage and the later verses: lines 134–135, ὑδάτ‹εσσ›ι δ' ἐπ Ἀσ[ω-/ποῦ echo lines 7–8, ὕδατι ... ἐπὶ ... /... Κασταλίας and within both scenes the singers introduce not just water but 'gates' or 'doors', and identify features of the landscape. Still following Hardie, but developing his argument, this final vignette may also glance back to the choral motif highlighted at the start;[62] for an audience well versed in abduction stories, and witnessing the dance now performed before their eyes, the account of how Zeus bore Aigina off from the portico of her home with her 'father' Asopos in close proximity, would bring to mind the scenario ubiquitous in visual and literary depictions of such 'choral snatches': that of a preeminent maiden with whom a man or god falls in love and abducts while she dances in the company of her

---

60 See Radt (1958) 128–129.
61 Folded into these images of drinks offerings is the theme of thirst that bears directly on Aigina's role at Delphi.
62 Hardie (1996) 230–231.

kin/age mates,[63] a group made up, in this instance, of Aigina's sister Asopids. In accordance with the template, a father figure appears nearby, and the dance occurs in a watery locale.

A series of vase representations clustered chiefly in the early fifth century – there are over thirty extant examples in the corpus – depict the abduction scene, many including Aigina's sisters witnessing the act;[64] the girls are regularly shown moving towards their father, assuming poses often indistinguishable from those used in contemporary representations of choral dancers.[65] The subject may also have appeared in Aiginetan statuary: the sculpture group originally designed for the east pediment of the temple of Aphaia on the island, and commissioned ca. 500 at the same time as the construction of the building, depicted the abduction. Although the Aiginetans replaced the image sometime in the next decades – there is debate as to precisely when, but most date it to the 480s[66] – excavators have unearthed the fragmentary remains from the site where the pedimental components were then exhibited, the stoa-like structures on either side of the Altar Court in front of the temple. There is no way of knowing whether the Asopids were included in the original scene, but, in the light of contemporary vase images, it seems at least plausible that they formed part of the multi-figured pediment. The maiden choruses that performed in the vicinity of the temple (see below) could have modeled themselves after the sorority portrayed on the pediment as originally conceived.

Korai found on the island supply additional evidence.[67] Three of the extant four, all dated to the first half of the sixth century, come from the Aphaia sanctuary; one is dressed in a tight-fitting chiton and belt, while the second has the same type of gown, with a central vertical meander-pattern border that runs between the leg; the third wears a belted chiton, earrings, and a taenia holding her distinctively styled hair. As many readings of korai suggest, the maidens could serve as offerings that instantiated in perpetuity *parthenoi* as they appeared decked out in their rich garments and jewelry while participating in choral pro-

---

[63] Among the numerous examples, Polymele at *Il.* 16.179–183, the disguised Aphrodite (*Hom. Hymn to Aphrodite* 117–120), Persephone with the Okeanids (*Hom. Hymn to Demeter* 5), Helen in Eur. *Hel.* 167–178.

[64] Smith (2011) 29–30.

[65] On the parallels between maidens dancing in choruses and in flight at abduction scenes, see the discussion of the confusion of the two motifs in representations of Nereids in Barringer (1995) 86–89.

[66] There is also debate as to whether Zeus' abduction of Aigina was originally a pedimental sculpture or whether it was designed as an independent votive offering; for a summary of divergent views, see Walter-Karydi (2006). For additional discussion, see Watson (2011) 80–88.

[67] For documentation, illustrations, and discussion, see Karakasi (2003) 109–112.

cessions and dancing; their continued presence in the shrine, and in proximity to current performances, commemorates and eternalizes their service to the deity. The find spots of the Aphaian korai well suit this account: not only would choral dancing have been integral to the rites celebrated on behalf of Aphaia, a goddess who, in her capacity as *kourotrophos*, presided over the coming of age rituals in which the Aiginetan maidens participated (dedications prove as much),[68] but all were set up in the north-east portion of the temenos, in the vicinity of the altar belonging to that section. According to Sinn's reconstruction, a smoothed rock surface that served as a stage for the performance of ring dances stood between the propylon and buildings in the southeast, while the colonnaded porch of the propylon and hall of the so-called Amphilopeion offered seating for audiences.[69]

For the Aiginetans in the audience gathered at the Delphic *theoxenia*, lines 134–135 of the Pindaric paean might not only recall a celebrated local monument and its (intended and recently relocated) decorative program, but would create a still tighter amalgam between the current performance site, where the Pindaric chorus (whether made up of Delphians, of Aiginetans or comprising two choruses, one picking up where the other had left off)[70] now dances and sings, and choral activity back home. With the correlation between the waters of Kastalia where *Paean* 6 situates itself and the Asopid banks to which line 134 clearly refers, the poem superimposes the dancing ground by the side of the Delphic spring onto the area adjacent to the Aiginetan river where, as other compositions by Pindar and Bacchylides illustrate, such performances routinely occurred. The effect is twofold: broadly, the move serves to bridge the distance between the remote and peripheral island and its local traditions and the panhellenic sanctuary, and to reinforce what the song has been doing all along, affirming the place of Aigina as integral to the Greek community and holding up its heroes as central to the well-being of the Hellene collective; more narrowly, it posits relations between the dancing Delphides visible at the poem's start and their Aiginetan counterparts, the maidenly Asopids.

Omitting discussion of the Asopos that appears in the prelude of Pindar's *Nem.* 3.3–5 – in this instance not so much the river as a spring identified in our sources with a daughter of Asopos, and evidently the nymph Aigina herself[71] – where the Pindaric chorus waits to perform, I turn instead to Bacchylides'

---

[68] See Sinn (1988) for evidence.
[69] Sinn (1988) 157.
[70] Kurke (2005) incisively treats the unresolved issue.
[71] Nagy (2011) 74. For detailed discussion of this Aiginetan Asopos, see Fearn (2007) 102–105 and Privitera (1988), together with *EM* (s.v. Ἀμφιφορίτης), which mentions just such an 'Asopid spring', the Ἀσωπίδα κρήνη, and Σ Pind. *Nem.* 3.1, iii. 42 Drachmann.

ninth ode, composed on behalf of the Nemean victory of Automedes from Phleious. Here the poet exploits the multiplicity of rivers all bearing the name Asopos: one formed the southern limit of Boiotia, the second, as just noted, was located on Aigina, and the third, featured in the song for the Phleian victor, traced its course through Phleious and into the Corinthian Gulf at Sikyon.[72] This is the Asopos, who, along with his progeny, receives explicit praise in lines 40–52, where the singers rehearse how the river-god's renown has traveled to the far points of the earth, further stoked by the fame of his daughters. Invoking Asopos, the singers hail their addressee before beginning their celebration (47–65):

στείχει δι' εὐρείας κελε[ύ-]
θου μυρία πάνται φάτις
σᾶς γενεᾶς λιπαρο-
ζώνων θυγατρῶν, ἃς θε[ο]ὶ
σὺν τύχαις ᾤκισσαν ἀρχα-
γοὺς ἀπορθήτων ἀγυιᾶν.
τίς γὰρ οὐκ οἶδεν κυανοπλοκάμου Θήβας ἐϋδμα[τον πόλι]ν,
[ἢ τὰν μεγαλώνυ]μον Αἴγιναν, μεγ[ίστ]ου
[Ζην]ὸς [ἃ πλαθεῖσα λ]έχει τέκεν ἥρω
[–]δε σω [--υ]ου,
[ὃς γ]ᾶς βασά[νοισιν Ἀχ]αιῶν
[ ]υ[ ]α[ ]
τ [--υ—υ--]
<α>[ ]ω[.......ε]ΰπεπλον [..].'[ ]
ἡ[δὲ Πειράν]αν ἑλικοστέφα[νον]
κ[ούραν, [– ὅ]σαι τ' ἄλλαι θεῶν
ε[ὐναῖς ἐδ]άμησαν ἀριγνώτ[ο]ις π[α]λαι[οῦ]
[παῖδες αἰ]δοῖ[αι] ποταμοῦ κε[λ]άδοντος·

> On a wide path travel in all directions the countless reports of your progeny, the shining-girdled daughters whom the gods with good fortune have settled as rulers of unsacked streets. Who does not know of the well-built town of dark-haired Thebe or of the renowned Aigina, who (came to) the bed of great Zeus and bore the hero ... whom the land of the Achaians by the tests ...? ... fair-robed ... and (Peirene the maiden) of the twirling garland, and all those who won glory when bedded by gods, venerable daughters of the ancient noisy river.

---

[72] There is actually a fourth Asopos; Herod. 7.199–200 mentions the existence of a Thessalian river named Asopos that flowed into the Gulf of Malis. For additional discussion see Nagy (2011) 52–54 (drawing on West [1985] 162–163) and the very detailed account of Kowalzig (2007) 195–201.

While the personified river serves, as it does so often, as the perfect means of establishing a 'natural' connection and two-way vector between the victor's home and the victory site, Asopos' multiple daughters occupy the chief portion of the celebration. As D'Alessio observes of the lines,[73] this is the 'passage which comes closest to a Hesiodic catalogue in the preserved songs of Pindar and Bacchylides', and he further notes that the ἤ at the start of line 62 (?) suggests that 'the list may have been coordinated through the distinctive particle, recalling the ἤ' οἵη formula' of the *Catalogue of Women*. But where D'Alessio identifies Bacchylides as borrower here, in the argument presented below I suggest a bi-directional, or even a reverse, trajectory.

A catalogic structure continues to inform the passage. Despite the lines' lacunose condition, we can assume that the singers would have listed at least some of the river's progeny: with Thebe and Aigina heading the enumeration as suits their particular pertinence to the victory, at least two or three other daughters would have been named, each picked out by an epithet.[74] Fearn suggests the inclusion of Kleona in line 61, and Peirene, the Corinthian spring, seems a likely candidate for 62.[75] The catalogue then ends in the fashion typical of hexameter lists, with a summary reference to 'all those other venerable daughters of the ancient sounding (ποταμοῦ κε[λ]άδοντος) river'.

But alongside the choice of the catalogue format for the presentation of the Asopids, their choral character is no less emphatic. Bracketing the geographical-mythical excursus are references to Automodes' victory and its celebration on native ground. In line 39, the pentathlete returns to the 'dark-eddying (πορφυροδίναν) river', a phrase which acts as lead in for the account of Asopos and his daughters; a second and matching mention of the river concludes the praise of the Asopids, signaling this embedded section's end and a return to where the song left off. With the river and its epithet in final position in the line, the lacunose phrase that follows moves directly back to the present occasion where the 'shouts of pipes' belonging to the ongoing performance simultaneously pick up on the noise just emitted by the water. The placement of the lines concerning the Asopids between two celebrations of the victor not only prompts the audience to perceive the connections that the poem suggests between the objects of praise – the Asopos, its offspring, and the local boy made good – but also draws attention to choral song and dance as the critical mechanism for the propagation of renown, a counterpart to the river/genealogical network that Bacchy-

---

[73] D'Alessio (2005) 237–238.
[74] Maehler (1982 vol. I) 186 makes various proposals concerning the other names.
[75] Fearn (2003) 361.

lides has traced out and that, like the river water with its self-diffusion through its progeny, is both synchronic and diachronic in scope.

By virtue of this triptych structure, the poet may additionally position Automedes not just as analogue to the renowned Asopids but even as participant in a chorus whose role it is to celebrate these once local and now trans-national *parthenoi*. Both *laudator* and *laudandus*, he becomes a present-day reconfiguration of those temporally distant but still sung-of maidens and a figure whose activity serves as model for the choristers in the here-and-now. One pointer to Automedes' likeness to the Asopids belongs to the pivot from the mythical excursus to the present occasion. If commentators correctly understand the reference to Aphrodite and the *erotes* in 66–73 as a nod to the victor's youth, loveliness and still unwed state, then this would make him, like the Asopids who aroused divine desire, a focus of erotic attention.[76] Enough remains of the fragmentary description of the maidens to indicate the poet's answering attention to their beauty and radiance-cum-moving brilliance. Styled 'shining-girdled' (λιπαροζώνων, 49) and, in the case of Peirene (?), 'of twirling garland', they resemble Automodes as depicted in the lines that precede this tribute to their charms. At 27–29 the poet describes how the victor 'shone out among the pentathletes as the bright moon in the mid-month night outshines the light of the stars', a simile that, in the standard view, echoes the lunar conceit in Sappho 96.6–10 Voigt.

But both this evocation of radiance and the subsequent account of the victor's athletic feats describing the 'flashing motion (ἀμάρυγμα) of his wrestlings' (36) include a second glance to the Lesbian poet and to her evocation of Anaktoria at the close of fr. 16 V:[77] recalling the departed maiden, the *persona loquens* describes how she longs to see 'the brilliant sparkle of [Anaktoria's] face' (κἀμάρυχμα λάμπρον ... προσώπω, 18). The visualization recalls the girl as she once performed as choral *première*, endowed with that sparkle and mobility characteristic of dancers which the term ἀμάρυχμα in both Sappho and Bacchylides conveys. Not only, as Fearn remarks, is Automedes 'thus attracted into the language register associated with the kinds of feminine mythological archetypes who appear in Bacchylides' central myth, the Asopids',[78] but also to the motions of both present-day and mythical choristers: already in Homeric song and the archaic hymnic repertoire, the phrase μαρμαρυγαί ... ποδῶν evokes the glint or sparkle emanating from a dancer's feet as he/she performs as chorus member

---

76 Fearn (2003) 364.
77 Also cited by Fearn (2003) 364 in passing; see too Cairns (2010) 256.
78 Fearn (2003) 364.

or *choregos* leading the ensemble (e.g. *Od.* 8.63, *Hom. Hymn to Apollo* 203). No less pertinent to *choreia* are the associations of the nighttime sky illuminated by the moon and attendant stars; already on the first band of the Iliadic Shield and in Alcman, these constellations are paradigmatic choral dancers, the less brilliant celestial bodies following the lead of, or circling about, their lunar *choregos*.[79]

The expression ἀμάρυγμα has additional significance here, supplying another possible glance to the 'Hesiodic' Asopids. Sappho's choice of term no less than that of Bacchylides, matches the formulaic phrase so frequent in the *Catalogue of Women*, Χαρίτων ἀμαρύγματα, a description repeatedly applied to the heroines celebrated for their beauty in the work. That Bacchylides' deployment of the noun for Automedes' 'flashy' moves is informed by the 'Hesiodic' text seems additionally likely in the light of the presence of the Asopids in both works. Also visible in the *Catalogue* is the lunar simile (in fr. 23a Leda is styled 'fair tressed like the rays of the moon') and the comparison could plausibly have been used of (one of) Asopos' multiple daughters. But again, I would question the assumption that the *Catalogue* supplies the 'source' for Bacchylides while Sappho furnishes the 'window text'; instead, the expressions and conceits are equally well grounded in the choral tradition from which hexameter poets are free to borrow, a practice already apparent in the Homeric Catalogue of Ships.

A series of terms in the section featuring the Asopids and the framing evocations of the ode's current enactment reinforces the choral motif by drawing attention to the performers' sounds and motions. Reviewing the different events in which Automedes competed at Nemea, the ode recalls his winning cast with the discus, a moment which supplies the tenor for the lunar simile: 'for he was conspicuous (ἐνέπρεπεν) among the pentathletes ...; even so (τοῖος) in the endless circle of the Greeks did he display his wondrous form casting the wheel-shaped (τροχοειδέα) discus' (30–32). The description privileges circularity: the athlete in the midst of his fellow contestants stands equivalent to the moon with its circlet of attendant astral bodies as he throws the rounded discus (a move which required the body to form an arc and then turn around its axis) while positioned in the centre of the surrounding crowd sounding its acclaim. The scene recalls not just *Od.* 8.370–380, where the chorus encircling the preeminent dancers performing their athletic dance likewise raises a loud sound; if the Homeric account of the chorus on Achilleus' Shield cited in section two reflects traditional notions of choral dancing, then the spin of the potter's wheel (τροχόν: *Il.* 18.600) supplies a canonical analogue for the gyrating chorus.

---

[79] For extensive discussion and examples, see Ferrari (2008) and Csapo (2008).

This circular motion proves characteristic of the Asopids and their father too. The epithet ἑλικοστέφα[vov used of one of the girls at 62 figures the twists and turns so regularly highlighted in choral contexts and which the dancers' accessories reflect, while fresh rotations belong to their watery progenitor, who, in a striking hapax, displays its 'purple eddies' (πορφυροδίναν, 39).[80]

Commentators regularly observe that the 'Hesiodic' *Catalogue* still more fully shapes the final text considered here, this one composed by a poet who, like the *Catalogue*'s putative author, was native to Boiotia.[81] Of course, any mention of Corinna comes surrounded by debates concerning the poet's date, the manner in which her songs were performed, and their intended audience, and I make two assumptions, both argued by other scholars,[82] in the reading that follows: first, that Corinna belongs to the fifth century, and second, that her poems were most likely composed for choruses of *parthenoi* in Tanagra and perhaps elsewhere in Boiotia. Among the more extensive fragments is the so-called 'Daughters of Asopos', a work whose extant portion occupies columns two to four of fr. 654 *PMG*. The Asopids are introduced in the early portion of the text and presented in the manner of a list that narrated the abductions and marriages of at least some of the nine heroines that the lines then number. The term ὧν, 'of these', suggests the start of the inventory, with Aigina in first position, followed, in rapid succession, by Korkyra, Salamis, 'lovely Euboia', Sinope and Thespia:

ὧν Ἤγ[ινα γε]νέθλαν
Δεὺς[ἀ]γαθῶν
Πατρο[ἐς,
Κορκού[ραν δὲ κὴ Σαλαμῖ-]
ν' εἰδ[' Εὔβοιαν ἐράνναν]

---

[80] See Csapo (2000) 418–424 for detailed discussion of Euripides' repeated use of ἑλίσσω, δινέω, and their cognates in his descriptions of choral performances in which the dancers turned in circles.

[81] Does Boiotia have a strong tradition of catalogues in choral form? – hence the initial focus on Boiotia in the Catalogue of Ships, as though a nod to this tradition, as well as the geographic orientation of the Odyssean catalogue of heroines.

[82] Here I follow, among others, Stehle (1997) esp. 101–104, Larson (2002), Collins (2006) 19–20 (with an overview of the argument), Lardinois (2011) 165–168. The case for the choral character of Corinna's poetry rests on admittedly slender grounds. Fr. 655.1–16 *PMG*, which opens with an invocation to Terpsichora ('she who delights in choruses') and is spoken in the voice of a poet or that of the collective chorus, which announces that it proclaims the legends of its homeland, Tanagra in Boiotia, offers the most compelling evidence. In Stehle's reading, the fragment suggests that Corinna addresses two audiences for whom different songs are performed: first the collective audience made up of the women of Tanagra, and then the *parthenoi* with whom the stories 'from our fathers' time' seem to be connected.

Ποτι[δάων κλέψε πα]τείρ,
Σιν[ώπαν δὲ Λατοΐδα]ς
ἐσ[πιαν τ' ἔστιν ἔχων·

Of these (daughters) Zeus, giver of good things, (took) his child Aigina ... from her father's ... while Korkyra (and Salamis) and (lovely Euboia) (were stolen) by father Poseidon, and (Leto's son) is in possession of Sinope and Thespia ...

As Campbell's note points out, the catalogue would have ended with Tanagra, whom Hermes stole.

Fresh enumerative design follows when the singers remark at 33–40:

τᾶν δὲ πήδω[ν τρῖς μ]ὲν ἔχι
Δεὺς πατεὶ[ρ πάντω]ν βασιλεύς,
τρῖς δὲ πόντ[ω γᾶμε] μέδων
Π[οτιδάων, τ]ὰν δὲ δουῖν
Φῦβος λέκτ[ρα] κρατούνι,
τὰν δ' ἴαν Μή[ας] ἀγαθὸς
πῆς Ἑρμᾶς·

And of your daughters father Zeus, king of all, has three; and Poseidon, ruler of the sea, married three; and Phoibos is master of the beds of two of them, of one Hermes, good son of Maia.

A marked degree of the repetition characteristic of lists structures the account, with the phrase τὰν δέ standing at the start at each entry naming a god and the number of his conquests, almost like an inscribed victory list. In counterpoint to this homogeneity, but very much in keeping with catalogue design, the numbers gradually diminish, three apiece for the first two 'top' deities, two for Apollo, just one for Hermes.

As already noted, it has been commonplace to remark on the broader overlap between the subject matter, theme and arrangement of Corinna's extant poetry and that of the *Catalogue*, and nowhere is this more apparent than in fr. 654. The later poet's concern with genealogy and ancestry through maternity emphatic here recalls the *Ehoiai*, and Larson notes that line 9 'hints at familiarity with the *Catalogue*'; as she further comments, 'both the *Catalogue* and Asopid daughters provide a marked, hierarchical catalogue of progenitor gods who beget a race of semidivine heroes'.[83] The enumeration of the Asopids also points back to the Odyssean catalogue of heroines at 11.234–329, and not least for the Boiotian focus prominent in both; among those whom Odysseus encounters is Antiope, another daughter of Asopos in the 'Hesiodic' *Catalogue* (frr. 38–42), who

---

[83] Larson (2002) 50–51 with additional parallels.

has strong links to Boiotian sites and cults. The sequence of four that follows – Alkmene, Megara, Epikaste, and Chloris – all share connections to the region.[84]

As I argued for Bacchylides' original composition for Automedes, Corinna's song simultaneously taps into the chorality associated with the Asopids in the lyric and visual traditions. With Tanagra concluding the enumeration, the initial list seems designed so as to culminate in a final city, singled out by the performers for the closing and privileged position where it can claim expanded space and receive additional elaboration. Since Tanagra was the site of choral performances of Corinna's poetry by *parthenoi* in fr. 655 *PMG* (see n. 82), the passage offers a fresh instance of choral projection, with the role of the Asopids reenacted by the latter-day ensemble of maidens in Tanagra, also on the threshold of marriage and whose *choregos*, perhaps decked out in extra finery or with an added accessory, takes on the leading role afforded the local and hence preeminent daughter.[85]

Putting all these pieces together, the Asopids seem firmly grounded in two traditions, both on view in the songs of Bacchylides and Corinna. First, that of the genealogical poetry – the sources' chief interest in the maidens seems to be in their role as progenitors of the heroes whose lineage reaches down to historical times – that so readily lends itself to catalogue form. The tendency to figure the river's many daughters in the linear structure characteristic of these textual lists extends to 'visual representations'. Asopos and his daughters appear in the now lost bronze statue groups that Pausanias saw at Olympia and Delphi (5.22.6, 10.13.6), the former clearly depicting Aigina being abducted from the company of her sisters. Here Pausanias names Nemea, Harpinna, Korkyra and Thebe, with Asopos seemingly positioned last in the line. The language of the first of the passages, complete with the term διακοσμέω used in other sources for the marshaling-cum-arraying of choral processions as well as of troops,[86] leaves no doubt as to the group's linear presentation. Presumably reading off each name as inscribed beneath the successive images, Pausanias effectively performs a mini-catalogue, complete with internal repetition and a superlative name cap for the last item enumerated:

---

[84] As detailed in Larson (2000).
[85] Beyond that fragment, we have no references to choral activity in Tanagra, whether by *parthenoi* or other groups, although Calame (1997) 135 n. 131, citing Schachter (1981–1994 vol. I) 179–180 and 185–186, proposes that it might have been the site for an Agrionia, complete with a reenactment of the race, which could have been performed as a dance.
[86] E.g., *Il.* 2.476, Thuc. 6.47.1, Xen. *Ephes.* 1.2.4.

ἀνέθεσαν δὲ καὶ Φλιάσιοι Δία καὶ θυγατέρας τὰς Ἀσωποῦ καὶ αὐτὸν Ἀσωπόν, διακεκόσμηται δὲ οὕτω σφίσι τὰ ἀγάλματα. Νεμέα μὲν τῶν ἀδελφῶν πρώτη, μετὰ δὲ αὐτὴν Ζεὺς λαμβανόμενός ἐστιν Αἰγίνης, παρὰ δὲ τὴν Αἴγιναν ἕστηκεν Ἅρπινα..., μετὰ δὲ αὐτὴν Κόρκυρά τε καὶ ἐπ' αὐτῆι Θήβη, τελευταῖος δὲ ὁ Ἀσωπός.

> The Phliasians also dedicated a Zeus and the daughters of Asopos and Asopos himself, and the images are divided and marshaled thus: Nemea is the first of the sisters and after her comes Zeus seizing Aigina; next to Aigina stands Harpina ... after her is Korkyra with Thebe next; last of all comes Asopos.

As for the second generic tradition in which Asopos' daughters are embedded, that of choral songs, whether in the form of the *partheneia* performed by maidens in the regions with whom the mythical sisters were most closely associated, others by youths participating in different choral genres, this can be explained on several grounds. First, most simply, because the Asopids form an epichoric sorority, as do, loosely or formally, participants in the corresponding real-world ensembles. And second, because the heroines' 'histories' offer a prime instance of the types of myths, themes and concerns regularly articulated in *partheneia*, where composers typically select topics and motifs calibrated to their singer-dancers' gender and time of life. Ingalls details the contents of such works – those of Alcman, Sappho, Telesilla and Corinna among them – and argues that the issue of female sexuality, its positive and negative consequences and the need for its containment appear writ large in these pieces that serve a paideutic function for their performers and audiences.[87] Suggestive of a song designed for a chorus of *parthenoi* is not only the subject matter of Corinna's fragment, a group of maidens destined for marriage and abstracted one by one from their sorority, but also its resolution. In the conversation between Asopos and a local seer in which the just-cited list appears, the father learns that the gods will ultimately give him the compensation that recasts these abductions as sanctioned unions.[88] It needs no demonstration that unions between maidens, gods and heroes, some legitimate and orderly, others marked by violence or the transgression of regular practices, are the central concerns of the 'Hesiodic' *Catalogue*, which inscribes its women within larger genealogical hierarchies and focuses on their roles as wives and mothers. Courtship protocols both observed and violated (so the tale of Mestre) and marriage contests (that of Helen most obviously) also occupy a major place in the *Catalogue*,[89] as they do in the extant poetry composed on behalf of maiden choruses.

---

87 Ingalls (2000).
88 See Lardinois (2011) 166.
89 As closely argued and detailed by Ormand (2014).

Nor is explicit evidence for the Asopids' membership of a larger group of archetypal choral ensembles, chiefly parthenaic in character, wholly lacking. Instead it comes, albeit belatedly, in a passage in the third stasimon of Euripides' *Herakles*, where the chorus, rejoicing at the death of Lykos, invites the whole Theban topography to join in the dance and song being performed on the Attic stage (781–789):

Ἰσμήν' ὦ στεφαναφόρει
ξεσταί θ' ἑπταπύλου πόλεως
 ἀναχορεύσατ' ἀγυιαὶ
Δίρκα θ' ἁ καλλιρρέεθρος,
σύν τ' Ἀσωπιάδες κόραι
 πατρὸς ὕδωρ βᾶτε λιποῦσαι συναοιδοὶ
Νύμφαι τὸν Ἡρακλέους
καλλίνικον ἀγῶνα.

> Be wreathed o river Ismenos, and you polished streets of seven-gated Thebes, start the dance, and you lovely river Dirce, and you maidens, daughters of Asopos, leave your father's waters and come, Nymphs, to join in singing of the contest Herakles gloriously won.

Here the Asopids' classification as 'nymphs' goes some way to predetermining their participation in the celebration as they engage in the prototypical activity, dancing, routinely assigned these deities in visual and textual sources. But, in the proposal made here, Euripides also draws on the more specific and existing association between the daughters of Asopos and choral activity. Once again, a male chorus – and one whose dramatic identity is that of aged men – project themselves onto this archetypal ensemble and in so doing achieve the form of rejuvenation through *choreia* detailed in another of their songs in the play.

Mode of Performance

Chief among the many outstanding questions surrounding the *Catalogue of Women* concerns its mode of performance and the sites where recitations of the work might occur, and recent scholars have proposed various models and venues.[90] My closing suggestion draws on the arguments made in this chapter to introduce a fresh and necessarily speculative wrinkle to the debate. Granted, the *Catalogue* takes the form of hexameter poetry and would, in the consensus view, have been intended for delivery in the manner of the Homeric songs and in contexts where such epic performances took place. But, like the *Iliad*, *Odyssey*,

---

[90] For a handy summary, see Ormand (2014) 9–11.

and *Homeric Hymns*, the 'Hesiodic' piece reworks narratives that coexisted in other poetic genres and performance traditions, choral lyric among them, and which continued to be enacted at the different types of occasions for which they were designed. Might the *Catalogue* have, at least in part, taken its impetus from the compositions sung and danced by *parthenoi* within the context of civic and extra-urban rituals, chiefly those grounded in the coming-of-age festivals in which young girls participated and where, as nubile members of the community now ripe for courtship and marriage, they would rehearse their future roles as citizens' wives and mothers? And might the sixth-century work have grafted onto the existing epic tradition this very different type of song, embedding it within the catalogue structure with which these maidenly choral songs-and-dances have so many affinities?

Bibliography

Athanassaki, L. and E. Bowie (eds.) (2011). *Archaic and Classical Choral Song. Performance, Politics and Dissemination*, Berlin.

Barringer, J. (1995). *Divine Escorts. Nereids in Archaic and Classical Greek Art*, Ann Arbor.

Cairns, D. L. (2010). *Bacchylides: Five Epinician Odes (3, 5, 9, 11, 13)*, Cambridge.

Calame, C. (1997). *Choruses of Young Women in Ancient Greece. Their Morphology, Religious Role, and Social Function*, New York.

Carruesco, J. (2010). 'Prácticas rituales y modos del discurso: la coralidad como paradigma del catálogo en la poesía arcaica griega', in: J. F. C. Castro, J. Siles Ruiz, and J. de la Villa Polo (eds.), *Perfiles de Grecia y Roma. Actas del XII Congreso Nacional de Estudios Clásicos*. Vol II. Valencia, 271–277.

Carruesco, J. (2012). 'Helen's Voice and Choral Mimesis from Homer to Stesichorus', in: X. Rin and J. Pòrtulas (eds.), *Approaches to Archaic Greek Poetry*. Messina, 149–172.

Collins, D. (2006). 'Corinna and Mythological Innovation', *CQ* 56: 19–32.

Crowhurst, R. (1963). *Representations of Performance of Choral Lyric on the Greek Monuments, 800–350 B.C.* PhD diss., University of London.

Csapo, E. (2000). 'Euripidean New Music', in: M. Cropp, K. Lee and D. Sansone (eds.), *Euripides and Tragic Theatre in the Late Fifth Century*, *ICS* 24–5: 399–426.

Csapo, E. (2008). 'Star choruses: Eleusis, Orphism and New Musical Imagery and Dance', in: M. Revermann and P. Wilson (eds.), *Performance, Iconography, Reception. Studies in Honour of Oliver Taplin*, Oxford, 262–290.

D'Agostino, B. (2016). 'Potters and Painters: Schemata and Images', in: G. Colesanti and L. Lulli (eds.), *Submerged Literature in Ancient Greek Culture, vol. II: Case Studies*, Berlin, 243–258.

D'Alessio, G. B. (2005). 'Ordered from the Catalogue: Pindar, Bacchylides and Hesiodic Genealogical Poetry', R. Hunter (ed.), *The Hesiodic Catalogue of Women: Constructions and Reconstructions*, Cambridge, 217–238.

Faraone, C. (2013). 'The Poetics of the Hesiodic Catalogue', *TAPA* 143: 293–323.

Fearn, D. (2003). 'Mapping Phleious: Politics and Myth-Making in Bacchylides 9', *CQ* 53: 347–367.
Fearn, D. (2007). *Bacchylides*, Oxford.
Fearn, D. (ed.) (2011). *Aegina. Contexts for Choral Lyric Poetry*, Oxford.
Ferrari, G. (2008). *Alcman and the Cosmos of Sparta*, Chicago.
Hardie, A. (1996). 'Pindar, Castalia and the Muses of Delphi (the sixth *Paean*)', *PLLS* 9: 219–258.
Heiden, B. (2008). 'Common People and Leaders in *Iliad* 2: The Invocation of the Muses and the Catalogue of Ships', *TAPA* 138: 127–154.
Henrichs, A. (1994–1995). '"Why Should I Dance?" Choral Self-Referentiality in Greek Tragedy', *Arion* 3: 56–111.
Henrichs, A. (1996). *"Warum sol ich den tanzen?" Dionysisches im Chor der griechischen Tragödie*, Stuttgart and Leipzig.
Ingalls, W. B. (2000). 'Ritual Performance as Training for Daughters in Archaic Greece', *Phoenix* 54: 1–20.
Karakasi. K. (2003). *Archaic Korai*, Los Angeles.
Kavoulaki, A. (2011). 'Choral Self-Awareness: on the Introductory Anapests of Aeschylus' *Suppliants*', in: Athanassaki and Bowie, 365–390.
Kowalzig, B. (2007). *Singing for the Gods. Performance of Myth and Ritual in Archaic and Classical Greece*, Oxford.
Kurke, L. (2005). 'Choral Lyric as "Ritualization": Poetic Sacrifice and Poetic Ego in Pindar's Sixth Paean', *CA* 25: 81–130.
Langdon, S. (2008). *Art and Identity in Dark Age Greece, 1100–700 B.C.E*, Cambridge.
Lardinois, A. P. M. H. (2011). 'The *parrhesia* of Young Female Choruses in Ancient Greece', in: Athanassaki and Bowie, 161–172.
Larson, J. (2000). 'Boiotia, Athens, the Peisistratids, and the *Odyssey*'s Catalogue of Heroines', *GRBS* 41: 193–222.
Larson, J. (2001). *Greek Nymphs: Myth, Cult, Lore*, Madison, Wis.
Larson, J. (2002). 'Corinna and the Daughters of Asopos', *Syllecta Classica* 13: 47–62.
Lonsdale, S. (1993). *Dance and ritual play in Greek religion*. Baltimore.
Maehler, H. (1982). *Die Lieder des Bakchylides*. 2 vols., Leiden.
Martin, R. P. (2008). 'Keens from the Absent Chorus: Troy to Ulster', in: A. Suter (ed.), *Lament. Studies in the Ancient Mediterranean and Beyond*, Oxford, 118–138.
Minchin, E. (1996). 'The Performance of Lists and Catalogues in the Homeric Epics', in: I. Worthington (ed.), *Voice into Text. Orality and Literacy in Ancient Greece*, Leiden, 3–20.
Minton, W. W. (1962). 'Invocation and Catalogue in Hesiod and Homer', *TAPA* 93: 188–212.
Myers, M. (2007). 'Footrace, Dance, and Desire. The χορός of Pindar's *Pythian 9*', *SIFC* 5: 230–247.
Nagy, G. (1990). *Pindar's Homer. The Lyric Possession of an Epic Past*, Baltimore.
Nagy, G. (2011). 'Asopos and his Multiple Daughters. Traces of Preclassical Epic in the Aeginetan Odes of Pindar', in: Fearn, 41–78.
Notopoulos, J. A. (1949). 'Parataxis in Homer. A New Approach to Homeric Literary Criticism', *TAPA* 80: 1–23.
Ormand, K. (2014). *The Hesiodic Catalogue of Women and Archaic Greece*, Cambridge.

Peponi, A.-E. (2004). 'Initiating the Viewer. Deixis and Visual Perception in Alcman's Lyric', *Arethusa* 37: 295–316.
Perceau, S. (2002). *La parole vive. Communiquer en catalogue dans l'épopée homérique*, Louvain.
Power, T. (2000). 'The *Parthenoi* of Bacchylides 13', *HSCP* 100: 67–81.
Privitera, G. A. (1988). 'Pindaro Nem. III 1–5, e l'acqua di Egina', *QUCC* 58: 63–70.
Radt, S. L. (1985). *Pindars zweiter und sechster Paian. Text, Scholien und Kommentar*, Amsterdam.
Robbins, E. (1994). 'Alkman's Partheneion: Legend and Choral Ceremony', *CQ* 44: 7–16.
Sammons, B. (2010). *The Art and Rhetoric of the Homeric Catalogue*, Oxford.
Schachter, A. (1981–1994). *Cults of Boeotia*, 4 vols., London.
Sinn, U. (1988). 'Der Kult der Aphaia aud Aegina', in: *Early Greek Cult Practice: Proceedings of the Fifth International Symposium at the Swedish Institute at Athens, 26–29 June, 1986*, Stockholm, 149–159.
Smith, A. C. (2011). *Polis and Personification in Classical Greek Art*, Leiden.
Stehle, E. (1997). *Performance and Gender in Ancient Greece. Nondramatic Poetry in Its Setting*, Princeton.
Steiner, D. (forthcoming). *Choral Constructions. The idea of the Chorus in the Poetry, Art, Technologies and Social Practices of Archaic and Early Classical Greece*, Cambridge.
Swift, L. (2016). 'Visual Imagery in Parthenaic Song', in: V. Cazzatto and A. Lardinois (eds.), *The Look of Lyric: Greek Song and the Visual*, Leiden, 255–287.
Wachter, R. (2001). *Non-Attic Greek Vase Inscriptions*, Oxford.
Walter-Karydi, E. (2006). *How the Aiginetans Formed their Identity*. The Archaeological Society at Athens Library 243, Athens.
Watson, J. (2011). 'Rethinking the Sanctuary of Aphaia', in: Fearn, 79–113.
West, M. L. (1985). *The Hesiodic* Catalogue of Women, Oxford.

Malcolm Davies
The Origin of Things: A Study in Contrasts

Guthrie once memorably observed[1] that 'Homer was not interested in the origin of things, ... and his poems show only faint an occasional traces of a knowledge that it was not always so. In this the heroic epics are peculiar, for a consuming interest in beginnings is a characteristic of the Greeks'. This view is expressed in a rather eccentric form, since we cannot hope to know what Homer's personal view was on such matters; and to much present-day sentiment the *Iliad* and *Odyssey*'s shared generic status offers a far more important potential explanation for this lack observed in comparison with Hesiod's theogonic and wisdom literature than any personal preferences that might be inferred. But Guthrie's underlying aperçu is illuminating. Moreover, it is fully borne out by comparison with the genuine works of Hesiod. The *Theogony* and the *Works and Days* are far more interested in or explicit about what Guthrie terms 'the origin of things' than *Iliad* or *Odyssey*, as the Hesiodic accounts of the creation of the cosmos and the coming to power of the Olympian deities, the origins of sacrifice to these deities, the acquisition of fire by mortals, and the introduction of evil and suffering into the world all confirm.

In this respect, at least, the Hesiodic fragments closely resemble the authentic works of Hesiod. For instance, as we shall see, we know from fr. 4 of the *Catalogue* that the story of Deukalion as the first man featured therein, and from fr. 205.2–5 of the same poem that the inhabitants of the island of Aigina were descended from the men whom Zeus manufactured out of ants. Furthermore, hardly has the *Catalogue* opened than we are reminded (fr. 1.6ff.) that, in Guthrie's phrase, 'the world was once different from what it is now'. The poet recalls that, in the days when gods had intercourse with mortal women, gods and mortals dined together and shared council. The presupposed happy state of affairs involving a harmonious amity – here involving men and gods – which is doomed to end is a motif familiar throughout the world.[2] The 'fundamental change in the

---

In the following footnotes, 'West (1985) = M. L. West'. Fragments are cited by the numeration of Merkelbach and West's edition.

1 Guthrie (1961²) 851 (= 34 of the separate fascicle). Quotations from this chapter below are from this latter.
2 See Davies (2001) 199 and 208f. Cf. West, p. 3: the 'poet had a clearly defined and individual view of the heroic period as a kind of Golden Age in which the human race lived in different conditions from the present and which Zeus terminated as a matter of policy'.

conditions of life'³ which is the regular sequel to such a happy existence seems to be depicted in the lacunose fr. 205 where the effect of Zeus' plan to make human life a great deal harder is described. One might compare what an Old Testament scholar⁴ has said of the story of the tower of Babel in Genesis: 'the narrative in the form in which it lies before us is aetiological: behind it lies a query about a present situation which is explained by something that happened in the past. A series of narratives in Genesis 1–11 is concerned with the question of how the present situation came about from the earlier. All of them find that the present situation is worse ... The event that gave rise to the present is usually presented in the pattern of crime and punishment ... God's intervention ... is the beginning of a way of life that marks the transition from primal events to history'. The series of narratives here referred to also includes the expulsion from the Garden of Eden, and the *Theogony* of Hesiod clearly envisages Prometheus' achieving of the better portion of sacrifice for mortals as the crime that leads to the dissolution of the shared existence of gods and men. The crime in the *Catalogue*'s version of this pattern is less clear, perhaps due to the lacunose state of the relevant fragment.

As we have just reminded ourselves, the aspect whose absence from Homer Guthrie found so marked is known to experts in folk-tale as an *aetiological narrative*. One such expert⁵ has observed of this aspect as follows: 'narrators everywhere entertain an interest in the origin of things. In Europe and elsewhere, no phenomenon of note does not have a narrative to explain its current form. We find this need for causality in even the most basic realms of human life ... Was it always so? What was it like before? The question of cause develops only out of this interest in origins. Why did it change?' And the same scholar proceeds, in a direction that will steer our own inquiry onto the right course, to observe that 'the grandest aetiological narratives explain the creation of the world and the human race ... e.g. stories about the origin of mortality and reproduction'. This claim receives ample confirmation from the first group of Hesiodic fragments which I wish to adduce.

We may begin with the topic of *eponymous ancestors*.⁶ To select a few examples, in fr. 2. *Hellen* gives his name to the race of Hellenes and the land that is

---

[3] West (1985) 119. On the nature of this change as reported in the Hesiodic Catalogue and Zeus' decision to annihilate the ἡμίθεοί, see Scodel (1982) 37–40.
[4] Westermann (1984) 534f. For possible Old Testament and Ancient Near Eastern analogues to the *Catalogue*'s picture of a divine plan to destroy mankind, see Scodel (1982) 40–42.
[5] Röhrich (1991) 27.
[6] On ancestors in the *Catalogue*, see Kyriakou 135–161 (this volume).

Hellas. Cf. fr. 9 for his three sons, *Doros*, ancestor of the Dorians, *Xouthos*, grandfather of *Achaios*, ancestor of the Achaians, and *Aiolos*, ancestor of the Aiolids. Or again, in fr. 5.3 Pandora bears *Graikos* to Zeus. In fr. 7, *Makedon* is identified as the eponym of Macedonia and in fr. 183 the heroine *Thebe* gives her name to Thebes.[7]

The context of this last detail requires a little more examination. The husband of Thebe was Zethos, and fr. 182 relates how he and his brother Amphion built the walls of Thebes with the help of his *kithara*, so the origins of this famous city also fell within the poem. So did the building of Troy (fr. 235: see below). Other cities' origins and namings seem to have featured in fr. 19, where it is recorded that the Aloadai founded a city in Thessaly named Alos after their father. Also in fr. 185, if we can really discern in this lacunose papyrus fragment an allusion to Eleuther founder of Eleutheron and more specifically in v. 8 (Ἀστρηίδος ἠϋκόμοιο) the eponymous heroine of the Thessalian city of Asterion. Stephanus of Byzantium s.v. Lastly, fr. 234. (on which see further below), implies that Lokros was the eponymous ancestor of the Lokrians.

No treatment of origins can afford to omit the related topos of the *primus inventor* or πρῶτος εὑρετής, which figures so importantly in popular and primal belief, and yet is so shockingly absent from Homer's poetry, as I have observed and explained elsewhere.[8] In fr. 205.6–7 we learn that the Aiginetans were the first to travel by ship and employ sails, while in fr. 282 we are told that the Idaean Dactyls, another markedly unHomeric group, first discovered iron in Scythe.[9] In this area too illumination may be gained by quoting from the field of comparative folklore. Scholars in this field have long been aware that early Celtic literature is frequently eager to state how a given event was the first of its kind, as when, in the *Mabinogion*'s First Branch, we are reminded that a certain occasion was the first time the game of Badger in the Bag was played.[10] A pair of experts who assemble a list of instances of this process from Irish literature[11] append the gloss that, in one particular composition, 'care is taken to commemorate the oc-

---

[7] On Hellen, Graikos and their descendants, see West (1985) 52 f. and 59 f. (for the principle of and parallels for eponyms, see his General Index s.v.) and Fowler (2013) Index of Names and Subjects s.vv.

[8] See Davies (2001) 207 f.

[9] Note that as part of Zeus' plan to make human life more unpleasant 'man was to be forced to sail about the sea' (West 1985, 119). Ancient authors assigned the invention of sailing to a variety of individuals: see Pease on Cicero *de nat. deorum* 2.89.

[10] See S. Davies' translation (2007, 14) of the *Mabinogion*.

[11] Rees (1961) 105. Note that fr. 205 may represent the first *season* as such on earth: see West (1961) 131 and (1985) 133 f.

casions when things were done or experienced for the first time and to record the names of the persons concerned, the first to land, the first to die', etc., and they draw the conclusion that 'as with other traditional cultures, Celtic society could not function without precedents'.

To return to Hesiodic fragments, 297 on Palamedes may also be relevant, given that hero's status as πρῶτος εὑρετής. His is a *nom parlant* and we know that his father Ναύ-πλιος begot two further sons with etymologically significant names, Οἴ-αξ and Ναυσι-μέδων.[12] Culture heroes or first discoverers often bear such names. Some rather crude examples are to be found in Philo of Byblus (Eusebius *Praep. Ev.* 2.15), where the first parents, Ἀίων and Πρωτογόνος[13] produce three children Φῶς, Πῦρ and Φλόξ, who, unsurprisingly, invent the use of fire. A little later we read of Ἀγρεύς and Ἁλιεύς, inventors respectively of hunting and fishing.

This leads us neatly to the next point for discussion. We may start with what may seem a trivial instance of the origins of things: the process by which individuals acquired significant names, that is *the etymologies of names*. A significant distinction between the use of etymologies by Homer and the genuine Hesiod was pointed out by Ernst Risch[14] in an article whose conclusion I herewith excerpt and translate: 'Homeric epic is certainly aware of etymological word play but by and large ignores it. In this respect there is no significant difference between the *Iliad* and the *Odyssey*... But Homer employs elegant subtlety and is not invariably explicit, whereas Hesiod does not aim at the self-evident but laboriously works things out and employs involved and ponderous expressions'. Thus, to cull one or two instances from Risch, at *Th.* 143–145. we are told that the Kyklopes have a single eye in the middle of each of their heads and are called

---

[12] On etymology in Hesiod, see Kyriakou 151 n. 57 (this volume); Tsagalis 197, 202–203 (this volume); Cardin and Pontani 254, 256–257, 267, 269 (this volume).

[13] The name Πρωτογένεια occurs in other similar contexts: see West (1985) 52 n. 39. Deukalion and his creation of mankind from stones certainly featured in the *Catalogue*. For his likely status as culture hero, see Fowler (2013) 116 n. 11, and note Ap. Rh. 3.1088–1089, who describes Deukalion as the first to build cities and temples and first to rule as king over men. This use of symbolic names may be in origin a folk-tale feature: see Gaster (1967) 73, citing such instances as Cinderella and Snow White, or Cain (= Smith) and Abel (= Herdsman). Here at least there is a shared facet with Homer, for Gaster also cites, from *Od.* 8.111ff., the sea-faring names of the Phaiakians, e.g. Prymneus and Nauteus, which he Anglicizes as 'Helmsman' and 'Jack Tar'. This resembles somewhat the etymologies of Nauplios' progeny in fr. 297. That the Phaiakians inhabit a paradisiacal faraway island, or, at least, a transitional area between the fantasy world of Odysseus' travels and the real world of Ithaca, may be cited in mitigation.

[14] Risch (1947) 72ff. = *Kleine Schriften* (1981) 294ff. The passage I have cited comes from p. 89f. = p. 311f.

Kyklopes because of the circular eye in the middle: μοῦνος δ' ὀφθαλμὸς μέσσωι ἐνέκειτο μετώπωι· / Κύκλωπες δ' ὄνομ' ἦσαν ἐπώνυμον, οὕνεκ' ἄρα σφεων / κυκλοτερὴς ὀφθαλμὸς ἔεις ἐνέκειτο μετώπωι.

Nothing is left to the imagination, everything is expressed fully in a somewhat laboured manner. Similarly, though less loquaciously, with the explanation of Pandora's name at *Op.* 80–82: the gods called her Pandora because all the gods contributed their gifts to her creation. With this technique contrast, from Homer, the reference to the significance of Astyanax's name at *Il.* 6.402–403, where there is none of Hesiod's over-explicit underlining by repeated words: τόν ῥ' Ἕκτωρ καλέεσκε Σκαμάνδριον, αὐτὰρ οἱ ἄλλοι / Ἀστυάνακτ'· οἶος γὰρ ἐρύετο Ἴλιον Ἕκτωρ. Note too the compressed and sophisticated effect of Calypso's indirect allusion to the etymology of Odysseus' name at *Od.* 5.160: κάμμορε, μή μοι ἔτ' ἐνθάδ' ὀδύρεο.

The fragments of works attributed to Hesiod follow the genuine compositions in producing straightforward and explicit etymologies, as opposed to the more subtle and suggestive Homeric variety. Thus, in fr. 296.2–3, the gods used to call the island Abantis, but Zeus called it Euboia[15] by an obvious derivation: τὴν πρὶν Ἀβαντίδα κίκλησκον θεοὶ αἰὲν ἐόντες, / Εὔβοιαν δὲ βοός μιν ἐπώνυμον ὠνόμασε Ζεύς.[16]

Note again, as with the Kyklopes at *Th.* 143–145, the employment of related words in order to ram home, in cumbersome and laborious fashion, the obvious etymology. The word πρίν, and indeed the whole couplet, beautifully exemplify the generalisation about aetiological narratives cited above, with their concern to answer the questions 'What was it like before? ... Why did it change?' It is worth noting that the theme of naming often features in accounts of creation (compare Genesis), where the creator god both brings into being and names an entity. Here, rather remarkably, Zeus gives a name, which then endures, to a territory to which the other gods had given different nomenclature.

The sequence in question, 'once ... but now', seems discernable in the indirect quotation that is fr. 226: Salamis was once called Kychrea by an unknown hero, until the serpent from which this name was derived was driven out and received at Eleusis by Demeter. Note also fr. 184, from Strabo: Makareus lived in

---

[15] Naming is regularly the sequel to creating in aetiological narratives (see Westermann's commentary on Genesis 1–11, English Translation Index of Subjects s.v. 'Naming'). The idea of the king of the gods renaming something already named by the gods, however, is difficult to parallel, although the theme of 'changes of names of islands' was to become 'a matter of great interest to Hellenistic poets' (Harder [vol. II] on Callim. fr. 75.62–63).

[16] For the construction with ἐπώνυμος governing the genitive of the thing after which 'x' is named, cf. Lloyd-Jones (1966) 145 = *Academic Papers* ii (1990) 83 f.

Olenos, on Lesbos τῆς τότε μὲν Ἰάδος, νῦν δ' Ἀχαΐας καλουμένης. Note also, in connection with fr. 185. mentioned above, Steph. Byz. s.v. Asterion, who terms it a Thessalian city ἡ νῦν Πειρεσία ἀπὸ Ἀστερίου. Cf. fr. 185.11]Πειρεσίοιο.

Fr. 235 in particular displays the fullness so characteristic of the genuine Hesiod's etymologies: it deals with the name Ilieus[17] applied to a hero so called because (vv. 2–3, 4–5) Apollo lay with his mother after she had *taken pity* on him,[18] the day that he and Poseidon built Troy's walls: καὶ οἱ τοῦτ' ὀνόμην' ὄνομ' ἔμμεναι οὕνεκα νύμφην εὑρόμενος ἵλεων μίχθη ἐρατῆι φιλότητι. Not dissimilar is fr. 250, Aias so called[19] because his father Telamon was entertaining Herakles and happened to see an eagle passing (taken over by Pindar *Isthm.* 6.49 ff.).

Perhaps the most interesting etymology among the fragments is that of Orion's name (fr. 148b), derived from the act of begetting that hero by urinating[20] on the hide of an ox which was then buried for nine months, an act performed by the three gods, Zeus, Hermes, Poseidon, who had been hospitably received by Hyrieus and wished to repay him.[21] The similarity to the Old Testament tale of Abraham who likewise entertains three angels and is rewarded by release from the burden of childlessness (Genesis 18.1–9), has long been recognised.[22] The story, which recurs in Ovid's *Fasti* 5.494 ff., needs to be carefully analysed. How is it to be categorised? What labels will be most illuminating? Which aspects of the story are most significant? ('Child unexpectedly born to childless couple'? 'Gods wander in disguise through the world'? 'Hospitality rewarded'? 'The granted wish'?) The folk-tale number three here does not really help. Superficially, for instance, the tale seems akin to the Judgement of Paris, where again

---

[17] For other etymologies of the name Ilieus, see Hirschberger (2004) 428–430 and Davies and Finglass (2014) 577–578 on Stesichorus fr. 291 Finglass.

[18] This passage alone should confirm the unacceptability of Page's view (1959, 328) that naming an individual after an act associated with a parent of that individual, as at *Il.* 9.561–564, is eccentric and, in the case of the Iliadic passage, a sign of interpolation. See, on the contrary, apart from *Il.* 6.402f. cited above, *Il.* 22.506f. and Kakridis (1949) 31.

[19] For other etymologies of the name, see Finglass (2011) 265 on Soph. *Aj.* 431–432.

[20] For the equivalence of urine to sperm thus presupposed see Adams (1982, 142 and n. 3), who refers to the relevant story. Some authors (see following note), e.g. Euphorion fr. 101 Powell = fr. 65 Lightfoot, actually have the gods releasing sperm onto the ox skin.

[21] For a full list of authors who mention the tale see Fontenrose (1981) 24 n. 2. As he observes, the 'statement that Hesiod ... told a similar story is questionable, since in Hesiod's story as elsewhere reported Orion's parents were Poseidon and Euryale'. Merkelbach and West ad loc. are even more sceptical.

[22] See e.g. Westermann's commentary on Genesis 18.1–16 (1984, 275f.). For the primeval pattern of gods visiting men in disguise, see e.g. Gaster (1967) 158, 353f., and 701f.; Pax (1962) 832–909; West (2007) 132f.

three deities visit a lonely mortal. But that narrative involves a life choice with an appropriately young hero near the start of his existence, and no choice between the three deities confronted occurs in the 'Hesiodic' version. In the tale of Meleagros, not to mention the New Testament's Magi, three numinous figures, the Moirai, make their appearance in order to settle the fate of the newly-born child, but again this motif is not very similar.²³ A recent and ingenious interpretation²⁴ sees the story as implying the resuscitation of the slaughtered ox, comparing an Indian tale where the son granted to a poor beggar by a Brahmin grateful for hospitality 'plays the role … that an animal plays in the European tales: the son/animal is slaughtered, cooked, served as food and then magically resuscitated'. The pattern recalls the story of Pelops, of course, while the bringing back to life of a slaughtered animal is reminiscent of the treatment of Thor's goat from Norse mythology.²⁵

Norse literature may supply a further analogue, whose surface dissimilarities may have impeded until now recognition of more profound similarities. The story forms the basis of *Rigspula*, from the Poetic Edda, and relates how the peripatetic god Rigir, who gives the poem its name, successively visits on foot three childless households of ascending social rank and begets in each an offspring by the remarkable stratagem of accompanying the married couple in each to bed and lying in the middle with husband and wife on either side. The three domiciles and their progeny clearly reflect the three classes of Norse society.²⁶ My interest in the tale was first whetted by the remarks of Ursula Dronke, who writes in her commentary on the work:²⁷ 'there are other versions of this divine travelling.

---

23 See Davies (2013) 15.
24 Hansen (2002) 216 f. He also quotes (219) the Canaanite legend of Aqhat, where the childless David asks the gods he has entertained (whether in disguise or not is unclear) for a son. He further cites a nineteenth century German tale (212 f.) in which God visits two homes, one rich, one poor, and grants three wishes to each: 'the hospitable man employs his wishes wisely, the inhospitable unwisely'. It is notable that Ovid's *Fasti*, which stresses the *poverty* of Hyreus, does so alone of authors who treat the tale (others make him a king). This is pointed out by Bömer ad loc. (1958, 321), who explains the feature in terms of contamination with the story of Baucis and Philemon. But in the light of the Italian and German stories, Ovid may be preserving a primeval feature of the tale (for a parallel preservation by him, see 2004, 690).
25 These parallels suggest that, in the original story, the ox upon whose skin the gods urinated had been previously served up to them as a meal, as is explicitly stated in Hyginus *fab.* 195 (*de tauro quem Hyrieus ipsis immolarat*), where the antepenultimate and penultimate words constitute an absolutely certain and irrefutable emendation.
26 This pattern is of course relevant to Dumézil's famous three functions. See e. g. Dronke (1997) 186 f. and Dumézil (1982) 209 ff. The same scholar saw the same significance in Paris' Judgement between the three goddesses: see e. g. Ward (1970) 193 ff. and Scott Littleton (1970) 234 ff.
27 Dronke (1997) 191 f. For text and translation of the poem see 162 ff.

Three Germanic deities and an early Irish saint are characteristically associated with the peripatetic visitation of human society'. This looked promising as an analogue to the tale of Orion, but when she proceeds 'Nerthus, Freyr and St Brigida go by wagon. Odin goes on foot', and adds that 'the deities who visit on wheels are of course meant to be recognised as gods and feted. But Odin goes incognito, with secret purposes, ... like Rigir', the potential points of contact with the begetting of Orion seem to dwindle.

And yet perhaps we should think again. Elsewhere in folk-tales and in narratives influenced by them, the shifting of numbers between one and three seems to be observable.[28] In one of the most common narrative sequences throughout the world, *three* questing siblings *successively* encounter *one* helper or tester or tempter: the two elder siblings insult this figure and so fail in their quest, while the youngest shows a kindly attitude and is rewarded by help. The shifting of numbers referred to above occurs in the Judgement of Paris, where instead *one* hero *simultaneously* encounters *three* helpers, tempters or testers, and in effect alienates two and wins the support of one. If we apply the same principle to the stories of Rigir, Orion, and Abraham, something interesting occurs. In the Norse tale, *one* numinous figure *successively* encounters *three* families while, in the Mediterranean narratives, *three* numinous figures *simultaneously* encounter *one* family.

If we provisionally accept this equivalence and look for shared features, the following spring to mind:
(i) The real identity of the numinous figures goes unrecognised.
(ii) The family visited is childless (and in the case of Orion, Abraham and the first family visited by Rigir, very old).
(iii) The numinous beings are offered food (bread and meat) and hospitality.
(iv) In presumed gratitude, action from the numinous beings produces a child for the childless within the year.

These correspondences seem to me sufficient to justify adding the story of Rigir to the parallels cited above.

Within the *Fragmenta Dubia* of Merkelbach and West's edition comes the next item to be considered. Fr. 343 quoted by Chrysippus and Galen is another story involving unusual conception. It relates how Hera bore Hephaistos without the intervention of Zeus, and then how Zeus produced Athena (by swallowing Metis) without Hera's involvement. The sequence reads like a more explicit version of *Th.* 886–900 (Athena) and 924–929 (Athena and Hephaistos), while mak-

---

[28] See Davies (2003) 33.

ing the two younger divinities each a 'complement' to the other, as West's commentary on the *Theogony* passage points out. Homer characteristically says nothing of Athena's birth from Zeus' head, though he does not supply her with an alternative origin from a more normal mother, as he does in Aphrodite's case, where Zeus' consort Dione[29] replaces the severed genitals of Ouranos which feature in Hesiod's theogonic account.[30] As for Hephaistos, Homer is so inexplicit about his origins that he even provides two separate and incompatible accounts[31] of how he came to be made lame by a fall from Olympos.

Athena and Hephaistos are associated by later sources in the collaborative creation of mankind, an 'origin' for which neither Homer, nor even Hesiod or his imitators, explicitly account.[32] Fr. 4, however, tells us that Deukalion was the first man, and fr. 234 preserves a notice of how Zeus once created men for Deukalion. Verse 3 tells us that he made them ἐκ γαίης, which would lead one to infer an account in which men were manufactured out of earth or clay, a popular motif worldwide.[33] But our passage goes on to use the ambivalent word ΛΑΟΥϹ for the beings thus created, which suggests the likewise popular idea[34] that mankind was fashioned from stones. Compare fr. adesp. epic. *apud* Σ Pind. *Ol*. 9.70 ἐκ λίθων ἐγένοντο βροτοί, ΛΑΟΙ δὲ καλέονται. Such etymologising is common in creation. Note, for instance, the remarks of an Old Testament expert[35] on the creation of Adam from the dust of the earth in Genesis: 'one can

---

29 Ovid's Hyrieus is *senex* (v. 498), but the poet states that his wife is dead and he has vowed never to remarry (v. 528).
30 See Davies (2000) 21.
31 See Andersen (1990) 25–45 on such 'inconsistencies'.
32 Though note the suggestion of Merkelbach and West on fr. 268, from the Κήυκος γάμος, that the Greek word ἀπάτωροι there attributed to this poem may have formed part of a riddle which thus referred to the first men, of whom Juvenal *Sat.* 6.13 says *nullos habuere parentes*. On the apparent indifference to the creation of mankind see Lloyd-Jones (1971) 34 f.
33 See Gaster (1967) 8 ff. and 327 n. 4; Westermann (1984) 203 ff.; Guthrie (1957) 24 ff.
34 For instances from Greek and Latin literature, see Jacoby on Acusilaus (*FGrHist* 2 F 34/35) and Callimachus fr. 496 with Pfeiffer ad loc. That this latter fragment should be immediately followed by fr. 533 from the elegiac couplet ΛΑΟΙ Δευκαλίωνος ὅσοι γενόμεσθα < γενέθλης add. Naeke>/ πουλὺ θαλασαίων μυνδότεροι νεπόδων was shown by Irigoin (1960) 439 f. See Trypanis (1975, 261), where the fr. is translated as 'we, the race of stones, who are descended from Deukalion, much more silent than the children of the sea'. For folk-tale analogues see Röhrich's article s.v. 'Anthropogonie' in *EM* 1.583; cf. Fowler (2013) 114 n. 4. If the Kenning-like reference to the stones as 'bones of (Mother) Earth' in Ovid *Met.* 1.138 ff. goes back to earlier times, there may be no significant difference between birth from earth and birth from stones. For stones equivalent to 'earth's bones' as a primeval image in which the earth is treated as having bodily parts see West cited in (2007) 344.
35 Westermann (1984) 206.

derive neither the person from earth … nor earth from the person … rather, the same word is at the root of both, a word originally meaning "skin" or "surface" … The relationship attests that human beings and earth belong together, that the earth is there for humanity and human beings are there to populate it'.

The first line of our fragment names Lokros as leader of the Leleges whom Zeus had earlier created out of stones for Deukalion. We know from other sources that the first city founded by Deukalion and Pyrrha was Opous on the Lokrian plain and Pindar *Ol.* 9.43 ff. locates the stone throwing at Opous. The similar notion (fr. 205.2–5) that the inhabitants of the island of Aigina were descended from men whom Zeus created out of ants for Aiakos also has folk-tale parallels.[36] It may further, as West suggests,[37] confirm his idea that the *Catalogue*'s narrative of men created from stones does not presuppose that Deukalion and Pyrrha were the sole survivors of a flood, as in Ovid *Met.* 1 onwards. The two accounts may originally have confined themselves to the origins of purely local inhabitants. A remark of Guthrie's from a different context[38] may help us here: 'The Hebrews knew of only one man, Adam … Among the Greeks we find a very different state of affairs, due partly to their fertile and impressible imagination, but more to the fact that they were always divided into a number of small and highly competitive tribal and political units, each of which felt bound to put in its claim to be the oldest, and to possess its land by a better right than the others. Either each put forward a different ancestral hero … or the same hero appears to have been born in a surprising number of places'. The outcome of the process here summarised was that a number of Greek locales claimed to have witnessed the origins of mankind out of various entities. Hippolytus *refut. omn. haeres.* 5.17 = *PMG* 985 has a lengthy but by no means exhaustive list of local claimants to the title of first man.

I have kept back until the end the lengthiest relevant fragment dealing with an event's origins, since consideration of it may help explain by contrast that Homeric aversion to origins with which we began. The passage in question,

---

[36] See Klíma's article s.v. 'Ameise' in *EM* 1.448. The motivation mentioned at fr. 205.3 for the creation of men from ants (Αἰακὸς μοῦνος ἐὼν ἤσχαλλε) is reminiscent of God's reason for creating Woman in the J version of the Genesis creation story: 'it is not good that the man be alone. I will make a helper for him' (2.18). Tzetzes' reference to this fragment has Aiakos specifically *ask* Zeus for company (ᾐτήσατο τῶι Διί) and we recall that, in Apollodoros' account (1.7.2) of the creation of men from stones, Zeus sends Hermes with the message that Deukalion can have whatever he wishes. On Lokros and the Leleges, see Fowler (2013) Index of Names and Subjects s. vv.

[37] West (1985) 54 f., followed by Fowler (2013) 114. For flood narratives and Deukalion, see further Scodel (1982) 42–45.

[38] Guthrie (1957) 24.

fr. 204, is again from the *Catalogue*, and lists the suitors for Helen's hand in marriage. The folk-tale roots of the contest for a princess' hand have recently been explored,[39] but what I wish to concentrate upon is the motif of the ἀρχὴ κακῶν[40] as applied to the issue of the origins of the Trojan War. I say 'origins' advisedly, for different writers in antiquity devised different causologies for this event (the birth of Helen from the egg laid by Leda, the Judgement of Paris …). The *oath* imposed on his daughter's suitors by Tyndareus at fr. 204.78 ff., whereby they were to help recover her should she be abducted from her lawful husband, is clearly another example of an un-Homeric search for origins.[41] A debate raged in antiquity as to whether Homer knew of this tradition and, if he did, why he failed to mention it. The answer I should advance for this latter conundrum is that Homer did not wish to diminish his characters' heroism by having their participation in potentially deadly combat depend on a merely external obligation in the form of an oath.

But there may be another consideration, one which will return us at the end to the contribution by Guthrie with which we began, and allow us to confirm his remark that 'the tendency of the Homeric poems is towards universality'.[42] In the particular case we are examining, Homer *departicularises* or *universalises* war because he wants it to serve as apt symbol of the human condition, war being, regrettably enough, man's natural, or, at least inevitable, state. No specifying, therefore, of the oath or any other particular cause of this particular war. Although, as I said at the start, we cannot hope to know Homer's personal opinion on such matters, perhaps he would have agreed with Colonel à Court Repington,[43] who devised the phrase 'The Great War' in order 'to prevent the millennia folk from forgetting that the history of the world is the history of war'.[44]

---

[39] West (2007) 232 ff.; Cingano (2005) 118–152, esp. 124–127; Lyle (2008) 356 ff.
[40] See Davies and Finglass (2014) 320–322 on Stesichorus fr. 85 Finglass.
[41] See the commentary cited in previous note.
[42] Guthrie (1957) 42.
[43] Repington (1920) II, 291. The author was 'a clever and unscrupulous character who … had been forced to leave the army after a scandal involving a brother officer's wife' (Gilmour 1994, 298).
[44] It may be illuminating and relevant to quote from P. A. Brunt's review of A. Momigliano's *Secondo Contributo alla Storia degli Studi Classici* in *CR* 11 (1961) 142, where, warning against anachronistic twentieth century attitudes to war in antiquity, he writes: 'if war was "an ever present reality in Greek life", … it was not only natural but correct if ancient writers were satisfied with what may seem to us superficial explanations for particular wars. It was perhaps not till the nineteenth century that peace could be regarded as normal, and that deep-seated causes for wars needed to be found. In antiquity it is peace that may most need complex explanations'.

Bibliography

Adams, J. (1982). *The Latin Sexual Language*, London.
Andersen, Ø. (1990). 'The making of the Past in the *Iliad*', *HSCP* 93: 25–45.
Brunt, P. A. (1961). Review of 'A. D. Momigliano, *Secondo contributo alla storia degli studi classici e del mondo antico*', *CR* 11: 141–143.
Bömer, F. (1957–1958). *P. Ovidius Naso,* Die Fasten, Heidelberg.
Cingano, E. (2005). 'A Catalogue within a Catalogue: Helen's Suitors in the Hesiodic *Catalogue of Women* (frr. 196–204)', in: R. Hunter (ed.), *The Hesiodic* Catalogue of Women: *Constructions and Reconstructions*, Cambridge, 118–152.
Davies, M. (2000). 'Homer and Dionysus', *Eikasmos* 11: 15–27.
Davies, M. (2001). 'Homer and the Fable: *Odyssey* 21.293–306', *Prometheus* 27: 193–210.
Davies, M. (2003). 'The Judgements of Paris and Solomon', *CQ* 53: 32–43.
Davies, M. (2004). 'Aristotle fr. 44 Rose: Midas and Silenus', *Mnemosyne* 57: 682–697.
Davies, M. (2013). 'The Hero at the Crossroads: Prodicus and the Choice of Heracles', *Prometheus* 29: 3–17.
Davies, M. and P. J. Finglass (2014). *Stesichorus. The Poems*, Cambridge.
Davies, S. (2007). *The* Mabinogion, Oxford.
Dronke, U. (1997). The *Poetic Edda. Mythological Poems*, vol. II, Oxford.
Dumézil, G. (1982). *Apollon Sonore et autres essais*, Paris.
Finglass, P. J. (2011). *Sophocles,* Ajax. *Edition with introduction, translation, and commentary*, Cambridge.
Fontenrose, J. (1981). *Orion. The Myth of the Hunter and the Huntress*, Berkeley.
Fowler, R. (2013). *Early Greek Mythography*, vol. II, Oxford.
Gaster, T. H. (1967). *Myth, Legend and Custom in the Old Testament*, London.
Gilmour, D. (1994). *Curzon: Imperial Statesman 1859–1925*, London.
Guthrie, W. K. C. (1957). Guthrie, *In the Beginning: some Greek views on the origin of life and the early state of man*, London.
Guthrie, W. K. C. (1961²). 'The Religion and Mythology of the Greeks,' *CAH* ii: 851–905.
Hansen, W. (2002). *Ariadne's Thread*, Ithaca, NY.
Harder, A. (2012). *Callimachus:* Aetia. *Introduction, Text, Translation, and Commentary*, 2 vols., Oxford.
Hirschberger, M. (2004). Gynaikōn Katalogos *und* Megalai Ēhoiai. *Ein Kommentar zu den Fragmenten zweier hesiodeischer Epen*, Munich-Leipzig.
Irigoin, J. (196). 'Sur un distique de Callimaque (fr. 496 + 533 Pfeiffer)', *RÉG* 73: 439–447.
Kakridis, J. (1949). *Homeric Researches*, Lund.
Lloyd-Jones, H. (1971; rev. ed. 1983). *The Justice of Zeus*, Berkeley.
Lloyd-Jones, H. (1966). 'Menander Sikyonios' *GRBS* 34: 131–157 (= 1990. *Greek Comedy, Hellenistic Literature, Greek Religion and Miscellanea: The Academic Papers of Sir Hugh Lloyd-Jones*, 77–86).
Lyle, E. (2008). 'The Marriage and Recovery of the Young Goddess: Story and Structure', *JIES* 36: 356–370.
Page, D. L. (1959). *History and the Homeric* Iliad, Los Angeles.
Pax, E. (1962). 'Epiphanie', *Reallexikon für Antike und Christentum*, 832–909.
Pease, A. S. (1958). *M. Tulli Ciceronis De Natura Deorum libri secundus et tertius*, Cambridge, MA and London.

Rees, A. and B. (1961). *Celtic Heritage*, London.
Repington, Ch. à Court (1920). *The First World War, 1914–1918*, 2 vols., London.
Risch, E. (1947). 'Namensdeutungen und Worterklärungen bei den ältesten griechischen Dichtern', in: *Eumusia: Festschrift E. Howald*, Erlenbach-Zurich, 72–91 (= A. Etter and M. Looser (1981). *Kleine Schriften*, Berlin and New York, 294–313).
Röhrich, L. (1991). *Folktales and Reality*, translated into English by P. Tokofsky, Indiana.
Scodel, R. (1982). 'The Achaean Wall and the Myth of Destruction', *HSCP* 86: 33–50.
Scott Littleton, C. (1970). 'Some Possible Indo-European Themes in the *Iliad*', in: J. Puhvel (ed.), *Myth and Law among the Indo-Europeans*, Berkeley, 229–246.
Trypanis, C., Th. Gelzer, and C. Whitman (1975). *Callimachus:* Aetia, Iambi, Hecale *and Other Fragments. Musaeus:* Hero and Leander, Cambridge, MA and London.
Ward, D. (1970). 'The Separate Functions of the Indo-European Divine Twins', in: J. Puhvel (ed.), *Myth and Law among the Indo-Europeans*, Berkeley, 193–202.
West, M. L. (1961). 'Hesiodea', *CQ* 11: 130–145.
West, M. L. (1985). *The Hesiodic* Catalogue of Women: *Its Nature, Structure, and Origins*, Oxford.
West, M. L. (2007). *Indo-European Myth and Poetry*, Oxford.
Westermann, C. (1984). *Genesis 1–11: A Commentary*, translated into English by J. J. Scullion, London.

Part II: **The *Catalogue of Women***

Hugo Koning
Helen, Herakles, and the End of the Heroes

Generally speaking, early hexameter poetry is remarkably consistent in its view of the history and shape of the world. Notions of the relative chronology of the coming-to-be of the universe and its inhabitants (Titans-Olympians-heroes-men) and on the spatial organization of the world's most prominent places (especially the symmetrical position of Olympos and the Underworld) are mostly shared. Graziosi and Haubold argue persuasively for such a coherent worldview when comparing the poetry of Homer and Hesiod, and their point holds true for the three main Hesiodic poems as well: in general, the *Theogony*, *Catalogue* and *Works and Days* combine to present a generally consistent view of the genesis and place of gods and men.

Such unity should naturally be understood in terms of complementarity rather than strict narrative logic. In Hesiodic scholarship, the *Theogony* and *Works and Days* have often been seen as mutually supportive, an interpretive trend that has culminated in Clay's masterful *Hesiod's Cosmos*. Clay regards both poems as widely different but in perspective only: in the end, they purvey the same message about the power of the gods and the *condition humaine*. In Clay's view, this complementarity is fundamental and even intentional: Hesiod 'insists that we combine these two perspectives [i.e. from both poems] in order to grasp his cosmos.'[1]

The *Catalogue* is largely absent from the bipartite view of Hesiod's poetry expressed throughout *Hesiod's Cosmos*. Nonetheless, several scholars, including Clay herself, have argued for a strong thematic affiliation between the *Catalogue* and the other Hesiodic poems. Thus, the *Catalogue* can be seen as 'a perfect complement to heroic epic',[2] finding its natural place between the *Theogony*, focusing on the gods, and the *Works and Days*, with its central occupation with mankind. 'Suspended between two stages of world history'[3] as a 'giant system of cross-referencing to archaic epic',[4] the *Catalogue* can be regarded as a poem thematically connected not only with the other Hesiodic poems but with early hexameter poetry in general.

The fundamental coherence of the three poems is not disqualified by the impossibility of completely harmonizing their accounts. A case in point is the tale

---

[1] Clay (2003) 129; cf. her introduction, pp. 1–11.
[2] Clay (2005) 26.
[3] Haubold (2005) 96.
[4] Hunter (2005) 252.

of the origin of the separation of gods and men (fundamental to all poems), which is widely different in the three works. In the *Theogony*, the sacrifice at Mekone and the clash between Zeus and Prometheus articulate the division between divine and mortal inhabitants of the cosmos; in the *Works and Days*, this point in mythological time is marked by the tale of Prometheus (told in a form that differs from that of the *Theogony*) and the Myth of the Ages; in the *Catalogue*, the 'real separation point'[5] is provided by the Trojan War, caused by Zeus to bring an end to the heroic era. Obviously, the differences are there – but to allow for a thematic unity of the poems only when they present 'a single coherent narrative' to be assembled into a 'comprehensive mythic sequence'[6] is, in my view, rather anachronistic. To be sure: by (chrono)logical demands, it is impossible, for instance, to integrate the Mekone-affair and the Myth of the Ages – but strict logic is not what the poet is after. Rather, the poems each present their own perspective on the history of the world and the part that mankind plays in that history: 'there was a Golden Age once, there were heroes once who were bigger and better, but all that is gone now – our present Iron Age is the reality we have to cope with'.

Catalogue-poetry, 'a form of potentially limitless delays and expansions',[7] may at first seem a curious vehicle for the expression of a worldview that is teleological (in the basic sense that it covers an era from start to finish). In fact, scholars have often struggled with identifying a main thread of the *Catalogue*, its famous '*ehoie*'-connective often thought to be indicative of a rather loose and aimless structure. Catalogue-poetry *per se* is not hostile to teleology, however (witness the *Theogony*) – and in fact a teleological thrust can be discerned in the *Catalogue* when one focuses on two important characters in the work: Helen and Herakles. Both superhumans fit very well in the heroic world but, because of their awesome powers of destruction, are also instrumental in ending that world, thus being *telos*-bringers themselves. This paper is concerned with their function in the *Catalogue* and will focus on their similarities and differences, paying attention to the greater narrative as well. Before we start zooming in on Helen and Herakles, however, I will first further explore the distinct world of the *Catalogue* and its position between the *Theogony* and *Works and Days*.

---

5 Irwin (2005) 55; Irwin also briefly discusses some attempts at the synchronization of Hesiod's mythical accounts.
6 González (2010) 386.
7 Hunter (2005) 245.

The World of the *Catalogue*

The *Catalogue* does not just fit nicely between the *Theogony* and *Works and Days* because of the natural and oft-supposed (chrono)logical sequence of their respective protagonists, i.e. gods, heroes and men.[8] The *Theogony* is a story of coming-to-be, narrating the births and earliest clashes of the huge natural forces that are known as gods. It is a tale of disorder, discontinuity and chaos which under Zeus' rule slowly settles down into an organized and delineated cosmos. The *Works and Days* presents a world that is in its essence orderly and knowable – hence, it is possible for the poet to give us advice on how to deal with its patterns and cycles.

Between these realms of disorder and regularity lies the part-divine, part-human world of the *Catalogue*, a universe in the final throes of the birth of the cosmos as we know it. It is a place slowly arriving at the organized world of the *Works and Days*, but which has not yet reached that point. Nature does not yet operate according to fixed rules. One indication of this is the many 'freaks' inhabiting the poem. First of all, there are plenty of monstrous species, such as satyrs, griffins and harpies;[9] there are prodigies like Pegasos, Chimaira and the Minotaur;[10] miraculous people like the Half-Dogs, Long-Heads and Pygmies;[11] and instances of miraculous fertility (Aigyptos fathering fifty sons and Niobe bearing ten sons and ten daughters)[12] and sexuality (the possibly hermaphroditic Pleisthenes).[13] These biological novelties remind us of the unchecked fertilization taking place among divinities in the first days of the universe as told in the *Theogony*, appearing without boundaries for breeding (cf. e.g. the birth of the Giants from Ouranos' blood falling on Earth and the birth of Aphrodite from the genitals of Ouranos touching Sea). Secondly, some individuals have superhuman capabilities: Periklymenos and Mestra are shapeshifters, Iphiklos like an ancient Greek *Flash* races upon crops with such speed that he does not damage them, the master thief Autolykos can make things invisible, apparently by changing their color, and the musicians Zethos and Amphion were so

---

[8] See e.g. Tsagalis (2009) 159–160, Clay (2005) 26–27, and Haubold (2005) 96.
[9] Frr. 123, 152, 155 (the Satyrs are interestingly called οὐτιδανῶν, 'worthless' and ἀμηχανοεργῶν, 'unfit to work' (Most: 'frivolous'), pointing to their incompatibility with the Iron Age world dominated by the need for ἔργον). The order of the fragments follows the edition of Merkelbach and West (unless otherwise specified); all translations are taken from Most's Loeb edition.
[10] Frr. 43a and 145.
[11] Fr. 153.
[12] Frr. 127 and 183.
[13] Fr. 137c Most.

gifted they could move stones with their tunes and thus build the massive walls of Thebes.[14] These extraordinary capabilities reflect the fluid state of the world: not all shapes and appearances have definitely settled, and the solid boundaries existing in our time (such as those between man and beast, and between animate and inanimate) have not yet become final and definitive.

These characteristics of the *Catalogue* have a distinctly folkloristic taste, reminiscent of the fantastic world of books 9–12 of the *Odyssey*, although they are presented in a more evident and natural way. Rutherford characterizes such feats as 'magic',[15] but this is a somewhat misleading term. Rather, the prodigal creatures and capabilities belong to a world that is still unstable and seeking a definite form. They are the remarkable but natural features that belong to the pre-Iron Age universe.

In this universe, the most prominent actor checking the flux and bringing the world into order (apart, of course, from the narrator himself) is Zeus, setting limits and imposing boundaries. To a significant degree, the supreme god thus replays the role he had in the *Theogony*, but shifts his terrain from the divine realm to earth, the place where mortals live. In the *Catalogue*, Zeus intervenes quite regularly in the lives of the heroes, and his presence is far more manifest than in the *Works and Days*. His main concern, however, is very similar to that in both the *Theogony* and *Works and Days:* even though gods and humans once associated freely (fr. 1), they should in fact be separated. The gods are of a higher status, enjoying a blessed and carefree existence, whereas men toil and die. We thus see Zeus responding to transgressions by such mortals as Keyx and Alkyone, Salmoneus, Asklepios, Lykaon and Eetion, all adopting god-like behaviour and pretensions: Keyx and Alkyone used to address each other as 'Zeus' and 'Hera', Salmoneus similarly 'tried to be Zeus', and Eetion slept with Demeter.[16]

Zeus' responses to mortal pride and injustice fall roughly into two categories: he either kills the hybristic culprit (preferably by thunderbolt) or he imposes metamorphosis: Keyx and Alkyone are changed into birds, Atalanta ('who had seen [what it is not lawful] to see') is turned into a lioness (for a similar crime, Artemis changes Aktaion into a deer).[17] It is characteristic of the flux-

---

[14] Frr. 33a, 43b, 62, 67b and 182.
[15] Rutherford (2005) 102.
[16] Frr. 10d, 15/30, 51, 164, 177. The transgressive acts of Asklepios (reviving people who had died from disease) and Lykaon (killing his son and serving him to Zeus to test his omniscience) are known but not made explicit in the fragments. Hera punishes the Proetids for their lewdness in fr. 132.
[17] Frr. 10a/10d, 72, 346.

bound world of the *Catalogue* that even punishment for the rejection of newly-imposed borders by humans in fact crosses such borders. Forms are not quite final yet, and unusual circumstances or events can sometimes cause metamorphosis.[18]

Killing, naturally, imposes the ultimate boundary. We should be careful, however, of taking this for granted. To us, Zeus' capital punishment by thunderbolt is a well-worn theme, but to the mortals living in the world of the *Catalogue* it was not. Zeus' weapon was used in the *Theogony* of course, but against *gods*, in order to settle dynastic strife and, notably, to end disorder in the form of the truly chaotic monster Typhoeus.[19] To use this formidable weapon against mortals was probably new. Lightning causes a brutal and sudden end of human life, and as such functions as a forceful symbol of the new world order desired by Zeus. Before, gods and mortals interacted, sharing meals and knowledge (fr. 1). Without pressing the connection with the pre-Mekone, communal state mentioned in the *Theogony*, and without pushing the possibility that commensality implies the use of nectar and ambrosia by mortals (causing protracted youth), I think it is a safe hypothesis to say that Zeus did not use his thunderbolt against non-divine beings in the earliest stages of human development. His subsequent use of it against transgressors is a strong reminder of their mortality, stressing the relatively new boundary between divine and mortal. The thunderbolt is a riot gun, used to impose order – this means that someone like Salmoneus (or Asklepios, or Eetion) may be regarded as a mortal counterpart to the cosmic agent of chaos Typhoeus.

Zeus does more in the *Catalogue* than punish by death. He also hands out rewards, described, as could be expected, in terms of longevity. Mortals who are dear to him thus return to the presumably earlier human state of enjoying an extended life span. At the most extreme end, this means immortalization, as dealt out to Iphimede (= Iphigeneia) and, notably, to Herakles (his divinity being emphatically coupled to youth).[20] At the other end, long life can apparently qualify punishment, as in the case of Phineus, whose crimes led to divine displeasure – but he was allowed to live 'a long lifetime' while at the same time

---

18 Naturally, Zeus applies metamorphosis in other cases as well, for instance when changing Io into a cow (fr. 124) and ants into Myrmidons (fr. 205). Other gods change forms: Hera turns Arethousa into a fountain (fr. 188 A OCT) and Poseidon changes Kainis into a man (fr. 87), both at their own request.
19 See for Typhoeus as a chaotic, anti-cosmic force e.g. Blaise (1992), Clay (2003) 26 ('Typhoeus is *acosmia* incarnate') and Goslin (2010) with bibliography.
20 Fr. 23a (Iphimede). Herakles' immortality and eternal youth are both stated explicitly and symbolically (by his union with Hebe or 'Youth' on Olympos), see further below.

being stricken with blindness (fr. 157). Another case in point is Endymion, who was so dear to the gods that Zeus turned him into a 'dispenser' of his own death and old age (fr. 10a60–62). This power over one's own, individual fate is remarkable, not only because of its unique wording[21] but also for its connection to an earlier phase of humanity, expressed in the *Works and Days*. In the so-called Myth of the Races Zeus experiments with mortals and their conditions, life span being one of the parameters: witness the Silver Age and its extended childhood. That Endymion is allowed to measure out his own life serves as a reminder that large-scale experimentation with human characteristics is a thing of the past, but that anomalies still occur.

Also quite reminiscent of the Myth of the Races is the occasionally inclusive and 'pandemic' nature of Zeus' punishment, most prominent in his wish to wipe out the entire heroic race by use of the Trojan War. The sheer size of this scope may surprise us, but this is actually behavior quite typical of Zeus. In the Myth of the Races, Zeus removes several 'races' as a whole from the face of the earth. Notably, some are transposed to a better place, just as the heroes in the *Catalogue* are in fact transferred to the Isles of the Blest. Furthermore, there is a remarkable parallel for Zeus' inclusive punishment of Salmoneus, a sinner whose transgressions reflect on his entire city.[22] Because of his superhuman ambitions, Zeus descends from Olympos to 'wicked (ἀτασθάλου) Salmoneus' [people], who were quickly going [to suffer] destructive deeds because of their arrogant (ὑβριστὴν) king; [he struck them] with thunder and blazing thunderbolt. Thus he punished [the people] for their king's tresspass (ὑπερβασίην). ...] sons and wife and house-servants, ...] city and [ ]- flowing mansions, he obliterated them'. This is the same punishment that Hesiod warns us about in the *Works and Days:* 'Often even a whole city suffers because of an evil (κακοῦ) man who sins and devises wicked deeds (ἀτάσθαλα). Upon them, Kronos' son brings forth woe from the sky, famine together with pestilence, and the people die away; the women do not give birth, and the households are diminished by the plans of Olympian Zeus...'.[23]

---

[21] The word 'dispenser' (ταμίη) is unique in Hesiod. The word occurs quite often in Homeric epic, also on a (semi-)divine level: in *Od.* 10.21, we learn that Zeus turned Aiolos into the ταμίη of winds.

[22] Fr. 30. Salmoneus seems to be marked out as a particularly evil person; his punishment is described at some length in fr. 30, and he is already singled out as 'unjust' at his birth in fr. 10a. In this fragment, he is mentioned alongside Sisyphos, who is characterized as 'shifty-counseled' (a characteristic that returns later in the *Catalogue* as well, when it is mentioned twice that he may be very smart but cannot in fact 'perceive the mind of Zeus', frr. 43a.52 and 76–77).

[23] Fr. 30.16–21 and *Op.* 240–245. For Zeus the punisher, see also Davies (1992) 116–124.

As is quite usual in such cases of pandemic punishment, one or two individuals escape total destruction, a common motif in Greek myth and elsewhere. So we see Deukalion and Pyrrha surviving the Flood, and Salmoneus' daugher Tyro remaining unharmed by the decimation of her city and family. Similarly, some members of the heroic race come home after the Trojan War, most notably Helen, who in fact caused it. It is to this pivotal character in mytho-history that we will now turn.

Helen: A Second Pandora

In more than one sense, Helen in the *Catalogue* is the ultimate woman. She is (virtually) the last heroine mentioned in the poem, she is the most beautiful and eagerly wooed of all women (having a list of suitors that is easily the longest to survive),[24] and her function is apparently to end the lives of the demi-gods, and, less specifically, 'most of the race of speech-endowed human beings' (fr. 204.98–99). All the lists of the beautiful and much-desired women of the *Catalogue* lead to this final heroine. As the catalyst for the Trojan War, she is an agent of Zeus' will, playing a role that is rather unique in terms of divine determination: no other heroines in the poem seem to be specifically conceived to fulfill some kind of destiny.

Of course, the ability to inspire conflict is not restricted to Helen alone; in fact, all the heroines in the *Catalogue* seem to be closely linked to ἔρις. First of all, they practise ἔρις themselves, contending with the Olympian goddesses in terms of beauty: the phrase ἣ εἶδος Ὀλυμπιάδεσσιν ἔριζεν is used twice, of Iolaos' daughter Leipephile (fr. 252) and an unknown woman (perhaps Abas' wife Aglaia) in fr. 129. On many other occasions, the heroines are said to resemble the gods in terms of beauty or otherwise.[25] Naturally, there is no hint of transgression here; this kind of competition rather belongs to the domain of the good kind of ἔρις, the kind described by Hesiod in the beginning of the *Works and Days* (17–26).

Second, the near-divine beauty of women inspires ἔρις among the men who wish to marry them. The heroes have to vie with each other in order to win the hand of their beloved brides-to-be, mostly by bidding against each other. There

---

[24] It is in fact said of Demodike, daughter of Agenor, that it was her 'whom the largest number of human beings on the earth sought to wed' (fr. 22), since she had 'limitless beauty'; but her suitors are not named.
[25] Cf. fr. 195.11–13 (= *Aspis* 4–6), where it is said of Alkmene that no mortal women could contend with her in beauty, stature or mind.

may be exceptions to such a procedure (there can, for instance, arise ἔρις between the father of the bride and the aspiring bridegroom, or a god can snatch away a desired heroine for himself),[26] but wooing the heroines generally classifies as good ἔρις. It is simply part of the heroic world that women are beautiful and that men have to engage in conflict with each other to get them. There is nothing generically evil about the women,[27] nor about the men who marry them.

All this appears to change when Helen arrives at the scene. At first, the wooing of Helen seems to fit the usual pattern of the *Catalogue:* the woman in question is said to be very beautiful (fr. 196a.5–6), and the interested parties vie for her in a peaceful way, sending gifts and messages to Sparta.[28] We soon find out, however, that Zeus intends to use Helen's beauty as a catalyst for war, the ultimate manifestation of bad ἔρις (*Op.* 11–16); a war, moreover, of such scale that it is supposed to end the heroic era and usher in the Iron Age. As scholars have remarked, the tale of Helen's wooing clearly points ahead to the Trojan War: the catalogue of her suitors can be regarded as an introduction to the *Cypria* and *Iliad*.[29] The elaborate description of the well-known oath taken by the suitors is of course part of this introduction, but the oath itself seems to be a sign of a coming transition. In the *Catalogue*, mortals do not take oaths, and I believe that this is the case because oaths do not belong to their world. Oaths imply the existence of deception and evil, which belong to the evil Eris, who is in fact their mother, as we are told in both the *Theogony* and the *Works and Days*.[30] These two poems also stress, in remarkably similar wording, that oaths bring 'pain' to mortals. Oaths thus seem to belong to the Iron Age, a world that, according to the *Works and Days*, lacks Reverence and Indignation (Αἰδὼς καὶ Νέμεσις, *Op.* 200), and the oath among the heroes in the *Catalogue* is made precisely in case one of the suitors 'would seize [Helen] by force, and set aside indignation and shame (νέμεσίν ... καὶ αἰδῶ, fr. 204.82).' The mere possibility of this actually happening is a hint that the Age of Heroes is waning, and that a new Era is at hand.

---

[26] See fr. 43a.36–69 for the case of Mestra, wooed by Sisyphos for his son Glaukos. An ἔρις (and ν[εῖκος]) arose between him and her father, which was eventually settled by Athena. After that, Sisyphos lost her anyway because Mestra was taken away by Poseidon.
[27] Cf. Osborne (2005) 17.
[28] That the wooing proceeds in a fair way may be indicated by line 198c.20, saying that 'there was no deed of deception in Tyndareos' sons'; they apparently played a part in the procedure (but the line may also be connected to another matter).
[29] See e.g. Cingano (2005) 143.
[30] *Th.* 231–232, *Op.* 804.

Helen takes centre stage in the war that procures the transition. She is a liminal figure, not evil in herself, since she is a woman belonging to the Heroic Age, but nonetheless the cause of destruction on a global scale. In this, the ultimate woman Helen strongly resembles the world's first woman Pandora, famously described in the *Theogony* as a καλὸν κακόν, a 'beautiful evil'.[31] Pandora is a creature specifically designed to arouse 'desire' (see her description in both the *Theogony* and *Works and Days*), and the *Catalogue* stresses the desire felt by Helen's numerous suitors: the Euboean Elephenor (fr. 204.14) and two anonymous heroes (frr. 200.1, 204.2) 'wanted very much' to marry Helen;[32] and an anonymous hero 'desires' (ἱμείρων) to be her husband (fr. 199.2). Similarly, from all corners of the Greek world 'countless', 'seemly' and 'marvelous' gifts are sent to Helen, who is thus Pandora-like in this respect as well.[33]

Pandora was designed by Zeus to end an era (the 'Golden Age' of ease and plenty) and to usher in a a new one. The key to this transition is the *pithos* ('jar') that she brings, a curious item that is also relevant in the appraisal of Helen's role in the *Catalogue*. As is well-known, the pithos contains numerous evils which are scattered over the earth after Pandora's arrival; only Ἐλπίς ('Expectation') remains. The question of the pithos and its contents is notoriously unresolved, fraught as it is with logical inconsistencies.[34] I follow the structuralist interpretation which equates Pandora, the first woman, with the *pithos*: with the introduction of womankind the static, masculine society of the Golden Age is ended and mankind acquires a cyclic way of life: individuals grow old, become ill and die, but thanks to women new individuals come into existence. For Expectation to be in a jar together with other phenomena connected with such a

---

31 *Th.* 585; she is called a κακόν several times in the *Works and Days* as well.
32 This presumably goes for the Aetolian hero Thoas as well, see fr. 198.12.
33 Apparently, many suitors woo Helen without ever having seen her and rely on hearsay. The above-mentioned hero of fr. 199 'desires' to be Helen's husband 'although he neither knew her nor had seen her, but hearing what others said'. Many heroes do not visit Sparta but send messages and gifts. Not even Menelaos had seen Helen prior to marrying her but leaves the wooing to his brother Agamemnon (fr. 197.4–5). Much is being made of Idomeneus who 'did not send some other messenger as suitor but himself with a many-benched black ship came over the Ogylian sea through the black waves to Tyndareos' mansion, so that [he could see Argive] Helen, and not merely hear what others [said]...' (fr. 204.18–23). I wonder if this remarkable detail can also be linked to the story of Pandora, who is married by Epimetheus who, only after accepting her, 'when he already had the evil, understood' (*Op.* 88–89). The *Works and Days* generally reflect on the difficulty of getting a good wife because you don't really know what you've got until after you have married her.
34 See e.g. Fraser (21–22) for a clear exposition of the logical problems that trouble modern interpreters.

cyclic existence makes perfect sense, and that *elpis* is kept in a *pithos* (a container designed for the storage of life-supporting items that are to be used in the future) makes sense as well, especially when we consider that the jar can be equated with the womb. In the Iron Age, women are the vessels of expectation as they prevent utter destruction and perpetuate the human race.

Similar to Pandora, Helen is designed by the gods to end an era, not the Golden Age but that of Heroes, still a better one than the present Iron Age. However, Helen's own affinity with the heroic world of the *Catalogue* makes her differ from Pandora in two important aspects. First of all, even though she is fathered by Zeus she is not actually 'fabricated' by him as Pandora was – the cyclic existence of mankind forms part of the age of heroes. And secondly, whereas Pandora, as a primordial woman, is supposed to be a part of the age that she ushers in, Helen is in fact part of the world that is supposed to be destroyed. Pandora is part of the future, hence her association with Ἐλπίς or Expectation, indicating a new way of continuity for the human race. By contrast, Helen is a *terminus*, an agent of discontinuity. When this force of anti-expectation in fact bears a child, this is highly 'unexpected', ἄελπτον.[35] The line of heroes must be broken, not continued. The birth of Hermione thus becomes a wake-up call for Zeus to further set in motion the Trojan War.

The new age of evil ἔρις has begun, and the first signs are immediately visible on Olympos itself: 'all the gods were divided in spirited in strife' (204.95–96). Such is the remarkable power of Helen.

Herakles: A Second Zeus

The only other semi-divine being in the *Catalogue* with a power comparable to Helen's is Herakles, also a child of Zeus. This superhero's position in the heroic world of the *Catalogue* is a fascinating one, studied in depth by Haubold, who focuses on Herakles' ambiguous and problematic role.[36] In his view, the well known performer of labors and helper of mankind is in the *Catalogue* embroiled

---

[35] Fr. 204.95. This broader context for the interpretation of ἄελπτον may seem far-fetched, but the use of the word is a remarkable detail that is curiously unexplained in modern scholarship. A common interpretation, that Helen was too old to bear children (cf. the *Hom. Hymn to Demeter*, lines 219 and 252), or the suggestion of Doherty (2008, 317), that a male heir was expected, are arbitrary. Like Hirschberger ad loc., I believe that the birth of Hermione is an 'unmittelbare Anlaß' for Zeus to spring into action.

[36] Haubold (2005); see also Davies (1992) 101–105.

in various κακά: he is sacking cities 'for no apparent reason',[37] killing heroes that seem not to deserve such a fate, and marries women wherever he goes. Haubold contrasts this Herakles to the monster-slayer of the *Theogony* (which mentions such ἀέθλοι as Geryoneus, Kerberos, the Hydra, and the Nemean Lion): 'whereas the *Theogony* concentrates on Herakles' so-called labours, the *Catalogue* appears to be more interested in the exploits he undertook after having parted with Eurystheus.'[38] In a recent article, Stamatopoulou similarly distinguishes a theogonic Herakles, who promotes order by the will of Zeus, and the 'epic aggressor against men and gods' we meet in the *Catalogue*.[39]

The ambiguity found in the figure of Herakles by Haubold and Stamatopoulou is intriguing and illuminating but I think mostly one of perspective.[40] In general, I do not believe that the roles of Herakles in the *Theogony* and the *Catalogue* are discontinuous; in my view, we see essentially the same Herakles at work in both poems. We could perhaps label Herakles as an 'epic agressor' in the *Catalogue*, but there is no reason to believe he is not promoting order by the will of Zeus or engaging in activities that are morally questionable. In fact, I believe Herakles can be regarded as an earthly double of Zeus, imitating the behavior of his father and through his apotheosis rising above all moral or mortal blame, like all the gods, and especially Zeus.

The first indication of Herakles' likeness to Zeus is found immediately at the programmatic beginning of the *Catalogue*, where the poet sets out to describe the 'tribe of women', organizing them (here, at least) according to their divine lovers – naturally, he names Zeus first, but after some other divinities comes Herakles, who is thus associated with the gods right from the start. As in the case of Zeus, who appears regularly in the *Catalogue*, sleeping with women and undertaking many other interventions, Herakles' numerous appearances in the poem are foreshadowed by association. Zeus dominates the *Catalogue* through the women he 'overpowers', and so does Herakles, 'the single most prominent man in this text about women'.[41] The fragments we have mention two of his partners, Deianeira and Auge (frr. 25 and 165), apart from his divine wife Hebe (frr. 25 and 229).

As we have seen above, an important goal of Zeus in the *Catalogue* is to install patterns in the world and to terminate factors of instability and change; one way of doing that is by killing transgressors and agents of chaos. Herakles' best-described opponent in the *Catalogue*, Neleus' son Periklymenos, is exactly such

---

37 Haubold (2005) 90.
38 Haubold (2005) 93.
39 Stamatopoulou (2013) 275.
40 This is also put forward by Haubold (2005) 96–98.
41 Haubold (2005) 87.

a force. Like others gifted by Poseidon, Periklymenos is a shapeshifter, a prodigal being that is 'a wonder to see'.[42] There is a brief list of the different shapes he can assume, one of them a snake described in terms vaguely reminiscent of Typhoeus, the ultimate chaotic monster, destroyed by Zeus in the *Theogony*.[43] Moreover, the changeling is said to have received, perhaps in addition to the one given to him by Poseidon, 'gifts of all kinds, unnamable' (fr. 33a.17–18), the last word stressing Periklymenos' otherwordliness. He is favored by the gods until Athena somehow grows angry with him; she switches sides and then helps Herakles to kill Periklymenos, who had just assumed the shape of a bee. The reason for Athena's change of mind is not given; she is a god and no explanation is needed for her actions. In this episode, Herakles obviously functions as an instrument of the gods.

The killing of Periklymenos is part of the battle of Pylos, won by Herakles and its army after its main defender is killed in action. After this, the other sons of Neleus are killed off by Herakles, that is to say, the ten other sons who defend the city – the Neleid Nestor 'escaped from death and black fate' only because he happened to be somewhere else.[44] The destruction of the Neleids is a supposed mark of Herakles' heroic aggression, Hesiod's tale sounding 'alarmingly' like Nestor's own account of it in the *Iliad*.[45] There is no sign in the text, however, that Herakles is working against the will of the gods; nor is there a reason to suppose that his actions are to be classified as evil;[46] the poet, who in general does not shrink from using evaluative words, does not condemn Herakles' performance in battle. He is simply engaged in war, killing heroes by the handful. In this, he also resembles Zeus.

This resemblance is even closer if we take a look at the scale of the destruction wrought by Herakles. As Zeus destroys cities and even entire races, so does Herakles 'sacker of cities' (frr. 229.17 and presumably 25.23) wipe out entire communities. Apart from destroying Pylos, we are told that he attacked Troy and 'slew the tribe of the great-spirited Dardanians' (fr. 165.12); on his way back,

---

[42] Fr. 33a.15: θαῦμα ἰδέσθαι.
[43] Fr. 33a.17. δεινὸς ὄφις, *Th.* 825 ὄφιος δεινοῖο.
[44] Fr. 35.9. There is a parallel here with individuals like Tyro who escape pandemic punishment by Zeus (see above).
[45] Haubold (2005) 91.
[46] According to Haubold, 'the monsters have turned into victims' as the sons of Neleus are described as 'good' (ἐσθλοί), and Neleus himself is now awarded the same epithet (ταλασίφρων, 'patient-minded') that described Herakles when his troops were facing destruction at the hands of Periklymenos. I believe that these epithets are generic; they describe the heroes whose business it is to fight and kill one another. The surprising repetition of the otherwise un-used ταλασίφρων may indicate fitness for battle.

he sacked the 'lovely city' of Kos, 'for small cause' (ἐξ ἀρχῆς ὀλίγης), and afterwards 'ravaged the villages' (fr. 43a.61–62). This passage is vital to Haubold's picture of Herakles as a morally ambiguous character, and we can easily see why. In my view, however, there is not enough here to cast Herakles in a dubious light. I consider the epithet 'lovely' to be more or less generic (even though it is not applied to other cities in the Hesiodic corpus), and I see no compelling reason to take ἐξ ἀρχῆς ὀλίγης as a *moral* comment by the narrator; it might just as well be a (true enough) statement that epic conflicts usually start out as small disputes (see the proem of the *Iliad*).

Moreover, the passage on Herakles' rampage is immediately followed by a verse saying that he 'in Phlegra slew the presumptuous Giants' (fr. 43a.65). The direct juxtaposition of the destruction of Kos and the slaying of the Giants undermines the split image of Herakles the epic aggressor and Herakles the theogonic agent of order. There appears to be only one Herakles, and he destroys Koans just as easily as Giants who are presumptuous; he kills a prodigal Neleid as he slays the Hydra of Lerna.[47] Searching to understand his actions in a moral sense seems to be much akin to trying to understand Zeus in such a way. Herakles, the second Zeus, is divine in his indifference to human evaluation.

Incidentally, it is remarkable that Herakles' acts of destruction are twice mentioned in a Trojan context: in Troy itself, he slays and scatters the inhabitants, and it is on his way back from Troy that he wreaks havoc on Kos. It is not likely that the so-called 'first' Trojan War, consisting of Herakles' expedition to get hold of the horses of Laomedon, was described at length in the *Catalogue*; perhaps because it could not easily be accommodated with the truly Pan-Hellenic view of the Trojan War of a generation later.[48] The references are nonetheless important, I believe, to prefigure Troy as a place of pandemic destruction: Herakles destroys the entire 'tribe' (φῦλον) of Dardanians, and drives them out of the 'whole country' (γῆς ... πάσης). This points ahead to the 'real' Trojan War, the site of human destruction on an even bigger scale, designed to end the γένος ... πολλόν ('most of the race').

Back to Herakles' Zeus-like characteristics. In my view, Herakles' apotheosis is a way of stressing Herakles' departure from the human condition and all the flaws that are rapidly becoming an integral part of it. The κακά he leaves behind are not in any way self-incurred by questionable behavior,[49] but the dreadful

---

[47] Cf. also Clay (1993) 111 on the 'paradoxical nature' of heroes; they are just as mixed as the monsters.
[48] This possible explanation was suggested to me by Christos Tsagalis; see also Tsagalis (2014).
[49] Cf. Haubold (2005) 94: '... the *Catalogue* tells of the 'evils' (κακά) into which this man got himself'.

qualities of the life of mortals. Herakles' deification is mentioned twice (frr. 25 and 229), and in both cases his condition as a god is described in negative terms: in contrast to mortals, he is now 'untroubled' (ἀπήμαντος), 'unharmed' (ἀκηδής), 'immortal' (ἀθάνατος) and 'un-aging' (ἄγηρος). In his shining negation of the human condition, he is married on Olympos with Hebe, goddess of youth. Herakles had during his life on earth been tainted by the evils of the post-Golden Age era, and it is exactly these qualities that are rubbed off at his deification. Here, too, the general mythical image is in keeping with that of the *Theogony* and *Works and Days*. Apart from the Golden Age-terminology used for his Olympian existence, we see that Herakles dies at the hands of a woman, the prototypical bringer of death (and life), more specifically his own wife,[50] who 'committed terrible deeds' because she was stricken by ἄτη (ἀάσατο, fr. 25.20), an Iron Age quality of mankind the destructive nature of which is mentioned several times in the *Works and Days*.[51]

Unlike Helen, Herakles is not to stay on earth and suffer the same fate as the rest of his generation. He is more like the divinities Aidos and Nemesis, who cannot stay among mankind and are withdrawn to Olympos.

Conclusion

The mythical material in the three main Hesiodic poems shares an essentially univocal view on gods, heroes and humans. Naturally, this does not mean that the myths presented in the poems can be neatly aligned in a logical sense. The myth of Pandora and the birth of womankind, the myth of the Five Races and the fall from the Golden Age, and the myth of Herakles and the corruption of mankind cannot be assimilated into one chronological, coherent whole. The myths, however, do have their essential worldview in common. They tell us how originally gods and men interacted freely in an age of bliss; how gods and men were separated; how the human condition was changed for the

---

[50] Who, incidentally, presents a rather literal interpretation of Hesiod's warning in the *Works and Days* (704–705) that a bad woman 'singes' her man alive, 'powerful though he be'.

[51] See *Op.* 216, 352 and 431 (in the good city, there is no ἄτη, 231). One might even go so far as to see that the ambiguity that is so typical of the world of humans is cast off in Herakles apotheosis: on earth, he was hated by one god but loved by another. In the world of the gods, as in the world of the *Theogony*, things are unambiguous. In both frr. 25 and 229, we hear that 'Previously the goddess, white-armed Hera, hated him more than any of the blessed gods and any mortal human beings, but now she loves him, and honors him beyond the other immortals, except for Kronos' mighty son himself'.

worse; how women can be both harmful and beneficial; how the present world has come to be full of misery and ambiguity; and how Zeus' mind cannot be fathomed. This is the same mythological blueprint of the history and of the nature of the world to which all three poems adhere.

The *Catalogue* plays a pivotal role in this global scheme. Hedged in between the *Theogony*'s tale of the genesis of the cosmos through divine breeding and conflict, and the *Works and Days*' focus on the Iron Age condition of man and the best strategies for dealing with the fixed patterns of human life, it focuses on the world of heroes and the slow but certain settling of the world of humans. It has all the sex, monsters and violence of the *Theogony* (and its lists of offspring and family relations), though on a human scale; and, at the same time, there are signs of the imminent transition to the Iron Age and the definitive disappearance of the heroes and heroines.

The thematic unity of the three poems raises questions concerning their composition, especially that of the *Catalogue*. Dates as far apart as ca. 700 and 520 BC have been proposed,[52] depending on the evaluation of dating criteria such as linguistic phenomena and historical or intertextual references. In this debate, I favor an older date, relatively close to 700 and thus close to the composition of the *Theogony* and *Works and Days*. In the present paper, however, the exact date of the *Catalogue*'s composition is hardly relevant: even before it was fixed in its present form a century later, it was certainly current as an oral poem already endowed with distinctly Hesiodic features, such as its language and style, but especially its thematic affiliation.

This I hope to have shown in the present paper, focused as it is on the heroes that are of central concern in the dynamic tale of the *Catalogue:* Helen and Herakles, both emblematic for the poem's middle position of change and transition. They are both put to use by Zeus to end the period of chaos on earth and in this capacity deal massive damage to those inhabiting the world of heroes. Their *modus operandi* differs according to gender: Helen by her supernatural beauty attracts a large list of powerful suitors who first compete amongst themselves and are then drawn into a cataclysmic war; Herakles is a superhuman force that kills everything and everyone in his path until the world has changed enough for him to be extracted from it. Helen's model is Pandora, the ultimate 'beautiful evil'; Herakles' model is Zeus, the ultimate destroyer of monsters of chaos, who regularly wipes out entire races. Together, they leave next to nothing of the tribe of heroes, and so fulfill the will of Zeus.

---

[52] See e.g. Janko (1982) and (2015) for an early date, and West (1985) 136 for a late one.

Bibliography

Andersen, Ø. and D. D. Haug. (eds.) (2015). *Relative Chronology in Early Greek Epic Poetry*, Cambridge.
Blaise, F. (1992). 'L'épisode de Typhée dans la *Théogonie* d'Hésiode (v. 820–885): La Stabilisation du Monde', *REG* 105: 349–370.
Clay, J. S. (1993). 'The Generation of Monsters in Hesiod', *CP* 88: 105–116.
Clay, J. S. (2003). *Hesiod's Cosmos*, Cambridge.
Clay, J. S. (2005). 'The beginning and end of the *Catalogue of Women* and its relation to Hesiod', in: Hunter, 25–34.
Davies, D. R. (1992). *Genealogy and Catalogue: Thematic Relevance and Narrative Elaboration in Homer and Hesiod*, Ph.D. Diss., University of Michigan.
Doherty, L. (2011). 'Putting the Women Back into the Hesiodic *Catalogue of Women*', in: Zajko and Leonard, 297–325.
Fraser, L.-G. (2011). 'A Woman of Consequence: Pandora in Hesiod's *Works and Days*', *Cambridge Classical Journal* 57: 9–28.
González, J. M. (2010). 'The *Catalogue of Women* and the End of the Heroic Age (Hesiod fr. 204.94–103 M-W)', *TAPA* 140: 375–422.
Goslin, O. (2010). 'Hesiod's Typhonomachy and the Ordering of Sound', *TAPA* 140: 351–373.
Graziosi, B. and J. Haubold. (2005). *Homer: The Resonance of Epic*, London.
Haubold, J. (2005). 'Heracles in the Hesiodic *Catalogue of Women*', in: Hunter 85–98.
Hirschberger, M. (2004). Gynaikôn Katalogos *und* Megalai Êhoiai: *ein Kommentar zu den Fragmenten zweier Hesiodeischer Epen*, Munich.
Hunter, R. (ed.) (2005). *The Hesiodic* Catalogue of Women. *Constructions and Reconstructions*, Cambridge.
Hunter, R. (2005). 'The Hesiodic *Catalogue* and Hellenistic poetry', in: Hunter, 239–265.
Irwin, E. (2005). 'Gods among men? The social and political dynamics of the Hesiodic *Catalogue of Women*', in: Hunter, 35–84.
Janko, R. (1982). *Homer, Hesiod and the Hymns: Diachronic development in epic diction*, Cambridge.
Janko, R. (2015). 'πρῶτόν τε καὶ ὕστατον αἰὲν ἀείδειν. Relative chronology and the literary history of the early Greek epos', in: Andersen and Haug, 20–43.
Montanari, F., A. Rengakos, and C. Tsagalis (eds.) (2009). *Brill's Companion to Hesiod*, Leiden.
Most, G. (2007). *Hesiod: The* Shield, Catalogue of Women, *Other Fragments*. Cambridge, MA and London, England.
Rutherford, I. (2005). 'Mestra at Athens: Hesiod fr. 43 and the poetics of panhellenism', in: Hunter, 99–117.
Stamatopoulou, Z. (2013). 'Reading the *Aspis* as a Hesiodic poem', *CP* 108: 273–285.
Tsagalis, C. (2009). 'Poetry and Poetics in the Hesiodic Corpus', in: Montanari, Rengakos, and Tsagalis, 131–177.
Tsagalis, C. (2014). 'γυναίων εἵνεκα δώρων: Interformularity and Intertraditionality in Theban and Homeric Epic', *Trends in Classics* 6.2: 357–398.
West, M. (1985). *The Hesiodic* Catalogue of Women, Cambridge.
Zajko, V. and M. Leonard (eds.) (2006). *Laughing with Medusa*, Oxford.

Kirk Ormand
Helen's Phantom in Fragments

Τῶν ἐκ τῆς Ἑλλάδος ἀρίστων ἐπὶ μνηστείαν τῆς Ἑλένης παρόντων διὰ γένος καὶ κάλλος, Τυνδάρεως ὁ πατὴρ αὐτῆς, ὥς τινες φασί, φυλασσόμενος, μή ποτε, ἕνα αὐτῶν προκρίνας, τοὺς ἄλλους ἐχθροὺς ποιήσηται, κοινὸν αὐτῶν ὅρκον ἔλαβεν, ἦ μὴν τῶι ληψομένωι τὴν παῖδα, ἀδικουμένωι περὶ αὐτὴν, σφόδρα ἐπαμυνεῖν. διόπερ Μενελάωι αὐτὴν ἐκδίδωσι, καὶ μετ' οὐ πολὺν χρόνον, ἁρπαχθείσης ὑπὸ Ἀλεξάνδρου, ἐκοινώνησαν τῆς στρατείας διὰ τοὺς γενομένους ὅρκους. Ἡ ἱστορία παρὰ Στησιχόρωι.

When the noble men of Greece were present for the wooing of Helen because of birth and beauty, Tyndareos, her father, as some say, being on guard so that having chosen one of them he would not make the others his enemies, took a common oath from them: that they would immediately come to aid against one who intended to snatch the girl, doing wrong concerning her. Wherefore he entrusted her to Menelaos, and after a not very long time, when she had been seized by Alexander, they took common part in an expedition because of the oath that had taken place. This story is in Stesichoros.

(Σ [D] Hom. *Il.* 2.339 = Stesichorus fr. 87 Finglass)[1]

The most remarkable thing about the scholium quoted just above is the last four words (five in English). The scholium itself is a comment on a speech of Nestor, in which he upbraids his comrades for disobeying the oaths they have taken in coming to Troy. We should note that Nestor does not refer directly to the oath of Tyndareos, which is never mentioned in the *Iliad*, so it is the assumption of the scholiast that he refers to that particular oath.[2] This was a reasonable assumption: the story of the oath of Tyndareos was well-known in antiquity. Indeed, the story is told at some length in the Hesiodic *Catalogue* (fr. 204.78–85), and the narrative there is such that the scholium above – minus the attribution at the end – could be taken as a summary of it.[3] The Hesiodic passage uses different vocabulary, but all the same themes are there: Tyndareos requires an oath of all the suitors, specifically that if anyone should take Helen by force (*bie*) and in so doing set aside retribution (*nemesis*) and shame (*aidos*), the others would set out together to extract punishment. It is almost impossible not to see Stesichorus' narrative of injustice (*adikomenos*) – as recorded by the scholiast – as a reference to the *Catalogue*-poet's identification of the man

---

[1] All references to the fragments of Stesichorus come from the edition of Davies and Finglass (2014). All translations are my own, and are intended to be as literal as possible.
[2] Davies and Finglass (2014) 326 *ad* fr. 87.
[3] See Cingano (2005) 127; Ormand (2014) 188–189 for brief discussions of this difficult passage.

who puts aside *nemesis* and *aidos*.⁴ This, I suggest, is not an isolated incident: rather, we should see significant interaction between the poetry of Stesichorus, known in antiquity as being the 'most Homeric' of the lyric poets, and the hexameter poetry of the Hesiodic *Catalogue*. Perhaps due to the accidents of transmission, this relationship is seen most clearly in both poets' treatment of Helen.

That provocative statement immediately calls to question a fundamental issue for readers of archaic Greek poetry, especially poetry which, like the *Catalogue* and the works of Stesichorus, exists only in fragments. Namely, when two poems appear to have an unusually close correspondence of treatment or of language, should we understand that one poet is making a reference to the other? Or is this correspondence simply what, in studies of intertextuality in Latin poetry, is sometimes dismissed as 'accidental congruence'?⁵ Particularly when we have two poems on the same subject – such as the wedding of Helen and Menelaos – how much overlap in structure and language is inevitable, unintentional, and therefore ultimately unmeaningful? In the world of Latin literature, the tendency in recent years has been to perceive intertextual meanings as a function of the reader as much as the author: if a reader perceives and echo or reference, then it can be taken to produce meaning even if not the result of the ever-elusive authorial 'intent'.⁶

Similarly, recent readings in the Greek hexameter tradition have argued for an understanding of such poetry as 'intertextual', in a certain sense. As Tsagalis suggests, each performance of an oral hexameter poem takes place in an interconnected web of competing traditions – here, as he says, different versions of a narrative '… function like nodes opening up the entire horizon of diverse mythical traditions in which the listeners have been immersed during their entire lives'.⁷ In this understanding of archaic hexameter, *every* text, indeed every performance of a particular narrative has the potential to be, in a sense, 'intertextual', even when we are dealing with an orally performed poem. A key point of de-

---

4 With most scholars, I do not see the *Catalogue* as having been composed by the same poet who wrote the *Theogony* and *Works and Days*. See discussion with commentary at Ormand (2014) 1–15. On these questions, see Graziosi and Haubold (2005) 37–40. For an argument that the author of the *Catalogue* may be the same as that of the *Theogony*, see Janko (2012) 41–43.
5 On these issues, a good summary (with bibliography) can be found in Hinds (1998). See also Trinacty (2014) 16–23.
6 See Hinds (1998) 34, and the warning against 'an intertextualist fundamentalism – which privileges readerly reception so single-mindedly as to wish the alluding author out of existence altogether' (48). See also Burgess (2009) 66–67 on the sometimes 'embarrassing' need to invoke authorial intent in discussing intertextuality.
7 Tsagalis (2008) xiii. See also the excellent discussion in Burgess (2009) ch. 4.

bate has been whether such 'intertextual' moments are allusions to specific oral *poems* or to a somewhat more vague body of shared mythic knowledge.[8] Even for critics who see the Homeric poems working with specific epic material in an intertextual, allusive manner, we can only rarely identify references to specific, known, written narratives.[9] In addition, one of the great problems that we face is that the vast majority of the texts known from this period are lost, as Kelly notes.[10] What we may perceive as references to one of the few still extant texts could, and very likely do, refer to multiple other texts that are no longer extant.

Although recent critics have borrowed the word 'intertextual', then, archaic Greek literature does not function within the same sort of intertextual tradition as post-Augustan poetry, not least because we do not think of it as having been primarily transmitted in written form. The complexities of oral composition for the tradition of archaic hexameter – especially Homer, Hesiod, and the Homeric Hymns – necessitates that certain phrases, formulas, and even entire lines will be repeated verbatim. Thus, for strict 'oralist' interpreters, such repetitions carry no particular intertextual meaning.[11] Indeed, it is difficult to argue that such repetitions have the same intertextual valence as, say, an apparent refer-

---

8 The first systematic application of intertextual theory to this mode of neoanalyst interpretation is Burgess (2006), who argues for an intertextual understanding of the Homeric texts, though he sees the target of the intertext as a general body of myth rather than specific identifiable poems (esp. 153). Burgess argues cogently, however, that the Homeric texts engage in a process of 'motif transference' with 'meaningful poetic results' (170). See also Burgess (2012), where he argues for 'surprisingly detailed examples of the *Iliad*'s textless yet allusive intertextual engagement with the epic tradition from which it stems' (183). Tsagalis has gone a step further in seeing specific intertextual referents, arguing not only that poems of an advanced oral tradition acquire characteristics of 'textuality', but that we can see 'allusive intertextuality... operating between gradually fixed performance traditions' (Tsagalis 2011, 228; see also 231–232 and n. 75; Tsagalis (2014a) provides a brief summary of the arguments for quotation from specific, known epics in the Homeric poems). Currie (2012) has also argued for references to specific poems, discernible in specific phraseology as well as in the phenomenon of motif transference. Currie (2012) 207 n. 117 delineates the difference between his approach and Burgess' particularly clearly. Rutherford (2012) takes as given that archaic oral poets engaged in 'creative imitation' of other poets and narratives, and explores the theoretical implications of seeing this imitation as 'intertextuality' as opposed to 'traditional referentiality'. Tsagalis (2014b) provides an extensive argument for a deep intertextual relationship at the level of phraseology as well as motif between the epic narratives of the Trojan and Theban wars.
9 Burgess (2009) 56, 60.
10 Kelley (2015) 26.
11 Explained clearly by Burgess (2006) 155.

ence to Catullus in Horace or Vergil.¹² One of the important aspects of intertextual readings of the Latin tradition is the understanding that when a later text makes reference to an earlier one, it also engages in a process of creating its own literary tradition, and thus affects the way that we read the earlier text as well as the later, referring text. As Hinds puts it, '[e]very allusion made by a poet, in epigram and epic alike, mobilizes its own *ad hoc* literary historical narrative ... and a subjectivized literary history is the total of many such narratives'.¹³ It is difficult to see exactly this process of reading, re-reading, and re-interpreting the past while creating the present in the constantly shifting tradition of oral hexameter poetry.

While the repetition of a given word or sentence may not have precisely the sort of intertextual force that it would in a written text from later traditions, however, Burgess, Tsagalis, and Currie have argued for the phenomenon of 'motif transference' as an indicator of another specific narrative, lurking behind the narrative being performed.¹⁴ In brief, motif transference takes place when a theme or idea that seems to belong organically in one narrative pops up in another – not infrequently with a sense that the motif does not quite belong in the text in which it is found.¹⁵ As Burgess suggests, '[r]esulting contextual inappropriateness is not unskillful composition but rather a trigger toward recognition of another narrative'.¹⁶ Indeed, this particular form of intertextuality seems to grow organically from the practice of oral composition. As Burgess has argued, the presence of transferred motifs '... grew out of methods of comparison, reflection, and doubling that were inherent in oral traditions and is derived from observable techniques in early epic ...'¹⁷ Careful attention to motif transference, then, allows us to step closer to an understanding of epic repetitions and borrowings as something like the intertextual practices of more recent

---

12 See Burgess (2016) 18: 'Advocates of early epic intertextuality need to provide an explanation of its circumstances, and their choice of scenario will necessarily limit the extent of their argument'.
13 Hinds (1998) 133; see the full discussion 123–142. See also Barchiesi (2001) 142: 'The new text rereads its model, while the model in turn influences the reading of the new text – indeed when recognized, it often has the power to do so'.
14 See Burgess (2006), (2009), (2012); Tsagalis (2008), (2011), (2014); Currie (2012).
15 See Burgess (2009) 62–69. Also Tsagalis (2008) xii.
16 Burgess (2009) 66. In recent years a number of works have focused on the narratives that seem to be lurking, but repressed, in the Homeric texts: see for example Frame (2009); Sammons (2010) (focusing especially on the function of the catalogue); Tsagalis (2008). Currie (2012) 197–198 argues that in such instances, 'the traditional narrative is both superseded and left vestigially present in the text'.
17 Burgess (2009) 69.

literary traditions. The borrowing of a motif both allows us to read the motif in the original text differently, and to see how the original text has helped shape the text at hand.[18]

Recently, however, Kelly has argued that only with Stesichorus do we see the kind of direct, intentional interaction with a specific *poet* (in this case Homer) that we might call fully 'intertextual'.[19] In earlier lyric poets who have treated themes from the epic tradition (including the Cyclic epics), he argues, it is simply not possible to determine if they are referring specifically to Homer, or merely writing about the same well-known themes. With Stesichorus, as the recent spate of excellent work on him has shown, it is clear that we are seeing something different.[20] Stesichorus does not merely refer obliquely to other, possibly lost, poetic traditions; rather, he engages with the Homeric texts directly, deliberately, and in the process calls attention to the ways in which he is changing them.[21]

Stesichorus' direct interaction with Homer is most evident in his most well-known poem, the *Palinode* concerning Helen, from which we have only a few direct lines:

οὐκ ἔστ' ἔτυμος λόγος οὗτος,
οὐδ' ἔβας ἐν νηυσὶν ἐυσσέλμοις
οὐδ' ἵκεο πέργαμα Τροίας,

This story is not true,
you did not set out on the well-benched ships
nor did you arrive at the towers of Troy.

Stesichorus fr. 91a Finglass

The story that is not true is, of course, that which is already well-known from the epics of Homer. In the narrative that surrounds the *Palinode*, it appears that Stesichorus had already told a version of the abduction of Helen that corresponded with the Homeric version; but having been struck blind, he had the sense that Homer lacked, modified his story, and had his sight returned.[22] This is not just

---

[18] Tsagalis (2014a) 244 argues that this operation is characteristic of the *Iliad* and *Odyssey*, as does Burgess (2006) 170; (2012) 181; Currie (2012) 197–203. For an example of this mode of reading see Ormand (2014) 119–151.
[19] Kelly (2015) 44, Finglass and Kelly (2015). See also Davies and Finglass (2014) 39.
[20] Though Carey (2015) 55 points out that the titles of Stesichorus' poems seem to point to the epic cycle as much as to the poems we think of as Homeric.
[21] See especially Kelly (2015) 44; Davies and Finglass (2014) 32–39.
[22] See Davies and Finglass *ad* 91a.1: 'Stesichorus' οὗτος must be referring back to something already mentioned'.

a playful reference to a known text, but rather a narrative about the production of narrative in relation to that known text; Davies, Finglass, and Kelly are right to see in Stesichorus a new form of literary sensibility.

Recent work on the Hesiodic *Catalogue of Women*, however, has also seen in that poem a degree of full intertextuality.[23] I have argued elsewhere that certain fragments of the extant *Catalogue* take motifs from the *Iliad* and *Odyssey* and transfer them, with various literary effects, to entirely different narratives.[24] In terms of date, this does not necessarily contradict Kelly's assertion; both the *Catalogue* and Stesichorus are of uncertain date, but both seem to fall in about the same range, roughly 580–540 BC.[25] It may be the case that the *Catalogue*-poet picked up on a technique of his contemporary Stesichorus, or it may be that Stesichorus developed and further complicated a feature of the Hesiodic *Catalogue of Women*; or the two may have been involved in a contemporary literary development. What seems not to have been noted to date is an unusually high correspondence between Stesichorus and 'Hesiod'; not the Hesiod of the *Theogony* and *Works and Days*, but specifically of the 'Hesiod' who composed the heroic compendium that is the *Catalogue of Women*.

We have considerable evidence that Stesichorus and the *Catalogue of Women* contained significant areas of overlap: Stesichorus fr. 87 Finglass (above) sounds like a summary of something remarkably similar to frr. 199–204 of the *Catalogue of Women*. We are told by an ancient commentator (Stesichorus fr. 90 Finglass) that he criticized both Homer and Hesiod, probably in connection with the story of Helen (though why he criticized Hesiod is not specified). In his *Oresteia*, Philodemus tells us, Stesichorus 'followed' Hesiod in making Iphigenia into He-

---

[23] As Rutherford (2012) points out, the *Catalogue* intersects with other archaic epic at several points, in part because of its form as a compendium of heroic myth (156).
[24] Ormand (2014) 119–179.
[25] The dates of both poets are highly contested. For likely dates of the *Catalogue of Women*, see the summary in Ormand (2014) 3–7 and 3 n. 5. Hirschberger would date the *Catalogue of Women* a bit earlier, to c. 630–590. The one significant outlier is Richard Janko, who sees the *Catalogue of Women* as contemporary with, or even earlier than, the *Theogony* on the basis of statistical analysis of archaic linguistic forms in the *Catalogue* and other hexameter texts. See now Janko (2012). West (1985) 133–135 discusses the relative chronology of the *Catalogue of Women* and Stesichorus, reaching no firm conclusion as to precedence. Rutherford (2012) 166–167 suggests that some material in the *Catalogue* may pre-date even the Homeric poems, in the form of a 'proto-*Catalogue*'; he expresses some unease about the hypothesis of a 'proto-version' as being 'a scientific way of saying that we do not know when it was written, and of keeping the option open for its relation to other poems...' (154). Questions of priority are always problematic in instances of motif transference in oral traditions; see, e.g., Currie (2012) 184; Burgess (2012) 170–171; Tsagalis (2011) 218.

kate (Stesichorus fr. 178 Finglass, discussed further below). Another fragment, a summary in a scholium to Euripides' *Orestes* 249, explicitly links Stesichorus' treatment of Tyndareos' daughters with that of Hesiod (Stesichorus fr. 85 = *Cat.* fr. 176).[26] The similarities deserve a brief analysis, though I will not go into all the complex issues raised.

> οὕνεκα Τυνδάρεος
> ῥέζων ποκὰ πᾶσι θεοῖς μόνας λάθετ' ἠπιοδώρου
> Κύπριδος· κείνα δὲ Τυνδαρέου κόρας
> χολωσαμένα διγάμους τε καὶ τριγάμους ἐτίθει
> καὶ λιπεσάνορας.

> Because when Tyndareos
> was sacrificing to all the gods, he forgot only the soothing-giver
> Kypris; and she, angry at the daughters of Tyndareos,
> made them twice-married and thrice-married
> and husband-leavers.
>
> Stesichorus fr. 85 Finglass

The scholiast who recorded this short bit of Stesichorus noted the similarities to a passage in Hesiod, which he recorded immediately following:

> τῆισιν δὲ φιλομμειδὴς Ἀφροδίτη
> ἠγάσθη προσιδοῦσα, κακῆι δέ σφ' ἔμβαλε φήμηι.
> Τιμάνδρη μὲν ἔπειτ' Ἔχεμον προλιποῦσ' ἐβεβήκει,
> ἵκετο δ' ἐς Φυλῆα φίλον μακάρεσσι θεοῖσιν
> ὣς δὲ Κλυταιμήστρη <προ>λιποῦσ' Ἀγαμέμνονα δῖον
> Αἰγίσθωι παρέλεκτο καὶ εἵλετο χείρον' ἀκοίτην·
> ὣς δ' Ἑλένη ᾔσχυνε λέχος ξανθοῦ Μενελάου

> Looking at them, laughter-loving Aphrodite was angry
> and she threw an evil reputation on them.
> Timandre, when she had gone away, leaving Echemos,
> came to Phyleus, dear to the blessed gods,
> and thus Klytaimestra, having left godlike Agamemnon
> went to bed with Aigisthos and chose a worse husband;
> and thus Helen disgraced the bed of blond Menelaos.
>
> *Cat.* fr. 176

As Davies and Finglass note, it seems unlikely that in the *Catalogue*'s version Tyndareos neglected to sacrifice to Aphrodite; though both poets record her

---

[26] See the full and useful discussion in Davies and Finglass (2014) 319–322 *ad* fr. 85. Also West (1985) 133.

anger, the cause in the *Catalogue of Women* is unspecified.[27] What is particularly interesting, however, is the way that the two fragments interlock, as the scholiast seems to have observed. In the *Catalogue of Women* the shame that Aphrodite intends is made explicit, and we read a narrative of how that shame played out in action. The fragment from Stesichorus, in so far as the scholiast's words can be taken to reflect Stesichorus', reads as a gloss on this passage: he adds a reason for Aphrodite's anger and then generalizes the punishment of the daughters, leaving the resulting ill-repute and shame implicit in the terms διγάμους, τριγάμους, and λιπεσάνορας.[28] It is possible to imagine that Stesichorus is not just treating the same theme, but interacting deliberately with the particular version in the *Catalogue of Women*.[29] In what follows, however, I will argue that this poetic interaction did not flow in only one direction: I will also argue for an intertextual reference on the part of the *Catalogue*-poet to the famous *Palinode* of Stesichorus.

Eidola

Let us now turn to the two poets' treatments of the myth of Helen, and particularly Stesichorus' most famous addition to this narrative, namely the introduction of Helen's *eidolon*.[30] We are faced immediately with the somewhat dizzying, slightly different *testimonia* regarding Stesichorus' *Palinode*.[31] While it seems clear that Stesichorus was the poet best known for the introduction of the *eidolon*, this part of the story is not recorded in the direct fragments that we have. Instead it is referred to on a papyrus fragment commenting on some lyric poetry, which appears to contain two brief quotations of Stesichorus not relevant to my discussion. The scholiast tells us as follows:

[μέμ-
φεται τὸν Ὅμηρο[ν ὅτι Ἑ-
λέ]νην ἐποίησεν ἐν Τ[ροίαι
καὶ οὐ τὸ εἴδωλον αὐτῆ[ς, ἔν
τε τ[ῆι] ἑτέραι τὸν Ἡσίοδ[ον

---

[27] Davies and Finglass (2014) 321 *ad* fr. 85 Finglass.
[28] It is also possible that the influence goes the other way: Stesichorus discussed the punishment in vague terms, and the *Catalogue*-poet wrote a version in which he glossed Stesichorus' terms with specific examples. I cannot determine with certainty which text had priority.
[29] Or possibly another work of the Hesiodic corpus, as Most (2007) 318–319 n. 32 suggest.
[30] See the excellent discussion of Davies and Finglass (2014) 299–307.
[31] Brilliantly sorted out by Davies and Finglass (2014) 330–343, *ad* frr. 90–91j Finglass.

μέμ[φετ]αι· ...
αὐ-
τὸ[ς δ]έ φησ[ιν ὁ] Στησίχορο[ς
τὸ μὲν ε[ἴδωλο]ν ἐλθεῖ[ν ἐς
Τροίαν τὴν δ' Ἑλένην π[αρὰ
τῶι Πρωτεῖ καταμεῖν[αι·

> He criticizes Homer because he placed Helen in Troy and not her *eidolon*, and in another poem he criticizes Hesiod...
> Stesichorus himself says that the *eidolon* went to Troy, but Helen stayed with Proteus.
> Stesichorus fr. 90.1–6, 11–15 Finglass[32]

Fortunately, the idea of the *eidolon* as Stesichorus' invention – or at least as central to his poem – is confirmed by a fragment from Plato's *Republic* (9.586c = Stesichorus fr. 91b Finglass):

τὸ τῆς Ἑλένης εἴδωλον ὑπὸ τῶν ἐν Τροίαι Στησίχορός φησι γενέσθαι περιμάχητον ἀγνοίαι τοῦ ἀληθοῦς.

> Stesichorus says that the *eidolon* of Helen was fought over by those in Troy, out of ignorance of the truth.

This much confirms that Stesichorus' narrative had an *eidolon* at Troy, though it leaves somewhat unclear how the *eidolon* got there and whether Helen ever did run away with Paris.[33]

Was Stesichorus the only poet to introduce this striking idea, however? A statement made in a periphrasis to the *Alexandra* of Lycophron suggests otherwise: πρῶτος Ἡσίοδος περὶ τῆς Ἑλένης τὸ εἴδωλον παρήγαγε ('Hesiod first introduced the *eidolon* concerning Helen, *Catalogue of Women* fr. 358). The suggestion of priority here is irrelevant; if the author of the periphrasis found this story in a text ascribed to Hesiod – such as the Hesiodic *Catalogue of Women* – he would have assumed that it was earlier than Stesichorus, regardless of the actual dates of the two texts.[34] But someone in antiquity thought that Hesiod had a story about Helen's *eidolon*, a point to which I will return. As luck would have it, we almost certainly have the text in question, a curious fragment from the *Catalogue of Women* about the daughters of Tyndareos. While this fragment

---

[32] As Davies and Finglass (2014) 310–311 note, the phrasing here suggests that the scholiast's source for the first part of this passage (1–6) is Chamaileon, and that he switches to Stesichorus himself at line 11. The comment about criticizing Hesiod is tantalizing; see, however, the comments of West (1985) 134: 'It may mean only that he criticized a story which Chamaileon found in a Hesiodic poem, and there is no guarantee that it was a story about Helen'.
[33] See Davies and Finglass (2014) 340 *ad* fr. 91 h Finglass, citing Solmsen (1934) 119 n. 4.
[34] March (1987) 88.

has been extensively discussed elsewhere (and is carefully considered by Davies and Finglass), I suggest that it should be read intertextually with the *Palinode* of Stesichorus; one of the two poets is, I believe, borrowing from the other. While we may not be able to determine which way the borrowing goes – and indeed, much in this discussion must remain speculative – we should consider how this intertext might have functioned, and what it tells us about the literary communication between these two important archaic poets. The relevant passage of the Hesiodic fragment is as follows:

> γῆμ[ε δ' ἐὸν διὰ κάλλος ἄναξ ἀνδρ]ῶν Ἀγαμέμνων
> κού[ρην Τυνδαρέοιο Κλυταιμήσ]τρην κυανῶπ[ιν·
> ἣ τ[έκεν Ἰφιμέδην καλλίσφυ]ρον ἐν μεγάρο[ισιν
> Ἠλέκτρην θ' ἣ εἶδος ἐρήριστ' ἀ[θανά]τηισιν.
> Ἰφιμέδην μὲν σφάξαν ἐυκνή[μ]ιδες Ἀχαιοὶ
> βωμῶ[ι ἔπ' Ἀρτέμιδος χρυσηλακ]άτ[ου] κελαδεινῆς,
> ἤματ[ι τῶι ὅτε νηυσὶν ἀνέπλ]εον Ἴλιον ε[ἴσω
> ποινὴ[ν τεισόμενοι καλλισ]φύρου Ἀργειώ[νη]ς,
> εἴδω[λον· αὐτὴν δ' ἐλαφηβό]λος ἰοχέαιρα
> ῥεῖα μάλ' ἐξεσά[ωσε, καὶ ἀμβροσ]ίην [ἐρ]ατε[ινὴν
> στάξε κατὰ κρῆ[θεν, ἵνα οἱ χ]ρὼς [ἔ]μπε[δ]ο[ς] ε[ἴη,
> θῆκεν δ' ἀθάνατο[ν καὶ ἀγήρ]αον ἤμα[τα πάντα.
> τὴν δὴ νῦν καλέο[υσιν ἐπὶ χ]θονὶ φῦλ' ἀν[θρώπων
> Ἄρτεμιν εἰνοδί[ην, πρόπολον κλυ]τοῦ ἰ[ο]χ[ε]αίρ[ης.

He married her, because of her beauty, lord of men Agamemnon,
Klytaimestra daughter of Tyndareos, dark-eyed.
She bore lovely-ankled Iphimede in the halls,
and Elektra who contended with the immortals in beauty.
The well-greaved Achaians sacrificed Iphimede
on the altar of Artemis of the golden spindle, and noisy,
on that day when they sailed with their ships into Ilion,
to extract revenge for the lovely-ankled Argive woman,
an image; but her the deer-shooting arrow-shooter
very easily saved and poured lovely ambrosia
over her head, so that her skin would remain firm,
and she made her immortal and ageless for all time.
This one the tribe of people on the earth now call
Artemis of the road, temple-servant of the famous arrow-shooter.

Cat. fr. 23a.13–26

The *eidolon* in line 21 has been much-discussed; for my purposes, let us assume that this is the passage that the paraphrasist of Lycophron had in mind.[35] Much

---

35 Solmsen (1981) 355 neatly sidesteps all problems by assuming that lines 21–26 were added

has been restored in this passage, and as March pointed out some time ago, the ending of the word *eidolon* cannot be determined from the papyrus.[36] It is possible that what the poet wrote here was not the text as printed by Merkelbach and West, but rather, as March suggests, εἰδώ[λου· κούρην δ' ἐλαφηβό]λος ἰοχέαιρα ...[37] In that case, the *eidolon* here would not be one of Iphimede, but rather of Helen herself; and we would have a mention, either contemporary with or earlier than Stesichorus (assumed by the paraphrasist of Lycophron as earlier).

This suggestion has not met with general approval. Most commentators, including Austin as well as Davies and Finglass in their new commentary on Stesichorus, believe that the *eidolon* here refers to Iphimede, and is the key to her escape from sacrifice. Davies and Finglass are rightly suspicious of the reliability of the paraphrasist of Lycophron (who makes errors in his summary of the account in Herodotus). More importantly, they argue that in the passage above, '... a glancing mention of Helen's εἴδωλον would be quite out of place, whereas Iphimede's εἴδωλον has an important part to play in ensuring the rescue of the real Iphimede'.[38] This is reasonable enough, and the 'glancing mention' of the *eidolon* is certainly troubling. But let us interrogate this interpretation a bit further. If we assume, as most scholars have, that the word *eidolon* here must refer to Iphimede, we are immediately faced with two rather serious problems. First, it is far from clear that it is possible to sacrifice an *eidolon*.[39] Although Euripides' version of Helen's *eidolon* seems to have been surprisingly lifelike – more on the order of an android than a sculpture – no other *eidolon* in Greek literature receives a wound or simulates the act of dying. Even more difficult, we have to accept the fact that this aspect of the Hesiodic narrative has left virtually no mark on the later literary tradition concerning the sacrifice of Iphimede/Iphigeneia: although there is strong evidence that later authors associated this text with the sacrifice of Iphigeneia at Aulis, no other author suggests that the girl was rescued by substituting an *eidolon*. As Hirschberger notes, '[i]n verschiedenen Ver-

---

by a rhapsodist, and are therefore of no literary interest. Austin (1994) provides a full and lively discussion; he assumes that the *eidolon* is of Iphimede, and that the paraphrasist of Lycophron has either mis-read or mis-remembered the passage. Rutherford (2012) 159 discusses the passage briefly, and notes the overlap with Stesichorus.

36 March (1987) 88. A high-resolution image of the papyrus is available online: http://quod.lib.umich.edu/a/apis?type=boolean;view=thumbnail;rgn1=apis_inv;q1=P.Mich.inv.%25206234. There is no recovering the last two letters of the word *eidolon*.
37 March (1987) 89.
38 Davies and Finglass (2014) 303; quotation from 303 n. 32.
39 Pointed out by Hirshberger (2004) 212, *ad* fr. 15.21 [= 23a.21].

sionen des Mythos ist das Ersatzopfer eine Hirschkuh (*Cypria* Procl. *Chrest.* 31 Kullmann. Eur. *IA* 1585–1589; *IT* 28–29. Ov. *Met.* XII 32–34. Nonn. *Dionys.* XIII 104–119.), ein Rind (Nikandros *Heteroiumena* F 58 Schneider = Ant. Lib. XXVII 3) oder eine Bärin (Phanodemos *FGrHist* 325 F 14), worin sich Artemis' Verbindung mit diesen Tieren in verschiedenen Lokalkulten widerspiegelt'.[40] An animal of some sort – sacred to Artemis – can be the ritual substitute for Iphigeneia (or, perhaps, Iphimede). In no other text is an *eidolon* used in this way.

Arguments from silence are never as strong as we would like, but here we should note that we have two apparent ancient references to exactly this passage, and neither mentions an *eidolon* in Iphimede's place. Pausanias tells us, somewhat problematically:

> οἶδα δὲ Ἡσίοδον ποιήσαντα ἐν Καταλόγωι Γυναικῶν Ἰφιγένειαν οὐκ ἀποθανεῖν, γνώμηι δὲ Ἀρτέμιδος Ἑκάτην εἶναι.
>
> I know that Hesiod said in the *Catalogue of Women* that Iphigeneia did not die, but is Hekate by the will of Artemis.
>
> Pausanias 1.43.1 = *Cat.* fr. 23b

If we take this to be a reference to fr. 23a M.-W. (as most scholars do) it appears that Pausanias has gotten two details wrong, but both are explicable: he has identified Iphimede as Iphigeneia, which is easy enough given the narrative circumstances, and he has identified 'Artemis Enodie' as Hekate, also a common ancient association.[41] This understanding of Pausanias' comment seems to be further supported by a brief passage from Philodemus:

> Στη-
> [σίχορο]ς δ' ἐν Ὀρεστεί[-
> αι κατ]ακολουθήσας
> Ἡσιό]δωι τὴν Ἀγαμέ-
> μνονος Ἰ]φιγένειαν εἶ-
> ναι τὴ]ν Ἑκάτην νῦν
> ὀνομαζ]ομένην...
>
> Stesichorus in his *Oresteia*, following Hesiod, [makes] Iphigeneia the daughter of Agamemnon [into] the one now called Hekate...
>
> Philodemus *De* Pietate B 8364–70 Obbink = Stesichorus fr. 178 Finglass

---

40 Hirschberger (2004) 211 *ad* fr. 15.17 [= 23a.17]. 'In various versions of the myth the false sacrifice is a doe..., a cow..., or a female bear..., where Artemis' connection with these animals in different local cults is reflected'.
41 See the useful comments of Davies and Finglass (2014) 502 *ad* fr. 178 Finglass. Also Austin 1994, 106–110.

We should not ignore the fascinating information that Philodemus thinks Stesichorus is following Hesiod in this narrative when it comes to his *Oresteia* – and it seems that the text in question must be *Catalogue of Women* fr. 23a. This is evidence of a sense in antiquity that Stesichorus knew, and responded to, the *Catalogue of Women*. For my present purposes, however, what is important is that Philodemus seems to know a text in which Hesiod makes Iphigeneia (Iphimede again?) into Hekate (Artemis of the crossroads again?). It is possible that Hesiod's version and Stesichorus' differ in precisely these details, i.e. Stesichorus' narrative has Iphigeneia sacrificed but turned into Hekate, and that Pausanias is confusing Hesiod and Stesichorus; but it seems more likely that both poets have produced overlapping narratives once again. And still more important, neither Pausanias nor Philodemus seems to suggest that Iphimede/Iphigeneia was rescued by means of an *eidolon*.

Finally, it is worth considering the nature of the enjambment of the word *eidolon* in line 21. Regardless of the case of the word, it is an odd enjambment; but how likely is it to signal, as the reading εἴδωλον requires, a change of object and operative verb, back to Iphigeneia? Austin notes the difficulties and the ambiguities:

> 'A cursory reading of lines 20–21, particularly for readers versed in the epic style, could easily mistake *eidolon* as the qualification added to Argeione in line 20 – fair-ankled Helen – particularly since the name is in the genitive case, which, construed as a possessive, could leave the reader with a first impression that the Achaeans had sailed to Troy to exact reparations for "Helen's eidolon". But no, the enjambment directs us to overlook Helen and return to Iphimede, who is named four hexameters earlier … In fact the addition of the word *eidolon* completely undermines the whole sentence. The sacrifice of Iphimede at Aulis was, it now transpires, a false assumption'.[42]

The shift of object makes this into a highly unusual use of enjambment, requiring us to ignore Helen and the verb that governs her, and seek Iphimede in apposition to *eidolon*, jumping back as well to the verb 'sacrificed' (*sphaxan*, fr. 23a.17) four lines earlier to find its grammatical function. I have scanned all the extant lines of the *Catalogue of Women* and can find no parallels. Though the case of the run-over word does not always agree in case with the word to which it stands in reference, enjambment is never used to change the subject (or object) of the immediately preceding clause. To take one example, consider a battle description from fr. 33a:

---

[42] Austin (1994) 108–109. See also Solmsen (1980) 354: 'The word εἴδωλον whick lacks an organic syntactical connection with the preceding lines is a clumsy way of introducing a correction of the original story'.

> πολέας δ' ἀπόλεσσε καὶ ἄλλους
> μαρνάμενος Νηλῆος ἀγακλειτοῦ περὶ τεῖχος
> ο[ὗ] πατρός, πολέας δὲ μελαίνηι κηρὶ πέλασσε
> κ]τείνων. ἀλλ' ὅτε δή οἱ ἀγάσσατο Παλλὰς Ἀθήνη,

> He killed many others,
> fighting around the wall of very famous Neleus,
> his father, and he brought many close to black death,
> killing. But when Pallas Athena became angry with him...
>
> *Cat.* 33a.19–22

In neither of the two enjambments in this brief passage – 'his father' in line 21 and 'killing' in line 22, does the grammar require the kind of leap of attention that *eidolon* does in fr. 23a.21. In the case of 'father', the run-over word modifies Neleus in the previous line and is in the same case; the word 'killing' is in agreement with the subject of the clause immediately preceding it.[43] Given these real syntactic problems with the reading *eidolon*, it is at least possible that March is correct to suggest that the form on the papyrus was originally εἰδώλου, referring to Helen.[44]

We have, then, two interesting and interlocking questions: first, it would be useful to know which of these texts was actually first to introduce the *eidolon*; and second, was the *eidolon* of Helen or of Iphimede? Of the four possible outcomes of these interlocking variables, I think that we can safely eliminate two: despite the belief of the paraphrasist of Lycophron, I do not believe that Hesiod can have introduced the theme of the *eidolon*, whether of Helen or of Iphimede. If, as I think we should, we accept the reading εἰδώλου, then Hesiod's mention of the *eidolon* of Helen simply cannot be its introduction to Greek poetry; in the text above, he says

> The well-greaved Achaians sacrificed Iphimede
> on the altar of Artemis of the golden spindle, and noisy,
> on that day when they sailed with their ships into Ilion,
> to extract revenge for the lovely-ankled Argive woman,
>   an image...
>
> *Cat.* 23a.17–21

And there the narrative stops. The rest of the immediate story has to do with the rescuing of Iphimede. As Davies and Finglass suggest, this 'glancing' reference

---

[43] Similar uses of enjambment in the *Catalogue of Women* can be found at frr. 30.2–3, 204.94–5; *Aspis* 31–32.

[44] If this is reading is correct, it would be similar to other uses of enjambment in the *Catalogue of Women* in being followed by an immediate change of subject; see frr. 30.2–3 and 204.94–95.

simply does not present enough narrative to justify its introduction via an enjambment; the result of listeners could only be puzzlement. If, on the other hand, Hesiod did introduce the word in the accusative case, referring to Iphimede, then it is surely remarkable that no other ancient author picked up this narrative variant, and still more remarkable that Stesichorus introduced an *eidolon* of Helen without apparent reference to this passage.

There is, however, another possibility. We believe that Stesichorus and the *Catalogue*-poet were roughly contemporaries. What if Stesichorus' *Palinode* – destined to make something of an impression – was current when the *Catalogue of Women* was being molded into it's final form, and the poet chose, in this brief early mention of Helen, to nod to Stesichorus' bold suggestion that what the Greeks and Trojans were fighting over was not, as they thought, a real woman but an image, an idea?[45] First, this notion enhances our reading of the *Catalogue of Women*. Any reader of the extant fragments will quickly note that the primary feature of the women in the *Catalogue* is beauty, often denoted with forms of the word *eidos*.[46] In the fragment in question, both Phylonoe and Elektra are said to 'compete with the goddesses in *eidos*'. The theme of *seeing*, and especially seeing beauty, is critical to the narratives of the *Catalogue of Women*; indeed, it is the motivating force of the 'plot of attraction' that structures the *Catalogue of Women* as a whole.[47]

Helen is, of course, most famous of all for her *eidos*, a point that is emphasized by two of her suitors who take opposing approaches to it:

ἱμείρων Ἑλένης πόσις ἔμμεναι ἠυκόμοιο,
εἶδος οὔ τι ἰδών, ἀλλ' ἄλλων μῦθον ἀκούων.

...desiring to be the husband of fair-haired Helen,
not having seen her form, but hearing the stories of others.

Cat. fr. 199.2–3

οὐδέ τινα μνηστῆρα μ[ε]τάγγελον ἄλλ[ον ἔπεμψεν,
ἀλλ' αὐτὸς [σ]ὺν νηΐ πολυκλήϊδι μελαίνῃ[ι

---

[45] Davies and Finglass (2014) 303–304 argue that 'the story of the phantom would be inconsistent with the *Catalogue*. The phantom should exculpate Helen, yet that poem describes her guilt in strong language'. I cannot see where Helen's guilt is specified in the *Catalogue of Women*, unless Davies and Finglass are referring to fr. 176 (discussed above), which may not belong to the *Catalogue of Women*. If Janko (2012) is correct about the early date of the *Catalogue*, then we must presume that the lines in question are, in fact, later additions; that does not negate their possible intertextual meaning.
[46] See Osborne (2005) 10–13 for a substantial list of the women who are praised for their beauty, and the terms of that praise.
[47] On the 'plot of attraction', see Osborne (2005).

βῆ ὑπὲρ Ὠγυλίου πόντου διὰ κῦμα κελαιγ[ὸν
Τυνδαρέου ποτὶ δῶμα δαΐφρονος, ὄφρ[α ἴδοιτο
Ἀ]ρ[γείην] Ἑλένην, μηδ' ἄλλων οἷογ̣ ἀκ[ούοι
μῦθον

... nor did he [Idomeneus] send another messenger as a suitor,
but he himself with his many-benched black ship
went over the Ogylian sea thorugh the dark waves,
to the house of prudent Tyndareos, so that [he could see
Argive] Helen, and not hear the stories of
others...

Cat. fr. 204.58 – 63

In the *Catalogue of Women*, it is important that the suitors *see* Helen, and in particular see her *eidos*, her form. The idea, then, that it is not Helen that they end up fighting for, but rather an image of her, the form of her form, takes on additional potency. Keyed to this understanding of Helen, it becomes possible to imagine fr. 23a as building on Stesichorus' contemporary *Palinode* and, in the language of modern intertextual readings, 'mobilizing an ad hoc literary historical narrative' for that poem. At the moment that the *Catalogue*-poet introduces the daughters of Tyndareos (and their daughters), he comments briefly on the futility of the quest for Helen's return. Not only is Iphimede (nearly) sacrificed, but all of it was for an image, not even the Argive woman herself.[48]

There is still another possibility, one which the preceding discussion has foreclosed, but to which we might now turn. Perhaps I am wrong, and the reading in line 21 should be εἴδωλον, referring to Iphimede. If this is the case, and if we are nevertheless willing to imagine a scenario in which the *Catalogue*-poet is reacting intertextually to the new, exciting *Palinode* of his contemporary Stesichorus, new horizons of meaning open up. As Austin has argued (above), the enjambment of the word *eidolon* is significantly difficult and ambiguous in the text as we have it.[49] Coming, as it does, immediately after the mention of the famous 'Argive woman', it becomes possible to read it, even if it refers grammatically to Iphimede, as a brief, coded reference to Stesichorus' radical re-envisioning of the

---

[48] There is another problem in that here it does not appear that Helen is listed as a daughter of Tyndareos; see the useful comments of West (1985) 123 – 124. She is one of the three daughters of Tyndareos at *Catalogue of Women* fr. 176; in his recent edition, however, Most suggests that this fragment may not belong in the *Catalogue of Women* as it seems to repeat information from fr. 23a M.-W. (= Most fr. 19); he suggests that it may be from the *Megalai Ehoiai*. (Most 2007, 318 – 319 n. 32 *ad* fr. 247 [176 M.-W.]. Helen is clearly married from Tyndareos' household in frr. 199 – 204 M.-W., which suggests that she was, in this poem, his daughter.
[49] See also Solmsen (1981) 354.

Iliad. It is, if correctly restored here, the only use of the word *eidolon* in the Hesiodic corpus (regardless of case); this usage cannot be dismissed as 'accidental congruence'. Though there are many ancient versions of the sacrifice of Iphigeneia in which she is rescued by Artemis, there seem likewise to have been versions in which she is not.[50] The poet has not only chosen this version, but has done so using the highly unusual word *eidolon*. We might see the *Catalogue*-poet, then, as referring to Stesichorus' re-invention of Helen with a corresponding re-invention of the sacrifice of Iphimede. And we could then see Stesichorus' response when he 'follows Hesiod' (as recorded by Philodemus) in making Iphigeneia into Hekate in his *Oresteia* (discussed above). The world of archaic poetics, in this imagining, becomes significantly more literate and more open to notions of intertextual interpretation.

Relations and Intertexts

I would like to suggest, then, that if we see an intertextual reference to Stesichorus' *Palinode* here, it has broad implications for how we read the *Catalogue* and sixth-century poetry generally. It is still true, as Tsagalis suggests, that for the poets who produced the Homeric and Hesiodic poems, including the Cyclic Epics, 'a highly interactive character and self-consciousness indicate that allusive intertextuality was indeed operating between gradually fixed performance traditions'.[51] But the kind of reading that I am suggesting here goes further than that, and piggybacks on the idea that Kelly, Davies and Finglass have put forward for Stesichorus: namely that with his poetry we see a kind of literary revolution in which true inter*text*tuality becomes an operative strategy, in which intertextual allusions creatively re-write the literary history to which they refer.[52]

The idea of an *eidolon* of Helen, which came to be so strongly associated with Stesichorus, goes beyond the sort of narrative variants that we have come to see as suppressed by the master-narratives of Homer and Hesiod. This is not as simple a case as, for example, the suppression of a meeting between Achilleus and Helen in the *Iliad*, or even the sort of elegant interplay with tradition that we find in in the deaths of Patroclus and Achilleus and recently argued

---

[50] See March (1987) 92–98.
[51] Tsagalis (2011) 228. See also Tsagalis (2008) xiii, 'there is no almighty author but an omnipotent song-tradition weaving its own nexus of associations, evoking other traditions or versions at will, immersing its listeners to an *intertext* of mythical cross-references'.
[52] Davies and Finglass (2014) 39: 'Any later poet who interacts creatively with Homeric epic is following and implicitly paying tribute to the first poet to perfect this technique: Stesichorus'.

for by Burgess.⁵³ Rather, as Austin notes, this is the sort of variation that upends things entirely: '... the function of Helen's *eidolon* is to declare the whole issue of the Trojan War a perceptual error'.⁵⁴ If we accept that the *Catalogue*-poet has made an intertextual reference to this radical break, then we must admit that already we are in a world something like that of the Augustan poets, in which poets know each others' written work and refer to it in order to make their own, meta-narrative points. Given its rarity, we cannot in any case see the word *eidolon* in fr. 23a.21 as an instance of 'accidental congruence'; rather, we must see the *Catalogue*-poet adopting this radical re-imagining and referring to it somewhat obliquely. For that reference to have meaning to his audience, we also have to imagine that his listeners (or readers?) *also* knew Stesichorus – that the *Palinode* was, in effect, already celebrated enough for the audience to respond to the *Catalogue*'s enjambment with a knowing wink rather than confusion and puzzlement.

As Carey has recently pointed out, though Stesichorus seems to have been known for his interaction with Homer, '... it is not the Homer text as we understand it but the cycle (with lower case) as the body of heroic narrative before, after, and around Homer which leaps out when one looks at the surviving titles/themes of the lost works'.⁵⁵ Though I agree with Carey's observation, I want to take it a step further: Stesichorus is not just interacting with heroic myth (of which the *Catalogue of Women* was, in any case, a handy compendium), but seems at times – in quite a few places, from the fragments that we have – to have interacted with this specific text. And if I am right about the use of *eidolon* in fr. 23a, the *Catalogue*-poet was also interacting with Stesichorus, at some moment, in some performance, which became, in ways that are still not clear to us, our written text.

One of the more curious traditions about Stesichorus' life is that he was the son of Hesiod.⁵⁶ That story is not true, as Stesichorus might say, but the high number of interactions between Stesichorus and the 'Hesiod' who wrote the *Catalogue of Women* suggests one reason why this tradition might have sprung

---

53 On the meeting of Achilleus and Helen, see Tsagalis (2008) 93–111; on the deaths of Patroklos and Achilleus see Burgess (2012) 173–179; Currie (2012) 192–193.
54 Austin (1994) 112.
55 Carey (2015) 55.
56 Recorded in the Aristotelian *Constitution of the Orchomenians* (Arist. fr. 579 Gigon) and in Philochorus (*FGrHist* 328 F 213). See the useful discussion in Davies and Finglass (2014) 4–5, from whom I have taken these references.

up.⁵⁷ Stesichorus tended to take moments from the heroic tradition and expand them in writing, what West referred to as 'epic lyric'.⁵⁸ In this regard, Stesichorus' interactions with the heroic texts seem similar in technique to Ovid, who created narrative expansions of moments from specific epic texts in his *Heroides*.⁵⁹ Stesichorus' relation to the *Catalogue of Women* also appears to have been one of careful selection, expansion, and intervention. If I am correct about the *Catalogue*-poet's use of Stesichorus' *eidolon*, however, we must see this interaction as even more dynamic, and potentially flowing in both directions. The *Catalogue*-poet – whom our ancient sources were unanimous in calling 'Hesiod' – must also have been interacting with Stesichorus' re-writings of Homeric epic. Stesichorus and 'Hesiod' were not father and son, but competing poets engaged in a mutually playful process of composition, reference, and recomposition. This understanding places not only Stesichorus, but also the *Catalogue*-poet, in a thoroughly literary tradition.

Bibliography

Andersen, Ø. and D. T. T. Haug (eds.). (2012). *Relative Chronology in Early Greek Epic Poetry*, Cambridge.
Austin, N. (1994). *Helen of Troy and Her Shameless Phantom*, Ithaca, NY.
Barchiesi, A. (2001). *Speaking Volumes: Narrative and Intertext in Ovid and Other Latin Poets*, ed. and trans. M. Fox and S. Marchesi, London.
Burgess, J. (2004). 'Performance and the Epic Cycle', *CJ* 100: 1–23.
Burgess, J. (2006). 'Neoanalysis, Orality, and Intertextuality: An Examination of Homeric Motif Transference', *Oral Tradition* 21: 148–189.
Burgess, J. (2009). *The Death and Afterlife of Achilles*, Baltimore.
Burgess, J. (2012). 'Intertextuality Without Text in Early Greek Epic', in: Andersen and Haug, 168–183.
Burgess, J. (2016). 'Origins and Reception of the Trojan Cycle', in: F. Gallo (ed.), *Omero: Quaestiones Disputatae*, Biblioteca Ambrosiana, 13–30.
Carey, Ch. (2015). 'Stesichorus and the Epic Cycle', in: Finglass and Kelly, 45–62.
Currie, B. (2012). 'Perspectives on Neoanalysis from the Archaic Hymns to Demeter', in: Andersen and Haug, 184–209.
Davies, M. and P. J. Finglass (2014). *Stesichorus: The Poems*, Cambridge.
Finglass P. J. and A. Kelly (2015). 'The State of Stesichorean Studies', in: Finglass and Kelly, 1–17.

---

57 Graziosi (2002, 168) argues cogently that ancient 'discussions about authors were a powerful way of expressing thoughts about the poetry, especially at a time in which written texts were not the focus of attention'.
58 Carey (2015) 56; West (2015).
59 See, e.g., Barchiesi (2001); Michalopoulos 219–243 (this volume).

Finglass P. J. and A. Kelly (eds.). (2015). *Stesichorus in Context*, Cambridge.
Graziosi, B. (2002). *Inventing Homer: The Early Reception of Epic*, Cambridge.
Hinds, St. (1998). *Allusion and Intertext: Dynamics of Appropriation in Roman Poetry*, Cambridge.
Hirschberger, M. (2004). Gynaikôn Katalogos *und* Megalai Ehoiai: *Ein Kommentar zu den Fragmenten zweier hesiodeischer Epen*, Munich and Leipzig.
Hunter, R. (ed.) (2005). *The Hesiodic* Catalogue of Women: *Constructions and Reconstructions*, Cambridge.
Janko, R. (2012). 'πρῶτόν τε καὶ ὕστατον αἰὲν ἀείδειν: Relative Chronology and the Literary History of the Early Greek Epos', in: Andersen and Haug, 20–43.
Kelly, A. (2015). 'Stesichorus' Homer', in: Finglass and Kelly, 21–44.
March, J. (1987). *The Creative Poet: Studies on the Treatment of Myths in Greek Poetry*, London.
Merkelbach, R. and M. L. West (1990³). *Hesiodi. Fragmenta Selecta*, Oxford and New York.
Most, G. (2007). *Hesiod II. The* Shield, Catalogue of Women, *Other Fragments, Edited and Translated by G. W. Most*, Cambridge, MA and London.
Ormand, K. (2014). *The Hesiodic* Catalogue of Women *and Archaic Greece*, Cambridge.
Osborne, R. (2005). 'Ordering Women in Hesiod's *Catalogue*', in: Hunter, 5–24.
Rutherford, I. (2012). 'The Catalogue of Women within the Greek Epic Tradition: Allusion, Intertextuality and Traditional Referentiality', in: Andersen and Haug, 152–167.
Sammons, B. (2010). *The Art and Rhetoric of the Homeric Catalogue*, Oxford.
Solmsen, F. (1934). 'ΟΝΟΜΑ and ΠΡΑΓΜΑ in Euripides' *Helen*', *CR* 48: 119–121.
Solmsen, F. (1981). 'The Sacrifice of Agamemnon's Daugher in Hesiod's *EHOEAE*', *AJP* 102: 353–358.
Trinacty, C. (2014). *Senecan Tragedy and the Reception of Augustan Poetry*, Oxford.
Tsagalis, C. (2008). *The Oral Palimpsest: Exploring Intertextuality in the Homeric Epics*, Cambridge, MA.
Tsagalis, C. (2011). 'Towards an Oral, Intertextual Neoanalysis', *TC* 3.2: 209–244.
Tsagalis, C. (2014a). 'Preface', in: C. Tsagalis (ed.). *Theban Resonances in Homeric Epic*, *TC* 6.2: 239–244.
Tsagalis, C. (2014b). 'γυναίων εἵνεκα δώρων: Interformularity and Intertraditionality in Theban and Homeric Epic', in: C. Tsagalis (ed.). *Theban Resonances in Homeric Epic*, *TC* 6.2: 357–398.
West, M. L. (1985). *The Hesiodic* Catalogue of Women: *Its Nature, Structure, and Origins*, Oxford.
West, M. L. (2015). 'Epic, lyric, and lyric epic', in: Finglass and Kelly, 63–80.

Irini Kyriakou
Female Ancestors in the Hesiodic *Catalogue of Women*

What has survived from the monumental poem known as the *Catalogue* is only fragments and remnants of its glorious past.[1] Nevertheless, the fragmentary state of this epic does not prevent us from understanding its general structure.[2] In modern editions the papyrological evidence is presented alongside sources that reference the poem, consequently reconstructing the version closest possible to what once was the Hesiodic *Catalogue*.

In this article I aim at demonstrating how and why the *Catalogue* is a female catalogue in which women protagonists are above all recognized as ancestors. This reading, which focuses on the discursive and narrative function of the genealogical references naming the female ancestors, proposes to rethink kinship in epic Greek poetry according to the criteria of gender. By doing so, this study challenges the long-standing assumption that dactylic hexameter poems are the vestige of a patrilineal system within which female ancestors have neither place nor status.[3]

It is true that the *Catalogue* has been subjected to various reformulations and transformations since the archaic period. Nevertheless, what seems to stand out, even within its current form, is that its overall structure is narratively organized as a female catalogue. Ancient scholars never questioned this characteristic and the *testimonia* describe the poem as a genealogical catalogue centered on female protagonists.[4] However the *Catalogue* has a complex structure, since it presents genealogical material fused with narrative sections.[5]

The role of female ancestors in the *Catalogue* has never been fully studied. Modern scholars almost unanimously conclude that the heroines of this epic enable the transition from one genealogical branch to another and offer the host-

---

[1] West (1985) 125.
[2] The surviving vestiges of the *Catalogue* represent one-third or one-quarter of the poem. See West (1985) 1 and 31 and Osborne's argumentation (2005) 6–8.
[3] Specialists in other disciplines, such as anthropology and sociology, also reproduce this idea. Even regarding studies that focus on the anthropology of kinship, Ghasarian (1996, 245) admits the existence of a 'hidden' face in our understanding of kinship because the proposed perspective is mostly male.
[4] Regarding the *testimonia* about the *Catalogue*, see Merkelbach and West (1967) 1–3 and Most (2006) 201–205.
[5] With respect to the complex structure of the *Catalogue*, see e.g. Tsagalis (2009) 160.

https://doi.org/9783110537581-010

ing framework for the development of 'male' stories.⁶ Thus, even though the necessity to read the *Catalogue* by adopting a gendered methodology has been indirectly stressed, modern scholarship projects onto this poem numerous preconceived ideas concerning the poetical representation of gender.

I here analyze the role of the female protagonists in the *Catalogue* within a gender theory framework. Gender is here used as an instrument of interpretation which permits us to understand the poetic manifestations of gender within genealogical references.⁷ That is to say, it allows us to comprehend how and why the poet refers to the mother, the father, or both parents in a given instance. This study aims to explore the genealogical references in the poem according to gender criteria, taking under consideration the narrative context and the unique characteristics of the poem regarding the representation of its heroines. The *Catalogue* is not only an autonomous and detailed female catalogue⁸ praising female figures, but is also in genealogical terms a female-centric poetic creation. In the following sections I discuss the complex narrative features that allow us to see these distinctive gendered characteristics of the poem. Taken together, these features establish the framework in which genealogy is referenced. These complex narrative features are based neither on the presence of female figures in the poem nor on the presupposition that other dactylic hexameter poems exclude female voices.⁹

---

6 Fowler (1998, 6) considers the women in the *Catalogue*'s genealogical presentation to be the 'glue' holding together the 'building blocks' that pertain to the role of the male characters. Ormand (2014) adopts Fowler's arguments and, even if he recognizes a certain importance in the role held by female figures within the institution of marriage (see p. 49), he still declares that: '(…) it seems clear enough that the *Catalogue*'s real concern is not the women but rather the famous heroes to whom they give birth (p. 46)'. Cf. Rutherford (2000) 86. For an opposing view see Doherty (2006).
7 Joan Scott, 24 years after the publication of her famous article 'Gender: A Useful Category of Analysis' (1986), where gender capitalizes on the social relationships between the two sexes and allows the apprehension and exercise of power, she treats gender as 'une question *ouverte*, qu'il faut apprendre à poser dans un contexte donné', (Scott et Perreau 2010). Regarding the use of the gender in the reading of ancient sources, see for example Cuchet and Ernoult (2007), Boehringer and Cuchet (2011). Cf. Schmitt (2001); Schmitt Pantel (2002) and Holmes (2012).
8 By the term 'detailed catalogue' I designate the catalogic form based on the introduction of developed lemmas, in contrast to the 'enumerative catalogues' that match a list composed by the simple juxtaposition of objects, people, or places. Regarding the various definitions of 'catalogue' as a poetic form see Perceau (2002) 1–14. Cf. Sammons (2010).
9 A strict dichotomy of 'genres' made between Homeric heroic epic and Hesiodic poetry of the *ehoie*, the former supposedly centered only on male figures and the latter supposedly centered only on female figures, is problematic. Firstly because we find masculine and female figures in all dactylic hexameter poetry and secondly because epic diction does not necessarily correspond

The ἢ' οἵη Expression

Even if the expression ἢ' οἵη / ἢ' οἷαι ('or one like her' / 'or those like her') that gives the *Catalogue* its second title, *HOIAI*, is mentioned only six times in the papyri, the frequent use of the ἢ' οἵη expression by the ancient authors who refer to or quote the *Catalogue* shows that it likely was used systematically in the poem.[10]

As Rutherford characteristically put it, the ἢ' οἵη expression 'has never been fully explained'.[11] Nonetheless, scholars have demonstrated that the function of the ἢ' οἵη formula would be to introduce new entries in the *Catalogue* starting with a female figure mentioned in the previous genealogical section.[12] This expression is considered to be a structural feature of the *Catalogue*; a mechanism of lemmatization, which at same time ensures the continuation of the genealogical record.[13]

Given that genealogical material is not necessarily presented or organized in a catalogue form, the use of the ἢ' οἵη expression demonstrates that the *Catalogue* is a poem which spans and combines three different registers: genealogy, narration, and catalogue.[14] The most important observation for the purpose of

---

to a poetic genre that can be easily identified; rather it is a combination of several poetic forms such as narration, catalogue and genealogy, conditioned by internal and external pragmatics. For example, in the *Iliad* we find male as well as female catalogues. For an example of this generic separation, see Ziogas (2013) 8 ff.

10 Frr. 23a.3, 26.5, 43a.2, 58.7, 59.2, 195.8. Unless otherwise indicated, the citations in this paper follow Merkelbach and West's 1967 edition.

11 Rutherford (2000) 83.

12 According to West (1985) 56, this first ἢ' οἵη would introduce Pyrrha in the *Catalogue*. Cf. Rutherford (2000) 83 and Tsagalis (2009) 165.

13 See West (1985) 39: 'Even those sections introduced by ἢ' οἵη clearly do not represent the start of a new family but the resumption of a collateral branch'. Cf. Rutherford (2000) 83–85 and Tsagalis (2009) 160–161. 'According to Rutherford's analysis, the *ehoie*-formula is nothing more than a "vestigial" element within the overall organization of the *CW*', Tsagalis (2009), 161. For the 'archaeology' of the ἢ' οἵη expression, see Rutherford (2000).

14 The use of the ἢ' οἵη expression could be also proof of the genealogical presentation's flexibility in the *Catalogue:* several parts of the poem and especially the parts introduced through this expression could have been developed and exist independently of the whole poem. We have an eloquent example: the ἢ' οἵη of Alkmene, which opens the Hesiodic *Aspis* (l. 1–56). In addition, in fragment 52 a reference occurs to a 'catalogue of the Leukippides' that could indicate the existence of another, more expanded version of Leukippides' story. Such a use of the *ehoie* is also implied by the existence of the *Megalai Ehoiai*, which is perhaps an extended or alternative version of some parts of the *Catalogue*. Regarding the flexibility of the *Catalogue*, see Rutherford (2000) 88–89. For a comparison between the *Catalogue* and the *Megalai Ehoiai*,

this present study is that the use of the ἢ' οἵη formula as a lemmatization device for the internal organization of the poem indicates that the *Catalogue* is a female catalogue. The role played by the ἢ' οἵη expression as a method for introducing women within the *Catalogue* is also employed in other Greek epic poems through other expressions. These other female catalogues are the catalogue of the goddesses united with mortal men at the end of the *Theogony*, the catalogue of Zeus's lovers in *Iliad* 14, and the catalogue of the heroines in *Odyssey* 11.

Seen through a wide lens, the presentation of Aiolos' descendants in the *Catalogue* is a significant example of the female-centered catalogal structure of the poem based on the ἢ' οἵη expression. In fr. 10a.[15] the poet makes an allusion to Aiolos' sons before proceeding to the presentation of his daughters and their offspring. The demonstration of the descendants of Aiolos' sons starts with fr. 30. Some of Aiolos's sons are introduced in the poem through a narration centered on female figures: Deion is mentioned in the ἢ' οἵη concerning his daughter Asterodeia (fr. 58), Sisyphos in the ἢ' οἵη of Mestra (fr. 43a) and Kretheus appears in a fragment narrating Tyro's biography (fr. 30.29). Within this section, which presents Aiolos' sons, we also find some other ἢ' οἵη, like the one presenting Atalanta and the one introducing Leukon's daughters.[16] Therefore, by using the ἢ' οἵη formula the poet focuses specifically on female figures even when the genealogical material introduces male descendants.

The use of the ἢ' οἵη expression is relative to the female-centered subject of the poem. It follows that, in a broad sense, it is necessary to define the subject of the poem in terms of gender and, on a more detailed level, it is necessary to examine the description of its female protagonists. The study of the discursive form of genealogical references in the *Catalogue* will thus allow us to question the relation between the organization of the catalogue form based on female figures and the narrative function of the genealogical references. Consequently this study will determine whether or not the poem offers a distinctive way of referencing the female ancestors in relation to its semantic macrostructure.

---

see Cohen (1986). Cf. Hirschberger (2004) 81–86, D'Alessio, (2005) 176–216 and Cingano (2005) 118–121.
15 West published this fragment in 1981. Cf. West (1985) 31. In Most's edition (2007) this is fr. 10 and in Hirschberger's (2004) fr. 5.
16 See West (1985) 65–69.

The *Catalogue of Women* as Glorification of Female Figures

The *Catalogue* begins with an invocation to the Muses. Within this proem the poet unveils the purpose of the song: to sing of the excellent mortal women who united with gods. If the ἤ' οἵη expression shows that the catalogue form is *structured* on women, the proem proclaims that the *Catalogue* is a poem that *sings* of women.

> Νῦν δὲ γυναικῶν [φῦλον ἀείσατε, ἡδυέπειαι
> Μοῦσαι Ὀλυμπιάδε[ς, κοῦραι Διὸς αἰγιόχοιο,
> αἳ τότ' ἄρισται ἔσαγ[
> μίτρας τ' ἀλλύσαντο .[
> μισγόμεναι θεοῖσ[ιν¹⁷
>
> And now sing of the generation of women, sweet-voiced
> Olympian Muses, daughters of aegis-holding Zeus
> those who were the best at the time
> and they loosened their girdles
> mingling with gods

Cat. fr. 1.1–5

Through the use of the adjective ἄρισται ('excellent', l. 3), the proem of the *Catalogue* indicates a female ἀριστεία ('excellence') parallel to the one claimed by the heroes of epic Greek poetry, who are often qualified as ἄριστοι. The female figures of the poem share some common characteristics such as beauty and fecundity.[18] However, their rich representation in the poem shows that, these qualities notwithstanding, each of their respective biographies also exemplifies different forms of female ἀριστεία.[19] Ultimately though, in the *Catalogue* as in the *Iliad*,

---

[17] Most (2007) adopts Merkelbach's addition for the third line: καὶ κάλλισται κατὰ γαῖαν ('and most beautiful on the earth'). This addition seems valid and justified, since the female protagonists of the *Catalogue* are also exalted because of their beauty. Hirschberger (2004) follows Merkelbach and West's 1967 edition.

[18] Examples include: ἠύκομος: frr. 25.17, 37.8, 37.21, 200.2, 204.3; ἐυπλόκαμος: fr. 171.5; καλλίσφυρος: fr. 23a.15, 129.14, 195.4, 204.94; καλλιπλόκαμος: fr. 129.18 βοῶπις: 23a.9, fr. 129.20; καλλίζωνος: fr. 26.27; κυανῶπις: fr. 23a.14 and the expressions ἐπήρατον εἶδος ἔχουσαν: fr. 25.39; περικαλλέα κούρη: fr. 193.11; ἣ εἶδος ἔχε χρυσῆς Ἀφροδίτης: fr. 196.5; ῥοδόπηχυς: fr. 35.14; ἣ εἶδος ἐρήριστ' ἀθανάτῃσιν: fr. 23a.10, 23a.16, 35.12, 36.3, 180.14.

[19] Similarly, '(...) dal più vecchio al più giovane, dal più feroce al più mite, dal più coraggioso al più prudente, gli eroi di Omero agiscono distintamente perché rappresentano persone e quindi individualità – definite nella loro totalità – entro una collettività fortemente caratterizzata su di

one's claim to ἀριστεία depends on the consent of all the community members: to be excellent is to be recognized as such.[20]

Besides the descriptions of their physical characteristics that indicates different aspects of their beauty,[21] the *Catalogue's* female figures are exalted for their mental capacities. Deianira is 'intelligent', Mestra 'prudent', and Eurydike 'wise'.[22] In addition, some heroines 'know how to accomplish very beautiful deeds' and others have thoughts equal to the goddesses,[23] while the use of the adjective δῖα ('divine') reveals a parallelism with the description of epic heroes.[24] Meanwhile, the description of Chloris and Laothoe stresses their royal status.[25] Furthermore, Tyro is described as 'dear to the blessed gods',[26] an expression generally attributed to male figures.[27] The aligned description of heroes and heroines in the *Catalogue* suggests a certain parallelism in the representation of male and female figures.

In terms of social status, the heroines of the *Catalogue* are either παρθένοι, not married, or γυναῖκες, married.[28] The former, παρθένοι, are mostly mothers, yet their representation in the *Catalogue* is not uniform; on the contrary, each

---

un piano sociale', Di Donato (2006) 46. According to Lévy (1995) 182–183 'c'est aussi pourquoi des frères n'ont pas nécessairement la même *arétè*'.

20 'Or, une *arétè* qui n'agit pas, n'est plus une *arétè*. Et, comme *l'arétè* doit aussi se montrer et se faire reconnaître, elle est aussi et surtout diminuée par toute atteinte à la réputation', Lévy (1995) 185. 'L'aristia non comincia né si svolge in disparte ma coinvolge il centro dello scontro generale. *L'aristeus* non è un isolato ma è individuo che compie al meglio la sua parte in mezzo ai compagni', Di Donato (2006) 50. See also Bouvier (2002) 57–61. The ἀρετή as a 'visible action' proves, against preconceived ideas, that women were not enclosed in their foyers. In order to recognize the characteristics that make a woman ἀρίστη, she has to be seen, acknowledged, and judged by her social milieu.

21 These epithets, which describe in the *Catalogue* the beauty of the heroines, are often used in Homer and in the *Theogony* to describe the beauty of immortal goddesses. This usage could indicate the intention of the *Catalogue's* poet to assign to his heroines a mythical and divine beauty. For example, consider the adjective βοῶπις attested seventeen times in the *Iliad*, fourteen times to describe Hera, and one time to describe the Nereides. Cf. Cohen (1989/90) 26–27.

22 Ἐπί[φ[ρ]ονα: fr. 25.17; πολύϊδρις: fr. 43a.57; ἐϋ πραπί[δεσσ'] ἀρα[ρυῖα]ν: fr. 129.13.

23 Περικαλλέα ἔργ' εἰδυῖαι: fr. 23a.4, 26.6, 129.23; νόεσκε γὰρ ἶσα θεῆισι: fr. 43a.72.

24 Δῖα: fr. 25.34 (Hypermestre), 64.14 (Philonis), 73.2 (Atalanta), 76.5 (Atalanta), 76.20 (Atalanta), 190.3 (Hippodameia).

25 Fr. 33(a) and 26.

26 Φίλη μακάρεσσι θεοῖσι: fr. 30.24.

27 Frr. 14.6, 23a.33, 136.19, 176.4.

28 The status of νύμφη, married woman with no children could not be assigned to the women of the *Catalogue* since all the wives are mothers. Regarding the three status παρθένος, νύμφη and γυνή, see Calame (1996) 140–145 and 185. Concerning παρθένος and παρθενία, see Sissa (1987).

heroine has her own story and within that story her individual characteristics are developed. Unmarried female figures could be hunters, such as Kallisto and Atalanta,[29] priestesses including Io, sacrificed heroines like Iphigeneia, or female figures that achieve immortality, such as Phylonoe in fr. 23a. In this category we could also integrate heroines who were lovers of a god before marrying a mortal hero, like Tyro or Europe, and also women lovers of gods who never married, like Demodike. Consequently, παρθενία applies to a wide-ranging group of women.

Using as operative models the two types of marriage 'mariage en bru' and 'mariage en gendre',[30] we could argue that heroines-γυναῖκες ('wives' having a child while married) are not presented in the *Catalogue* as an exchange object between the paternal house and the house of the future husband. The ἕδνα and the δῶρα ('marriage gifts' and 'presents') and the motif of ἀγών according to which one or many suitors compete to claim the hand of a heroine, indicate that a suitor has, above all, to prove himself worthy to become husband to one of the *Catalogue*'s heroines. The absence of the institution of dowry, προίξ, favors this interpretation.[31] Furthermore, in the story of Demodike, Agenor's daughter, narrated in fr. 22, we find mutual love postulated as a precondition for the accomplishment of marriage.

Based on this brief analysis of the poetic representation of female figures in the *Catalogue*, we can argue that in the poem, heroines are also protagonists of the narrative action, since their personal stories are portrayed in a recognizable way. The fact that women in the *Catalogue* never deliver any direct speech does not, in my opinion, contradict this statement.[32] Direct speech, being extremely rare in the surviving fragments of the poem, can be considered a narrative char-

---

29 The erotic description of Atalanta, runner and huntress, in fr. 75, puts forward her beauty and not her physical strength. Her strength may have been exalted within the lost narration of the running competition between the heroine and Hippomenes.
30 According to Leduc (2002) 309–382, there are two ways to marry a girl in Homeric society, 'la mariée donnée en bru' and 'la fille mariée à un gendre'. According to the first, the suitors are obliged to present wedding gifts, the ἕδνα, and presents, the δῶρα. As for the second, the father of the girl wants to attract a groom into his house, regardless of whether he has a son. Within the 'marriage en bru', the suitor must not present ἕδνα and instead the father offers the gifts to his daughter. Consequently, the groom and the children belong to the house of the bride's father.
31 On προίξ and ἕδνα see Ormand (2014) 52–81.
32 Ormand (2014) 45, uses the lack of direct speech addressed by women as a proof for his argument that '(...) the women rarely seem to be the most important characters in the narratives in which they appear'.

acteristic of the *Catalogue*[33] which merely happens to appear in given places and thus not a deciding factor in determining whether or not women are represented as full-blown actors on par with the male heroes of the narrative development. Female heroines enjoy the status of full protagonists in the narrative regardless of their never utilizing direct speech. Nevertheless, the glorification of female figures in the *Catalogue* does not imply that heroes are absent nor that they are illustrated in a negative way. On the contrary, within some long fragments we can observe a focus on the actions of heroes whereas in some other (long fragments) the narration revolves around female figures.[34] Thus, the male and the female protagonists of the poem create a complementary conglomerate. Consequently, the *Catalogue* should not be considered to be just another glorification of male excellence hidden behind a female-centered catalog, but rather an all-encompassing glorification of excellence regardless of gender.

Genealogical References in the *Catalogue of Women*

The discursive analysis of the genealogical references in the *Catalogue* allows us to question the function of the genealogical representation of the protagonists in relation to (a) the subject of the poem as it is announced in the proem, (b) the structure of the catalogue form based on the female figures, and (c) the description of the heroines. In order to analyze the discursive form of genealogical references in the *Catalogue*, I will focus my attention only on the direct tradition of the poem that offers most of the actual 'text' of the *Catalogue*.

The uses of kinship references in the *Catalogue* could be categorized into two groups according to the number of parents mentioned. By adopting this criterion we can distinguish between the genealogical references that name one parent and those that name both parents.

In statistical terms, restricting the focus to this epic, naming the two parents of an individual is the most frequent discursive form of genealogical reference. In the context of genealogical presentation, naming the two parents of an indidivid-

---

[33] Rutherford (2000) 88 and 94. Rutherford discusses the absence of direct speech in the *Catalogue* with respect to the Odyssean *Nekyia*, which, according to his suggestion, represents an earlier stage of the non-genealogical *ehoie*-poetry. Cf. Tsagalis (2009) 169–170.
[34] See for example fr. 33a.10–36 revolving around Periclymenos, son of Nileus and Chloris and frr. 73 and 75 concerning Atalanta. Cf. Tsagalis (2009) 170 as far as it concerns a zero-degree-plot-line of the *Catalogue*.

ual functions as a mechanism of advancing the narrative. References to two parents correspond to a model that could be codified as X+Y = XY (X = parent 1; Y = parent 2; XY = descendant). This model has a prospective dimension because it is introducing new descendants in the genealogical narrative. The lodestones of the genealogical model's expressions are verbs, which denote birth. In the *Catalogue*, the subject of verbal forms such as τέκεν and γείνατο is always a female figure. The name of the father is often placed in the dative:

τοὺς δ' ἄλλους Οἰνῆϊ [τέκ'] Ἀλθαίη κυα[ν]ῷ[π]ις

And other children, dark-blue-eyed Althaia [bore] from Oineus[35]

Cat. fr. 25.14

In the poem, genealogical references naming two parents are often enriched with expressions concerning the marriage or the reproductive union.[36] Furthermore, in this context, the parents are sometimes described in genealogical terms:[37]

Ἠλεκτρύων ἵπ[π]οισι καὶ ἅρμασι κολλητ[οῖσιν
ἤγαγε Λυσιδίκην] Πέλοπος περικαλλέα [κούρην.
ἥ οἱ γείνατο παῖδ]ας ὁμὸν λέχος εἰσαναβ[ᾶσα

Elektryon with horses and closely-joined chariots
led off Lysidike, Pelops' very beautiful daughter.
She bore him sons, having gone up in the shared marriage-bed

Cat. fr. 193.10–12

There is a distinctive feature present in the discursive form of genealogical references which names the two parents of an individual, present both in the *Cata-*

---

35 Most translates: 'The others dark-eyed Althaea [bore] to Oeneus'. Throughout his translation of the poem, Most systematically translates the dative indicating the father as 'to + name of the father/masculine pronoun'. I think that the name of the father in dative could be translated as 'from + name of the father'. This translation can be also applied in the following examples, where a pronoun in dative – most of the times οἱ – indicates the father. In my opinion, the translation I am proposing fits better the context of the genealogical exposé because it allows more clearly to insist on the genealogical provenance of a descendant. Furthermore, from a gender perspective, the translation 'from + name of the father/masculine pronoun' is most adequate regarding my interpretation of the preeminent role hold by female ancestors in the *Catalogue*. Even if I follow Most's translation I add my suggestion of the translation of the dative in parentheses.
36 Rutherford (2000, 83) and Tsagalis (2009, 164–165) identify the expressions concerning the marriage and the reproductive union as *formulae* attested to in the *ehoie*.
37 Moreover, within these developed genealogical references the physical characteristics or the social status of the male and the female figures are often mentioned.

logue and in the *Theogony:* that is, the female figure-mother is systematically placed at the center of the genealogical narrative. After the description of the marriage or the reproductive union between the two parents, who are sometimes also described by brief genealogical references and adjectives, the mother is reintroduced in the narrative via the expression ἥ + verb of birth.

Νηλεύς,] καί ῥα θύγατρ' Ἀμφίονος Ἰασίδα[ο
Χλῶριν ἐ]ύζωνον θαλερὴν ποιήσατ' ἄκ[οιτιν.
ἥ δέ οἱ ἐν μ]εγάροισιν ἐγείνατο φαίδιμα τέκ[να

Neleus,] and the daughter of Iasos' son, Amphion
Chloris], he made his well-girdled vigorous [wife.
She bore him in the halls splendid children

Cat. fr. 33(a).6–8

ἥ'] οἵην ἵππο[ισι καὶ ἅρμασι κολλητοῖσι
Φ]ῶκος ἐυμμ[ελίης δόμον ἠγάγετ'³⁸ Ἀστερόδειαν
ἐκ] Φυλάκης κ[ούρην μεγαθύμου Δηϊονῆος·
ἥ τέκετο Κρῖ[σον καὶ ὑπέρθυμον Πανοπῆα
νυκτὶ μ[ι]ῆ[ι].[

Or one like her, with horses and closely-joined chariots
Phokos, well armed with ashen spear, led off to his home Asterodeia,
from Phylake, the daughter of the great-spirited Deion.
She bore Krisos and high-spirited Panopeus
in one night

Cat. fr. 58.7–11

Ἀμύ]κλας[
Λαπί]θαο θύγατ[ρα
χθονίοιο[
θεῶν ἄπ]ο κάλλος ἔ[χουσαν
ἐυπλ]όκαμον Δ[ιομ]ήδ[ην·
ἥ δ' Ὑάκινθον ἔτικτεν ἀμύ]μονά τε κρατερόν τε

] Amyklas [
Lapithes'] daughter
] of the earthly
possessing] beauty [from the gods
] beautiful-haired Diomede;
she bore Hyakinthos,] excellent and strong

Cat. fr. 171.1–6

---

38 Addition proposed by Merkelbach.

In addition to the ἥ' οἵη expression that indicates a female centered catalogic organization, the use of the ἥ γείνατο / τέκεν expression shows that the genealogical presentation of the poem is also based on female figures. Within the narrative function of the ἥ γείνατο / τέκεν expression which is to structure the genealogical narrative leading to the entry of a new offspring, we observe a particular focalization on the female mother-figure introduced by the pronoun ἥ and used as the syntactical subject of the verb denoting birth. Moreover, this expression could be considered a discursive form of a genealogical reference which only names the mother, while the father is mentioned as far as it concerns the marriage or the reproductive union. It is true that in our examples the father appears as the subject of a verb of marrying. That could lead to the argument that the focus of the passage is actually the offspring of the man who marries a woman. Nevertheless, the placement of the pronoun ἥ or the ἥ γείνατο / τέκεν expression at the beginning of the verse indicates a change of focus from the marriage to the birth of the offspring. And the introduction of the descendants operates through a focus on the mother, the subject of the verb denoting birth. This opinion is reinforced by the punctuation marks (full stop or semicolon) that precede the pronoun ἥ. I will examine in detail the function of the ἥ γείνατο / τέκεν expression in the following section.

It is necessary to add here that this particular focus on female ancestors, who hold a prominent role in the genealogical presentation of the *Catalogue*, is not connected, as Ormand argues, to the fact that the fathers are usually gods and thus not attached to a specific geographical region and thence a political structure.[39] As we can see from the examples presented in this paper, the poem deals at great length with the offspring of various women and their mortal male relatives.

Before presenting the genealogical references that name solely one parent in the *Catalogue*, we have to acknowledge that the mention of two parents can also have a retrospective dimension. This type of references is brief, infrequent, and corresponds to the general model XY (descendant of) = X (parent 1 in the genitive) + Y (parent 2 in the genitive). This discursive form is an inversion of the frequently used model X + Y = XY.

Ἀλκμήνη δ' ἄρα] μούνη ἐλ[είπ]ετο χάρμα γο[νεῦσι,
Λυσιδίκης κο]ύρ[η] καὶ ['Ηλ]εκτρύων[ος ἀγαυοῦ

---

[39] 'Those geographically local genealogies could be kept in their context only by arranging them according to the women who bore the heroes, for a simple reason: many of the *hemitheoi* are the offspring of a potent panhellenic male god and a mortal woman', Ormand (2014) 47.

> Alkmene alone was left behind as joy to her parents,
> daughter of Lysidike and illustrious Elektryon
>
> Cat. fr. 193.19–20

As suggested before, the expressions introduced by ἥ γείνατο / τέκεν can be considered as genealogical references dedicated only to the mother of an individual. Alongside this type of reference, we also find some other references that name only the father of a female or male figure. These allusions have a retrospective dimension and they follow the schema υἱός ('son') / θυγάτηρ ('daughter') / κούρη ('daughter') / παῖς ('child') / + the name of the father in genitive.[40] The reference solely to the father occurs when the descendants are the subject of the verbal forms γένοντο or ἐξεγένοντο; this discursive expression is rare[41] and its use does not exclude the presence of the mother:

> ἥ' οἷαι κο]ῦραι Πορθάονος ἐξεγέν[οντο
> τρε[ῖς, ο]ἷαί τε θεαί, περικαλλέα [ἔργ' εἰδυῖα]ι·
> τ[ά]ς ποτε [Λ]αο[θό]η κρείουσ' Ὑπερηῒς ἀ[μύ]μων
> γεί]νατο Παρθᾶνος [θ]α[λ]ερὸν λέχ[ος] ε[ἰσ]αναβᾶσα
>
> Or like them: the daughters who were born from Porthaon,
> three, like goddesses, [skilled] in very beautiful [works];
> whom once [Laothoe], blameless ruler of Hyperesia,
> bore after she went up into Porthaon's vigorous marriage-bed.
>
> Cat. fr. 26.5–8

In fact, genealogical references mentioning only the father of an individual are abundant in the last section of the poem dedicated to the presentation of Helen's suitors. Within this catalogue, every hero is introduced by the expression ἐκ + place of origin + verb (ἐ)μνᾶτο;[42] the portrait of a suitor is completed by the use of genealogical references,[43] which are, only in this part of the poem, exclusively dedicated to the father. Cingano observes a change between the female-centered structure of the *Catalogue* and the 'male focus' of the presentation of Helen's suitors, a part of the poem that ensures the transition to another subject: the Trojan War and the annihilation of the demi-gods.[44] Yet Helen's wooers are competing in wealth because it is the richest man who will win her hand. Con-

---

[40] Among a plethora of examples see frr. 37.9, 43a.2, 58.9, 70.9, 198.9, 199.5, 200.2 and 204.56.
[41] See also fr. 26.29. Cf. fr. 35.10.
[42] See for example frr. 197.7, 198.2, 199.4, 200.3, 204.44. For a detailed analysis see Cingano (2005) 131–133. I add the expression ἐκ τῆς + γένετο ('from her was born'), fr. 70.36.
[43] Only Ajax's ancestors are not mentioned, fr. 204.44.
[44] Cingano (2005) 122–124 and 131–132. Cf. Ziogas (2013) 20–27.

sequently, these suitors in the *Catalogue* are deprived of any kind of physical or spiritual description, in contrast to the description of the commander chiefs in the *Catalogue of Ships* in the *Iliad* where the status and martial capacities of each hero are emphasized.⁴⁵ In this last section of the *Catalogue*, genealogical references naming only the father elucidate the wealth of each suitor, a necessary condition for marrying Helen.⁴⁶

Female Ancestors

The development of the genealogical narrative in *the Catalogue* is based on kinship references that make an allusion to the two parents. Giving a prospective dimension to the poem, this kind of referencing is structured around a verb of birth and guarantees a central place to female figures who are the subjects of the verbal forms τέκεν and γείνατο. Moreover, the focus on female figures operates through the frequent use of the expression ἥ γείνατο / τέκεν, which reintroduces the female character. In order to discuss the narrative function of this expression I will use fr. 23a as an example.

The genealogical narrative of this fragment begins with the daughters of Thestios and Eurythemiste (Leda, Althaia, and Hypermestra). This particular genealogical branch, which represents the seventh-generation offspring of Aiolos' daughter Kalyke, is remarkably long and stands before the presentation of Aiolos' sons.⁴⁷ Thestios' name does not occur in fragment 23a but, according to West, he would be introduced in the poem within an ἥ' οἵη dedicated to his mother, Demodike, daughter of Agenor and lover of Ares (fr. 22). The name of Thestios' spouse, Eurythemiste, appears in fr. 26.⁴⁸ In fact, Eurythemiste and Thestios are cousins since she is the daughter of Porthaon, Demodike's brother.

---

45 'The catalogue of Helen's suitors is a good example of how the *Catalogue* reduces the heroes of the *Iliad* to a footnote', Ziogas (2013) 27. Only Ajax is described as an excellent warrior, fr. 204.44. Moreover the genealogical references to the chiefs in the Catalogue of Ships are not exclusively dedicated to male ancestors. On the contrary the female ancestors are also mentioned. See for example *Il.* 2.513, 658 and 714–715.
46 The patronymic is another discursive form of the genealogical references naming solely the father. Having a retrospective dimension the patronymics do not occur in the prospective references structuring the genealogical narrative but they do describe a male or female figure when he/she is mentioned as ancestor. Patronymics are frequent in the *Catalogue* and even more so in the *Helenae Proci* section.
47 As it has been mentioned above, the marriages and the offspring of Aiolos' daughters precede those of his sons. See West (1985) 39 and 62–63.
48 Εὐρ]υθεμίστην τε Στρατ[ο]νίκην [τ]ε̣ Σ̣τ[ε]ρ̣ό̣π̣ην τε, fr. 26.9.

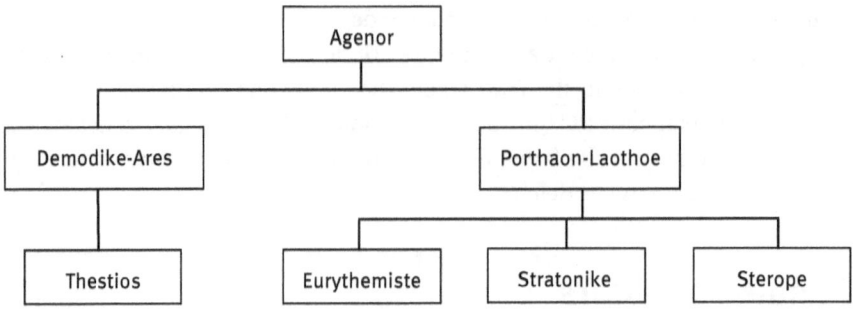

The marriage between these two cousins is mentioned at the end of fr. 26:

Θέσ[τ]ιος ἱππόδ[α]μος δ[
ἠγάγεθ' ἵππ[ο]ισίν τε [καὶ ἅρμασι κολλητοῖσι
μυρία ἔ[δ]να [πο]ρώ[ν

horse-taming Thestios [
he led off (scil. to marriage) with his horses [and closely-joined chariots
presenting] countless wedding-gifts [

Cat. fr. 26.35–37

If we accept the order of the fragments in the edition by Merkelbach and West, we observe a chronological problem in the narrative timeline: Eurythemiste and Thestios' marriage (fr. 26) is presented after the ἠ' οἵη concerning their daughters (fr. 23a). It could be possible that the descendants of Eurythemiste and Thestios were also mentioned in fragment 26 as we only have access to parts of it. If that is the case, then Leda, Althaia, and Hypermestra would be mentioned twice in the *Catalogue:* one time in the ἠ' οἵη of Demodike, their paternal grandmother (fr. 23a), and one time in the ἠ' οἵη of Porthaon's daughters, their maternal grandfather (fr. 26). Regardless of the possibility that they may be mentioned twice, we could consider changing the order of the fragments and place fr. 26 before 23a.[49] Given the flexibility that characterizes the catalogue form,[50] we could also suggest that the ἠ' οἵη of Eurythemiste and Thestios' daughters such as it is presented in fragment 23(a) could also be part of fr. 26. Either way, the possibility of the double mention of Eurythemiste and Thestios' daughters shows that the genealogical presentation of Agenor's descendants is structured around female

---

49 Concerning the order of the fragments, see the West's argument (1985) 62. In the most recent editions, Hirschberger (2004) and Most (2007), the editors did not question the order of these fragments in Merkelbach and West's edition.
50 Cf. note 14.

figures placed at the center of the narrative because of the use of the ἡ' οἵη expression and the use of the ἥ + birth verb expression.

Returning to the analysis of fragment 23a, the introduction of Leda, Althaia, and Hypermestra is followed by a description and by the adjective (θεαί, l. 4) that suggests a parallelism[51] between the three figures and the goddesses.[52] According to Hirschberger, what is left from the sixth line could be a designation of Leda introduced via Aitolos' name, one of her ancestors (of a fifth generation).[53] The focus on Leda becomes more obvious from the seventh verse, beginning with the relative pronoun ἥ. Through the use of this pronoun, Leda stays in the center of the brief description concerning her fecund union with Tyndareos.

With a retelling of her beauty (l. 9), Leda preserves her lead role as the subject of the verb of birth. In this context, Tyndareos is not mentioned. The beauty of Leda's daughters (Timandra, Klytaimestra, and Phylonoe) is, like her own, praised. In particular, Phylonoe resembles the goddesses, just like her female ancestors (l. 10). Moreover, she is immortal like the divinities. Her description serves to introduce us to the motif of the immortalization of παρθένοι bestowed by Artemis.[54]

τὴν[   ]ἰο]χέαιρα,
θῆκ[εν δ' ἀθάνατον καὶ ἀγήραον ἤ]ματα πάντ[α

She   ] Arrow-shooter,
and she made [her immortal and ageless all her days.

Cat. fr. 23a.11–12

Starting from the next verse, the focus shifts to Klytaimestra, Leda's second daughter:

γῆμ[ε δ' ἑὸν διὰ κάλλος ἄναξ ἀνδρ]ῶν Ἀγαμέμνων
κού[ρην Τυνδαρέοιο Κλυταιμήσ]τρην κυανῶπ[ιν·
ἣ τ[έκεν Ἰφιμέδην καλλίσφυ]ρον ἐν μεγάρο[ισιν
Ἠλέκτρην θ' ἣ εἶδος ἐρήριστ' ἀ[θανά]τῃσιν.

Because of her beauty] Agamemnon, [lord of men,] married
Tyndareos'] daughter, dark-eyed [Clytemestra;
she [bore beautiful-ankled Iphimede] in the halls
and Elektra who contended in beauty with the immortal goddesses.

Cat. fr. 23a.13–16

---

51 On parallelism as a stylistic feature of the *Catalogue*, see Tsagalis 199–201, 212 (this volume).
52 In addition, Hypermestra is described individually: βοῶπις ('cow-eyed', l. 5).
53 Hirschberger (2004) 207.
54 Regarding Phylonoe see also Apollod. *Bibl.* 3.10.6 and Hirschberger (2004) 208–209. Concerning the immortalization of young girls by Artemis, see for example Larson (1995) 116–118.

Klytaimestra's story begins with her wedding to Agamemnon. The motive for this marriage is clearly explained in line 13: her beauty. The allusion to Klytaimestra's beauty, a common characteristic of Eurythemiste and Thestios' female descendants, is continued to the next line where the heroine's portrait is enriched further by a short genealogical reference dedicated to her father. Paternal reference alone is a frequently feature employed to describe the context of a marriage since it allows for the legal identification of a person and explains the alliance between two kingdoms. But more than just indicating the alliance between Sparta and Mykenai, this particular reference to Tyndareos echoes the section devoted to Helen's suitors, where Agamemnon is presented as γαμβρός ('son-in-law', fr. 197.4–5) of Klytaimestra's father and the Dioskouroi. Explaining the relationship between Agamemnon and Tyndareos serves not just to clarify the right under which the king of Mykenai woos Helen on behalf of his brother, but also to elucidate why he himself is not one of the suitors.[55] Furthermore, this reference to Klytaimestra's father could be making a distinction between the children of Leda and Tyndareos and the children of Leda and Zeus.[56]

Klytaimestra and Agamemnon's children are introduced in fragment 23a by the expression ἣ τέκεν (l. 15). This discursive form not only reintroduces Klytaimestra in the genealogical narrative but also brings a different focus to the female figure, as mother, the only protagonist of the action of birth. Agamemnon is mentioned as husband – he is the subject of the verb of marrying (l. 13) – but not as a father. As discussed before, the episode of the marriage is separated from the introduction of the offspring, initiated by the expression ἣ τέκεν (l. 15) at the beginning of the verse, which is preceded by a semicolon. The expression ἣ τέκεν designates Klytaimestra, who gives birth to three children, Elektra, Iphimede, and Orestes, the daughters as beautiful as their female ancestors. Elektra, like her aunt Phylonoe (l. 10), even rivals the immortal goddesses in beauty (l. 16).

After this brief description of Elektra, and before the introduction of Orestes, the genealogical presentation is interrupted by the lengthy story of Iphimede (l. 17–26). Like Helen, and of course Achilleus, Iphimede plays an important role in the beginning of the expedition to Troy. In fragment 23a her sacrifice is the necessary condition for the Achaians to leave Aulis (l. 17–19) but due to

---

[55] Agamemnon's role in the catalogue of Helen's suitors is discussed in Cingano (2005) 135–140.
[56] See n. 62.

the intervention of Artemis the young girl is saved and becomes immortal and ageless (ll. 21–24).⁵⁷

From a philological point of view, this episode is considered a later interpolation in the *Catalogue*.⁵⁸ Without entering into this debate, I would like to stress that this narrative part of fragment 23(a), dedicated to a female figure, reinforces the argument that this fragment focuses on female protagonists.

The linear genealogical presentation that was interrupted continues in line 27 via a new focus on Klytaimestra, subject of the verb of birth (γείνατο, l. 28) placed at the beginning of the verse. This is true even if her union with Agamemnon is mentioned in the context of the sexual union:

λοῖσθον δ' ἐν μεγά[ροισι Κλυτ]αιμήστρη κυα[νῶπις
γείναθ' ὑποδμηθ[εῖσ' Ἀγαμέμν]ον[ι δῖ]ον Ὀρέ[στην

As the last one in the [halls, the dark-eyed Clytemestra,]
overpowered by [Agamemnon], bore godly Orestes.

Cat. fr. 23a.27–28

The two following lines are introduced with the pronoun ὅς, putting Orestes in the center of the narration, thus concluding the biography of Klytaimestra:

ὅς ῥα καὶ ἡβήσας ἀπε[τείσατο π]ατροφο[ν]ῆα,
κτεῖνε δὲ μητέρα [ἣν ὑπερήν]ορα νηλέι [χαλκῶι

who (sc. Orestes) when he reached puberty [took vengeance] on his father's murderer, and he killed his [over-manly] mother with the pitiless [bronze.

Cat. fr. 23a.29–30

---

57 Iphigeneia is named Iphimede in the *Catalogue*. It is interesting to note that 'Iphigeneia' means 'the strength of the *genos*' and Iphimede 'the strength of μέδομαι', "thinking". The adjective Ἀργειώνης in line 20 of fragment 23a designates Helen who is often named Ἀργείη in the *Catalogue*: frr. 200.2, 204.4, 204.55, 204.62. Cf. Hirschberger (2004) 211. Regarding Iphigeneia and Helen, see Lyons (1997) 161: 'If Helen is the *casus belli*, without Iphigeneia the Trojan War could not have taken place'. Cf. *ibid.* 138–139, 148–149 and 162. Iphigeneia's sacrifice resembles Polyxene's, daughter of Priamos and Hekabe, which takes place at the end of the Trojan War. In both cases Achilleus is involved. See Hughes (1991) 189. In Eur. *IA* 1574, Achilleus says that Iphigeneia was offered to Artemis in Aulis because of her 'pure blood': ἄχραντον αἷμα καλλιπαρθένου δέρης. According to Sebillote Cuchet (2004, 145) 'plutôt que son sexe, l'intouché est bien son sang qui est encore celui de son père, tant qu'elle ne l'a pas mêlé en ses enfants, à celui d'autre *génos*'. This argument could further be accentuated by the etymology of Iphigeneia's name.

58 See Solmsen (1981) 353–358, Hughes (1991) 84–85 and Lyons (1997) 142; see also Ormand 126–133 (this volume).

Even if the narrator designates the conditions of Agamemnon and Klytaimestra's death and also her relationship with Aigisthos,[59] he does not centralize its narration on this part of Klytaimestra's biography. On the contrary, in the fragment 23a the ancestral status and the beauty of the heroine loom large (βοῶπις fr. 23a.9 and κυανῶπις, fr. 23a.14, 27).[60] This focus on Klytaimestra as protagonist indicates that in the *Catalogue* female figures are not judged but glorified like heroes. However, since in the *Catalogue* the deaths of the heroines are not mentioned, Klytaimestra's death may be the only example.[61]

After the presentation of Klytaimestra's offspring, the genealogical narrative continues to Timandra's story:

Τιμάνδρην δ' Ἔχε[μος θαλερὴν] ποιήσατ' ἄκ[οιτιν,
ὃς πάσης Τεγ[έης ἠδ' Ἀρκαδίης] πολυμήλου
ἀφνειὸς ἤνασ[σε, φίλος μακάρεσσι θ]ε̣ο[ῖ]σιν·
ἥ οἱ Λαόδοκο̣ν μ[εγαλήτορα ποιμένα] λαῶν
γ]ε̣ίνα[θ]' ὑποδμη[θεῖσα διὰ] χρυσῆν Ἀφ[ροδίτην.

Echemos made Timandra his vigorous wife,
he who over all of Tegea [and Arkadia] rich in sheep
ruled, wealthy, [dear to the blessed gods;
she bore him Laodokos, [great-hearted shepherd] of the people,
overpowered because of golden [Aphrodite.

Cat. fr. 23a.31–35

After mentioning Timandra and Echemos' marriage, the poet focuses on the social status of the husband. Presenting Echemos as a glorious king has a double function: to underline the alliance between his rich kingdom and that of his spouse and also to clarify why their son, Laodokos, becomes a magnanimous king. However, the birth of Laodokos is mentioned in relation to his mother, introduced by the pronoun ἥ. The fact that Timandra and Echemos are not described by their own genealogical antecedents means that the focus lies on their descendant.

Although the last verses (37–40) of fr. 23(a) are dedicated to Kastor and Polydeukes, the Dioskouroi, the fragmentary state of these lines does not preserve any information regarding their birth and ancestry. According to a Pindar scho-

---

[59] Cf. fr. 176.
[60] Only the adjective ὑπερήν]ορα (l. 30), an addition proposed by West, describes Klytaimestra in a negative way.
[61] See Rutherford (2000) 86 and 93–96. Just like in the *Iliad* heroes earn immortality through poetry, in the *Catalogue* the heroines benefit from the poetic *kleos*. This observation is in favor of the argument that in the *Catalogue* excellent female protagonists are glorified.

liast, (*Nem.* 10.150a [iii 182.18–26 Drachmann]) the Dioskouroi were, in the *Catalogue*, sons of Leda and Zeus. We could thus argue that fragment 23(a) was divided in two parts: the presentation of Leda and Tyndareos' children and the presentation of Leda and Zeus' children.[62]

A careful study of frr. 25 and 26, which share linguistic and discursive analogies with fr. 23a, shows that they are similarly structured around female figures. But based on the above reading of fr. 23a we can draw some conclusions concerning the organization of the genealogical presentation within the fragment *and* concerning the function of the discursive form of the genealogical references in the *Catalogue*.

In fact, the arrangement of the genealogical presentation in fragment 23(a) is based on female figures who are the subjects of the birth verbs that lead to the entry of the new offspring and structure the genealogical narrative. In addition, the non-genealogical parts of the fragment are dedicated to biographies of female characters such as Phylonoe and Iphimede, while all the female figures are amply described through the use of adjectives and expressions exalting their beauty or other qualities. The male figures of the fragment are used in order to provide information regarding the marriage, and it is within this context that the royal status of Agamemnon and Echemos emerges. Furthermore, Echemos' description serves to explain the royal status of his son, while Tyndareos' name appears only in the context of his union with Leda.

Moreover, the systematic use of the expression ἣ + birth verb in fragment 23(a) places the female ancestors in the center of the genealogical presentation. This expression has a double function: the first is a narrative one, as it moves the genealogical presentation forward; the second is a semantic one, since the history and continuation of a *genos* depends on the act of birth. More than a genealogical reference naming the two parents, the discursive expression of kinship in this fragment presents the female ancestors as the protagonists of the act of birth, who are not only in charge of physically perpetuating a *genos* but are also those who authorize the genealogical identity to the newly born. In contrast to the ostensible agnatic filiations that scholarship has detected in Greek epic poems, the *Catalogue* offers another way of reading genealogies, where the moth-

---

[62] Helen does not appear in the last fragmentary lines dedicated to the descendants of Leda and Zeus. According to a Pindar scholiast (*Nem.* 10.150a [iii 182.18–26 Drachmann]) Helen wasn't Leda's daughter in the *Catalogue*. Nonetheless, in the last part of the poem, *Helenae Proci*, she is presented as the Dioskouroi's sister residing in Tyndareos' palace.

er holds an ancestral status and where the continuation of lineage depends on her.[63]

While the female figures of fr. 23a are related within a direct mother-daughter filiation, those of fr. 129 are related within an indirect filiation. Fr. 129 begins with an allusion to the myth of the Danaids and the vengeance of Lynkeus against Danaos.[64] Lynkeus and Hymermestra have a descendant, Abas.[65] The fifth line of the fragment perhaps introduces to the narrative Aglaia,[66] who rivaled the Olympian goddesses in beauty (ἣ εἶδος Ὀλυ]μπιάδεσσιν ἔριζεν, l. 5). The union of Aglaia and Abas is most likely described in the second half of line 7 ('and she went up into the common marriage-bed', καὶ ὁμὸν λέχος εἰσαναβῆναι). The birth of Proitos and Akrisios is described in line 8 starting with Aglaia:

ἣ δ' ἔτεκε Προῖτόν τ]ε̣ καὶ Ἀκρίσιον βασιλῆα[ ]
καὶ τοὺς μὲν διένασ]σε πατὴρ [ἀν]δρῶν τ[ε θε]ῶν τε·

She bore Proitos and Akrisios, king
and these the father of the men and gods settled separately

Cat. fr. 129.8–9

Verse 9 alludes to the twins' dispute,[67] resolved through Zeus' intervention: Akrisios is the king of Argos and Proitos of Tiryns. Inversing the order of the initial presentation of the twins (l. 8), the genealogical exposé continues with Akrisios:

Ἀκρίσιος μὲν ἄρ' Ἄ]ργει ἐυκτ[ίτ]ωι ἐμβασί[λ]ευεν
[   ]..ρεν ὀκριόεντ[.].[.].[
[Εὐρυ]δίκην Λακεδαί[μο]νο[ς   ]ι̣[.]
[καλλι]πάρηον ἐὺ πραπί[δεσσ'] ἀρα[ρυῖα]ν
ἣ δ' ἔτεκεν   Δανά]ην κ[α]λλίσφυρο[ν ἐν μεγάλ]ρ̣[οισιν,
ἣ Περσῆ' ἔτεκεν κρα]τε̣[ρὸ]ν μ[ήσ]τωρ[α] φόβοιο.

---

63 Patrilineal filiation is also called 'agnatic'. However, the latter term 'emphasizes the fact that the transmission of kinship is guaranteed by the male (...) In the patrilineal-filiation system, belonging to a kinship group is a right obtained through the father and the relationship with the other members of this group is exclusively structured around the male relatives (*les agnants*)', Ghasarian (1996) 60 (the translation is my own).
64 See Hirschberger (2004) 294–295. Cf. fr. 128.
65 Most translates the fragmentary third verse (ἔπειτα ἀμύμ[ονα τίκτ]εν Ἄβαντα) as 'then he (scil. Lynkeus) begot excellent Abas'. Within this translation Lynkeus is the subject of the birth verb. We can, though, consider that Hypermestra is the subject of τίκτ]εν and opt for the following translation: 'then she begot excellent Abas'.
66 See Hirschberger (2004) 295 and the critical apparatus in Merkelbach and West's edition.
67 Hirschberger (2004) 295.

Akrisios] ruled in well-founded Argos
                    ] rugged [
                    ] Lakedaimon's daughter Eurydike [
        ] beautiful-cheeked, well-fitting in her thoughts;
she bore   ] beautiful-ankled Danae in the halls
who bore Perseus,] strong counselor of fear.

Cat. fr. 23a.10 – 15

The king of Argos is joined in matrimony with Eurydike, Lakedaimon's daughter. Through the expression ἥ ἔτεκεν, the beautiful and wise Eurydike has a central place in the exposé. Her daughter, Danae, whose beauty is also mentioned, gives birth to Perseus (ἥ ἔτεκεν). The use of the expression ἥ + birth verb in two successive lines emphasizes the female figures. The fact that the name of Perseus' father, Zeus, is not even mentioned favors this interpretation.[68]

The description of Proitos, which introduces the presentation of his descendants, stresses his royal status; a description aligned with the one dedicated to his brother in the line 10.

Προῖτος δ' αὖ Τίρυ]νθα ἐυκ[τ]ίμε[νο]ν πτολίεθρον
νάσσατο καὶ κούρη]ν μεγαλήτορος Ἀρκασίδα[ο
γῆμεν Ἀφείδαντο]ς καλ[λι]πλόκαμον Σ[θ]ενέβοι[αν
              ].[..].ες [
       ].σοι Σθεν[έ]βοια βοῶπις
       ]ὁμὸν λέχος εἰσαναβᾶσα
κούρη Ἀφείδαντος με]γαλήτ[ο]ρο[ς] Ἀρκασίδα[ο
       περικ]αλλέα ἔργ' εἰδυίας
Λυσίππην τε καὶ Ἰφι]νόην καὶ Ἰφιάνασσαν

But Proitos dwelt in Tiryns,] the well-founded city,
and the daughter of Apheidas,] great-hearted Arkas' son,
he married,] beautiful-haired Stheneboia
                    ][
                    ]cow-eyed Stheneboia
       ], going up into the shared marriage-bed,
the daughter of Apheidas,] great-hearted Arkas' son,
              ] skilled in very beautiful works:
Lysippe and Iphinoe] and Iphianassa.

Cat. fr. 129.16 – 24

Proitos marries Stheneboia, the daughter of Apheidas, son of Arkas. The genealogical reference to the male ancestors of Stheneboia is repeated three lines later in order to accompany anew the name of the heroine. This retrospective genea-

---

[68] Zeus is perhaps mentioned as Perseus' father in fragment 135. See Hirschberger (2004) 296.

logical reference concerns firstly Stheneboia and secondly her father. Arkas is not directly presented as her grandfather, but as Apheidas' father.

Through this double allusion to her male ancestors, Stheneboia is described as an Arkadian heroine; her female ancestors are also related to Arkadia.[69] This suggests an alliance between the kingdom of her father in Arkadia and her husband's kingdom in Tiryns, perhaps formed against the kingdom of Argos ruled by Akrisios. In an analogous way the reference to Lakedaimon, the father of Eurydike, wife of Akrisios (l. 12), could reinforce the twin's claim to Argos. In fr. 129 the female figures are introduced in the narrative through retrospective genealogical references dedicated to their fathers; here these references have an essential function in showing the formation of the region's geopolitical map.

Stheneboia gives birth to three girls, generally known after their patronymic Proitids. Unfortunately, the verb of birth is not preserved in this context, but for the present we may consider that the supplementation of γείνατο in line 21 as valid. According to indirect sources, the story of Lysippe, Iphinoe, and Iphianassa was recounted in the *Catalogue*.[70]

Based on this reading of fr. 129 we can suggest that the expression ἥ + birth verb is used in the context of the genealogical presentation not only to introduce a direct female filiation, as in the case of fr. 23a (Leda – Klytaimestra – Iphimede), but also to describe the act of birth by a female ancestor introduced in the genealogical narrative as spouse (Aglaia – Akrisios and Eurydike – Danae).

---

69 Arkas rules the Pelasgians of Peloponnesos, hence the denomination 'Arkadians'. With the Nymph Hamadryad Chrysopeleia he has two sons, Apheidas and Elatos, who share the kingdom of Arkadia with Azan, his third son mothered by the nymph Erato:

Kallisto – Zeus
|
Arkas – Crysopeleia
|
Apheidas

70 The reference to the house of their father in l. 25 (δώματα πατρός) suggests that their story was also told in the missing lines of fr. 129. This story is already mentioned in another context (fr. 37) and it is the subject of frr. 130–133, through an indirect tradition. According to frr. 131 and 132, Proitos' daughters would have been struck by mania because they rejected Dionysos' rituals. Proitos asks Melampous to cure his daughters and Melampous asks for two-thirds of his kingdom in exchange. Melampous gives one-third to his brother Bias. On the triple division of Tiryns' kingdom, see Finkelberg (1991) who demonstrates, based on a comparison between the male and female genealogical lines of Tiryns' royal house, that the queens have access to the throne following a mother-daughter criterion. Meanwhile, the kings who come from Megapenthes, Melampous and Bias succeed to the throne in rotation. According to Finkelberg (1991) 311, the purpose of this arrangement is to ensure male succession based on marriage with women coming from the same royal lineage.

Hence the expression ἤ + birth verb functions on multiple levels: it operates as a narrative focus on a female figure but also indicates the bond between the wife and the genealogical line of her husband; this connection is assured through the act of birth, which concerns the mother and the child. Regardless of whether the mother is introduced as a spouse or as a descendent, it is still the female figures that assure, through the act of birth, the integration of a descendant into a genealogical line and the *genos*' legitimacy. Consequently, and because of the systematic use of the ἤ + birth verb expression in the *Catalogue*, I suggest that the female ancestors are poetically recognized as ancestors even when the female figure appears in a genealogical line as a spouse. That is how the status of the heroines is acknowledged and glorified within the poem.

The prominent role of mothers in the genealogies of the *Catalogue* is also supported by the fact that in other epic poems, male father figures are sometimes presented as the subjects of verbs denoting birth.[71] Thus the absence of such syntax in the *Catalogue* indicates that the placement of the mothers as subjects of the birth verbs is a narrative choice that leads to the poetic recognition of female ancestors.

The notoriety of their status is further attested through the ἤ' οἵη of Mestra, the daughter of Erysichthon and spouse of Glaukos, son of Sisyphos (fr. 43a).[72] Despite his intelligence, Sisyphos could neither prevent nor stop Mestra's escape who, after her marriage, goes back to her father's house. Sisyphos' efforts to make her return to her husband's house are in vain because:

ὡς οὔ οἱ δοῖεν Γλαύκωι γένος Οὐρανίωνες
ἐκ Μήστρης καὶ σπέρμα μετ' ἀνθρώποισι λιπέσ[θαι.

That Sky's children would not grant to Glaukos a race
Arising from Mestra and progeny to be left among human beings.

Cat. fr. 43a.53–54

Within this phrase, which concludes the episode concerning Mestra and Glaukos, the heroine is recognized as the potential founder of a generation that would continue Sisyphos' *genos*. More than the title of the mother, the acknowledgement attributed to Mestra is her role as the essential ancestor. Without her the *genos* is doomed to disappear.

With Glaukos' second spouse, Eurynome, Sisyphos' hopes are restored. But her child, though born in the palace of her husband, is the fruit of her union with

---

71 See for example, *Il.* 2.628, 5.800, 13.451, 20.237; *Od.* 16.118, 19.113; *Th.* 233.
72 Regarding the ἤ' οἵη of Mestra, see the analysis of Rutherford (2005) and Ormand (2014) 85–118.

Poseidon (fr. 43a.81). Glaukos, like other heroes in the *Catalogue*, becomes the mortal father of this child who is none other than Bellerephon (l. 82). From a narrative point of view, Sisyphos' efforts to secure the perpetuation of his *genos* are expressed in two different parts of the fragment, which focus on Mestra's and Eurynome's stories. That proves a poetic recognition of the role held by female figures in the continuation of a genealogical line.

Euemon's birth, himself probably a son of Euippe, one of Leukon's daughters, is expressed in analogous terms with the phrase ἐκ Μήστρης:

ἐκ τῆς δ   ]μων γένετο κρατερός τε μέγας τε

from her was born (sc. Euemon) strong and magnanimous

Cat. fr. 70.36

What seems to be the most interesting part of fr. 70 is the genealogical presentation of Eteoklos, Euippe's husband, because it names his male ancestors, going back three generations:

....]ην Ἀνδρεΐδης Ἐτέοκλος ὄπυιεν
..... Ὀρχομ]ενοῖο πάϊς Μινυηϊάδαο·

] Andreus' son Eteoklos married
] of Orchomenos, son of Minyas;

Cat. fr. 70.34–35

If West's hypothesis that Minyas is the seventh son of Aiolos is correct, Eteoklos would then be the grandchild of the grandchild of Aiolos:

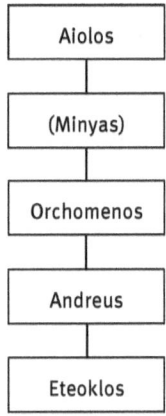

In addition, his spouse would also be a third-generation descendant of Aiolos. The male-centered genealogical references that describe Eteoklos indicate a relationship between husband and wife. But the discursive form of the kinship references shows that the narrator can go back up to three generations of an individual's male genealogical line in order to indicate its origins and royal status.

I will conclude by comparing the discursive form of the male genealogical references of frr. 70 and 165:

ἣ τέκε] Τήλεφον Ἀρκασίδην Μυσῶν βασιλῆ[α,
μιχθε]ῖσ' ἐν φιλότητι βίηι Ἡρακληείηι

She bore Telephos, Arkas' descendant, king of the Mysians
mingling] in the desire of Herakles' force.

Cat. fr. 165.8–9

The syntactic subject of the birth verb τέκε is Auge: she is Aleos' daughter, who is the son of Apheidas, one of Arkas' three sons. Telephos then, son of Auge and Herakles, is described as Ἀρκασίδης that refers to his fourth-generation maternal ancestor. It is possible that through this reference, the poet aims to dissociate Telephos from the other descendants of Herakles and to reinforce his Arkadian origins coming from his mothers' side. Regardless, this fragment testifies to the use of a term that names a maternal ancestor of four generations before the individual, which is significant for the poetic recognition of female ancestors.

In both frr. 70 and 165, the genealogical references have a retrospective dimension. In fr. 70, the genealogical identity is expressed through the use of successive references to the father that go back progressively, generation by generation, until the male ancestor of the third generation, Eteoklos. In fr. 165, though, the narrator does not follow the same procedure. Given the fact that Arkas is the fourth-generation ancestor in Telephos' maternal genealogical line, the poet does not trace progressively the genealogical line of Auge. In place of the references that individually name the fathers in fr. 70, Telephos' genealogical identity is described with the patronymic Ἀρκασίδης. Through his mother he is directly attached to the *genos* of Arkas, without needing to name each of his maternal ancestors tracing back to Arkas. Through the discursive form of the genealogical references in these two fragments we could thus suggest that the narrative function of genealogical references to the mother is, in part, to link a descendant directly to a kinship group. In the *Catalogue*, female ancestors continue a *genos* and carry its story forward. The discursive form of the genealogical references to the male ancestors, naming directly only the ancestors of the first generation before an individual (father-descendant) indicates that the male ancestors can only be recognized through their first-degree kinship relationships.

Bibliography

Boehringer, S. and V. Sebillotte Cuchet. (2011). *Hommes et femmes dans l'antiquité grecque et romaine*, Paris.
Bouvier, D. (2002). *Le sceptre et la lyre. L'Iliade ou les héros de la mémoire*, Grenoble.
Calame, C. (1996). *L'Eros dans la Grèce antique*, Paris.
Cingano, E. (2005). 'A catalogue within a catalogue: Helen's suitors in the Hesiodic *Catalogue of Women* (frr. 196–204)', in: Hunter, 118–152.
Cohen, I. M. (1986). 'The Hesiodic *Catalogue of Women* and the *Megalai Ehoiai*', *Phoenix* 40: 127–142.
Cohen, I. M. (1989/90). 'Traditional language and the women in the Hesiodic *Catalogue of Women*', *Scripta Classica Israelica* 10: 12–27.
D'Alessio, G. B. (2005). 'The *Megalai Ehoiai*: a survey of the fragments', in: Hunter, 176–216.
Depew, M. and D. D. Obbink (2000). *Matrices of genre: authors, canons, and society*, Cambridge.
Di Donato, R. (2006). *"Aristeuein" : premesse antropologiche ad Omero*, Pisa.
Doherty, L. (2006). 'Putting the Women Back into the Hesiodic *Catalogue of Women*', in: Zajko-Leonard, 297–325.
Finkelberg, M. (1991). 'Royal succession in heroic Greece', *CQ* 41: 303–316.
Fowler, R. L. (1998/1999). 'Genealogical thinking, Hesiod's *Catalogue*, and the creation of the Hellenes', *PCPS* 44: 1–19.
Ghasarian, C. (1996). *Introduction à l'étude de la parenté*, Paris.
Hirschberger, M. (2004). Gynaikōn Katalogos *und* Megalai Ēhoiai. *Ein Kommentar zu den Fragmenten zweier hesiodeischer Epen*, Munich-Leipzig.
Holmes, B. (2012). *Gender: Antiquity and its Legacy*, London and New York.
Hughes, D. (1991). *Human Sacrifice in Ancient Greece*, London.
Hunter, R. (2005). *The Hesiodic* Catalogue of Women: *constructions and reconstructions*, Cambridge and New York.
Larson, J. (1995). *Greek Heroine Cults*, Madison.
Leduc, C. (2002). 'Comment la donner en mariage? La mariée en pays grec (Ixe–IVe s. av. J.-C.)', in: Schmitt Pantel, 309–382.
Lévy, E. (1995). '*Arétè, timè, aidôs* et *némésis:* le modèle homérique', *Ktèma* 20: 177–211.
Lyons, D. (1997). *Gender and Immortality. Heroines in Ancient Greek Myth and Culture*, Princeton.
Merkelbach, R. and M. L. West (1967). *Hesiodi Fragmenta Selecta*, Oxford.
Montanari, F., A. Rengakos and C. Tsagalis (2009). *Brill's Companion to Hesiod*, Leiden and Boston.
Most, G. (2006). *Hesiod I. Theogony, Works and Days, Testimonia, Edited and Translated by G. W. Most*, Cambridge, MA and London.
Most, G. (2007). *Hesiod II. The* Shield, Catalogue of Women, *Other Fragments, Edited and Translated by G. W. Most*, Cambridge, MA and London.
Ormand, K. (2014). *The Hesiodic* Catalogue of Women *and Archaic Greece*, New York.
Osborne, R. (2005). 'Ordering women in Hesiod's *Catalogue*', in: Hunter, 5–24.
Perceau, S. (2002). *La parole vive. Communiquer en catalogue dans l'épopée homérique*, Louvain and Paris.

Rutherford, I. (2000). 'Formulas, voice and death in the *Ehoie*-poetry, the Hesioc *Gynaikon Katalogos* and the Odysseain *Nekuia*', in: Depew-Obbink, 81–96.

Rutherford, I. (2005). 'Mestra at Athens: Hesiod fr. 43 and the poetics of panhellenism', in: Hunter, 99–117.

Sammons, B. (2010), *The Art and Rhetoric of the Homeric Catalogue*, Oxford.

Sebillotte Cuchet, V. (2004). 'La sexualité, une histoire problématique pour les hellénistes. Détour par la "virginité" des filles sacrifiées pour la patrie', *Mètis* 2: 137–161.

Sebillotte Cuchet, V. and N. Ernoult (2007). *Problèmes du genre en Grèce Ancienne*, Paris.

Sissa, G. (1987). *Le corps virginal*, Paris.

Schmitt, J.-C (2001). *Eve et Pandora. La création de la première femme*, Paris.

Schmitt Pantel, P. (2002). *Histoire des femmes en Occident*, vol. 1: *L'Antiquité*, Paris.

Scott, J. W. (1986). 'Gender: A Useful Category of Historical Analysis', *American Historical Review:* 91/5, 1053–1075.

Scott, J. W. and B. Perreau, (2010). 'La question du genre. Entretien avec Joan Scott', *Genre, Sexualité et Société:* 4 (online).

Solmsen, F. (1981). 'The sacrifice of Agamemnon's daughter in Hesiod's "EHOEAE"', *AJP* 102: 353–358.

Tsagalis, C. (2009). 'Poetry and Poetics in the Hesiodic Corpus', in: Montanari, Rengakos, and Tsagalis, 131–177.

West, M. L. (1985). *The Hesiodic* Catalogue of Women: *its Nature, Structure and Origins*, Oxford.

Zajko, V. and M. Leonard (2006). *Laughing with Medusa*, Oxford.

Ziogas, I. (2013). *Ovid and Hesiod. The Metamorphosis of the* Catalogue of Women, Cambridge.

Benjamin Sammons
The Hesiodic *Catalogue of Women*: A Competition of Forms

It cannot be said that Homeric poetry delights in genealogy as a poetic form. Given that most of its major heroes have an impressive lineage to tell, it is remarkable how seldom they actually do so, beyond merely naming a father or grandfather.[1] Significantly, other passages suggest that the poet's avoidance of extended genealogy is deliberate and pointed, his engagement with the form itself polemical.[2] Particularly striking in this regard is the famous 'Catalogue of Women' in Book 11 of the *Odyssey* (225–330). The passage is essentially a list of women interviewed by Odysseus in the Underworld. There is no evident arrangement or basis for selection except in the fact that Odysseus uses his sword to force the shades to approach his pool of blood in single file so that he can interview them one at a time. Yet it has long been noted that many of the women enumerated belong to the genealogical stemma of the Aiolids. Indeed, several of them are closely related. The poet seems almost to go out of his way to order the women without regard for genealogy; for example, Chloris is the daughter-in-law of Tyro but the two women are separated by five entries and nothing is made of this connection.[3] By scrambling the underlying genealogical and chronological order implied in the women's identities, the poet ensures that the entries of this catalogue have no apparent relation to one another except their shared suitability to the catalogue's stated rubric, 'wives and daughter of

---

[1] Striking examples include Glaukos' recitation of his lineage to Diomedes (*Il.* 6.150–211), that of Aineas recited to Achilleus (*Il.* 20.215–241), and that of Theoklymenos recounted by the poet when Theoklymenos encounters Telemachos (*Od.* 15.238–257). Both Glaukos and Aineas preface their performances with words that appear to question whether it is worthwhile to tell or ask one's lineage. More typical is Diomedes' speech at *Il.* 14.114–125: He does indeed trace his lineage back to a great-grandfather, Portheus, but puts all the emphasis on the excellence of his own father's career (vv. 119–25), believing that this is what justifies his right to speak amongst the Achaian leaders.
[2] E.g., *Il.* 2.100–108, the famous 'genealogy of the scepter' where the poet recounts the successive owners of Agamemnon's scepter rather than (as might be expected in the context) the genealogy of the king himself. In doing so the poet alludes indirectly to the dynastic struggle between Atreus and his brother Thyestes. The passage is heavily ironic within the already ambiguous representation of Agamemnon as leader in Book 2.
[3] Cf. Steinrück (1994) 91–92, Rutherford (2000) 94, Sammons (2010) 82 (where I exaggerated the case by mistakenly calling Chloris daughter of Tyro).

heroes'.⁴ In only one case does the poet slip from the truly catalogic mode to that of genealogical narrative, namely when he names Pero as the daughter of Chloris and then goes on to tell of Pero's own wooing and marriage.⁵ This at least raises the possibility that more of the catalogue's disjointed entries could be so connected; as it is, the passage devolves into the form of a 'bare list' (consisting simply of names and epithets). Here and elsewhere Homer shows his awareness that catalogue can be constitutive of narrative, even if he seems to downplay its role in his own narrative art. In fact, these seemingly disparate forms are closely related, particularly within the context of epic tradition, in which there are many catalogic or catalogue-like narrative forms, including that of genealogical narrative.⁶

Precisely this tension between genealogy, a catalogic narrative form, and catalogue proper can be observed in the Hesiodic tradition, particularly in the *Theogony* but also (as this paper will argue in detail) in the *Catalogue of Women* or *Ehoiai* that was regularly appended to ancient texts of the *Theogony*. To judge from its proem, we would think the *Catalogue* to have been precisely what either of its titles implies, a list of exemplary women, in particular those who were able to attract divine lovers and thereby became progenitors of the heroic race of *hemitheoi* (fr. 1.1–5):⁷

> Νῦν δὲ γυναικῶν ⸤φῦλον ἀείσατε, ἡδυέπειαι
> Μοῦσαι Ὀλυμπιάδες, κοῦραι Διὸς αἰγιόχοιο,
> α̣ἳ τότ' ἄρισται ἔσαν̣ [καὶ κάλλισται κατὰ γαῖαν
> μίτρας τ' ἀλλύσαντο δ[ιὰ χρυσέην τ' Ἀφροδίτην
> μισγόμεναι θεοῖσ[ιν

> But now sing the tribe of women, beautiful-voiced
> Olympian Muses, daughters of aegis-bearing Zeus,
> those who were best in that time [and were most beautiful in the world
> and they loosened their girdles [and because of golden Aphrodite
> mingling with gods....

---

4 For the terminology see Sammons (2010) 9.
5 See my discussion in Sammons (2010) 79–81.
6 For this relation between catalogue and narrative and the category of 'catalogic narrative', see Sammons (2010) 206–208. Many notable examples can be found in Homer's own battle narratives, not only the clearly list-like sequences but also the more integrated form of the typical *aristeia*. Homer displays a playful tendency to downplay the narrative potentialities of catalogue passages despite his own reliance on the catalogue form; Hesiod's attitude is quite different, as I argue with regard to the *Theogony* in Sammons (forthcoming).
7 I cite the Loeb text of Most (2007).

Hearing these words one could well expect a poem that simply lists exemplary women who consorted with gods, each entry introduced with the formula ἠ' οἵη 'or such a one as...'. This would indeed be something very like what we see in *Odyssey* 11.[8] Yet this idea of a simple catalogue of women is not borne out by the fragments, which reveal a complicated genealogical account of the heroic race, somewhat along the lines of the *Theogony*, although considerably more complicated because of the variety of epichoric figures and traditions that had to be worked into numerous discrete genealogical stemmata.[9] Yet even to call the poem a complex genealogical narrative would be misleading. Examination of lengthier fragments reveal that Hesiod puts into play several competing structures, each of which could be seen as a distinct sub-genre of epic poetry, broadly defined: One structure is that of the catalogue, its presence sometimes (but not always) signaled by the *ehoia* formula that would be appropriate to a catalogue-poem like that staged by Homer in *Odyssey* 11. As we shall see, in the *Catalogue* as in Homer and other Hesiodic poems, catalogues provide a context not only for listing people or things, but for establishing or modifying important mythic paradigms. Another is genealogy proper, which can be regarded as catalogic narrative since it lists individuals but follows a temporal and causal sequence. Finally, there is non-catalogic structure of individual myths told in narrative digressions within catalogic or genealogical frameworks, in some cases freely developed so as to dwarf these contexts.[10] Any of these forms can work together or against one another. Catalogue proper is indispensable to genealogical narrative (e.g., to list multiple offspring of a single set of progenitors), yet the purely catalogic mode evoked by the *ehoia* formula (poem as list of exemplary women) is necessarily in tension with the genealogical program, which aims to be comprehensive rather than exemplary.[11] The simple narrative element can complement the *ehoia* structure (women are named as exemplary precisely because there is a story to tell about them) but can also be introduced as essentially digressive elaborations within the genealogical framework (whenever an individual is named, a story might be told of him or her). The *ehoia* can be used to soften the necessarily abrupt transition when an increasingly complicated genealogical narrative forces the poet to move from one branch to another. At the same time the *ehoiai*, since they apparently featured tales of women seduced or raped by gods, maintain this dominant paradigm as a central

---

[8] Rutherford (2000) 93–94, Hirschberger (2004) 30–31.
[9] Cf. Hirschberger (2004) 67–70.
[10] As the tale of Bellerophontes does in the genealogy of Glaukos from *Iliad* 6.
[11] Cf. Rutherford (2000) 91–93.

leitmotiv within the larger genealogical aim of the poem.[12] Yet narrative digressions can either hinder or aid the advance of the genealogical program (e. g., stories about women often narrate their resistance or acquiescence to sexual advances). Finally, it appears that narrative digressions within the genealogical program could be used to tell stories of broader scope than could be communicated in a single passage. So the myth of Herakles was told piecemeal, and perhaps in reverse chronological order, through various narrative elaborations scattered throughout the genealogical framework,[13] and there is much to suggest the poem as a whole developed into an historical narrative explaining the origins of the Trojan War.[14]

Such an interplay of forms can be observed in the *Theogony*. Here, too, we see a catalogic genealogical narrative that soon becomes too complicated to follow in a straight chronology, forcing the poet to make various jumps in time to pursue different genealogical branches. Here, too, we see the element of pure catalogue, particularly where many offspring of a single set of parents are listed, and free use of such contexts to pursue themes or paradigms that in turn become important to the poem.[15] Here, too, we see narrative digressions, at least two of which (the story of Prometheus and Zeus' battle with Typhoeus) are pursued at such length as to overshadow their immediate context. The *Theogony* also traces a larger historical narrative, the so-called 'Succession Myth', which tells of how Zeus and the Olympians came to power. It can be argued further that this poem stages a competition of forms of the kind I have suggested for the *Catalogue*: It begins as a predominately genealogical poem, interspersed with catalogues and relatively brief narrative digressions, but as the Succession Myth begins to take on historical shape and the purely narrative element begins to dominate over the genealogical element, an evolution of forms unfolds that closely parallels the changing form of the cosmos this poem describes.[16]

Since it undertook to treat the entire history of the heroic age, the *Catalogue* could not possibly have had the same kind of unity as the *Theogony*. Neverthe-

---

[12] Cf. Ziogas (2013) 66.
[13] Haubold (2005) 86–94.
[14] Clay (2005), esp. 29–32.
[15] Effects can range from the purely thematic, as in the almost allegorical shape of the catalogue of Nereids or the progeny of Night (cf. Brown 1953, 85–87, Solmsen 1949, 38–40), to a truly paradigmatic dimension that emphasizes the repetition of narrative patterns, as in the catalogue of Iapetids that gives rise to the major narrative concerning Prometheus (Muellner 1996, 82–87, Loney 2014, 506–510). For the paradigmatic dimension of Homeric catalogues, see Sammons (2010) 208–209.
[16] I argue this in detail in Sammons (forthcoming).

less, lengthy fragments preserved through papyri, largely from the popular first half of the poem, allow us to see a complicated interplay of forms, and perhaps even the nature of their evolution as the poem itself progressed. The introduction of the first major genealogical stemma, that of the Aiolids, features a methodical opening that ramifies into a complex interplay of genealogical narrative, catalogue proper, and free narrative elaboration, each form being used to generate paradigmatic themes and to modify themes that are already well-established in the text. The *ehoia* device may have been used, as noted above, to bridge discontinuities when complex genealogical stemmata made back-tracking necessary, but this does not seem to be the whole story. It also serves as a marker for lengthier narrative elaborations, some of which complicate or pointedly retard the advance of the genealogical program, and may have continued to evoke an idea that the poem was, in a more than vestigial sense, a list of exemplary women. In an interesting development which we will have occasion to observe, the formula could be used to introduce not only individual women but sets of women, i.e., miniature catalogues of women embedded within the genealogies.

The Family of Aiolos: Getting Started

Aiolos appears first as one of the three sons of Hellen in fr. 9:[17]

Ἕλληνος δ' ἐγένοντο φιλοπτολέμου βασιλῆος
Δῶρός τε Ξοῦθός τε καὶ Αἴολος ἱππιοχάρμης

From Hellen the war-loving king were born
Doros and Xouthos and Aiolos who delights in horses.

Fr. 10 shows a characteristic method of the poet: He will name the offspring of a single progenitor in the form of a list, with no elaboration beyond the occasional formulaic epithet. He then inserts the individuals named into his genealogical program through a more elaborate catalogue whose entries include the descendants of each individual up to several generations. In this expansion of list into catalogue[18] the poet also makes room for the development of themes, paradigmatic patterns, and larger historical form. Accordingly, the three brothers listed in fr. 9 are taken up in fr. 10 through just such an elaborate catalogue, each occupying an entry featuring further genealogical information. They are taken up

---

[17] For a skeptical assessment of this fragment (not explicitly attributed to Hesiod) see Heilinger (1983) 28–29.
[18] For the distinction between list and catalogue, see Sammons (2010) 9–10.

in the order in which they are listed, the first two with relative brevity, the last in a way that provides a gateway to still further ramifications of the genealogical program.[19] The highly lacunose verses 1–19 record the birth from Doros of Aigimios, father in turn of Dyman and Pamphylos (v. 7), and Iphthime along with perhaps four other daughters (cf. fr. 11) ancestors of nymphs, satyrs and Kouretes (vv. 13–19). Xouthos is dealt with even more briefly (fr. 10.20–24):[20]

> Ξοῦθ]ος δὲ Κ[ρείουσαν ἐπή]ρατον εἶδος ἔχ[ουσαν
> κούρ]ην καλλ[ιπάρηον Ἐρε]χθῆος θείοιο
> ἀθανά]των ἰ[ότητι φίλην ποι]ήσατ' ἄκ[οι]τιν,
> ἥ οἱ Ἀ]χαιὸν ἐγ[είνατ' Ἰάον]ά τε κλυ]τόπωλ[ο]ν
> μιχθεῖσ' ἐν [φιλότητι καὶ εὐε]ιδέα Διομήδην.

> Xouthos married Kreiousa who had a beautiful appearance
> the lovely-cheeked daughter of divine Erechtheus
> by the will of the gods he made her his dear wife
> she bore to him Achaios and Ion famous for his horses
> mingling with him in love, and beautiful Diomede.

Aiolos comes next with a list of his sons (25–30):

> Αἰολίδαι δ' ἐγένοντο θεμιστοπόλοι βασιλῆες
> Κρηθεύς τ' ἠδ' Ἀθάμας καὶ Σίσυφος αἰολομήτης
> Σαλμωνεύς τ' ἄδικος καὶ ὑπέρθυμος Περιήρης
> Δηϊών] τε μέγ[ας   ] τ' ἀριδείκετος ἀνδρῶν
> οἵ πατρὸς ὑψηλοῖς ἐν δώμ]ασιν ἡβώοντες
>   [τ]έκοντό τε κύδιμα τέκνα·

> But these children of Aiolos were born, scepter-bearing kings:
> Kretheus and Athamas and swift-thinking Sisyphus
> and Salmoneus the unjust and arrogant Perieres
> and Deion,] huge and distinguished among men.
> They in their father's lofty house] coming to manhood
> ...] begat famous children ...

After this brief indication that the sons themselves generated notable offspring, the poet immediately offers a list of Aiolos's daughters (31–34):

---

[19] Doros and his descendants occupy verses 1–19, Xouthos verses 20–24, while Aiolos' descendants were pursued apparently through the rest of Book 1 and perhaps further. Admittedly we don't know how many lines were devoted to Doros before the beginning of fr. 1.
[20] In the case of such lacunose fragments I do not try to work the bracketing into my translation.

αὖτις δ' Αἰναρέτη τέκεν Αἰόλωι] εὐνη[θεῖσ[α
ἠϋκόμους κούρας πολυήρ]ατον ε̣ἶδος ἐχούσας,
Πεισιδίκην τε καὶ Ἀλκυόνη]ν Χ[αρ]ί̣τ̣ε̣σσιν ὁμοίας
καὶ Καλύκην Κανάκην τε καὶ ε]ὐ̣ειδέ[α] Π̣ε̣ριμήδην·

Going to bed [with Aiolos, Ainarete bore to him]
lovely-haired daughters] holding a very beautiful appearance,
Peisidike and Alkyone,] like to the Graces,
and Kalyke and Kanake] and beautiful Perimede.

As is readily apparent, the text here is highly fragmentary, preserving only the name of Perimede. The rest of fr. 10 virtually guarantees the identity of the other daughters, and the order in which they are named in the restored text is at least highly probable for reasons discussed below.[21] The further descendants of Aiolos, through these daughters and sons, will be developed in great detail in the ever-more elaborate genealogical program – indeed, according to West's reconstruction, this work occupied the remainder of Book 1 and some of Book 2.[22] We will trace this further, but here it is worth noting that the catalogue of the sons of Hellen shows three types of genealogical outcome: Doros is ultimately the progenitor of mythical or semi-divine races, i.e., nymphs, satyrs and Kouretes. Xouthos is ultimately the progenitor of two major Greek ethnic groups through his sons Achaios and Ion. Aiolos's line, finally, leads into the race of heroes proper, which was evidently the subject of the poem as a whole. The first two outcomes are, as it were, genealogical dead-ends.[23] It is only the third that really moves the genealogical program forward.

The Daughters of Aiolos

It was evidently the poet's standard procedure, when dealing with a larger brood including both sons and daughters, to take up the daughters first and then backtrack to give an account of the sons. Accordingly, we see in the remains of fr. 10

---

[21] Peisidike is named in lines 100, Alkyone in line 96 (where the mythic content guarantees her identity anyway). An account of Kalyke's famous son Endymion can be discerned in vv. 60–62. Kanake is restored to the list from the closely related account of Apollodoros (*Bibl.* 1.7.3), where all the other names are found.
[22] West (1985) 41–42.
[23] As West (1985) 59 notes, 'Achaios and Iaon .... were probably not mentioned again. We understand that they gave their names to peoples; they need no sons. Aiolos' children are listed in the succeeding verses, introducing the whole vast section of the poem devoted to their descendants'.

that the poet takes up the daughters of Aiolos first and leaves the sons for later.[24] As with the sons of Hellen, the poet uses the procedure of first naming the daughters in a simple list and then introducing them to the genealogical program with a more elaborate catalogue. What is interesting here is that while at least several of these daughters stood at the head of lengthy branches of heroic genealogy, the poet takes care to introduce them to the genealogical program *en bloc* and without letting the genealogical narrative get away from him:

1. Perimede (vv. 35–57) bore children to the river Achelous, among them the hero Hippodamas. Hippodamas begat Antimachos and Eurite, Eurite married Porthaon and bore Oineus and his brothers. The passage ends with a brief notice of how Oineus' son Tydeus killed one or more of these uncles because they had usurped power from his father.

2. Kalyke (vv. 58 to at least 74) married Aethlios and gave birth to Endymion, who was allowed by Zeus to choose his own time of death; the section is carried on through at least four generations of his offspring.[25]

3. Alkyone (up to verse 98) married Keyx. The highly fragmentary text reveals no offspring but clearly reflects a narrative of the couple's disastrous impiety towards Zeus and Hera (νόου βεβλαμμέγ[οι ἐσθλοῦ, 88). They were so fond of each other that they called each other 'Zeus' and 'Hera' (cf. fr. 12), so an angry Zeus turned them both into birds.

4. Peisidike (vv. 99–101) married Myrmidon and gave birth to Antiphos and Aktor.

5. Many see in the final fragmentary lines (102–107) the beginning of a fifth section, presumably devoted to Kanake:

ἣ δὲ Ποσειδάω[
Αἰολὶς ἠ[ύκ]ομ[ος
δὶς τέκε

---

[24] How and where the sons were re-introduced remains unclear; see below.
[25] The relation of the Deidameia mentioned in line 74 is uncertain; six further missing lines mean that one or two more generations could have been given, though by line 85 we are in the midst of the story of Alkyone and Keyx.

This is enough to show that a descendant of Aiolos had sex with Poseidon and 'gave birth twice' (vv. 102–104). It is conceivable that the text relates to a further descendant of Peisidike, but the use of the patronymic 'Aiolid' would be less appropriate for such a person, while it would serve perfectly to transition quickly from Peisidike to the last of the daughters of Aiolos, Kanake.[26]

In this way the poet introduces the daughters into his larger genealogical framework, yet the passage shows an orderly and circumscribed form that is distinctly catalogic. He does not pursue the descendants of each daughter in an open-ended genealogical narrative, but typically restricts himself to giving three or four generations of offspring for each before moving on to the next daughter. Further generations were reserved for later in the poem, as separate fragments reveal; the focus here is on treating all the daughters of Aiolos within a relatively short span.[27] The consequence is that each daughter occupies a relatively brief entry within a catalogue of probably less than 150 verses – a catalogue that is in itself an elaboration of the list in verses 31–34, where besides the names there was only room for a handful of formulas or epithets.

Despite the fragmentary character of the text, the artful arrangement of this catalogue is immediately clear. If we accept the ordering of the names in West's supplemented text, it follows that the daughters are taken up into the genealogical program in reverse order of their naming in 31–34, with the one exception of the fourth-named daughter, Kanake, who ought to be taken second, after Perimede, but actually comes last.[28] Though nothing can be said about Kanake's entry, the other entries are carefully balanced. Perimede's entry occupies about 22 verses. Kalyke's entry starts at verse 58 and ends somewhere between 75 and 83 (where the poet is already speaking of Alkyone and Keyx), while Alkyone's entry begins somewhere before 83 and ends at 98, hence each of these entries was about 20 verses in length. It is striking therefore that Peisidike receives only three lines; yet such variation is highly characteristic of catalogues both in Homer and Hesiod, and this may have served to draw still more attention

---

[26] As Ziogas (2013: 106) notes, Kanake refers to herself as 'Aiolis' twice in Ovid, *Heroides* 11 (5, 34). Of the two other candidates mentioned by Hirschberger (2004, 195), Iphimedeia (granddaughter of Kanake) would hardly have come in here before Kanake herself had been enrolled in the genealogical program, whereas Moline (wife of Peisidike's son Aktor) was probably not a descendant of Aiolos. For the possible place of Iphimedeia within this immediate context, see below.

[27] Cf. West (1985) 46–47. In some cases the genealogies are taken up later through the *ehoia* formula, as we shall see in the case of the daughters of Thestios, who are descendants of Perimede.

[28] For more on the arrangement, with comparison to Apollodoros, see Dräger (1997) 56–59.

to the final entry, that of Kanake, which is already notable for appearing out of order.[29]

The first and the last entries are occupied by girls wooed by gods, Perimede by the river Achelous and Kanake by Poseidon. The conventional tale of a girl loved by a god is, of course, the dominant paradigm for the whole poem, as announced programmatically in its proem (quoted above). Naturally, little can be said about other similarities the framing entries may have shared. Perimede's entry traces her descendants for four generations, as far as Tydeus, but there ends on a dark note with the story of how Tydeus killed one or more of his uncles, who had perhaps dethroned his father. If Kanake's descendants were followed as far as Perimede's, the final entry could have included an account of her granddaughter Iphimedeia, who had an affair with Poseidon and gave birth to the notorious *theomachoi* Otos and Ephialtes, who were struck down by Zeus.[30] At the risk of excessive speculation, this would imply in turn a subtle contrast: While Perimede's entry ends with a messy act of familial homicide in the midst of a very human dynastic struggle, Kanake's entry would end with deaths resulting from conflict between gods and demi-gods or giants in the midst of a cosmic struggle.

The three girls in the middle do not, it seems, attract immortal lovers, but nevertheless two of them present contrasting relationships with Zeus. Kalyke's son Endymion is so favored by Zeus that he is given the gift of controlling the time of his death (61–62):

[τὸν δὲ Ζεὺς τίμησ]ε, περισσὰ δὲ δῶρα ἔδωκεν,
ἵν δ' αὐτῶι, θανάτου ταμίης καὶ γήραος ἦεν.

[But Zeus honored him] and gave him outstanding gifts
and he was steward of his own death and old age.

Alkyone and her husband Keyx, by contrast, incurred the displeasure of Zeus and were changed into birds (89–90):

---

[29] Faraone (2013) 300–301 cites *Theogony* 132–138 as an example of how relatively cursory treatment of penultimate entries can bring prominence to a more developed final entry. Sometimes catalogues simply dwindle towards their end, as with the Catalogue of Myrmidons (*Il.* 16.168–197) and indeed in the Catalogue in *Odyssey* 11 (where the brevity of the final entries may reflect Odysseus' eagerness to end his account). Of course, we cannot know for certain whether Kanake's entry was much longer than Peisidike's.

[30] Cf. West (1985) 61, Fletcher (2005) 307. The story is attested for Hesiod in fr. 16. Iphimedeia features prominently in the catalogue of *Odyssey* 11 (305–320), where the tale of her sons' death is heavily focalized through the mother's implied voice: Cf. Hirschberger (2001) 142, Sammons (2010) 87–88.

Ζ[εὺς δὲ ἰδὼν νεμ]έ̣σησεν ἀπ' αἰγλήεντος Ὀλύμπ[ου,
καὶ τὴν μὲν ποί[ησε πατὴρ ἀνδρῶν τε θεῶν τε
ἀλκυόν', ἥ τ̣[

But Zeus [seeing it] found fault from shining Olympus
and made her....
a kingfisher, which....

If the framing entries engage with the poem's dominant paradigm (girl attracts god), the entries within explore other, more complicated relationships between mortal women, their husbands or offspring, and the gods. These, in turn, contrast with one another: One presents a positive paradigm (Zeus loves and gives favors), the other a negative one (Zeus finds fault and punishes). Each of these alternative paradigms has a certain effect, in turn, within the genealogical program: The descendants of Kalyke are listed at greater length than in any other entry of the catalogue; indeed, she has still more descendants for the poet to deal with later in his work. This suggests that divine favor in general (not only divine sexual favors) can ensure the survival of families. Alkyone and Keyx, on the other hand, seem to have produced no children. Yet the negative paradigm of divine disfavor ensures a different access to posterity for the fond lovers. As is typical in myths of metamorphosis, the transformation is not a death but translation to an eternal, everlasting state (94–96):

Κήϋξ δ' οὔτε π[
παύεται ἀΐσσω[ν
ἵεται Ἀλκυόνη[ς

Keyx never ...
stops leaping ...
he longs for Alkyone ...

One is tempted to say that the poet devotes little space to Peisidike simply because there is nothing special to tell – her straightforward marriage to the hero Myrmidon exemplifies neither the dominant paradigm nor any interesting variation to it. Since, however, Myrmidon is the eponymous hero of the Myrmidons, one might see this as a genealogical dead-end like that of the children of Xouthos: Having established a people the poet seeks no further for heroes.[31]

---

[31] As West (1985, 141 and 163) notes, Aktor was the father of Menoitios and grandfather of Patroklos according to Homer (Il. 11.785), but the Hesiodic poet apparently supplies a different genealogy for these heroes.

Table 1

Daughter	Consort/Offspring	Narrative/paradigm
Perimede	Achelous + four generations	Dominant paradigm (girl wooed by both god). Ending: Tydeus kills his uncles.
Kalyke	Aethlios + four/five generations	Zeus honors – Endymion enjoys long life.
Alkyone	Keyx [no offspring?]	Zeus hates and punishes – eternal metamorphosis
Peisidike	Myrmidon + one generation	Ordinary marriage.
[Kanake]	Poseidon + [some generations]	Dominant paradigm (girl wooed by both god). [Ending: Gods kill Otos & Ephialtes?]

The Daughters of Thestios

As I note above, the poet's evident desire to treat the daughters of Aiolos within a circumscribed, catalogic structure necessitated that he limit himself to at most four or five generations for each. That is to say, the genealogical dimension had to be reined in for the sake of the catalogic form of the whole. Nevertheless, since some of these genealogical lines continued on for many generations, it was necessary for the poet to backtrack and take them up again in what must have quickly become a more loosely structured and desultory genealogical exposition, supported at times by ancillary use of the *ehoia* formula. According to West, papyri show that some of this work was done *before* the poet returned to the sons of Aiolos, particularly as regards the numerous descendants of Kalyke.[32] We recall that within the catalogue of Aiolos's daughters, Kalyke's descendants were traced at greatest length: Her son Endymion begat Aitolos, who begat Pleuron, who begat Agenor and Polykaste, who in turn married Elektor. The Deidameia mentioned in line 74 could indicate that this was carried even further. Yet fragments 18 and 19 show that this line was pursued still further in the following part of the poem. Fr. 18 records the wooing of Demodike, the daughter of Agenor. Among her children were Thestios, Euenos, Molos and Pylos. Fr. 19 records the three daughters of the first, Thestios, beginning with the *ehoia*-formula and a simple list of the three daughters (19.3–5):

---

[32] West (1985) 63.

ἠ' οἷαι κ[οῦραι
τρεῖς ο[ἷαί τε θεαί, περικαλλέα ἔργ' εἰδυῖαι,
Λήδη[τ' Ἀλθαίη τε Ὑπερμήστρη τε βοῶπις

Or such as [the daughters . . . . .
three [like goddesses, knowing very beautiful works
Leda and [Althaia and oxen-eyed Hypermestra

It may well be that the *ehoia* formula is used here to hearken back to an unfinished genealogical line. More interesting, however, is its use to introduce not an exemplary individual but a list, since this seems to run counter to what is generally supposed to have been its original function (i.e., to name exemplary individuals).[33] Following his usual procedure, the poet develops this unadorned list of women into a fully elaborated catalogue. Fragments 19 and 22 together reveal that the three women were thereby introduced in the genealogical program in the order in which they are named in the list,[34] the descendants of each being recounted only to a few generations. The procedure is therefore similar to that observed with the daughters of Aiolos. Yet this catalogue, though it features three women rather than five, is complicated by two factors: First, the fact that Leda, who is taken up first, herself has three daughters who are treated in detail in a series, creating a kind of catalogue of three daughters within a catalogue of three daughters. Second, the fact that the whole context, and especially the already complicated entry of Leda, is particularly prolific in narrative elements and recurrent mythological paradigms.

Beginning with Leda, the poet first lists her three daughters, Timandra, Klytaimestra, and Phylonoe (19.7–10):

ἣ μὲν [Τυνδαρέου θαλερὸν λέχο]ς εἰσαναβᾶσα
Λήδη ἐ[υπλόκαμος ἰκέλη φαέεσσ]ι σελήνης
γείνατ[ο Τιμάνδρην τε Κλυταιμήστρ]ην τε βοῶπ[ιν
Φυλο[νόην θ' ἣ εἶδος ἐρήριστ'] ἀθαν]άτηισι.

She going into [the flourishing bed of Tyndareus
Leda [beautiful-haired, like the rays] of the moon
bore [Timandra and Clytaemestra] the oxen-eyed
and Phylonoe [who vied with goddesses in beauty.

---

[33] This is no aberration since the poet does it again with the three daughters of Porthaon (fr. 23.5).
[34] Admittedly that order depends on the editor's supplement; the identity of the three is not be doubted based on frr. 19–22.

He takes these up in reverse order, as he had done by and large with the daughters of Aiolos. Phylonoe receives a mere two lines recording that she was made immortal by Artemis (11–12):[35]

τὴν [ἰο]χέαιρα,
θῆκ[εν δ' ἀθάνατον καὶ ἀγήραον ἤ]ματα πάντ[α.

this one the arrow-shooter
made [immortal and ageless] for all her days

Timandra is taken last with a relatively brief notice of her marriage and offspring (31–36):

Τιμάνδρην δ' Ἔχεμος θαλερὴν̣ ποιήσατ' ἄκ̣οιτιν,
ὃς πάσης Τεγ[έης ἠδ' Ἀρκαδίης] πολυμήλου
ἀφνειὸς ἤνασ[σε, φίλος μακάρεσσι θ]εο[ῖ]σιν·
ἥ οἱ Λαόδοκον μ[εγαλήτορα ποιμέν]α̣ λαῶν
γ]είνα[θ]' ὑποδμη[θεῖσα διὰ] χρυσῆν Ἀφ[ροδίτην
[ἐ]μβασ[ίλευε]η̣..[.].[

But Timandra Echemos made his flourishing wife
he who ruled all Teg[ea and Arkadia] with many flocks
a rich man, dear to the blessed gods.
She gave birth to Laodokos, great-hearted shepherd of the people
being subdued through golden Aphrodite
he was king . . .

This entry did not go on much further since the Dioskouroi are mentioned three lines on; this must represent a continuation of the account of Leda's offspring, the poet following his usual procedure in treating sons after daughters. Although we cannot know for sure, it seems highly probable that he would have registered the ultimate fate and immortalization (or partial immortalization) of the two brothers. Whether the poet went on to mention Helen, as another child of Leda by Zeus, is impossible to say exactly; but it does not appear that Helen, if mentioned here, received a very elaborate description.[36]

---

35 For Phylonoe's immortalization see Apollod. *Bibl.* 3.10.6.
36 The issue is complicated by fr. 21, a scholion to Pindar according to which Hesiod did not make Helen Leda's daughter at all, but said that she was born from a daughter of Okeanos and Zeus. While this is not generally accepted for the *Catalogue*, there is something to be said for it since already in the *Cypria* Helen was represented as daughter of Nemesis (indeed the scholion alludes to this tradition as well, implicitly remarking on a general tendency to aggrandize Helen's divine lineage). West (1985, 43, 96, 123) argues that Helen would have been named as daughter of Leda and Zeus but the extended narrative of her wooing was told in connection

The whole intervening space within the fragment is occupied by Klytaimestra, who married Agamemnon and gave birth to Iphimede (also known as Iphigeneia), Elektra and Orestes. The passage is worth quoting (fr. 19.13–30):

γῆμ[ε δ' ἑὸν διὰ κάλλος ἄναξ ἀνδρ]ῶν Ἀγαμέμνων
κού[ρην Τυνδαρέοιο Κλυταιμήσ]τρην κυανῶπ[ιν·
ἣ τ[έκεν Ἰφιμέδην καλλίσφυ]ρον ἐν μεγάρο[ισιν
Ἠλέκτρην θ' ἣ εἶδος ἐρήριστ' ἀ[θανά]τῃσιν.
Ἰφιμέδην μὲν σφάξαν ἐυκνή[μ]ιδες Ἀχαιοὶ
βωμῷ[ι ἔπ' Ἀρτέμιδος χρυσηλακ]ά̣τ̣[ου] κελαδεινῆς,
ἤματ[ι τῶι ὅτε νηυσὶν ἀνέπλ]εον Ἴλιον ε[ἴσω
ποινὴ[ν τεισόμενοι καλλισ]φύρου Ἀργειώ[νη]ς̣,
εἴδω[λον· αὐτὴν δ' ἐλαφηβό]λος ἰοχέαιρα
ῥεῖα μάλ' ἐξεσά[ωσε, καὶ ἀμβροσ]ίην [ἐρ]α̣τ̣ε̣[ινὴν
στάξε κατὰ κρῆ[θεν, ἵνα οἱ χ]ρὼς [ἔ]μπε[δ]ο̣[ς] ε̣[ἴη,
θῆκεν δ' ἀθάνατο[ν καὶ ἀγήρ]αον ἤμα[τα πάντα.
τὴν δὴ νῦν καλέο[υσιν ἐπὶ χ]θονὶ φῦλ' ἀγ[θρώπων
Ἄρτεμιν εἰνοδί[ην, πρόπολον κλυ]τοῦ ἰ[ο]χ[ε]αίρ[ης.
λοῖσθον δ' ἐν μεγά[ροισι Κλυτ]αιμήστρη κυα[νῶπις
γείναθ' ὑποδμηθ[εῖσ' Ἀγαμέμν]ον[ι δῖ]ον Ὀρέ[στην,
ὅς ῥα καὶ ἡβήσας ἀπε[τείσατο π]ατροφο[ν]ῆα,
κτεῖνε δὲ μητέρα [ἣν ὀλεσήν]ορα νηλέι [χαλκῷ.

Agamemnon lord of men married on account of her beauty
Klytaimestra, the dark-eyed daughter of Tyndareus,
who bore beautiful-ankled Iphimede in his house
and Elektra who vied with the goddesses in beauty.
Iphimede the well-greaved Achaians slaughtered
upon the altar of Artemis of the golden staff, the dinning one,
on that day when they were sailing to Ilion in their ships
to exact punishment for the beautiful-ankled Argive woman.
Her image they slaughtered; the girl herself the deer-shooting goddess
easily rescued, and dripped lovely ambrosia
over her head, in order that her skin would be unchanging;
she made her immortal and ageless all her days.
The tribes of men upon the earth call her
'Artemis in the road', servant of the famous shooter.
Lastly in the house dark-eyed Klytaimestra
bore god-like Orestes, being subdued by Agamemnon;
Orestes, when he reached manhood, avenged his father's killer
and killed his own overweening mother with the pitiless bronze.

---

with Tyndareus himself towards the end of the poem. For criticism of this last assumption, see Heilinger (1983) 31. In view of the paradigmatic complexity of fr. 19, the banal fr. 247, which lists Timandra, Klytaimestra and Helen as paradigms of the unfaithful wife, is appropriately excluded from the *Catalogue* by Most (against West).

The tale of Iphimede begins with horror, her sacrifice recounted as though it were a real death, though the poet immediately assures us that she ultimately met a fate not unlike that already recorded for her aunt, Phylonoe. It is perhaps a piquant touch that even in this fully narrative corner of his poem the poet follows his usual procedure of naming girls before boys: Orestes' birth is reported paratactically, as though it happened after the seeming death of his sister, in a dense series of revelations that disclose at once the fate of Agamemnon, Klytaimestra and the unnamed Aigisthos. The listener is left to imagine the role of the famously childless Elektra.

Leda, as beloved of Zeus, participates in the poem's dominant paradigm. But the catalogue of her children by Tyndareus offers a series of competing paradigms of a kind that run counter to any straightforward genealogical program. Apotheosis, the fate of both her daughter Phylonoe and her granddaughter Iphimede, is a dead end from the genealogical perspective, similar in this regard to the ambiguous immortalization of Alkyone and Keyx. As I note above, it seems not unlikely that the Dioskouroi, mentioned towards the end of the fragment, were also presented as participating in the paradigm of immortalization. What is most interesting, however, is the juxtaposition of this paradigm of immortalization with the story of Klytaimestra, the centerpiece of the catalogue of daughters. Here no god is involved. Rather, the transgression of Aigisthos and Klytaimestra, and the horrific murders that result, reflect on what humans are capable of when they act without or against the advice of the gods.[37] The whole complicated story is sandwiched suggestively between the sublime but uncomplicated fate of Phylonoe, the assurance of immortality for the innocent Iphimede, and the apparently quite ordinary and uneventful marriage of Timandra.

From a more strictly formal standpoint the passage is interesting because it shows a relative disengagement of themes from structures. We recall that the daughters of Aiolos were presented in a catalogue quite artfully arranged, with instantiations of the poem's dominant paradigm in the framing entries and variations contained within. Here, where we are dealing with a catalogue within a catalogue, themes and paradigms begin to develop freely across formal boundaries. I note in particular how variations on the pattern of apotheosis and immortalization appear both within the catalogue of Leda's daughters (Phylonoe, Iphimede), external to this catalogue but within Leda's entry in the larger catalogue of Thestios's daughters (the Dioskouroi, most likely) and, as we shall see, in one

---

[37] As Zeus famously remarks in the *Odyssey* (1.32–43).

and perhaps both of the two remaining entries of the latter (Herakles, Amphiaraos).

Let us return then to the larger structure listing the daughters of Thestios. Fr. 22 shows that Althaia was introduced second, followed by Hypermestra. The fragment begins with praise of Meleagros, Althaia's son by Ares, and a brief account of his death at the hands of Apollo while fighting the Kouretes around Pleuron (vv. 1–13). What is perhaps most surprising here is that the poet eschews the famous tale of the Kalydonian boar hunt and Meleagros' tragic death at his mother's instance. It seems that at the beginning of the fragment Meleagros was compared favorably with Herakles, and this in fact looks forward to the major narrative development of Althaia's entry. This comes at the end of the list of her children by Oikles with mention of Deianeira, who marries Herakles and causes his death, though we are assured by the poet that he now lives as one of the immortal gods (fr. 22.18–33):

> ... Γόργην τ' ἠΰκομον κ[αὶ ἐπί]φ[ρ]ονα Δηϊάνειραν,
> ἣ τέχ' ὑποδμηθεῖ[σα βίηι Ἡρ]ακλη[ε]ίηι
> Ὕλλον καὶ Γλῆνον κα[ὶ [Κτή]σιππον καὶ Ὀνείτην·
> τοὺς τέκε καὶ δείν' ἔρξ[', ἐπεὶ ἀάσατ]ο μέγα θυμῶι,
> ὁππότε φάρμακον .[ἐπιχρί]σασα χιτῶνα
> δῶκε Λίχηι κήρυ[κι] φ[έρειν· ὃ δὲ δῶ]κεν ἄνακτι
> Ἀμφιτρυωνιά[δ]ηι Ἡ[ρακλῆϊ πτολιπό]ρθωι.
> δ[εξ]αμένωι δέ ο[ἱ αἶψα τέλος θανάτοι]ο παρέστη·
> καὶ] θάνε καί ῥ' Ἀϊδ[αο πολύστονον ἵκε]το δῶμα.
> νῦν δ' ἤδη θεός ἐστι, κακῶν δ' ἐξήλυθε πάντων,
> ζώει δ' ἔνθά περ ἄλλοι Ὀλύμπια δώματ' ἔχοντες
> ἀθάνατος καὶ ἄγηρος, ἔχων καλλ[ίσ]φυρον Ἥβην,
> παῖδα Διὸς μεγάλοιο καὶ Ἥρης χρυσοπεδίλου·
> τὸν πρὶν μέν ῥ' ἤχθηρε θεὰ λευκώλενος Ἥρη   30
> ἔκ τε θεῶν μακάρων ἔκ τε θνητῶν ἀνθρώ[πων,
> νῦν δ' ἤδη πεφίληκε, τίει δέ μιν ἔξοχον ἄλλ[ων
> ἀθανάτων μετά γ' αὐτὸν ἐρισθενέα Κρ[ο]νίωνα.

and beautiful-haired Gorge and prudent Deianeira,
who was subdued by the strength of Herakles and bore
Hyllos and Glenos and Ktesippos and Oneites.
These she bore and did a terrible thing, since she was greatly blinded in her heart,
when having anointed a cloak with a drug
she gave it to Liches the herald to carry. He gave it to the lord
son of Amphitryon, Herakles the sacker of cities.
The end of death was immediately present for him when he took it.
And he died and went into the groan-filled house of Hades.
But now he is a god and has escaped from all evil.
He lives there where the others who hold Olympian homes
immortal and ageless, holding the beautiful-ankled Hebe

child of great Zeus and Hera of the golden slipper.
Before white-armed Hera hated him
most of all the blessed gods and mortal men,
but now she loves him exceedingly, and honors him before all other
immortals after the wide-ruling son of Kronos himself.

The story brings together two themes already established in Leda's entry: A man killed by his wife who then experiences apotheosis and immortality.[38] Hypermestra's entry is clearly incomplete, with the fragment breaking off with the mere listing of her children (fr. 22.34–40):

δ[ῖα δ'] Ὑπερμήστρη λαῶν ἀγὸν Ἀμφιάρηον
γε[ί]νατ' Ὀϊκλῆος θαλερὸν λέχος εἰσαναβᾶσα
Ἄ[ρ]γει ἐν ἱπποβότωι πολέων ἡγήτορα λαῶν·
ὅς ῥ' ἀγαθὸς μὲν ἔην ἀγορῆι, ἀγαθὸς δὲ μάχεσθαι,
ἐ[σ]θλὸς δ' ἐν πραπίδεσσι, φίλος δ' ἦν ἀθανάτοισι·
γείνατο δ' Ἰφιάνειραν ἐπήρατον εἶδος ἔχουσα[ν
Ἐνδηόν τε ἄνακτ' ἀνδρῶν ἠΰν τε μέγαν τε

God-like Hypermestra bore Amphiaraos leader of hosts,
going into the flourishing bed of Oikles,
[Amphiaraos] leader of many hosts in horse-pasturing Argos.
He was good in assembly, good at fighting,
good in his wits, and dear to the immortals.
She begat Iphianeira having a lovely apperance
and Endeos, lord of men, good and big....

But the fact that these children include Amphiaraos suggests the possibility of an engagement with the major epic cycle of the seven against Thebes. Most versions of this tale involve some kind of chthonic apotheosis of Amphiaraos, the faultless prophet forced to participate in the enterprise against his will. The account of Amphiaraos could have combined the theme of apotheosis with that of the heroic death exemplified by Meleagros, just as Herakles had combined it with the theme of domestic murder. Between them the three daughters of Thestios produce allusions to three major epic sagas: The Trojan War through Leda, the myth of Herakles through Althaia, and the Theban Wars through Hypermestra. We can also note surprising omissions: Whether Helen was named or not among the children of Leda is not known, but there was no space here for the

---

38 Cf. Haubold (2005) 91–92. Most reports that lines 26–33 are obelized in P.Oxy 2075, but the present argument shows that the poet not only does not avoid tales of immortalization of heroes but actively lists them in paradigmatic sequences; he is unlikely therefore to have omitted the most famous instance in Greek mythology, least of all in this particular context.

extended narrative of her wooing that probably featured much later in the poem.³⁹ The Kalydonian boar hunt, Meleagros' murder of his uncle, and his death at the hands of his mother are likewise omitted. The poet clearly aims to use the entry for introducing the tale of Herakles, starting with the hero's death and apotheosis in what is likely to be the first detailed account of him in the poem. The relatively minor tradition of the boar hunt would merely distract from this. For the same, reason it is no accident that in Althaia's entry the poet departs from his usual practice of taking daughters before sons; the famous Meleagros should be dispensed with so that mention of Herakles and the account of his death can receive an unexpected emphasis.⁴⁰ Indeed, by comparing Meleagros to Herakles near the beginning of the entry the poet already signals his goal. Omission or relatively cursory treatment of Helen is more puzzling if the poet aimed to evoke the Trojan War through Leda, but a few points may help to explain this: By emphasizing the sinister Klytaimestra and her crimes, the poet may signal a less positive or Philhellenic aspect of the Trojan War myth in favor of a more pessimistic vision focused on its unhappy aftermath. Indeed, given the disposition of the text here, it would be churlish to deny the poet a vision comparable to that of Aeschylus, who sets the whole Trojan War within a string of impieties connected with the curse of the house of Atreus. Such a pessimistic vision would not be amiss for a poet who saw this war as marking the twilight of the heroic age.

The daughters of Thestios are thus catalogued in essentially the same manner as the daughters of Aiolos. The most noticeable difference is the proliferation of short narratives involving their children and grandchildren. Viewed from a paradigmatic perspective, these present less of a balanced series in comparison with the paradigmatic form of the earlier catalogue; rather, there is a noticeable insistence on the paradigm of apotheosis and immortalization of heroic men and women. The poet draws on multiple traditions to create virtually a paradigmatic catalogue of tales featuring this theme, while discovering ways in which other themes (the heroic death, the treacherous wife) can be actively combined with it.⁴¹

---

39 Cf. West (1985) 96; Cingano (2005) 120–121.
40 As West (1985, 47) notes, this also creates a chiastic arrangement with the previous entry: While the poet began with Leda's children by Tyndareus and moved on to her children by Zeus, with Althaia he begins with her child by Ares and moves on to her children by Oineus. Ovid's *Metamorphoses* perhaps outdoes the *Catalogue* in re-joining the full story of Meleagros' death with that of Herakles' death and apotheosis: cf. Ziogas (2013) 133–134.
41 Such 'paradigmatic catalogues' (i.e., actual catalogues of *paradeigmata*) are rare in the Homeric poems but become wildly popular in Hellenistic poetry and the Roman tradition, especial-

Table 2

Daughter	Consort	Offspring	Narrative/Paradigm
1) Leda	Zeus/Tyndareus		Dominant Paradigm
		a) Timandra	immortalization
		b) Klytaimestra	murder/revenge
		c) Phylonoe	immortalization
		d) Dioskouroi, sons of Zeus [Helen, daughter of Zeus?]	immortalization
2) Althaia	Ares/Oineus		Dominant Paradigm
		a) Meleagros, son of Ares	heroic death
		b) Deianeira, daughter of Oineus	murder/immortalization (of Herakles)
		c) other children of Oineus	–
3) Hypermestra	Oikles		Ordinary Marriage
		a) Amphiaraos	[heroic death/ immortalization?]
		b) Iphianeira, Endeos	–

The Sons of Aiolos

As I note above, fr. 10 shows the poet first listing the sons of Aiolos, then his daughters, then proceeding to register the daughters into his genealogical program through a more elaborate catalogue recounting their marriages, offspring and fates. Further fragments reveal that the genealogical lines created in this context were taken and continued by the poet later in the work, in a more open genealogical narrative in which the *ehoia*-formula may have been used, among other devices, for navigating from one collateral line to another. What, then, of the sons of Aiolos? Since the poet's usual practice is to deal with daughters first, then sons, one should expect that the poet returned to the sons of Aiolos at some point after dealing with the daughters and their many descendants. By analogy with the daughters, one might expect further that he would take each of the sons in order (or perhaps reverse order) and recount the descendants of

---

ly Ovid: See Sammons (2010) 23–24. The *Catalogue* surely represents an intermediate stage in this development.

each for up to several generations, i.e. to create a catalogic context for the sons as for the daughters. This does not appear to be the case, however. Particularly important in this regard is fragment 60, which records how the daughter of Deion, Asterodeia, married the hero Phokos (fr. 60.7–11):

ἠ'] οἵην ἵππο[ισι καὶ ἅρμασι κολλητοῖσι
Φ]ῶκος ἐυμμ[ελίης δόμον ἠγάγετ' Ἀστερόδειαν
ἐκ] Φυλάκης κ[ούρην μεγαθύμου Δηϊονῆος·
ἣ τέκετο Κρῖ[σον καὶ ὑπέρθυμον Πανοπῆα
νυκτὶ μ[ι]ῆ[ι].

Or such as her whom with horses [and well-joined chariots
Phokos of the ash-spear [led to his house, Asterodeia
from] Phylake, [the daughter of great-hearted Deion.
She gave birth to Kri[sos and high-hearted Panopeus
in a single night.

The poet went on to relate how these twins fought even in the womb. If Deion were introduced into the genealogies formally as in a catalogue, clearly his immediate offspring and further descendants would be listed there.[42] The poet's resort to the *ehoia* formula to introduce Deion's daughter suggests that Deion himself did not stand at the head of a genealogical line; rather, this mention of him is his *first* appearance in the poem since the list quoted already from fr. 10. This supports West's view that the poet actually introduced the sons of Aiolos as best he could in connection with the running genealogies, relying on the *ehoia* formula when necessary.[43] The contrast is telling: While the poet introduced the girls to the genealogies by precisely cataloging them, he may have introduced the sons largely through *ehoiai* – which is to say, cataloguing men by cataloguing women.[44]

---

[42] It must be confessed that the restoration of the text is unusually shaky in this case. While Apollodoros does mention an Asterodeia born to the Aiolid Deion (*Bibl.* 1.9.4), we rely on the scholia to Lycophron for a statement that this person was the bride of Phokos. Another candidate, named by Pausanias, is Antiope. See the note of Hirschberger (2004, 446), who places the fragment with the *Megalai Ehoiai*. For some historical considerations see Fowler (1998) 13–14.
[43] West (1985) 63–64. Admittedly the poet may be taking up the sons of Aiolos more or less methodically; since these verses are preceded by mention of Asklepios, a descendant of Perieres, the poet may use the *ehoia* of Asterodeia to return to Deion, the next figure in a notional list of Aiolids waiting to be registered in the program: Cf. West (1985) 68; Rutherford (2000) 85.
[44] The poet's dependence on *ehoiai* in this regard is far from certain, though, as will be clear from what follows. For Athamas and Perieres there is precious little evidence to determine what role they played in the poem, let alone how they were formally introduced to the genealogical program. For Athamas we have only fr. 39, mentioning that Zeus stole his wits, and fr. 43, which

There is further support for this idea in the joint appearance of Salmoneus and Kretheus in fr. 27. The opening lines of the fragment reveal the end of the narrative of Zeus' revenge against Salmoneus and his people. Tyro, Salmoneus' pious daughter, was apparently the only survivor (fr. 27.15–35):

βῆ δὲ κατ' Ο]ὐλύμποιο [χο]λούμενος, αἶψα δ' ἵκανεν
λαοὺς Σαλμ]ωνῆος ἀτ[ασ]θάλου, οἳ τάχ' ἔμελλον
πείσεσθ' ἔρ]γ' ἀΐδηλα δι' ὑβ[ρ]ιστὴν βασιλῆα·
τοὺς δ' ἔβα]λεν βροντῆι [τε κ]αὶ αἰθαλόεντι κεραυνῶι.
ὣς λαοὺς ἀπε]τίνεθ' ὑπερβ[ασίη]ν βασιλῆος.
.... (.)].ς παῖδάς τε γ[υν]αῖκά τε οἰκῆάς τε,
..... πό]λιν καὶ δώμα[τ' ..]ίρρυτα θῆκεν ἀΐστως,
τὸν δὲ λα]βὼν ἔρριψ' ἐς Τ[ά]ρταρον ἠερόεντα,
ὡς μή τις] βροτὸς ἄλλος [ἐ]ρίζοι Ζηνὶ ἄνακτι.
τοῦ δ' ἄρα] παῖς ἐλέλειπτο φίλη μακάρεσσι θεοῖσι
Τυρὼ ἐυπ]λόκαμος ἰκέλη χ[ρ]υσῆι Ἀφρο[δ]ίτ[ηι,
οὕνεκα νε]ικείεσκε καὶ ἤρ[ισε] Σαλμωνῆϊ
συνεχές, οὐ]δ' εἴασκε θεοῖς [βροτὸν ἰσ]οφαρίζειν·
τούνεκά] μιν ἐσάωσε πατὴρ ἀνδρῶν τε θεῶν τε.
...... ἐ]ς Κρηθῆος ἀμύμονος ἤ[γ]αγεν οἶκον
ὅς δὲ μιν ἀσ]πασίως ὑπεδ[έ]ξατο καί ῥ' ἀτίταλλεν.
αὐτὰρ ἐπεί] ῥ' ἥβης πολυηράτου ἐς τέλος ἦλθεν
...... τῆ]ς γ' ἐράεσκε Ποσειδάων ἐνοσίχθων
..........] φιλότητι θεὸς βροτῶι, οὕνεκ' ἄρ' εἶδος
πασάων προὔχεσκε γυναι]κῶν θηλυτεράων.
ἡ δ' ἐπ' Ἐνιπῆος πωλέσκετο] καλὰ ῥέεθρα ...

He came] down from Olympos in anger, and soon he came
to the people] of arrogant Salmoneus, who were about
to suffer] destruction because of their violent king.
These] he struck with the lightning bolt and smoking thunder.
On the people] he thus took vengeance for their king's transgression.
...] children, wife and house-holders,
city and homes ... he made them utterly vanish,
but Salmoneus] he seized and cast into gloomy Tartaros
so that no] other mortal would vie with lord Zeus.
But his] child had been left behind, a girl dear to the immortals
Tyro] with beautiful hair, like to golden Aphrodite,
because] she faulted and quarreled with Salmoneus
constantly] and did not allow him [though mortal] to call himself equal to gods.
For this reason] the father of gods and men saved her.

---

states that his daughter Euippe bore Eteokles to Andreus. The first is just enough to suggest the famous tale of Athamas' madness and pursuit of Ino, but nothing more can be said. For Perieres we hear only that his son, Leukippos, was the father of Arsinoe, who begat Asklepios to Apollo (frr. 52, 53a).

> ...] he led her to the house of blameless Kretheus,
> ...] he received her gladly and cherished her,
> but when] she reached a very beautiful youthful prime,
> ...] Poseidon the earth-shaker loved her
> ...] a god in love with a mortal, because in appearance
> she surpassed all] mortal women.
> But she used to walk along Enipeus'] lovely currents ...

The poet went on to relate how the girl was seduced by Poseidon and gave birth to Neleus and Pelias. Fragments 31–33 make clear that the poet provided a detailed account of these heroes and their offspring, including the famous shape-shifter Periklymenos and the Iliadic Nestor. Tyro's removal to her uncle's house makes probable that the *Catalogue* followed the tradition, attested already in the *Odyssey*, that Tyro married her uncle Kretheus.[45] For our purposes what is really interesting is that, through Tyro, Salmoneus and Kretheus appeared in conjunction with one another, not through the paratactic arrangement of a catalogue but in connection with a running narrative of which Tyro is clearly the centerpiece.[46] Naturally, we would like to know how the poet first introduced the story of Salmoneus' destruction. It would be most interesting if the larger context were in fact an *ehoia* of Tyro, who through her affair with Poseidon and splendid heroic offspring conforms perfectly to the dominant paradigm of a girl loved by a god. It is intriguing, to say the least, that Tyro occupies one of the longest entries in the catalogue of *Odyssey* 11 (235–259). The entry is almost entirely dominated by a vivid account of her seduction by Poseidon (posing as the river Enipeus), including the only passage of direct speech in the catalogue. Only the last two lines mention her children with Kretheus, and no mention is made of Salmoneus' destruction. There is probably some irony in the fact that Tyro introduced herself to Odysseus as 'offspring of blameless Salmoneus and wife of Kretheus, son of Aiolos'.[47] This is preicsely how the woman would have introduced herself, but the vivid narrative of the love affair, which is understood to be based on Tyro's own account to Odysseus, reveals the truly defining moment of her career.

The later appearance of Sisyphos is equally intriguing. We encounter him in fr. 69, where he plays a role in the tale of Mestra, the shape-shifting girl who uses her powers to marry and then abandon a series of prospective husbands in order to care for her father, Erysichthon, who is cursed with insatiable hunger. Sisy-

---

[45] Cf. Apollod. *Bibl.* 1.9.10. The fragments do not record their union, but Aison, father of the famous Jason, was generally considered to be their child (cf. frr. 36–37).
[46] Cf. West (1985) 64; he argues that Salmoneus and Kretheus are the first of the sons of Aiolos to reappear in the poem.
[47] ἣ φάτο Σαλμωνῆος ἀμύμονος ἔκγονος εἶναι, / φῆ δὲ Κρηθῆος γυνὴ ἔμμεναι Αἰολίδαο.

phos attempts to win her for his son Glaukos. When Glaukos falls victim to the fraud, Sisyphos goes to law with Erysichthon, before the judgment of Athena, and apparently wins his case. Nevertheless, his son does not get the girl, who is carried off to Kos by Poseidon, where she gives birth to the founding hero Eurypylos.[48] Mestra apparently returns to her father, and we next meet Sisyphos trying to obtain Eurynome for his son. This marriage succeeds, but apparently without legitimate offspring; here the poet explains that Sisyphos has been cursed by the gods to have no offspring. Eurynome, like Mestra, is seduced by Poseidon and bears children to the god rather than to her mortal husband (69.94–107):

ἢ οἵη Νίσο]υ θυγάτηρ Πανδιονίδαο
Εὐρονόμη τὴ]ν ἔργα διδάξατο Παλλὰς Ἀθήνη
    ]εουσα, νόεσκε γὰρ ἶσα θεῆισι,
τῆς καὶ ἀπὸ χρ]οϊῆς ἠδ' εἵματος ἀργυφέοιο
    ]θεου χαρίεν τ' ἀπὸ εἶδος ἄητο·
τῆς μὲν Σίσυφο]ς Αἰολίδης πειρήσατο βουλέων
βοῦς ἐλάσα[ς· ἀλλ' οὔ τι Διὸ]ς νόον αἰγιόχοιο
ἔγνω· ὁ μ[ὲν ἕδνοις διζ]ήμενος ἦλθε γυνα[ῖκα
βουλῆι Ἀθ[ηναίης· τῶι δὲ] νεφεληγερέτα Ζεὺ[ς
ἀθανάτωι ἀ[νένευσε] καρήατι μή ποτ' ὀπίσ[σω
ἔσσεσθαι γ[ενεὴν εὐγν]ητου Σισυφίδαο.
ἡ δὲ Ποσε[ιδάωνος ἐν] ἀγκοίνηισι μιγεῖ[σα
Γλαύκωι ἐγ[ὶ μεγάροις τέκ'] ἀμύμονα Βελλε[ροφόντην,
ἔξοχον ἀνθ[ρώπων ἀρ]ετῆι ἐπ' ἀπείρονα γ[αῖαν.

Or such as] the daughter of Nisos, son of Pandion
Eurynome, to whom] Pallas Athena taught works
…] she had a mind like the goddesses
and from her skin] and shining clothes
…] a graceful, divine beauty wafted.
Sisyphos] son of Aiolos made trial of her prudence
rustling cattle, but the mind of aegis-bearing Zeus
he did not know at all. He came, seeking a wife with gifts
on the advice of Athena. But cloud-gathering Zeus
denied with a shake of his immortal head that ever
there be [offspring for the well-born] son of Sisyphos.
The girl, on the other hand, mingling in the arms of Poseidon
bore in the house to Glaukos blameless Bellerophontes
outstanding in virtue among men throughout the wide world.

---

[48] Cf. frr. 70–71, and careful explication of the story in Rutherford (2005) 103–107; Ormand (2015) 87–96.

What was the larger context for of this? Most, and West before him, take that context to be an *ehoia* of Mestra, supplementing fr. 69.2–3 as follows:

ἢ' οἵη θυγάτηρ Ἐρυσίχθονος ἀντι]θέοιο
   ]ου Τριοπίδαο
Μήστρη ἐυπλόκαμος, Χαρίτων ἀ]μαρύγματ' ἔχουσα·

[Or such a one as the daughter of god-like Erysichthon]
   ...] son of Triopas.
[Mestra with beautiful hair,] holding the gleam [of the Graces.

As can be seen from fr. 69.94 above, Most suggests that Eurynome, too, was introduced as an *ehoia*. Although the line-beginnings are lost, there is some reason to accept the theory, given the sort of praise that follows each girl's introduction and the fact, highly relevant for our purposes, that the girl herself becomes the real protagonist of the narrative elaborations that follow,[49] and of course the conformity of these stories to the dominant paradigm announced in the proem. The stringing together of two *ehoiai* suggests we are truly in the midst of a 'catalogue of women', yet what the two women here have in common is that they were both wooed by Sisyphos on behalf of his son. The first line of the papyrus mentions Polymela, daughter of the famous thief Autolykos, who was also connected with Sisyphos. The larger context could then be a more general narrative of Sisyphos' life and deeds, how he met his match in the person of the shape-shifting girl Mestra, and even with Eurynome failed to produce the descendants he sought through his son. The story of Mestra overshadows his failed attempt, and even if Mestra and Eurynome are not actually *ehoiai*, we can still see here that the dominant paradigm (girl loved by gods) reasserts itself in spite of Sisyphos' efforts: His would-be daughters-in-law apparently produce no offspring with Glaukos, but do with Poseidon. Hence it is a case where the dominant paradigm quite literally *rescues* the genealogical program, for the gods who would deny Sisyphos a posterity cannot themselves refrain from producing children with these women.[50]

---

49 Cf. Rutherford (2005) 102. Differently Ziogas (2013) 138, who argues that 'in Ovid and Hesiod, Mestra provides a narrative framework, but is not really a protagonist'.
50 According to Rutherford (2005) 102–103, 'the Sisyphus story as a whole seems to undercut the idea of stable genealogy' since 'Mestra's Coan descendants are killed by Heracles' and the divine parentage of Bellerophontes contradicts Glaukos' version of his genealogy in *Iliad* 6. But these two points show exactly how the dominant paradigm allows for the continuation of the heroic race and therefore of heroic tales.

The similarities between this and the Tyro passage are too numerous to be coincidental: In each case there are father figures (Salmoneus, Erysichthon, Sisyphos) whose impiety and punishment by the gods has forced the poem from a strict genealogical format into a more complicated narrative mode. In each case the narrative follows not the male figures but the female one, who becomes the real object of interest. In each case this female figure attracts the god Poseidon, leading to a mortal/divine sexual union that gets the genealogical program back on track, while also conforming to the dominant paradigm announced at the beginning of the poem – precisely the narrative paradigm of an *ehoia*, or mortal woman who conceives children with a divine lover. Uncertainty over whether Tyro and Mestra were actual *ehoiai* should not obscure the fact that they represent considerable expansions, on a narrative level, of the dominant paradigm which the *ehoiai* are meant to exemplify, expansions that are precisely necessary to keep the poem itself underway.[51]

Conclusions

While one cannot speak to the form of the poem as a whole, it does seem that within the major stemma of the Aiolids the poet stages an evolution of poetic forms: A simple genealogical format in which the catalogue is an ancillary device quickly becomes too complicated to follow in a straight line: The narrative element, with or without the use of the *ehoia* formula, clearly becomes an important device for bringing coherence to the poem once the complexity of the genealogical program forces the poet to indulge in chronological and geographical shifts and transitions. At this point the catalogue becomes a device for ordering portions of the poem and for intensive development of competing paradigms, like the paradigm of apotheosis that is developed within the account – marked by the *ehoia* formula – of the daughters of Thestios. Once the poet gets around to the sons of Aiolos, however, there are hints that free narrative elaboration has become the dominant form: Hence Salmoneus and Kretheus appear to come into the poem in connection with the story of Tyro, Sisyphos in connection with the story of Mestra. If these girls were, indeed, *ehoiai*, we could imagine a poem that only slowly takes on the form that is implied by its proem – a poem that does not begin as, but becomes, a catalogue of women.

It is remarkable that several of the most secure *ehoiai* in the fragments relate to sets of daughters rather than individual women. As I remark above, this would

---

[51] Cf. Rutherford (2000) 86.

seem at first glance to run counter to what we imagine to have been the original function of the formula, i.e. to introduce successive entries in catalogues of exemplary women. It is used in these cases rather to set small catalogues into broader genealogical contexts. I would argue that this hints at the poet's awareness that such catalogic contexts could be used to develop new paradigms or to modify existing ones; in other words, the catalogue was a context that could help him move beyond simple iteration of a single dominant paradigm.

The *ehoia* proper remained a powerful device, probably with a range of functions that were not merely vestigial or ancillary. Tyro and Mestra are examples of women whose stories could be used to bring in the many heroes whose inclusion in the poem through a purely genealogical narrative would become overwhelmingly complicated, as in the case of the sons of Aiolos who are left far behind by the extended genealogical lines descending from his daughters. Their attractions bring the genealogical program back on track, particularly where the impiety of male forebears threatens to create a genealogical dead-end, as with Salmoneus and Sisyphos.[52] It is worth considering as well that the *ehoia* did not merely serve to shore up necessary segues for a complicated genealogical structure, but actually had a kind of competitive and destabilizing relationship to the genealogical program: The generally more colorful and engaging narratives surrounding exemplary women so introduced, the usefulness of their stories as introductions to some of the most important cycles in heroic mythology, empowers the *ehoia* to take control of the poem, placing the heroines in a more powerful, constitutive role than mere genealogy would grant them. Perhaps it was this tendency of the poem that led to its being titled *Catalogue of Women* and *Ehoiai*. Indeed, our own insistence that it was 'something more than this' might appear mere pedantry if the whole poem could somehow come to light. Merkelbach originally suggested an orderly movement from genealogies to *ehoiai*, a theory now discredited by our fuller body of fragments; but there may be something to the idea that the *ehoia*, as a constitutive, structuring device and element of genre, tended to outcompete the strictly genealogical format as each stemma wore on.

---

52 As Ziogas (2013, 11) puts it: 'Female renown is the poetic core around which the program of the catalogue revolves, and female beauty is the force that creates and drives its genealogical narrative'.

Bibliography

Brown, N. O. (1953). *Hesiod's Theogony*, New York.
Cingano, E. (2005). 'A catalogue within a catalogue: Helen's suitors in the Hesiodic *Catalogue of Women* (frr. 196–204)', in: Hunter, 118–152.
Clay, J. S. (2005). 'The beginning and end of the *Catalogue of Women* and its relation to Hesiod', in Hunter, 25–34.
Dräger, P. (1997). *Untersuchungen zu den Frauenkatalogen Hesiods*, Stuttgart.
Fletcher, R. (2005). 'Or such as Ovid's *Metamorphoses* …', in: Hunter, 299–319.
Fowler, R. (1998). 'Genealogical Thinking, Hesiod's *Catalogue*, and the Creation of the Hellenes', *PCPS* 44: 1–19.
Haubold, J. (2005). 'Heracles in the Hesiodic *Catalogue of Women*', in: Hunter, 85–98.
Heilinger, K. (1983). 'Der Freierkatalog der Helena im hesiodeischen Frauenkatalog I', *MH* 40: 19–34.
Hirschberger, M. (2001). 'Die Erzählungen der Frauen in der *Nekyia* der *Odysee*', in: M. Païsi-Apostolopoulou (ed.), *Eranos: Proceedings of the 9th International Symposium on the Odyssey*, Ithaki, 123–149.
Hirschberger, M. (2004). Gunaikôn Katalogos *und* Megalai Êhoiai: *Ein Kommentar zu den Fragmenten zweier hesiodischer Epen*, Leipzig.
Hunter, R. (2005). *The* Hesiodic Catalogue of Women: *Constructions and Reconstructions*, Cambridge.
Ormand, K. (2014). *The Hesiodic* Catalogue of Women *and Archaic Greece*, Cambridge.
Loney, A. C. (2014). 'Hesiod's Incorporative Poetics in the *Theogony* and the Contradictions of Prometheus', *AJP* 135: 503–531.
Most, G. (2007). *Hesiod II: The* Shield, Catalogue of Women, *Other Fragments*, Cambridge, MA.
Muellner, L. (1996). *The Anger of Achilles:* Mênis *in Greek Epic*, Ithaca.
Rutherford, I. (2000). 'Formulas, Voice, and Death in *Ehoie*-Poetry, the Hesiodic *Gunaikon Katalogos* and the Odysseian *Nekuia*', in: M. Depew & D. Obbink (eds.), *Matrices of Genre: Authors, Canons, and Society*, Cambridge, MA, 81–96.
Rutherford, I. (2005). 'Mestra at Athens', in: Hunter, 99–117.
Sammons, B. (2010). *The Art and Rhetoric of the Homeric Catalogue*, New York.
Sammons, B. (forthcoming). 'Hesiod's *Theogony* and the Structures of Poetry', in S. Scully & A. Loney (eds.), *The Oxford Handbook of Hesiod*, New York, forthcoming.
Solmsen, F. (1949). *Hesiod and Aeschylus*, Ithaca.
Steinrück, M. (1994). 'Die fremde Stimme: der Erzähler und das Schweigen der Frauen im 11. Buch der *Odysee*', *Kleos* 1: 83–128.
Ziogas, I. (2013), *Ovid and Hesiod: The metamorphosis of the* Catalogue of Women, Cambridge.

Christos Tsagalis
Sound-Play in the Hesiodic *Catalogue of Women*

Although much work has been done with respect to the formulaic diction of the Hesiodic *Catalogue of Women*,[1] scholars have not shown similar interest in studying its style.[2] Part of the explanation is that catalogic poetry seems unattractive for stylistic studies because of the lack of continuous narrative and the high proportion of proper names. Add to the above the fragmentary condition of the *Catalogue* and the scholarly neglect of the stylistic features of this epic is explained.

Scholars have basically focused their attention on Hesiodic diction.[3] As in antiquity so in modern times, they have been principally concerned with its relation to Homeric phraseology.[4] This line of investigation is understandable, since the shadow cast by the monumental Homeric compositions has resulted in 'anchoring' Hesiod to Homer. It is also pertinent to questions of relative chronology and the overall evolution and shaping of epic diction in the archaic period. On the other end, it is fair to say that a work like the *Catalogue*, the Hesiodic authorship of which has been forged by the tendency to attribute much of non-Homeric archaic epic to the poet from Askra, is a very different case. First and foremost, it is not a narrative but a special sort of catalogue-poetry. As such, it is marked by stylistic devices that are part and parcel of its being a catalogue-*ehoie* blend. Seriation (catalogue) and lemmatization (*ehoie*) require a delicate balance between the smooth flow of information and the selective highlighting of specific entries. Style in all its aspects (sound, figures of speech, word-patterns in proper names) is crucial for an epic marked by the generic

---

1 See e.g. Krafft (1963); Neitzel (1975); Meier (1976); Mureddu (1983), (2008) 97–112; Cohen (1986) 127–142, (1989) 12–27; Davies (1992).
2 A notable exception is Hunter (2009, 253–269; 2014, 282–315), but his approach mainly concerns the way the ancients treated Hesiod's style. Hunter's focus is on the *Theogony* and the *Works and Days*.
3 On this point, see Richardson (1980) 284: 'The modern tendency to pay special attention to traditional or formulaic character of the verse does not encourage sensitivity to the way in which the poet fits sound to sense in particular contexts, whereas the ancient emphasis on *mimesis* naturally led to appreciation of this'.
4 See the bibliography cited in n. 1 (above).

https://doi.org/9783110537581-012

crossing of *ehoie*-poetry over to catalogue-poetry.⁵ In this novel mixture, style has a new role to play.

Sound-Play

One of the most notable aspects of style is sound-play, especially in a poetic tradition with a clear oral background. Aural effects are not, of course, restricted to oral poetry, but they are systematically exploited in oral media, since they constitute an essential aspect of performance. These observations are extremely relevant to Ancient Greek, 'a euphonious language, with a high proportion of vowels, less collocation of consonants than many languages, and no heavy stress accent'.⁶ In this chapter I intend to explore the full range of sound-play in the 'Hesiodic' *Catalogue*. Classification of the relevant phenomena will be undertaken, but with an aim both to enhance interpretation and to make general judgments with respect to the sophistication and poetic qualities of this generic hybrid.

Assonance (παρήχησις)

The Greeks were alert to the significance of assonance, especially with respect to whether a given sound was appropriate for the meaning of a specific passage. Sound effects had been discussed by ancient critics, e. g. Aristotle (*Rhetoric*), [Demetrius] (*On Style*), Dionysius of Halikarnassos (*Comp.*), and Philodemus (*Rhetoric, On Poems*), and in the post-classical period theories of sound were developed, the best known being that of the so-called 'euphonists' who claimed that sound was more important than content.⁷ Since in antiquity there was no overall consensus with respect to terminology, I have decided to use modern classifications, although ancient Greek terms will creep in from time to time. The most straightforward approach is that of Silk in the entry 'assonance' of the *OCD*. It is his categorization that I will hereby follow. My only addition is the Greek term παρήχησις ('resemblance in sound', 'assonance'), which is used by Hermogenes (*Inv.* 4.7), and under which I group (1) alliteration, (2) vocalic repetition, (3) syllabic repetition or near-repetition of stem syllables, (4) syllabic rep-

---

5 On this generic crossing, see Rutherford (2000) 93–94; Tsagalis (2009) 171–172.
6 Edwards (1987) 117.
7 See Janko (2000) 120–200; Nünlist (2009) 217.

etition or near-repetition of final syllables, and (5) more complex cases marked by a combination of some of the above.[8]

1 Alliteration (Word-Initial Rhyme)

Under the term 'alliteration' I group cases of consonantal repetition (word-initial or stem-initial). In the *Catalogue* alliteration is the least employed of the five forms of assonance described above. Alliteration often draws attention to the link between the various constituent items.

In the *ehoie* of Mestra the alliteration of –d- first highlights the inability of mortals to decide about whether Erysichthon/Aithon or Sisyphos is right (43a.38: ο]ὐδ' ἄρα τις **δ**ικάσαι [**δύ**]νατο βροτός· ἀλλ' αραπ[), and then showcases the ability of a goddess or woman to make this decision (43a.40: ἀ]τρεκέως **δ**ιέθηκ[ε] **δ**ίκην **δ**.[).[9] The effect of this sound-play is further enhanced by the syllabic repetition of the stem syllable –ep- in the ensuing verse (43a.39: **ἐπ**]έτρεψαν καὶ **ἐπή**ινεσαν·ἣ δ' ἄρα τοῖ[σιν). Father and husband left it to Athena or Mestra to decide who is right and who is wrong. The syllabic repetition links the two verbs (**ἐπ**]έτρεψαν and **ἐπή**ινεσαν) and intensifies the joint decision of the two opposing sides.

Sometimes alliteration acquires a 'proleptic' function.[10] It draws the listener's attention to two items whose initial sound will be soon repeated within the aural environment of a different alliteration. In cases like this, the former alliteration works as a bridge to the latter. The result is that what is linked here are not simply two items but two chains of items by means of two alliterative devices. In fr. 43a.62 (ἔπραθεν ἱμερόεντα πόλιν, **κ**ε[ρ]άϊξε δὲ **κ**ώμας) the consonantal repetition of –k- highlights the plundering of Koan villages by Herakles. A few verses later (43a.66: Μήστρη δὲ **π**ρο]λι**π**οῦσα **Κ**όων **π**οτὶ **π**ατρίδα γαῖαν), we are told that Mestra left Kos to return to her fatherland. The placement of the word Κόων within the three items of the alliterative unit (**π**ρο]λι**π**οῦσα **Κ**όων **π**οτὶ **π**ατρίδα) interrupts its autonomy and invites the audience to connect the idea of Mestra's return home with Herakles' ravaging of Kos. The word-initial –k- sound in the word Κόων facilitates the 'carrying over' of the initial alliterative repetition of –k- to the triple consonantal repetition of –p- a few lines later.

---

8 For this categorization, see Silk *OCD*, s.v. 'assonance', p. 186.
9 It is not clear who this woman is, Athena (West, crit. app. of editio maior; 1985, 169) or Mestra (Kakridis 1980, 150–151); on this problem, see Hirschberger (2004) 277 on *Cat.* fr. 37.38–39 (= fr. 43a.38–39 M.-W.).
10 On 'aural preparation', see Silk (1974) 187–191.

There are cases in which alliteration is not an isolated aural phenomenon but interacts with other forms of sound-play occurring in its immediate context. Thus, ἵκετο δ' ἐς Φυλῆα φίλον μακάρεσσι θεοῖσιν (fr. 176.4) is interwoven within a nexus of aural associations involving the preceding and two following verses that intensify and deepen the meaning of the relevant passage:

Τιμάνδρη μὲν ἔπειτ' Ἔχεμον <u>προλιποῦσ'</u> ἐβεβήκει,	3
ἵκετο δ' ἐς Φυλῆα φίλον μακάρεσσι θεοῖσιν·	4
ὡς δὲ Κλυταιμήστρη <u><προ>λιποῦσ'</u> Ἀγαμέμνονα δῖον	5
Αἰγίσθωι παρέλεκτο καὶ εἴλετο χείρον' ἀκοίτην	6

The Timandra left behind Echemos and ran away,
and came to Phyleus, who was dear to the blessed gods:
so too, Klytaimestra, leaving behind godly Agamemnon,
lay beside Aigisthos and preferred a worse husband;
so too Helen shamed the marriage-bed of blond Menelaos

The vocalic repetition of –e- in ἔπειτ' Ἔχεμον προλιποῦσ' ἐβεβήκει is contrasted to the alliteration of Φυλῆα φίλον in the next verse. Timandre, Tyndareos' first daughter, left Echemos and went to Phyleus, who was dear to the gods. Klytaimestra, Tyndareos' second daughter, left Agamemnon and joined Aigisthos, who (contrary to Phyleus) was not dear to the gods – in fact he was a worse husband. This contrast is aurally stressed for the listeners by a new sound-play, the vocalic repetition of –a-, which provocatively correlates Ἀγαμέμνονα, Αἰγίσθωι and ἀκοίτην. This time the operative words are apart but complex patterning (παρέλεκτο καὶ εἴλετο) both within the sub-unit of the couplet pertaining to Tyndareos' second daughter (Klytaimestra) and between the sub-units of Timandra and Klytaimestra (προλιποῦσ' – <προ>λιποῦσ') bring into focus the overall contrast: rejection of marriage for a new household.

Alliteration can also be used to conjure an image or to give vividness to an existing image. In μαρνάσθην [ἔτι] μητρ[ὸς ἐόντ' ἐν γαστέρι κοίληι (fr. 58.13) the alliterative link created by the word-initial consonantal repetition of *m* illuminates the image of the twins Krisos and Panopeus fighting in their mother's womb. Action (fighting) and place (mother's womb) are aurally associated, as they are associated in the actual image described here.

Alliteration is also employed to build a link between its constituent items. Here belongs σὺν τῶι πῦρ [πνείουσαν ⏑–⏑⏑–⏑ Χίμαιραν (fr. 43a.87). No particular effect is discernible, only a stress on a given activity, i.e. that the emphasis is on the fact that Chimaira breaths fire.[11]

---

[11] I have not taken into account fr. 43a.77 (ἔγνω· ὁ μ[ὲν δώροις διζ]ήμενος ἦλθε γυνα[ῖκα) be-

Dead alliteration is likely to occur in conventional collocations and formulas.[12] Here the aural link is downplayed by the fact that the listener's ear hears the two words as a single semantic unit. So, in Φθίην ἐξίκετο **μη**τέρα **μή**λων (frr. 211.1 and 212.8) the perceptibility of the aural association is low.

2 Vocalic Repetition

Vocalic repetition can isolate a given term from its context. The reason for this isolation is not always obvious nor is there any general rule that is applied here. When dealing with proper names, vocalic repetition aims at stressing a specific list-entry. A case worth examining is offered by fr. 25.16 (Τοξέα τε Κλύμενό[ν τε ἄνακ]τ' ἀτάλαντ[ον] Ἄρηϊ). The syntagma ἄνακ]τ' ἀτάλαντ[ον] Ἄρηϊ (fr. 25.16) is a *hapax* in Hesiod. In Homer only the formula ἀτάλαντον Ἄρηϊ (*Il*. 5.576; 15.302; 17.72) is used, which is likely to have a limited perceptibility as far as the word-initial vocalic repetition is concerned. The Hesiodic syntagma ἄνακ]τ' ἀτάλαντ[ον] Ἄρηϊ seems to be an expansion of the Homeric formula and is clearly built on vocalic repetition. The series of five consecutive –*a*- sounds and (after the brief interruption of an –*o*- sound in ἀτάλαντ[ον]) a sixth word-initial –*a*- sound (Ἄρηϊ) isolates the proper noun Klymenos which it modifies from the 'naked' reference to Toxeus in the same verse (Τοξέα τε Κλύμενό[ν τε ἄνακ]τ' ἀτάλαντ[ον] Ἄρηϊ). As noted above, the reason for this isolation is not clear, but it may be the case that for some reason Klymenos, the last entry in the short list of Althaia's sons (other than Meleagros) needs to be highlighted. Isolation of a term stresses its importance for a given scene or episode. Fragment 165 begins with the tattered remains of a speech that ends by stressing that somebody (offering hospitality and raising Auge) would be very pleasing to the immortals (165.3: ....]μάλα δ' εὔαδεν ἀθα[νάτοισιν]). We do not know who is the speaker but we know that the addressee is Teuthras, who agreed to do as the gods commanded. The narrator's text following the speech picks up the last word ἀθα[νάτοισιν and reiterates it in the second-to-next line (165.5):[13] ἀθανά]των οἵ οἱ τότ' ἐναργέες ἄντ' ἐφάνησαν. Repetition is strengthened by the assonance of οἵ οἱ that functions as an isolation mechanism keeping

---

cause I regard the supplement ἕδνοις instead of δώροις as being much more plausible because of *Od*. 16.391 and 21.161 (μνάσθω ἐέδνοισιν διζήμενος; see Hirschberger (2004) 283 on fr. 37.77 (= 43a.77 M.-W.); ἕδνοις is also printed in Most's Loeb edition.
12 See Silk (1974) 174 and *OCD* s.v. 'assonance', p. 186.
13 On adjacency across lines, see Guggenheimer (1972) 114–116; Frédéric (1985) 48; Lausberg (1990³) 314–315; Wills (1996) 394–397.

ἀθανά]των apart. This time, aural isolation is ancillary to verbal repetition. Together they corroborate the content of the passage: Teuthras abided by the will of the gods and they were pleased with him.[14]

Vocalic repetition is wont to be noticed by listeners, even within a formulaic environment, under the proviso that it is based on intensive recurrence. Unlike its Homeric counterpart ἐπήρατον ἐντὸς ἔεργεν/-ει (Il. 18.12/Il. 22.121), the Hesiodic formula ἐπήρατον εἶδος ἔχουσα[ν (frr. 25.29; 136.2: [ἐ]πήρατον [εἶδος ἔχουσαν) is used to draw attention to the formula's meaning, as sound repetition aims at underlining the formula's expressive force: excessive beauty. The same is the case with ἣ εἶδος ἐρήριστ' ἀθανάτηι]σιν (frr. 35.12; 180.14), in which the triple word-initial vocalic recurrence of the sound -e- stresses the content of the expression (i.e. that a mortal woman rivals the immortal goddesses), as well as with Ἑλένη]ς ἕνεκ' ἠϋ[κόμοιο (fr. 200.11), in which the word-initial -e- sound, enhanced by the liquid/nasal sequence in the first two words within a series of six -e- sounds in total, binds Helen and 'fair-haired' together, underscoring her beauty. Another relevant expression is ἀνδράσι τ' ἀλφηστῆισιν ἀρῆς ἀλκτῆρα φυτεῦσαι (fr. 195.36 = Sc. 29). The juxtaposition of two formulas, each consisting in two words beginning with the -a- sound (followed by nasals or liquids) creates a firm joint that highlights the content of the verse: Herakles will be a protector of mortal men. To this end, the placement of θεοῖσιν (that syntactically plays the same role with ἀνδράσι) at the very end of the previous verse makes it fade. The main role of Herakles is to ward off evil from humans. The aural association of the two formulas is so strong that it does not seem excessive to argue that it also exploits 'traditional' sound-patterns that are particular to Herakles. In this light, the interplay effected by the -a- sound (followed by nasals or liquids) would have aurally 'recalled' the typical patronymic Ἀλκείδης, partly echoed in the expression πάϊς Ἀλκαίοιο that is used three lines before (195.33 = Sc. 26).

On the contrary, when low-level vocalic repetition is nested in a formula, it usually remains unnoticed by the audience. εἴαρο[ς ὥρηι (fr. 70.13) is such a case, the more so since the syllable repeated at the beginning of the two ensuing words is not exactly the same. The expression is imbued with a certain melody (perceptible when the verse is heard), but its only artistic purpose seems to be euphony.

Vocalic repetition can enforce an idea that has been already expressed by renewing its force or by following it to its next phase. In fr. 43.76–77, Sisyphos' efforts to get Eurynome are unable to win the mind of Zeus (ἀλλ' οὔ τι Διὸ]ς νόον

---

[14] On this fragment, see Merkelbach (1957) 40–41; Hirschberger (2004) 338–341.

αἰγιόχοιο / ἔγνω). This is a situation analogous to the one that already occurred when Sisyphos tried to get Mestra for his son Glaukos a few verses earlier (Fr. 43a.51–52: ἀ]νδρῶν δὲ προὔχεσκε **νοήματά** τε πραπ[ίδας τε / ἀ]λλ' οὔ πως ᾔδει Ζη**νὸς νόον** αἰγιόχοιο). In the case of Mestra, the semantic antithesis between Sisyphos' excessive mental skills and his inability to rival Zeus' mind is highlighted by the aural interplay between **νοήματα** and Ζη**νὸς νόον**.[15] In the analogous case of Eurynome, Sisyphos' second failure to 'read' Zeus' mind is initially expressed by the formula 'verb οἶδα + Διὸς/Ζηνὸς νόον'. This time, though, the essential idea is carried through to its next step: Zeus expresses his denial to Sisyphos' offer by throwing back his immortal head (43a.79: **ἀ**θανάτωι **ἀ**[νένευσε] **κ**αρήατι).

Aural association may explain the poet's choice of a dialectic form instead of the standard epic one. In fr. 70.21, the epichoric form Ἐρχομενοῦ (IG VII 3171) is employed instead of the form Ὀρχομενοῦ,[16] which may have been used two more times in the same fragment (see *70.30 and *70.35). The reason for this choice is probably the creation of an aural link in 70.23 (καί τε δι' **Ἐ**ρχομενοῦ **εἰ**λιγμένος **εἶ**σι δράκω]ν ὥς).[17] The aim is to attach aurally place-names to nearby terms (such as εἶσι) and thus generate an onomatopoeic effect.[18] Such a mechanism is not 'reserved' only to 70.23 but is observed (though through syllabic or near-syllabic repetition) in verses 70.18 (ὅς τε **Λι**λαίηθεν προΐει κα**λλίρ**]ροο[ν] ὕδωρ) and 70.21 (ὅς <τε> **παρὲκ Πα**νοπῆα διὰ γ]ληχῶνα τέρειναν).[19] The effect is impressive: the listeners follow the course of the river Kephisos from Lilaia to Panopeus to Erchomenos by means of aural links that emphasize each of the three phases of this 'journey'. A similar case is that of Ἄτλαντός τ' ὄρος] <u>αἰπὺ</u> κ[αὶ **Αἴτ**ν]ην <u>παιπαλόεσσαν</u> (fr. 150.25). The vocalic repetition of word-initial –a– connects Atlas' high and steep mountain to rugged Aitna and the link is further reinforced by the near-syllabic repetition between **αἰπὺ** and **παι**παλόεσσαν,

---

[15] It should be noted that the emphasis on mental ability may have been also expressed in the highly fragmented lines 43a.44–50 (e.g. 43a.50: …]εν ελασσωνουν[). Merkelbach (ap. app. cr.) restores verses 49–50 as follows: ὃς δή] τοι μακάρων, [οἳ Ὀλύμπια δώματ' ἔχουσιν, εἶχ]εν ἐλάσσω νοῦν.

[16] On these forms, see Hirschberger (2004) 261.

[17] Silk (1974, 184–187) presents various cases of alliteration as enforcement of interaction, especially in similes or simple comparisons. In fr. 70.23 the expression εἰλιγμένος … δράκω]ν ὥς is appropriate to the course of the river Kephisos but there is not any aural association at work whatsoever. Instead, it is only εἰλιγμένος that interacts with the place name Ἐρχομενοῦ and the verb εἶσι.

[18] On etymological links in the Catalogue, see below (this chapter) and Davies 86–92 (this volume).

[19] See section 1.3 (below).

which modify the two place names, Atlas' mountain and Aitna respectively. As in the previous example (fr. 70, see above), so here toponyms indicating the regions from which the Boreads pass in their pursuit of the Harpies are highlighted by means of sound-play: .... παρ' Ἠριδανοῖο βα[θυρ]ρ[ό]ου αἰπὰ ῥέεθρα (fr. 150.21)[20] and .... Ὀ]ρτυγίην Λαιστ[ρ]υ[γον]ίην τε γενέθλην (fr. 150.26).

Vocalic repetition can operate not just on the level of the verse but of a series of verses sharing a common idea. In the Atalanta-*ehoie* (frr. 73–76)[21] repetition of a word-initial –*a*- lays emphasis to the main idea of the passage, i.e. Atalanta's rejection of human beings and especially of men. Before I go on with further details, a necessary *caveat* must be presented and briefly discussed. It is true that 'recurrence over a longer space tends to be less perceptible',[22] but systematic repetition organized with respect to a theme lying at the kernel of a passage or section may counterbalance the disadvantage of textual dispersion. In fact, the sound-play orchestrated around the word-initial –*a*- is unfailingly tied to the thematic thread unraveled in the entire Atalanta-*ehoie*:

Fr. 73.1–5:

          ἀγακλε]ιτοιο ἄνακτος
[   ]σι ποδώκης δῖ' Ἀταλάν[τη
[Χαρί]των ἀμαρύγματ' ἔχο[υσα
[πρὸς ἀνθρώπων ἀ]παναίνετο φῦλον ὁμιλ[εῖν
ἀνδρῶν ἐλπομένη φεύγ]ειν γάμον ἀλφηστάων[.

        very gl]orious lord
[   ] swift-footed godly Atalanta
[   ] possessing Graces' radiance
she refused to associate with the tribe [of all human beings
hoping to escape] marriage [with men] who live on bread

Fr. 75.24:
]α ἀνιηρὸν ἄεθλον

] grievous contest

Fr. 76.4–6:
ἦχ' ὑποχωρήσασ'· οὐ γὰρ ἶσ[ον ἀμφοτέροισιν

---

20 Compounds like βαθύρρος were thought to convey grandeur and conciseness, since they could stand for an entire phrase; See [Demetrius] *On Style* 93: ὄνομα γὰρ τεθήσεται ἀντὶ ὅλου τοῦ λόγου ('One word will stand for an entire phrase', Innes 1995, 409).
21 On the Atalanta-*ehoie*, see Hirschberger (2004) 458–460. On the problem related to whether it belongs to the *Cat.* or the *Megalai Ehoiai* (*ME*), see D'Alessio (2005) 213–216 with further bibliography.
22 Silk (1974) 174.

ἆθλον ἔκειθ᾽· ἦ μέγ ῥα π[οδώκης δῖ᾽ Ἀταλάντη
ἵετ᾽ ἀναινομένη δῶρα [χρυσῆς Ἀφροδίτης

she, retreating a little; for unequal for the two of them
was the contest: for she, [swift-footed Atalanta,
sped refusing the gifts of [golden Aphrodite

The words beginning with an –a- aurally summarize the thematic nucleus of an essential part of the story: Atalanta of the flashing steps (Ἀταλάντη/ἀμαρύγματα), daughter of a famous king (ἀγακλειτοῖο ἄνακτος), refused the company of mortals and (trying to avoid marriage with) men (ἀνθρώπων ἀπαναίνετο / ἀνδρῶν ἀλφηστάων). [...] A troublesome prize was set (ἀνιηρὸν ἄεθλον) for the one who would surpass her in speed, a prize not equal to her and the one who would compete with her (ἀμφοτέροισιν / ἆθλον), for she was running because she refused Aphrodite's gifts (ἀναινομένη / Ἀφροδίτης), while he was running for his life.

Vocalic repetition can at times cooperate with other linking mechanisms (μέν-δέ) to enhance parallelism or to bring a given term in the limelight. In fr. 129, where we hear about the sons of Abas, word-initial vocalic repetition is balanced by syllabic repetition a few verses later (-to- / -ti- / -ti- / -to-): Zeus gives to Akrisios, one of the sons of Abas, the city of Argos (129.10: Ἀκρίσιος μὲν ἄρ᾽ Ἄ]ργει ἐυκτί[τ]ωι ἐμβασί[λ]ευεν) and to the other son Proitos the well-built citadel of Tiryns (129.16: Προῖτος δ᾽ αὖ Τίρυ]νθα ἐυκ[τ]ίμε[νο]ν πτολίεθρον). In fr. 165.11 (ἐν Ἀσ[ί]δι ἔτραφεν αἴηι), the vocalic repetition of –a- in word-initial position in the first *sedes* of feet 4 and 6 of the verse is reinforced both by the hyperbaton and metonymy (Ἀσ[ί]δι ... αἴηι). The result is the stress on Asia, the place where both the Herakles-Laomedon episode took place and the birthplace of Telephos.

3 Syllabic Repetition or Near-Repetition of Stem Syllables

Syllabic repetition or near-repetition of stem syllables is observable both on the level of a single verse and in longer units consisting either of couplets or a few lines of text. From a methodological point of view, though, textual space does not determine the role of syllabic repetition. In this light, it is better to present the results of my analysis on the basis of the function of this form of aural association.

The simplest form of syllabic or near-syllabic repetition occurs with respect to proper names, whether personal or place-names. In οἳ δὲ καὶ εἰς Ἄργος **Προῖ**[το]ν **πά**[ρα δῖον ἵκοντο (fr. 37.10), ὅς τε **Λι**λαίηθεν προΐει κα**λλίρ**]ροο[ν] ὕδωρ(70.18), and ὅς <τε> παρὲκ **Πα**νοπῆα διὰ γ⌊ληχῶνα τέρειναν (70.21) the aural associative link functions as an emphatic mechanism that brings a proper name into the spotlight.

A more intricate (and perhaps stylish) type of syllabic repetition or near-repetition of stem syllables aims at accentuating the content of a given verse or passage. In Ἄγριον ἠδὲ Λατῖνον ... / κούρη δ' ἐν μεγάροισιν ἀγαυοῦ Δευκαλίωνος / **Πα**νδώρη Διὶ **πα**τρὶ θεῶν σημάντορι **πά**ντων / μιχθεῖσ' ἐν φιλότητι τέκε Γραικὸν μενεχάρμην (fr. 5.1–4), the syllabic triplet *-pa-* in **Πα**νδώρη ... **πα**τρὶ ... **πά**ντων binds Pandora and Zeus together and aurally differentiates them from the previous verse in which Pandora had been designated as the daughter of Deukalion.²³ The transition from *koure* to *concubine* is thus visually represented by the shift from verse 2 to verse 3 and aurally by the emphatic link between the proper name (**Πα**νδώρη) and the periphrastic designation of Zeus. A bolder interpretive take on this fragment would even entertain the thought that parallelism (κούρη – Πανδώρη and δ' ἐν μεγάροισιν ἀγαυοῦ Δευκαλίωνος – Διὶ πατρὶ θεῶν σημάντορι πάντων) enhances this interplay and 'plays' with the idea that Zeus' extended designation as the 'father of all gods' replaces (as a lover!) Pandora's human father Deucalion. In τὴν **πέ**ρι δ]ὶς **πό**λεσαν **πε**ρί τ' ἀμφί τε κυκλώσαντο (fr. 150.28), the aural flanking of πόλεσαν by περί (in reversion the first time and tmesis the second) stresses through anaphoric duplication²⁴ the idea of the double (δ]ὶς) 'going around and encircling' of Ortygia. Emphasis on the content of a single verse is also observable in τάων ἃς **θνη**ταὶ **θνη**τοῖς τέκον εὐ**νη**θεῖσαι (fr. 195.13 = *Sc.* 6). Here, the word-initial suprasyllabic repetition of *–thnet-*, which is further enhanced by polyptoton, creates through aural association a solid joint that resonates in the second-to-next participial form εὐ**νη**θεῖσαι (*neth*) describing the sexual union between mortal women and men. Syntactical coordination between subject (**θνη**ταὶ), dative of accompaniment (**θνη**τοῖς), and verb (εὐ**νη**θεῖσαι) is thus 'imitated' by acoustical coordination. Sound mirrors syntax.

Syllabic repetition may acquire subtler forms. A relevant case is that with two examples of syllabic or near-syllabic chiastic gemination. In the first example, this phenomenon, observable in a single verse, follows a 'preparatory' manifestation of its constituent elements, whereas in the second it basically precedes its elaborate coagulation in the second verse of the relevant couplet. So, in Νέστορά τε Χ]ρομίον τε **Πε**ρι̱κλύμενόν τ' ἀγέρω̱χον, / ὄλβιον, ὧι⌋ **πόρε** δῶρα Ποσει-

---

²³ On Pandora, see Aloni 8–9 (this volume); Davies 85, 87 (this volume); Koning 105–108 (this volume); Cardin and Pontani 274, 276, 281 (this volume).
²⁴ On multiple anaphora in the same verse with examples from both Greek and Latin poetry, see Wills (1996) 363–371.

δάων ἐνοσίχθων / **παντο**]ῖ' (fr. 33a.12–14), the initial *-peri-* in the first part of the proper name Periclymenus is picked up by the chiastic *poRE ...RA po* (**πόρε** δῶρα Ποσειδάων) in the very next verse. Sophisticated syllabic interplay of this kind is attuned to the narrative unraveling of Pylos' siege by Herakles. Periklymenos, last in the list of Neleus' sons mentioned in the previous lines, is endowed by his father Poseidon with gifts of every sort (**παντο**]ῖ'). Perhaps his most impressive ability, no doubt a gift from his father, is his ability to change shapes. In fact, the ensuing narrative dwells on this special skill of Periklymenos whom Herakles is able to kill with Athena's help only after suffering severe casualties. Seen from this vantage point, the placement of the near-syllabic chiastic gemination at the outset of the Periklymenos narrative draws the audience's attention to the key element of the entire passage to follow. In ἔξοχον ἀνθ[ρώπων ἀρ]ετῆι **ἐπ'** ἀπείρονα γ[αῖαν. / τῶι δὲ καὶ η[...... **πα**]τὴρ **πόρε Πήγασο**[ν **ἵππον** (fr. 43a.83–84) the chiastic aural association of *re ... EP ... PE ... ro* (ἀρ]ετῆι **ἐπ'** ἀπείρονα) suggests through the aural link between terms that are juxtaposed but syntactically unconnected (ἀρ]ετῆι ἐπ' ἀπείρονα) that Bellerophon's virtue has no limit. This aural 'suggestion' is consonant with the meaning of the actual phrase, since we are told that his virtue spans the boundless earth. This elaborate aural association enhances a further interplay in the ensuing verse that is orchestrated initially by a further acoustic chiasmus repeating the two constituent items of the preceding line, and then by an intensification of one of them: **πα**]τὴρ **πόρε Πήγασο**[ν **ἵππον**. This double aural chiasmus, which is further strengthened by single syllabic near-repetition, is one of the most impressive sound-plays of the whole *Catalogue*. The result of this refined interplay in two consecutive verses is arresting: the second verse of the couplet discloses the recognition of Bellerophon's virtue on the boundless earth by his father Poseidon by means of the gift of the horse Pegasos.[25]

Syllabic repetition can also enhance parallelism by calling attention to a 'dormant' semantic relation between its constituent items. In [ἐ]πεὶ τέκε **πα**ῖδα Ποσειδάωνι ἄνακτι / [αἰν]όμορον **πα**τέρα ὃν **πο**ρσαίνεσκεν (43a.68–69), the aural symmetry ABAB (*pa-po / pa-po*) alludes to Mestra's balanced life as Poseidon's concubine and as Erysichthon's daughter: 'she bore a son to lord Poseidon – she provided for her doomed father'.[26]

---

25 Along this interpretive line, I would not be surprised if verse 85 (ὠκύτατον [............]μινε- πτε[ ) contained some form of the root πτερ- (Pegasos is after all a winged horse), as it has been suggested by Schwartz (*in apparatu critico editionis* M.-W.) who reads πτερ[όεντι.
26 Note the semantically antithetical but structurally parallel use of ἄνακτι – αἰνόμορον, the former modifying Poseidon, the latter Mestra's father Erisychthon.

A special kind of syllabic or near-syllabic repetition involves sound recurrence both at the end of a given verse and the beginning of the next verse. The phenomenon has been aptly called 'adjacency across lines'[27] and, although it has been initially employed with respect to word repetition, it is equally applicable to aural association. Adjacency of an aural pattern across lines leads to the carrying over of a sound, often to suggest or expand or specify a meaning or relation that is not explicit. In τῆς μὲν Σίσυφο]ς Αἰολίδης πειρήσατο **βουλέων** / **βοῦς ἐλ**άσα[ς (fr. 43a.75–76), the near-repetition of *boule* / *bousel* at the end of one verse and the beginning of the following creates an aural link and specifies how Sisyphos 'made trial of her (Eurynome's) plans, i.e. by 'driving away cattle'. The second constituent item in this sound-play is thus coordinated with the first, effecting a smooth transition to the next phase of Sisyphos' plan. Although it is not clear whose cattle Sisyphos steals – nor are details of this story in general clear – it is noteworthy that this plan that is aurally underscored by *boule* / *bousel* resonates in the expression βουλῆι Ἀθ[ηναίης (fr. 43a.78), which Sisyphos follows in his attempt to get Eurynome for his son Glaukos. The implicit point of this aural association is the triggering of a semantic interaction between the adjacent aural link of lines 75–76 and the 'will of Athena' in line 78: The cattle Sisyphos raided, which must have been connected to Eurynome, amount to literal or metaphorical marriage gifts,[28] per Athena's will. Another relevant example of near-syllabic adjacency across lines is attested in ἐν δ' ἄνδρες ναίουσι **πολύ**ρρηνες **πολυ**βοῦται / **πολλοί** ἀπειρέσιοι φῦλα θνητῶν ἀνθρώπων (fr. 240.3–4).[29] Prosodic variation in the first part of the adjacent compounds like **πολύρρηνες πολυβοῦται** is cut short (because the first *polu* scans as υ – (short / long) due to the double ρρ in **πολύ**ρρηνες, whereas the second *polu* scans as υυ (double short)), but the near-recurrence of the sound *poll* at the very beginning of the ensuing verse is very strong; so strong, that by carrying over the sense of 'mass numbers' to the next line it facilitates the asyndeton that spans this couplet. Syntax and sound are, therefore, effectively orchestrated in order to call attention to the fact that Ellopie is a region of multitude ('rich in sheep and rolling-footed cattle' (240.1–2: ἔστι τις Ἑλλοπίη **πολυλήϊος** ἠδ' εὐλείμων / ἀφνειὴ μήλοισι καὶ εἰλιπόδεσσι βόεσσιν) and of many inhabitants (240.4: **πολλοί** ἀπειρέσιοι φῦλα θνητῶν ἀνθρώπων).

Near-syllabic repetition can also highlight an etymological bond between two items. If they are adjacent, their association is characterized by high levels

---

[27] See Wills (1996) 394–397.
[28] Hirschberger (2004, 283 on fr. 37.76 = 43a.76 M.-W.) considers various scenarios, of which none is certain, as she rightly acknowledges.
[29] On this couplet, see also 'Complex Cases' (below).

of perceptibility. In θεσσάμενος γενεὴν **Κλεοδ**αίου **κυδαλ**ίμοιο (fr. 231), the proper name **Κλεοδ**αίου resonates in its bordering epithet **κυδαλ**ίμοιο. The repetition of –k- in word-initial position and the consonantal chiasmus *l-d / d-l* stresses the etymological link between these two *verba loquentia*. One may not be wrong to argue that κυδαλίμοιο has been used here simply to make sound and sense cooperate in highlighting the glory (*kleos*) of Kleodaios' race.[30]

Last, I will visit a case in which double syllabic repetition in word-initial position is illusive, despite the fact that it is observed in two adjacent words, i.e. in what is the 'default' mode of aural association. In [   ]ι **πολυ**στάφυλον **πο[λυ**γηθέα (70.6), the aural link between *polu-polu* is misleading, since the prosodic variation of the repetend (resulting from metrically different 'neighbors') undermines the acoustic connection which is only visual, i.e. created by the printed text. The first *polu* scans as υ – (short / long) because the cluster στ in πολυστάφυλον makes the syllable λυ long (πολυσ.τάφυλον), whereas the second *polu* scans as υυ (double short), since it is followed by the single consonant γ (πολυ.γήθεα).[31]

4 Syllabic Repetition or Near-Repetition of Final Syllables

Syllabic repetition or near-repetition of final syllables is a form of rhyme facilitating memorization and list-learning of proper names. In Ὕλλ**ον καὶ** Γλῆν**ον καὶ** [Κτή]σιππ**ον καὶ** Ὀνείτην (fr. 25.19), the first three proper names rhyme at word-terminal position. The effect is made clearer by the placement of καὶ after each name so as to make the preceding short syllable of second-declension nouns long by position. The last item in this verse tellingly begins with the same sound (Ὀνείτην) in which all previous three names end. Here, sound similarity draws attention to the last name but immediately differentiates it by means of prosodic variation (its initial syllable being short). The same euphonic and mnemonic effect is observed in Φηρ**έα** θ' ἱππόδαμ[ον καὶ εὐμ]μελίη[ν Ἀγέ]λαον / Τοξ**έα** τε Κλύμενό[ν τε ἄνακ]τ' ἀτάλαντ[ον] Ἄρηϊ (fr. 15.15–16) by means of parallel syllabic repetition of –*ea*- (reinforced by the same accentual pattern) and word-terminal –*on* that is lengthened by position or in Δηΐμαχ**όν τε**] καὶ Εὐρύβιον κλειτ**όν** τ' Ἐπίλα**ον** / Νέστορά τε Χ]ρομί**ον τε** Περικλύμεν**όν** τ' ἀγέρω[χον (fr. 33a.11–12) through a simple word-terminal assonance of –*on*

---

[30] On etymology in Hesiodic fragments, see Davies 86–92 (this volume).
[31] Hopkinson (1982, 162–177) offers a large number of cases of juxtaposed prosodic variants in Greek and Latin poetry; on variation of repetends, mainly but not solely in Latin poetry, see Wills (1996) 461–471.

and -*on t(e)*. In Εὐρ]υθεμίσ̱τ̱η̱ν̱ τε Σ̱τ̱ρατ[ο]ν̱ίκην [τ]ε̱ Σ̱τ̱[ε]ρό̱π̱ην τε (fr. 26.9), morphological correspondence of first-declension feminine nouns and syntactical coordination are fully exploited so as to a create a triple sound-play of -*en te*.

5 Complex Cases

Ἄκρως δὲ καὶ ἡ ἐπὶ ταὐτὸ σύνοδος τῶν σχημάτων εἴωθε κινεῖν, ὅταν δύο ἢ τρία οἷον κατὰ συμμορίαν ἀνακιρνάμενα ἀλλήλοις ἐρανίζηι τὴν ἰσχὺν τὴν πειθὼ τὸ κάλλος ('The combination of several figures often has an exceptionally powerful effect, when two or three combined cooperate, as it were, to contribute force, conviction, beauty').[32] What [Longinus] (*On the Sublime* 20) says with respect to figures of speech is also true for the combination of sound-patterns.

Under the category of 'complex cases' I group verses or passages in which more than one of the above forms of sound-play are orchestrated in order to facilitate interaction and create or emphasize meaning.

5.1 Progressively-Developed Aural Associations

Aural association can operate not only in single verses or couplets but also in longer stretches of text by means of various forms of acoustic links. The effect is to ease the flow of the narrative by aurally drawing attention to some of its constituent elements. In [   ]εος **γαιη̱ό̱χου ἐννοσιγαίου**· / ἢ δ' ἄρ' ἐνὶ μεγ]άροις **διδυμάονε** γείνατο τέκ[νω / **Ἄκτορι** κυσαμ]ένη καὶ **ἐρικτύπωι** ἐννοσιγαί̱[ωι, / ἀπλήτω, **Κτέα**]τ̱όν τε καὶ **Εὔρυτον**, οἷσι πόδες [μ]ὲ̱ν̱.[/ ἦν τέτορες, κ]εφαλα̱ὶ̱ **δὲ̱ δύω ἰδὲ** χεῖρες εεισ[..]ν̱ (fr. 17a.13–17), Poseidon's fatherhood is stressed by the 'preparatory' syllabic recurrence of *gai* in the first and second part of two adjacent compound adjectives (γαιη̱ό̱χου ἐννοσιγαίου) pointing to ἐννοσιγαί̱[ωι in the next line. This is however, only the first phase of aural associations that are effected as the narrative unravels. Later on the new fathering by Aktor will be presented next to that of Poseidon. Their being on par with one another is highlighted by both their syntactical coordination (καὶ) and aural chiasmus (Ἄκτορι ... ἐρικτύπωι), which will resonate in the hypogrammatic echo of the names of the male offspring (Κτέα]τόν ... Εὔρυτον) in the next verse.[33] Once this aural interplay is exhausted, the poet will re-activate an aural element

---

[32] Halliwell (1995) 237.
[33] See Watkings (1995) 189–190, who has unearthed various hypogrammatic echoes in Greek poets, among whom is Hesiod (*Op*. 1.1–2: **Μοῦσαι** Πιερίηθεν ἀοιδῇσι κλείo**υσαι**, / δεῦτε Δί' ἐννέπετε, σφέτερον πατέρ' ὑμνείo**υσαι**).

that was pregnant in the near-syllabic repetition of **διδυμάονε** that designated the twins to be born. The near-syllabic repetition of *de-du-de* in κ]εφαλαὶ **δὲ δύῳ ἰδὲ** χεῖρες echoes the twin nature (**διδυμάονε**) of Kteatos and Eurytos and brings this progressive aural interaction to completion.

In καὶ **δὴ** ἔχεν **δύο** μῆλα ποδώκης **δῖ**' Ἀτ[αλάντη· / ἐγγὺς δ' ἦν τέλεος· ὃ δὲ **τὸ τρίτον** ἧκε χ[αμᾶζε (fr. 76.20 – 21), the near-syllabic repetition of *de-du-di* underscores the link between Atalanta and the two apples that she catches, while the aural association between *to-t-to* acoustically reenacts the semantic differentiation between the first two apples and the third, which is paramount for the unraveling of this story.

Various forms of assonance can be progressively combined to draw attention to place names that delineate the geographical framework within which a given episode will take place. In ἡ' οἵη **Διδύμους** ἱερ**οὺς** να**ίουσα** κολων**οὺς**] / Δωτ**ίωι** ἐν πεδ**ίωι** πολυβότρυος ἄντ' Ἀ]μύροιο / νίψατο **Βοιβιά**δος λίμνης πόδα παρθέ]νος ἀδμής (fr. 59.2–4), the near-syllabic repetition of *di-du* (**Διδύμους**) is coupled in the same verse by the triple repetition of the word-terminal syllable –*ous* (Διδύμ**ους** ἱερ**οὺς** ... κολων**οὺς**) which is also repeated one more time in word-internal position (να**ίου**σα). In the next verse, the highlighting of place names is achieved by the word-terminal syllabic repetition of *ioi-ioi*, and is strengthened by a similar accentual pattern (Δωτ**ίωι** ἐν πεδ**ίωι**) and by syllabic repetition in word-initial position that is aurally facilitated by the ensuing nasals (ἄντ' Ἀ]μύροιο). Last, in 59.4 emphasis on lake Boibias is carried out by the near-repetition of *Boi-bia* (**Βοιβιά**δος).

5.2 Short-Range Aural Association

Aural links of different kinds operate even on the level of a single verse, so as to call attention to semantic association or to make semantic suggestions that are not explicitly expressed. Since there are numerous examples of this phenomenon, I will restrict myself only to those I consider most noteworthy.

In fr. 33a.28 (νήπιος, **οὐδ' ἔδδεισε** Διὸς ταλασίφρονα παῖδα) consonantal repetition of –*d*- in three adjacent syllables (**οὐδ' ἔδδεισε**) is immediately followed by the near-syllabic repetition of *se-os* (**ἔδδεισε Διὸς**) interrupted by a further d-beginning syllable (**ἔδδεισε Διὸς**). This elaborate chiasmus stresses the irony of Periklymenos' behavior. The point is that the man whom he did not fear was none other than Zeus' son, i.e. someone superior to any descendant of Poseidon (Periklymenos was Poseidon's grandson who had been endowed with the ability to shapeshift). In this way, the text, which had marked by ring composition the last phase of their encounter (33a.25: ἤ]τοι ὃ μὲν ζυγοῦ **ἄντα** βίης Ἡρακληείης – 33a.30: ἀλλὰ] τότ' ἀντίος ἦλθε βίης Ἡρακληείης), underscores the fated end of Periklymenos (called a 'fool' (νήπιος)) by Herakles.

Another relevant case of consonantal alliteration combined with adjacent near-syllabic repetition is offered by fr. 198.10 (δί]ου Ἀρητιάδαο· δί[<δ>ου] δ' ἀπε[ρείσια ἔ]δνα), fr. 204.61 (Τυνδαρέου ποτὶ δῶμα δαΐφρονος, ὄφρ[α ἴδοιτο), and fr. 204.136 (δεινὸς ὄφις κατὰ νῶτα δα[φοιν). In fr. 198.10 the nexus of aural associations highlights the offering of marriage gifts to Helen by Thoas, who is first in the list of suitors mentioned *after* Odysseus. By aurally emphasizing the offering of wedding gifts by Thoas, the poet of the *Catalogue* wanted to indicate to his audience the difference between him and Odysseus, who 'did not send any gifts for the long-ankled maiden' (198.4: δῶρα μὲν οὔ ποτ' ἔπεμπε τανισφύρου εἵνεκα κούρης). In fr. 204.61, the acoustic link between **δῶμα δαΐφρο**νος and **ὄφρ[α ἴδ**οιτο underscores the fact that Idomeneus did not send a proxy to Sparta but traveled on his own *so that he could see* Helen *in the house of wise* Tyndareos. The function of the nexus of assonantal devices is to draw attention to the semantic interaction of the two constituent items (**δῶμα δαΐφρο**νος and **ὄφρ[α ἴδ**οιτο), highlighting Idomeneus' deviation from the proxy-sending tactics of the other suitors. In fr. 204.136, the epithet **δα[φοινός** is prefigured by the preceding phrase **δεινὸς ὄφις** in the same verse.[34] Although the fragmentary condition of the text does not allow for further arguments, it may not be too bold to note that both the kenning 'hairless' (129: ἄτριχος)[35] and the typical designation of the snake (137: ὄφις) trigger aural associations in the immediate context.

Often highlighted by ancient scholiasts and grammarians, a repetition of consonantal clusters imitating by its harshness of sound Zeus' mighty thundering is observed in fr. 54a.7 (σκ]ληρ[ὸν] δ' ἐβ[ρόντησε καὶ ὄβριμον, ἀμφὶ δὲ γαῖα).[36] A closer look, though, shows that various 'ancillary' aural links are activated so as to make the most of the expressiveness of this harshness of sound: a consonan-

---

[34] See Watkins (1995) 189, who draws attention to an analogous phenomenon in *Hom. Hymn to Apollo* [3] 362 (φοινὸν ἀποπνείουσ', ὁ δ' ἐπηύξατο Φοῖβος Ἀπόλλων), in which word-initial segments of the sequence φοινὸν ἀποπνείουσ' refigure the word-initial segments of the god's name in the sequence Φοῖβος Ἀπόλλων.

[35] On ἄτριχος, see under 'middle-range aural association' (below); on kennings, see Waern (1951).

[36] See Goslin (2010) 364, who draws attention to the use of this formula, which is coupled in *Th.* 839–849 with another formula (σμερδαλέον κονάβησε) that 'regularly occurs in epic poetry to register the effect of a powerful force, whether a voice or physical blow, on its environment'. In both the Typhonomachy passage from the *Theogony* and in fr. 54a, harshness of sound pertaining to Zeus' activity is followed by a reference to the earth (*Th.* 839–840: σκληρὸν δ' ἐβρόντησε καὶ ὄβριμον, ἀμφὶ δὲ γαῖα / σμερδαλέον κονάβησε – *Cat.* fr. 54a.7–8: σκ]ληρ[ὸν] δ' ἐβ[ρόντησε καὶ ὄβριμον / ἀμφὶ δὲ γαῖα / κ[ι]νήθ[η]).

tal cluster *skl* is placed at verse-initial position, and moreover the repeated consonantal clusters tied to near-supra-syllabic repetition of sound (*ebr-obr*) and other near-syllabic repetition (*ond-ont*) create an impressive chiasmus (*ond – ebr – obr – ont*).

Although formulas are marked by a low perceptibility of aural effects, Ζεὺς δ' ἄμ]μ' ἐπιμάρτυρος ἔστω (fr. 75.17) seems to be an exception. For the homoeoteleuton[37] with the previous verse (75.16:]οι εἰρημένος ἔστω) and the assonance of –e- in word-initial position are carried over to the ensuing formula Ζεὺς δ' ἄμ]μ' ἐπιμάρτυρος ἔστω through parallel repetition (ἐπιμάρτυρος ἔστω). In this light, the *amm-ma* acoustic link is not hidden in the formulaic expression but flanked by the parallel assonance of –e- sounds. The result of this intricate interplay is the stress on Zeus' being witness to Schoineus' words, as if repetition of sound imitated the force of the oath.

Prosodic variation of supra-syllabic word-initial pendants can be combined with other aural associative devices such as near-syllabic repetition. In fr. 150.22 (]φέρβουσα π[ολ]υσπερέας **πολύφορβος**) prosodic variation of the supra-syllabic word-initial πολυ-pendants[38] (πολυσ.περέα – πολύ.φορβος) is flanked by stem repetition in word-initial and word-terminal position (φέρβ-φορβ). The modification of φέρβουσα by πολύφορβος is a *hapax* that has disturbed Rzach who thought it to be the result of the visual influence of the preceding φέρβουσα, arguing that the poet of the *Catalogue* had initially written πολυφύλους in asyndeton. I have decided to follow the transmitted text which is, correctly, in my view, printed in the standard modern edition by Merkelbach and West. The chiastic structure *pherb-polu-polu-phorb* is based on the fact that πολύφορβος echoes in reverse order the preceding **φέρβουσα π[ολ]υ**(σπερέας), intensifying what has already been expressed. This well-known form of repetition in ancient Greek can take various forms: noun- or pronoun-shifts (e. g. *Il.* 4.62–63: ὑποείξομεν ἀλλήλοισι, / **σοὶ** μὲν **ἐγώ**, **σὺ** δ' **ἐμοί**), verb-shifts (e. g. Sappho 117: †**χαίροις** ἀ νύμφα†, **χαιρέτω** δ' ὁ γάμβρος), and even category-shifts (e. g. *Il.* 5.560–561: κα**πεσέτην** ... / τὼ δὲ **πεσόντ**' ἐλέησεν).[39] Verse 150.22 resonates *Od.* 11.264–265 (... οἷά τε **πολλοὺς** / βόσκει γαῖα μέλαινα **πολυσπερέας** ἀνθρώπους), in

---

[37] On an ancient definition of homoeoteleuton, see [Demetrius] *On Style* 25: ὁμοιοτέλευτα δέ ἐστι τὰ εἰς ὅμοια καταλήγοντα, ἤτοι εἰς ὀνόματα ταὐτά ... ἢ ὅταν εἰς συλλαβὴν καταλήγηι τὴν αὐτήν ('Homoeoteleuton is when clauses end similarly, either with the same word ... or with the same syllable', translation by Innes 1995, 365).

[38] Repetition of the first part of a compound (like φιλο- and πολυ-, a preposition, and α privative) is common in many Greek authors; see Denniston (1952) 130.

[39] For a detailed study of this forms of repetition in Latin poetry (with some examples from Greek authors too), see Wills (1996) 272–328.

which not only similar vocabulary is employed but also a similar repetition pattern is used. The recurrence of the simple adjective πολλοὺς in the compound πολυσπερέας (*Od.* 11.364–365) is analogous to the repetition of the participle φέρβουσα in the compound πολύφορβος in fr. 150.22.[40] In fact, the *Catalogue* also offers an example of the reverse phenomenon, which involves what is known as 'compound-simplification'[41] (the repetition of only one part of a compound): ἐν δ' ἄνδρες ναίουσι **πολύρρηνες πολυ**βοῦται / **πολλοὶ** ἀπειρέσιοι φῦλα θνητῶν ἀνθρώπων (fr. 240.3–4).

5.3 Middle-Range Aural Association

In fr. 43a.41–42 (ε]ὖτέ τις ἀντ' **ὤνοιο** χατίζηι **χ[ρῆ]μ'** ἀνελ[έσθαι / ἀ]μφὶ μάλα **χρῆν ὤγ[ον** ....]. τῖμον [), syllabic repetition of *chre* capped by nasals (*m-n*) aurally associates **χ[ρῆ]μ'** and **χρῆν** in two successive verses. The function of this aural link is the creation of an elaborate chiasmus with **ὤνοιο / ὤγ[ον**. The distribution of the constituent items of the chiasmus in the two successive verses (**ὤνοιο ... χ[ρῆ]μ' / χρῆν ὤγ[ον**) aims at stressing the balance between the thing to be exchanged and its purchased price.[42]

In fr. 62.1–3 (ἄκρον ἐπ' ἀνθερίκων καρπὸν θέεν οὐδὲ κατέκλα, / ἀλλ' ἐπὶ πυραμίνων ἀθέρων δρομάασκε πόδεσσιν / καὶ οὐ σινέσκετο καρπόν), near-syllabic repetition at word-initial position (**ἄκρ**ον ... **καρ**πὸν ... **κα**τέκλα/ **καρ**πόν) reinforced by other aural forms of acoustic association like syllabic repetition (ἀν**θερί**κων ... **θέε**ν / ἀ**θέρ**ων) and word-terminal syllabic recurrence in the arsis or first *sedes* of two bordering feet (ἀνθερί**κων** καρ**πὸν** / πυραμί**νων** ἀθέ**ρων**) may be distributed in three successive lines, in order to draw attention to the content of the story: Iphiklos used to run (**θέεν**) on the 'fruiting tops of asphodel' (**ἄκρον** ἐπ' ἀν**θερί**κων **καρπὸν**) without breaking them (**κατέκλα**); he would race upon the wheaten tassels (πυραμί**νων** ἀθέ**ρων**) on his feet and would not damage the fruit"[43] (**καρπόν**).

The sound-play orchestrated by tectals[44] can be noteworthy. In fr. 133.3–5 the alliteration of *-k-* and *-kh-* together with syllabic repetition at word-initial

---

40 For the 'simplex-compound' association, see Wills (1996) 443–445.
41 See Wills (1996) 319.
42 I am hereby following the text printed in Casanova (1977, 25–30) and reprinted in Most (2007, 138 and 140). For the various problems concerning the meaning of these lines, see Hirschberger (2004) 277–278 on *Cat.* fr. 37.41–43 (= fr. 43a.41–43 M.-W.).
43 Translation by Most (2007) 129.
44 'Tectals' is the current scientific term for 'gutturals'; for ancient Greek, see *NE* s.v. 'gutturals' [Steinbauer].

position⁴⁵ spans three lines describing the disease sent by Hera as a punishment to the daughters of Proitos (καὶ γάρ σφιν **κε**φαλῆισι **κ**ατὰ **κν**⌊ύος αἰνὸν **ἔχευ**⌊εν· / ἀλφὸς γὰρ **χ**ρόα πάντα **κα**τέσ**χ**<εθ>εν, αἱ δέ νυ **χα**ῖται / ἔρρεον **ἐκ κε**φαλέων, ψίλωτο δὲ **καλὰ κά**ρηνα). Sound repetition allows the listener to follow mentally the spread of the illness on the heads of the Proitids: itching (**κν**⌊ύος) is 'poured on' (**κ**ατὰ **ἔχευ**⌊εν) their heads, dull-white leprosy spreads over their skin (**χ**ρόα ... **κα**τέσ**χ**<εθ>εν), their hair (**χα**ῖται) begins to fall from their heads (**ἐκ κε**φαλέων), their beautiful heads (**καλὰ κά**ρηνα) are made hairless.

The same mechanisms of aural highlighting (alliteration of –d- together with syllabic or near-syllabic repetition of adjacent words) are employed in fr. 141.1–3 and 6 (] **Δ**ιὸς **δ**μηθεῖσα **δ**όλοισι. / τῆι δὲ μίγη φιλότητι] πατὴρ καὶ **δῶ**ρον **ἔδω**κεν / πα]τρὶ φέρων· ὃ **δὲ δέ**ξατο **δῶ**ρο[ν). In this episode of the love affair between Zeus and Europa, her subjugation to Zeus' wiles is aurally associated with Zeus' ensuing offer to her of a golden necklace, which Hephaestus made and gave to Zeus in the first place.

The same phenomenon is observed in fr. 204.87–90: **π**λεῖ[στ]α **π**ορών. Χείρων δ' ἐν **Πη**λίωι ὑλήεντι / **Πη**λείδην ἐκόμιζε **π**όδας ταχύν, ἔξοχον ἀνδρῶν, / **παῖ**δ' ἔτ' ἐόν[τ·] οὐ γάρ μιν ἀρηΐφιλος Μενέλαος / νίκησ') by means of alliteration of –p- and syllabic repetition of *pe*. The stress is on the antithesis between the victory of Menelaos in the suitors' contest for the hand of Helen by means of multiple gifts (**π**λεῖ[στ]α **π**ορών) and the absence of Achilleus from the contest who was raised by Cheiron at mount Pelion. The passage is nicely flanked by a ring composition (85–86: ... ἀλλ' ἄ[ρα πάντας / Ἀτρε[ίδ]ης ν[ίκησε]ν ἀρηΐφιλος Μενέλαος and 89–90: οὐ γάρ μιν ἀρηΐφιλος Μενέλαος / νίκησ') that accentuates the nexus of aural links.

Other forms of alliterative and/or syllabic or near-syllabic repetition are found in fr. 204.94–95 (ἄελπτον. πάντες δὲ **θ**εοὶ δίχα θυμὸν **ἔθ**εντο / ἐξ ἔριδος· δὴ γὰρ τότε μήδετο **θέ**σκελα ἔργα), fr. 204.124–129 (πο]λλὰ δ' ἀπὸ γλωθρῶν δενδρέων ἀμύοντα χα**μᾶζε** / χεύετο καλὰ πέτηλα, ῥ**έεσκε** δὲ καρπὸς **ἔραζε** / π]γείοντος Βορέαο περιζαμενὲς Διὸς αἴσηι, / .]·λ**εσκεν** δὲ θάλασσα, τρόμ{ε}**εσκε** δὲ πάντ' ἀπὸ τοῖο, / τρύχ**εσκεν** δὲ μένος βρότεον, μινύθ**εσκε** δὲ καρπός), and fr. 204.130 (γ]αἱ[η]ς ἐν κευθμῶνι **τρί**τωι ἔτεῖ **τρία τέ**κνα). In the first case, the usual alliteration of –th- in θεοί-τίθημι/-μαι is combined with syllabic repetition of -*the*- pointing to the 'wondrous deeds' (θέσκελα ἔργα) devised by Zeus for the race of men. In the second case, the homoeoteleuton χα**μᾶζε** / **ἔραζε** calls into attention the falling of trees and leaves on the earth and

---

45 A single-verse example of aural association by tectals (gutturals) is offered by *Cat.* fr. 26.12: ἄ**κρ**ᾳ **κά**ρηνα; for Homeric examples, see Edwards (1991) 58.

paves the way, through the harshness of sound created by the five-fold supra-syllabic repetition –*eske*- (ῥέεσκε / .]·λεσκεν ... τρόμ{ε}εσκε / τρύχεσκεν ... μινύθεσκε), to the destruction caused by Zeus. In the third case, the chiasmus of near-syllabic repetition of *tri-te-tri-te* in four successive words (**τρί**τωι **ἔτεϊ τρί**α **τέ**κνα) emphasizes the connection between the birth of three offspring by the snake in the third year. This middle-range aural association may have been created under the influence of the phrase ὅτε τ' ἄτριχος οὔρεσι τίκτει (fr. 204.129) that is also marked by recurrence of –*t*- sounds in various combinations and is syntactically linked to **τρί**τωι **ἔτεϊ τρί**α **τέ**κνα. After all, the kenning 'hairless' (ἄτριχος) functions as an attention-drawing device by means of its colloquial character.

Fragment 204.131 (**ἦρο]σ** μὲν κατ' **ὄρος** καὶ ἀνὰ δρυμ{ν}ὰ πυκνὰ καὶ ὕλην) offers a rare (for the *Catalogue*) form of aural association: near-repetition of two almost adjacent words. This sound repetition seems to function as a link to **ὥρηι ἐν εἰαρινῆι**, ὅτε τ' ἄτριχος **οὔρεσι** τίκτει (two lines before). The near-repetition of **ἦρο]σ** – **ὄρος** recapitulates the **ὥρηι ἐν εἰαρινῆι** – **οὔρεσι** interplay,[46] as the focus is still on the snake giving birth in the spring and going along 'down from the mountain and up among the dense corpses and forest'.[47]

5.4 Long-Range Aural Association

Long-range aural association is based on the repetition of the same or similar sound in an extended textual segment. The 'nuclear' aural feature is first presented as an 'advance mention' only to be picked up later and then exhaustively employed. In σκληρὸν δ'] ἐ**βρ**όντ[ησεν ἀπ'] οὐρανοῦ ἀστερόεντος (fr. 30.13), the word-initial cluster *br* seems to interact with other preceding and ensuing consonantal clusters such as *skl-nd* (σκληρὸν δ') and *nd* (ἐ**βρ**όντ[ησεν), since harshness of sound created by series of consonants was thought to imitate noise, here the noise made by Zeus' thundering.[48] But the unraveling of the narrative shows that the poet aims at creating a much more sophisticated interplay, since Zeus' thundering will be aurally connected to the insolent king Salmoneus and the punishment of his transgression: βῆ δὲ κατ' Ο]ὐλύμποιο [χο]λούμενος, αἶψα δ' ἵκανεν / λαοὺς Σαλμ]ωνῆος ἀτ[ασ]θάλου, οἳ τάχ' ἔμελλον πείσεσθ' ἔρ]γ' ἄϊδηλα δι' ὑ**β**[**ρ**]ιστὴν **β**ασιλῆα· / τοὺς δ' ἔ**β**α]λεν **β**ροντῆι [τε κ]αὶ αἰθαλόεντι κεραυνῶι. / ὣς λαοὺς ἀπε]τίνεθ' ὑπερ**β**[ασίην] **β**ασιλῆος / τὸν δὲ λα]**β**ὼν

---

46 See also the sound-play in fr. 70.13 (ε**ἴαρο**[ς **ὥρη**ι) and my comments under 'vocalic repetition' (above).
47 Translation by Most (2007) 237.
48 On such effects with emphasis on the Homeric scholia, see Richardson (1980) 283–285.

ἔρριψ' ἐς Τ[ά]ρταρον ἠερόεντα / ὡς μή τις] **βρ**οτὸς ἄλλος [ἐ]ρ̣ίζο̣ι Ζηνὶ ἄνακτι (fr. 30.15–23). This is a telling example of how a 'nuclear' aural feature (*br*) functions as the vehicle for a long-range acoustic interplay that will make use of the same or similar sound pattern: ἐβρόντησεν, ὑβριστὴν βασιλῆα, ἔβαλεν βροντῆι, ὑπερβασίην[49] βασιλῆος, βροτός. In fact, this list of acoustically associated terms amounts to an 'aural summary' of the relevant episode.

The preparatory mention of a low-perceptibility 'nuclear' aural element occurs again in the same fragment, this time in the context of the Tyro-Poseidon episode. Tyro was the only member of Salmoneus' family who was dear to the immortal gods, since she constantly rebuked and contended with her arrogant father and let no mortal challenge the gods. This episode begins right after the completion of the one pertaining to the destruction of Salmoneus' house by Zeus. At the very first verse, the only person of Salmoneus' family escaping destruction is introduced first as πάις ... φίλη and then by her name (Τυρώ). The 'nuclear' aural associative mechanism (alliteration of the sound –*p*- in *pais-phile*) can hardly be noticed per se by the audience but the emphasis on the justification of Tyro's salvation would no doubt have attracted attention. The two lines devoted to it, which are both full of repetitive features underscoring her continuous rebuke of Salmoneus (νεικέεσκε, **συνεχές**, εἴασκε), are completed by the phrase **βρ**οτὸν ἰσοφαρίζειν, which echoes the 'nuclear' aural element of the previous episode. This elaborate interplay between sound and narrative unraveling can hardly be accidental. The continuation of the plot verifies this assumption. The alliterative 'nuclear' element –*p*- that introduced Tyro as πάις ... φίλη soon becomes the acoustic pivot around which the rest of a long-range aural association revolves. Verses 31–35 (αὐτὰρ ἐπεί] ῥ' ἥβης **πο**λυηράτου ἐς τέλος ἦλθεν / .... τῆ]ς γ' ἐράεσκε **Πο**σειδάων ἐνοσίχθων / ....] **φι**λότητι θεὸς **βρ**οτῶι, οὕνεκ' ἄρ' εἶδος **πα**σάων **προ**ὔχεσκε γυναι]κῶν θηλυτεράων / ἣ δ' **ἐπ**' Ἐνιπῆος πωλέσκετο] καλὰ ῥέεθρα) exploit an entire wealth of alliterative or near-syllabic recurrences rotating around the love affair between Poseidon and Tyro. When the young girl arrived at the end of her much-desired puberty (ἥβης **πο**λυηράτου), Poseidon fell in love with her, a god with a mortal (**Πο**σειδάων ... **φι**λότητι θεὸς **βρ**οτῶι), since she surpassed all mortal women in beauty (**πα**σάων **προ**ὔχεσκε), and she would travel to the river Enipeus (**ἐπ**'

---

49 The abstract noun ὑπερβασίη is attested one more time in the entire Hesiodic corpus; see *Op*. 828 and West (1977) 364–365 on *Op*. 828, who defends the verse as genuine against the view (Σ Hes. *Op*. 828; see also Paus. 9.31.5) that it (or 826–828) was added to make a transition to the poem *Ornithomanteia*, also attributed to Hesiod. Writing before the edition of Hesiodic fragments by Merkelbach and West (1967), Krafft (1963, 71) discussed ὑπερβασίη in *Op*. 828 as a *hapax legomenon*.

Ἐνιπῆος πωλέσκετο), where Poseidon, taking the form of the river-god, would make love to her. Thus, the long-range aural interplay follows and highlights the narrative: the young girl at her puberty, the god in love, the girl's excessive beauty, the river she frequents as the place of their intercourse, all crucial elements of this episode are accentuated by means of the associative (alliterative and near-syllable based) repetition of the sound –*p*-. The sound-play is in this example so elaborately constructed that it not only interacts with the aural associations of the previous episode (see fr. 30.27: **βροτὸν**) but tags them in their new environment, always in tune with the narrative content. I am referring to verse 33 (**φιλότητι** θεὸς **βροτῶι**) where the consonantal cluster –*br*- that aurally marked the previous episode is almost juxtaposed (tellingly interrupted by θεὸς) to the alliterative device –*p*- of this episode. Previously, one god (Zeus) destroyed a family of arrogant mortals, now another god (Poseidon) falls in love with the one among them who honored the gods.

Another noteworthy example of long-range aural association is found in fr. 33. As in the previous case, the 'nuclear' element surfaces early in the text, at a significant distance from the passage where its linking potential will be fully operable. To cater to its enormous separation from the 'target' text, its advance mention takes the form of a complete syllabic and near-syllabic repetition that marks an entire verse: Νηλέα κα]ὶ **Πελίην πολέσιν λα**οῖσι[ν ἄνακτας (33a.2). By employing the *le-pel-pol-la* aural chiasmus, the poet aims to introduce his listeners to the aural and rhythmic 'grammar' of the ensuing episode. The high-perceptibility of this full-fledged acoustic device can stay in the audience's mind, in order to be evoked later on when Herakles attacks Pylos. Periklymenos, one of Neleus' sons, 'destroyed many other men fighting around the wall of glorious Neleus, his father, and he brought many to black death by killing them' (33a.19–21: β[ο]υλ[ῆι] Ἀθηναίης· **πολέας** δ' **ἀπόλεσσε** καὶ **ἄλλους** / μαρνάμενος Νηλῆος ἀγακλειτοῦ περὶ τεῖχος / ο[ὑ̃] πατρός, **πολέας** δὲ μελαίνηι κηρὶ **πέλασσε**).⁵⁰ Definitive proof that this mechanism of aural association is at work in this episode is offered by fr. 35, which is concerned with the same theme, i.e. the struggle between Periklymenos and Herakles. In verses 2–5 (ὄφρα μὲν οὖν ἔζ]ωε **Περικλύ**[μ]**ενος** θε[ο]ειδής, / οὐκ ἐδύναντο **Πύ**]**λον πραθέειν** μάλα περ μεμαῶτες· / ἀλλ' ὅτε δὴ θανάτο]ιο **Π**[**ε**]**ρικλύμενον** λάβε μοῖρα, / ἐξαλάπαξε **Πύλοιο πόλιν** Δι]ὸς ἄ[λ]κιμο[ς] υἱός) near-syllabic repetition is evenly distributed in four consecutive verses and further reinforced by parallelism (*per-pyl-per-pyl*) and other aural devices underscoring the sack of Pylos (*pyl-pr, pyl-pol*).

---

50 Translation by Most (2007) 93.

5.5 Formula-Bounded Aural Elements Interacting with Other Features

Syllabic or supra-syllabic repetition or near-repetition can happen between aural elements contained in a formula and aural features beyond its borders. By creating an aural expansion of part of a formula, the poet reads the formula anew, suggesting to his audience a novel function that is determined by the particular semantic content of the narrated story. This is the case with τῆμος ἄρ' ἄγγελος ἦλθε **κόρ**αξ ἱερῆς ἀπὸ δαιτὸς / Πυθὼ ἐς **ἠ**γαθέην καί ῥ' ἔφρασεν ἔργ' ἀΐδηλα / Φοίβωι ἀ**κερσεκό**μηι, ὅτι Ἴσχυς γῆμε **Κόρ**ωνιν / Εἰλατίδης, Φλεγύαο διογνήτοιο θύγατρα (fr. 60.1–4). The *ake-eko* supra-syllabic near-repetition in the formula Φοῖβος ἀκερσεκόμης is flanked by the interplay between the two *kor* (**κόρ**αξ – **Κόρ**ωνιν). The selection of this formula may, in fact, have been conditioned by the poet's will to 'refresh' the aural association between **κόρ**αξ and **Κόρ**ωνιν which (because of their separation in the text) would be characterized by low perceptibility. The result is that the crow, Apollo, and Koronis are aurally linked just as they are semantically associated in this particular story. Likewise in Φοῖβος ἀ**κερσεκό**μης ἀ**έκ**ων κτάνε νηλέ]ϊ δίσκωι (fr. 171.8), the *ake-eko* supra-syllabic near-repetition of the formula Φοῖβος ἀκερσεκόμης is exploited by the poet who uses it to create an aural interaction with the ensuing ἀέκων, beginning with the sound *aek*. The placement of *ktane* immediately afterwards reveals the studied sound-play: Apollo killed Hyakinthos by accident.

Conclusions

The *Catalogue of Women* is a treasurehouse of sound-play ranging from simple alliteration to vocalic, syllabic, and near-syllabic repetition in both word-initial and word-terminal position. Sound-play operates not only on verse-level but also on short-, middle- and long-range parallel and corollary passages. It is preeminently, but not exclusively, in cases like these that entire nexuses of aural associations are orchestrated to highlight what is overtly expressed in the narrative snapshot of a given episode or part of an *ehoie*. Sometimes aural links are used covertly to 'suggest' an interpretation that is not explicitly stated in the text. From a generic perspective, the wealth, variety, and sophistication of sound-play that has been explored in this chapter must be understood together with the fact that the *Catalogue* represents a novel crossing-over of *ehoie*-poetry to catalogue-poetry. It is exactly under the scope of the generic fusion of these sub-species of Greek epic that we should be studying the richness and intricacy of sound-play. To put it simply, all of these features of sound-play may well reflect the efforts of a cross-generic hybrid like the *Catalogue* seeking to find its own style.

Bibliography

Casanova, A. (1977). 'Lite per un matrimonio truffaldino nella Grecia arcaica (Hes. fr. 43 M.-W.)', *Prometheus* 3: 21–38.
Cohen, I. M. (1986). 'The Hesiodic *Catalogue of Women* and the *Megalai Ehoiai*,' *Phoenix* 40: 127–142.
Cohen, I. M. (1989). 'Traditional Language and the Women in the Hesiodic *Catalogue of Women*', *SCI* 10: 12–27.
D'Alessio, G. B. (2005). 'The *Megalai Ehoiai* : a survey of the fragments', in: R. Hunter (ed.), *The Hesiodic Catalogue of Women: Constructions and Reconstructions*, Cambridge, 213–216.
Davies, D. R. (1992). *Genealogy and Catalogue: Thematic Relevance and Narrative Elaboration in Homer and Hesiod*, Ph.D. dissertation, University of Michigan.
Denniston, J. D. (1952). *Greek Prose Style*, Oxford.
Edwards, M. W. (1987). *Homer: Poet of the Iliad*, Baltimore.
Edwards, M. W. (1991). *The Iliad: A Commentary, vol. V: books 17–20*, Cambridge.
Frédéric, M. (1985). *La Répétition: Étude linguistique et rhétorique*, Tübingen.
Goslin, O. (2010). 'Hesiod's Typhonomachy and the Ordering of Sound', *TAPA* 140.2: 351–373.
Guggenheimer, E. H. (1972). *Rhyme Effects and Rhyming Figures: A Comparative Study of Sound Repetitions in the Classics with Emphasis on Latin Poetry*, The Hague.
Halliwell, S. (1995): see Innes D. C. et al.
Hirschberger, M. (2004). *Gynaikōn Katalogos und Megalai Ēhoiai. Ein Kommentar zu den Fragmenten zweier hesiodeischer Epen*, Munich and Leipzig.
Hopkinson, N. (1982). 'Juxtaposed Prosodic Variants in Greek and Latin Poetry', *Glotta* 60.3/4: 162–177.
Hunter, R. (2009). 'Hesiod's style: towards an ancient analysis', in: Montanari, Rengakos, and Tsagalis, 253–269.
Hunter, R. (2014). *Hesiodic Voices. Studies in Ancient Reception of Hesiod's Works and Days*, Cambridge.
Innes, D. C., S. Halliwell, and W. H. Fyfe (1995). *Aristotle: Poetics, Longinus: On the Sublime, Demetrius: On Style*, Cambridge, MA and London, England.
Janko, R. (2000). *Philodemus. On Poems Book I*, Oxford.
Kakridis, I. Th. (1980). *Προομηρικά, Ομηρικά, Ησιόδεια*, Athens.
Krafft, F. (1963). *Vergleichende Untersuchungen zu Homer und Hesiod*, Göttingen.
Lausberg, H. (1990³). *Handbuch der literarischen Rhetorik: Eine Grundlegung der Literaturwissenschaft*, Stuttgart.
Meier, W. D. (1976). *Die epische Formel im pseudohesiodischen Frauenkatalog. Eine Untersuchung zum nachhomerischen Formelgebrauch*, Zürich.
Merkelbach, R. (1957). *Die Hesiodfragmente auf Papyrus*, Leipzig.
Merkelbach, R. and M. L. West (1967). *Fragmenta Hesiodea*, Oxford.
Montanari, F., A. Rengakos, and C. Tsagalis (eds.), *Brill's Companion to Hesiod*, Leiden and Boston.
Most, G. (2007). *Hesiod: The Shield, Catalogue of Women, Other Fragments*, Cambridge, MA and London, England.
Mureddu, P. (1983). *Formula e tradizione nella poesia di Esiodo*, Rome.

Mureddu, P. (2008). 'Epiteti femminili nel *Catalogo* esiodeo', in: G. Bastianini and A. Casanova (eds.), *Esiodo. Cent'anni di papiri, Atti del Convegno internazionale di studi* (Florence, 7–8 June 2007), Florence, 97–112.

Neitzel, H. (1975). *Homer-Rezeption bei Hesiod. Interpretation ausgewählter Passagen*, Bonn.

Nünlist, R. (2009). *The Ancient Critic at Work. Terms and Concepts of Literary Criticism in Greek Scholia*, Cambridge.

Richardson, N. J. (1980). 'Literary Criticism in the Exegetical Scholia to the *Iliad:* A Sketch', *CQ* 30.2: 265–287.

Rutherford, I. (2000). 'Formulas, Voice, and Death in *Ehoie*-Poetry, the Hesiodic *Gunaikon Katalogos*, and the Odyssean *Nekuia*', in: M. Depew and D. Obbink (eds.), *Matrices of Genre. Authors, Canons, and Society*, Cambridge, MA, 81–96.

Silk, M. S. (1974). *Interaction in Poetic Imagery*, Cambridge.

Silk, M. S. *OCD*, s.v. 'assonance', p. 186.

Tsagalis, C. (2009). 'Poetry and Poetics in the Hesiodic Corpus', in: Montanari, Rengakos, and Tsagalis, 131–177.

Waern, I. (1951). Γῆς Ὀστέα. *The Kenning in Pre-Christian Greek Poetry*, Uppsala.

Watkins, C. (1995). *How to Kill a Dragon. Aspects of Indo-European Poetics*, Oxford.

West, M. L. (1977). *Hesiod:* Works and Days. *Edited with Prolegomena and Commentary*, Oxford.

West, M. L. (1985). *The Hesiodic Catalogue of Women*, Oxford.

Wills, J. (1996). *Repetition in Latin Poetry: Figures of Allusion*, Oxford.

Part III: Hesiod's Fragments in Rome and Byzantium

Andreas N. Michalopoulos
Hesiodic Traces in Ovid's *Heroides*

Hesiod's multifaceted influence on Latin literature, probably through the mediation of Callimachus and Aratus,[1] has been investigated considerably.[2] In Rome, as well as in Greece,[3] Hesiod was treated with respect as Homer's great rival.[4] He was recognized on the one hand as the poet of myth (*Theogony*) and on the other as the wise poet of agriculture, practical advice, and everyday life (*Works and Days*).[5] Catullus,[6] Lucretius,[7] Vergil,[8] Horace,[9] Cornelius Gallus,[10] Propertius,[11] Tibullus,[12] and Ovid[13] are only some of the Roman authors influenced by Hesiod, his themes, motifs, and poetics.[14]

---

1 On Hesiod's importance for 3rd century BC poetry see Wimmel (1960) 238–241; Reinsch-Werner (1976); Hunter (2005b) 239 n. 1; Schroeder (2006); Sistakou (2009) 220 n. 2; Koning (2010) 333–341. For the presence of the *Catalogue* in Hellenistic poetry see Casanova (1979); Cameron (1995) 362–386; Rutherford (2000) 90; Hunter (2005b); Asquith (2005); on Callimachus' *Aetia* as a neoteric version of the *Catalogue*, see Sistakou (2009) 238–244. For Aratus as the Hellenistic Hesiod, see Callim. *Epigr.* 27 with Farrell (1991) 44–46.
2 See Hardie (2005) 287 n. 1; Rosati (2009) 343 n. 1; Koning (2010) 343–346; Ziogas (2013) 1 n. 2.
3 See e.g. Hermesianax fr. 7.21–23 Powell: Φημὶ δὲ καὶ Βοιωτὸν ἀποπρολιπόντα μέλαθρον / Ἡσίοδον πάσης ἤρανον ἱστορίης / Ἀσκραίων ἐσικέσθαι ἐρῶνθ' Ἑλικωνίδα κώμην.
4 On the *Certamen Homeri et Hesiodi* see Hess (1960); West (1967); Richardson (1981); Heldmann (1982); Rosen (1997) 473–477; Graziosi (2001); Collins (2004) 185–191; Koning (2010) 248f.; Rosati (2009) 343f. For a discussion between Philip and Alexander on Homer and Hesiod, see Dio Chrys. *Orat.* 2.7ff.
5 See Rosati (2009) 352; Koning (2010) 157. Aulus Gellius (*Noct. Att. 1.*15) calls Hesiod the 'wisest of poets' (*poetarum prudentissimus*). See Holford-Stevens (1988) 171f.
6 See Pontani (2000) on theoxeny (in the sense of the intermingling between gods and mortals) in the *Catalogue* and Catullus 64.
7 See Gale (1994) 64–7, 161–174, and index s.v. Hesiod, Rosati (2009) 356f.
8 La Penna (1962), Hardie (2005) 287–292, Rosati (2009) 357–9, 362f., 368. Vergil calls his *Georgics* an *Ascraeum carmen* (*Georg.* 2.176).
9 Rosati (2009) 371f. with n. 79.
10 For Gallus' role in Hesiod's reception at Rome, see Clausen (1994) 177–178, 199–204; Cairns (2006) 120–131; Rosati (2009) 362f.
11 See Alfonsi (1949); Hardie (2005) 292–295.
12 For Tibullus' relationship with Hesiod, see Grimal (1962); Rosati (2009) 366–368.
13 See Gibson (2003) 86, Hardie (2005) 296–298, Rosati (2009) 360, 363–365, 370f., 372–374.
14 On Hesiod and Ennius, see Häussler (1976) 161f., 172–178, Rosati (2009) 344–346; on Hesiod and Seneca, see Mazzoli (1970) 165–168, Setaioli (1988) 66–68.

As regards Ovid, scholarly interest has mainly focused on Hesiod's influence on the *Metamorphoses*.[15] In this essay I will seek to trace the influence of the *Catalogue of Women*[16] on another Ovidian work, the *Heroides*, a subject not treated systematically thus far. I will look for thematic affinities, common motifs, markers of allusion, and similarities in diction which will speak for the interrelation between the Hesiodic[17] *Catalogue* and the Ovidian *Heroides*; I will attempt to explore the way in which Ovid elaborated on the tradition of the *Catalogue* in order to compose his own innovative work.[18] I will discuss the single *Heroides* and I will focus my attention on Deianira's letter to Hercules (*Her.* 9), which, as I suggest, displays some striking points of contact with the *Catalogue*.

Most scholars agree[19] that Ovid had firsthand knowledge of the *Catalogue*. My goal here is to offer more evidence confirming this view, even though Ovid does not mention the *Catalogue* anywhere in his work. Ovid mentions Hesiod al-

---

15 See Schwartz (1960) 601–603; Lafaye (1904) 4f.; Bilinski (1959); McKay (1962) 44; Ludwig (1965) 74–76, Hollis (1970) 128f.; Myers (1994) 29; Keith (1992) 250 with n. 71 and (2002) 250f.; Fletcher (2005); Rosati (2009) 363f.; Ziogas (2011). More recently Ziogas (2013) studied in detail the way in which Ovid cast his *Metamorphoses* in the tradition of Hesiodic epic by reformulating the structure and the themes of the *Theogony* and the *Catalogue of Women*. See also Papaioannou (forthcoming) 130–131 on the catalogue of the heroes participating in the Calydonian boar hunt (Ov. *Met.* 8.298–328) and the *Catalogue*.

16 For the title of the work, see West (1985) 1; Hirschberger (2004) 26–30. The alternative title, Ἠοῖαι, derived from the formula ἢ οἵη which occasionally signaled the transition from the one story to the other. On the meaning and function of this formula, see West (1985) 1, 56, 121f.; Rutherford (2000); Hirschberger (2004) 30f.; Hardie (2005) 293; Cingano (2009) 111; Tsagalis (2009) 160f. For *qualis* as a Latin equivalent of the *ehoie* formula see McKeown (1989) on *Am.* 1.10.1–2; Hardie (2005) 292–294. See Ziogas (2013) 8 for *qualis* as a Hesiodic marker picking up the generic dynamics of *ehoie*-poetry.

17 In antiquity the *Catalogue* was universally ascribed to Hesiod [see Cingano (2009) 105 with n. 33]; however, modern scholars have expressed their doubts. On this vexed and unresolved issue, see Hirschberger (2004) 42–48; Clay (2005); Haubold (2005) 87 n. 8; Rutherford (2005) 114–117. The Hesiodic authorship is defended by Casanova (1979); Dräger (1997); Arrighetti (1998) 445–447. For the Hesiodic nature of the *Catalogue*, see Tsagalis (2009) 158–170. The authorship of the *Catalogue* does not really affect my investigation here. For reasons of convenience I call the poet of the *Catalogue* 'Hesiod'. Scholars are also divided as regards the date of composition of the *Catalogue*. See Cohen (1983) 365–425; Rutherford (2000) 82; Hirschberger (2004) 42–51; Clay (2005) 25 n. 2, (2009) 165 n. 51.

18 Ov. *Ars* 3.345f. (referring to the *Heroides*): *vel tibi composita cantetur Epistola voce: / ignotum hoc aliis ille novavit opus.*

19 Hollis (1970) 129; Fletcher (2005) 301 n. 11; Hardie (2005) 298; Rosati (2009) 365 n. 70; Ziogas (2011) 254. On the contrary, McKay (1962) 44 rejects the possibility that Ovid drew directly on pseudo-Hesiod. According to Obbink (2004) 199, Philodemus and Ovid drew on the *Catalogue* via Apollodorus' Περὶ θεῶν.

ready in his first work, the *Amores*, as the author of the *Works and Days* (1.15.11–12): *vivet et Ascraeus, dum mustis uva tumebit, / dum cadet incurva falce resecta Ceres.* ['Hesiod, as well, will live, while the vintage ripens, while the crops fall to the curving blade.' (tr. Kline)] In the *prooemium* to the *Ars Amatoria* he portrays himself as a *praeceptor amoris* and claims that he knows his subject matter from experience and not from inspiration by the Muses, like Hesiod did (1.27–30):[20] *nec mihi sunt visae Clio Cliusque sorores / servanti pecudes vallibus, Ascra, tuis: / usus opus movet hoc: vati parete perito; / vera canam: coeptis, mater Amoris, ades!* ['I never caught sight of Clio or Clio's sisters while herding the flocks, Ascra, in your valleys: Experience prompts this work: listen to the expert poet: I sing true: Venus, help my venture!' (tr. Kline)] In the *Fasti* (6.13) Ovid calls Hesiod a *praeceptor arandi*,[21] whereas later, in his exile poetry, he cites the *senex agricola* from Askra as an example of a citizen who disparages his homeland[22] but not its inhabitants, like Ovid does now with Tomi, its cold climate and the surrounding enemies (*Pont.* 4.14.31–4): *esset perpetuo sua quam vitabilis Ascra / ausa est agricolae Musa docere senis, / et fuerat genitus terra qui scripsit in illa, / intumuit vati tamen Ascra suo.* ['Hesiod, ancient farmer, dared to sing of how his Ascra was a place to be constantly avoided: though the man who wrote it had been born in that land, still Ascra wasn't angry with its poet.' (tr. Kline)]

1.1 The *Catalogue* and the *Heroides*

The well-documented influence of the *Catalogue* on the *Metamorphoses* perfectly justifies the investigation of its influence on the *Heroides* as well. Unfortunately, the highly fragmentary state of the *Catalogue* poses a great problem. One should also consider that certain similarities between the *Catalogue* and the *Heroides* may not be due to direct influence on Ovid, but either to the mediation of other texts or to the large common mythical stock.

So far, important work has been done on the influence of the *Catalogue* on *Her.* 16–17, the correspondence between Paris and Helen. In his review of E.J. Kenney's commentary on the letters,[23] Alessandro Barchiesi alerted readers

---

20 See Rosati (2009) 349 f.
21 For Hesiod's (*Works and Days*) influence on Ovid's *Fasti* see Rosati (2009) 360.
22 Hes. *Op.* 640: Ἄσκρῃ, χεῖμα κακῇ, θέρει ἀργαλέῃ, οὐδέ ποτ' ἐσθλῇ.
23 Kenney (1996, 87) points out that Paris' statement that he fell in love with Helen before seeing her (Ov. *Her.* 16.36–38) recalls one of her suitors in the *Catalogue* (fr. 199.2–3). See also Ziogas (2011) 254.

to the possibility of the *Catalogue*'s influence on the *Heroides*:²⁴ 'I take this occasion to ask whether somebody is interested in a link between the *Eoeae* and the *Heroides* in general. The two poems share an important feature, the angle on famous women and their lovers, and the Ovidian work frequently refers back to a tradition on divine amours as a kind of previous stage, now that the single *Heroides* deal with the loves of half-gods and heroes, and the double *Heroides* move on to famous boy-meets-girl stories like Leander or Acontios. Perhaps the influence of *Catalogue of Women* deserves more attention.' Numerous points of contact between *Her.* 16–17 and the *Catalogue* show that not only did Ovid have direct access to the *Catalogue*, but he also used it as a model and an important intertext for his *Heroides*.²⁵

Because of its particular generic identity, the *Catalogue* constitutes a most appropriate model for Ovid to introduce female figures from the world of myth and epic into the elegiac and epistolary world of the *Heroides*. The 'epic' tradition of the *Catalogue* – which has aptly been named '*ehoie*-poetry' – is strikingly different from Homer's martial epic poetry.²⁶ Homer's world is male-dominated, filled with war and death; the heroic code of values prevails and the role of women is only secondary and peripheral. On the contrary, the *ehoie*-poetry subverts the male-oriented agenda of heroic epic. Attention is placed on life,²⁷ love, marriage, conception, birth, women²⁸ (fr. 1.1:²⁹ γυναικῶν φῦλον) and their sexual

---

24 Barchiesi (1996).
25 Ziogas (2013) explores the relation between the *Catalogue* and *Her.* 16–17. He rightly claims that Ovid's Paris, who is a protagonist in the Epic Cycle, is also a reader of the *Catalogue of Women*. See Ziogas (2013) 45. On numerous points of contact between Ov. *Her.* 16–17 and the *Catalogue*, see Ziogas (2013) 28–53. The list of the loves of Neptune, mentioned by Hero in her letter to Leander (*Her.* 19.129–38) may have been also drawn from the *Catalogue*, either directly or via Apollodorus' Περὶ θεῶν. See Obbink (2004) 199; Hardie (2005) 297f.; Rosati (2009) 365.
26 See Rutherford (2000) 89–93, who takes the *Catalogue* as the crossing of genealogical poetry that did not focus on women with catalogues of women that did not focus on genealogies. Tsagalis (2009, 173–175) places Rutherford's 'generic crossing' *after* the consolidation of the Homeric epics. See also Sammons (in this volume) on how the catalogic/paradigmatic form and the genealogical/historical form complement one another in the *Catalogue*. The *ehoie*-poetry as an epic genre is clearly distinguished from martial epic. See West (1985) 3–11; Rutherford (2000); Nasta (2006) 64–68; Arrighetti (2008). For a clear account of the cardinal features and the differences between these two epic traditions, see Tsagalis (2009) 167–170; Skempis (2011) 256–268; Ziogas (2013) 8f. For the relation of the *Catalogue* with the epic tradition (Trojan cycle, Theban cycle, Argonautic expedition), see Hirschberger (2004) 51–58.
27 On the rarity of death in the *Catalogue*, see Rutherford (2000) 86f.
28 For the importance and centrality of women in the *Catalogue*, see Rutherford (2000) 83, 86; Osborne (2005); Tsagalis (2009) 166. On the generally encomiastic nature of the *Catalogue*, see

affairs with gods; this world is structured genealogically and geographically. Ovid's *Heroides* are fully in line with the tradition of the *Catalogue*'s *ehoie*-poetry.[30] As in the *Catalogue*, the *Heroides* too focus on women. Most of them actually come from the world of epic and are introduced by Ovid into a new epistolographic-elegiac environment, in which they are offered the opportunity to express their innermost thoughts, hopes and emotions. Here, however, lies the greatest difference between the *Heroides* and the *Catalogue:* in the *Catalogue* – in the extant fragments at least – the women are not heard, they do not have a voice, they never speak;[31] even the embedded speeches of other characters, mortal men or gods, are scarce.[32] On the contrary, Ovid's heroines write in the first person and present their subjective view of life.

Hesiod was considered a poet of peaceful deeds (Velleius Paterculus 1.7.1: *otii quietisque cupidissimus*) in stark contrast to Homer, the poet of war. His alternative model of life coincides with the pacifist ideology of love elegy.[33] The women of the *Heroides* detest war, because it takes away their loved ones. In her programmatic letter (*Her.* 1)[34] Ovid's Penelope complains about the war of men, because she is left with no husband and she constantly worries about his safety (*Her.* 1.3f., 11–22, 41–50).[35] Because of the same war, the Trojan war – which significantly puts an end to the heroic age as recorded in the *Catalogue* – Laodameia (*Her.* 13) is forced to lose her husband, Protesilaus; he is destined to be kil-

---

Dio Chrys. 2.14: ἐκείνου [sc. Ὁμήρου] περὶ τῶν ἡρώων ποιήσαντος αὐτὸς [sc. Ἡσίοδος] ἐποίησε Γυναικῶν κατάλογον, καὶ τῶι ὄντι τὴν γυναικωνῖτιν ὕμνησε, παραχωρήσας Ὁμήρωι τοὺς ἄνδρας ἐπαινέσαι. On Hesiod's emphasis on the female in the *Catalogue* as a foil to Homeric epic, see Clay (2003) 165f.; Rutherford (2000) 89. For Hesiod's supposed effeminate style, see Koning (2010) 338f. Ziogas (2013) 178 notes: 'Ovid's *Metamorphoses* is for Vergil's *Aeneid* what the *Catalogue* is for Homer's *Iliad*. Hesiod and Ovid face epic tradition from a distance and redeploy the diction of martial epic in their love stories, deflating the battle narratives of their forerunners'.
29 I use Merkelbach and West's OCT edition. Translations from the *Catalogue* are taken from Most's 2007 LCL edition.
30 Ziogas (2013) 53: 'In the *Catalogue*, Ovid seems to have found a congenial poem to imitate.'
31 Rutherford (2000) 88.
32 Rutherford (2000) 87. Diomedes (Keil, *Grammatici Latini* 1.482–483) considers the *Catalogue* as a *poema exegeticum vel enarrativum*, without speeches of characters: '*exegetici vel enarrativi species sunt tres, angeltice, historice, didascalice...historice est qua narrationes et genealogiae conponuntur, ut est Hesiodu γυναικῶν κατάλογος et similia.*'
33 See Rosati (2009) 365–369. On the war-peace distinction between Homer and Hesiod, see Koning (2010) ch. 8.
34 For the programmatic function of the first letter of the *Heroides* see Kennedy (1984); Henderson (1986); Hinds (1985) 28; Barchiesi (1992) 15 n. 1 and 51f.; Knox (1995) 12, 86.
35 Michalopoulos (2008) 344–349.

led by Hector, as is foreshadowed by a number of allusions in her letter (*Her.* 13.85–90, 125f.).

Most letters of the *Heroides* share the same time zone with the *Catalogue* as they treat love stories that took place in the age covered by the *Catalogue*, i.e. the time before the Trojan war. Zeus' final plan to depopulate the earth (fr. 204.98 f.)[36] by means of the Trojan war puts an end to the mythic time of prehistory, a kind of a Golden Age, in which gods and humans intermingle freely at feasts and in sexual encounters,[37] and create a generation of children from gods and mortal women.[38] The final story of the *Catalogue* is the wooing of Helen by her suitors, an episode which will eventually lead to mythology's total and most devastating war. Of the fourteen single *Heroides*, the letters of Penelope (*Her.* 1), Phyllis (*Her.* 2), Dido (*Her.* 7), and Hermione (*Her.* 8)[39] are supposedly written *after* the Trojan war, while the letter of Briseis (*Her.* 3) is written *during* the war. Technically the above letters lie outside the age covered by the *Catalogue*, although, of course, these letters too bear similarities to the *Catalogue*. The majority of the letters, however, are supposedly written *during* the time covered by the *Catalogue*: Phaedra (*Her.* 4), Oenone (*Her.* 5), Hypsipyle (*Her.* 6), Deianira (*Her.* 9), Ariadne (*Her.* 10), Canace (*Her.* 11), Medea (*Her.* 12), Laodameia (*Her.* 13) and Hypermestra (*Her.* 14). In fact, in terms of dramatic time the letters of Oenone and Laodameia fall right on the verge between the two ages, since Oenone writes to Paris immediately after his return from Sparta with Helen by his side, and Laodameia writes while the Greek fleet is anchored at Aulis, ready to depart for Troy. Furthermore, it is highly significant that the first pair of the double letters of the *Heroides* (*Her.* 16–17) deals with the love affair of Paris and Helen, which triggered the Trojan war, thus setting in motion Zeus' plan to reduce the earth's population.

The points of contact between the *Catalogue* and the *Heroides* do not end here. In the *Catalogue* the women mingle with gods or demigods; in the *Heroides* the women mingle with mortals, most of whom were born from the sexual encounters recorded in the *Catalogue*. Ovid conceived the single *Heroides* as cata-

---

[36] Cf. the proem of the *Cypria* (fr. 1), where Zeus plans the Trojan war in order to lighten the burden of the earth.
[37] See fr. 1.5–7: μισγόμεναι θεοῖσ[ιν / ξυναὶ γὰρ τότε δαῖτες ἔσαν, ξυνοὶ δὲ θόωκοι / ἀθανάτοις τε θεοῖσι καταθνητοῖς τ' ἀνθρώποις.
[38] González (2010) notes that the end of the *Catalogue* marks the end of the heroic age precisely by ending sexual relations between mortals and heroes.
[39] Hermione's birth is noted at fr. 204.94 of the *Catalogue*: ἣ τέκεν Ἑρμιόνην καλλίσφυρ[ο]ν ἐν μεγάροισιν.

logue entries⁴⁰ containing variations on a common theme: love stories of (deserted) women. In fact, he presents the contents of the *Heroides* in the form of a list at *Am.* 2.18.21–34: *aut, quod Penelopes verbis reddatur Ulixi, / scribimus et lacrimas, Phylli relicta, tuas, / quod Paris et Macareus et quod male gratus Iason / Hippolytique parens Hippolytusque legant, / quodque tenens strictum Dido miserabilis ensem / dicat et Aoniae Lesbis amata lyrae. / quam cito de toto rediit meus orbe Sabinus / scriptaque diversis rettulit ille locis! / candida Penelope signum cognovit Ulixis; / legit ab Hippolyto scripta noverca suo. / iam pius Aeneas miserae rescripsit Elissae, / quodque legat Phyllis, si modo vivit, adest. / tristis ad Hypsipylen ab Iasone littera venit; / det votam Phoebo Lesbis amata lyram.* ['or I pen the words Penelope wrote Ulysses and your tearful ones, deserted Phyllis, the ones Paris, and Macareus, and ungrateful Jason, and Hippolytus's father, Theseus, and Hippolytus read, what poor Dido said with the sword tight in her hand or that lover from Ionian Lesbos with her lyre. How soon Sabinus, my poet friend, you returned, carrying replies from lands scattered through the world! Fair Penelope knew the seal of Ulysses: Hippolytus's stepmother recognized his script. Dutiful Aeneas has replied to wretched Dido, Phyllis, if she's alive, has a note too. A sad note from Jason reaches Hypsipyle: the lover of Lesbos offers Phoebus her lyre.' (tr. Kline)]

A key feature of the *Catalogue* are the extensive heroic genealogies covering the entire heroic age.⁴¹ This genealogical element is strong in Ovid's *Heroides* too: numerous family links join many of the letter-writers together and the same goes for their husbands and lovers. It is a complicated situation: Phyllis (*Her.* 2) is in love with Demophoon, the son of Theseus. Theseus is the husband of Phaedra (*Her.* 4) and the lover of Ariadne (*Her.* 10). Phaedra and Ariadne are sisters. They are the daughters of Pasiphae, whose brother, Aeetes, is the father of Medea (*Her.* 12), hence Phaedra, Ariadne, and Medea are cousins. Medea (*Her.* 12), Ariadne's cousin, and Hypsipyle (*Her.* 6), Ariadne's grand-daughter, are in love with the same man, Jason. Jason is the cousin of Protesilaus, the husband of Laodameia (*Her.* 13).⁴² Althaea, the mother of Deianira (*Her.* 9), is the sister of Leda, who is the grandmother of Hermione (*Her.* 8), hence Deianira is Her-

---

40 Hinds (1999) 127. For the *Heroides* as 'Ovid's own *Catalogue* of women', see Ziogas (2013) 4. On Ovid's love for lists of various kinds, see Hardie (2005) 296, who also notes (298): 'In reducing the variety and length of his own *Heroides* to a schematic list of women characterised by their essential qualities, Ovid registers his awareness of how the Hellenistic '*Catalogue* poems' themselves constitute, as Richard Hunter puts it [see Hunter (2005b) 259], a 'reduction of the rich scope and uneven texture of the *Catalogue* to its most memorable … repetitive feature'.
41 West (1985) 2, 3.
42 Jason's mother, Alcimede, and Protesilaus' father, Iphiclus, are siblings.

mione's aunt. This nexus of family and genealogical links can grow considerably denser, if one digs deeper into the world of mythical genealogies.

In the *Heroides* the letter writers often use genealogy, either their own or of their loved ones, as part of their argumentation. For instance, Hermione compares the origins and families of Orestes and Pyrrhus in a way highly reminiscent of the *Catalogue*, only that the roles are now reversed: in the *Heroides* it is a woman that writes the *ehoie* (or rather the *ehoios*) of Orestes (*Her.* 8.43–48): *ille licet patriis sine fine superbiat actis; / et tu quae referas facta parentis habes. / Tantalides omnes ipsumque regebat Achillem. / hic pars militiae, dux erat ille ducum. / tu quoque habes proavum Pelopem Pelopisque parentem; / si melius numeres, a Iove quintus eris* ['He may boast endlessly about his father's, Achilles's, deeds, you also have your father's actions to speak about. Agamemnon, Tantalus's scion, ruled over all, even Achilles: the latter a soldier, the former was lord of lords. You too have Pelops and his father, Tantalus, as ancestors: if you counted carefully, you'd be the fifth from Jove.' (tr. Kline)].[43]

---

43 Likewise, Briseis discusses Achilles' divine descent from Zeus, Aegina, Aeacus, Peleus, Nereus, and Thetis [(*Her.* 3.73 f.): *digna nurus socero, Iovis Aeginaeque nepote, / cuique senex Nereus prosocer esse velit* 'and she'll be worthy to be a daughter-in-law to her father-in-law Peleus, descendant of Jove and Aegina, of whom old Nereus well might wish to be a grandfather to the wife' (tr. Kline)]; Ariadne doubts that such a cruel man as Theseus is the son of Aegeus and Aethra [(*Her.* 10.131 f.): *nec pater est Aegeus, nec tu Pittheidos Aethrae / filius; auctores saxa fretumque tui* 'Your father's not Aegeus: Aethra, daughter of Pittheus, is not your mother: your creators were stone and sea' (tr. Kline)]; Phyllis questions Demophoon's divine origin from Neptune [(*Her.* 2.37 f.): *perque tuum mihi iurasti – nisi fictus et ille est – / concita qui ventis aequora mulcet, avum.* 'you swore by Neptune, your grandfather, unless that too is a lie, who calms the waters roused by the winds' (tr. Kline)]; and so does Dido with Aeneas' divine origin from Venus (*Her.* 7.31–39): *parce, Venus, nurui, durumque amplectere fratrem, / frater Amor; castris militet ille tuis. / aut ego quem coepi – neque enim dedignor – amare, / materiam curae praebeat ille meae. / fallor et ista mihi falso iactatur imago: / matris ab ingenio dissidet ille suae. / te lapis et montes innataque rupibus altis / robora, te saevae progenuere ferae / aut mare, quale vides agitari nunc quoque ventis.* 'Venus, spare your daughter-in-law, and Love, my brother, embrace your hard-hearted brother: let him serve in your ranks. So I, who began this love – I don't scorn indeed to say this – might offer him the substance of my affections. I'm cheated and this is a false idea I speak of: he differs from his mother in disposition. Begotten by stones, or hills, or native oaks on tall cliffs, by savage beasts, or by the sea such as you now gaze on, stirred by the winds' (tr. Kline)]

1.2 Love Affairs of Gods and Mortal Women in the *Heroides*

The intermingling of gods with mortals and the sexual relations between them are important themes and distinctive features of the *Catalogue*. On the other hand, the *Heroides* treat the love affairs of mortal women with mortal men, even if these are not ordinary mortals but rather great heroes (e.g. Odysseus, Paris, Jason, Orestes) or the sons of heroes (e.g. Demophoon, Hippolytus) or the sons of gods and goddesses (e.g. Achilles, Theseus, Hercules). Still, in the *Heroides* too one comes across love affairs of gods and mortal women taking place precisely in the age covered by the *Catalogue* and closely modeled on the *Catalogue*. Characteristic of such cases is the wedding of Ariadne to Dionysus after her abandonment by Theseus on the deserted Naxos. Phyllis knows all about this wedding and takes it as something totally normal (*Her.* 2.79 f.): *illa – nec invideo – fruitur meliore marito / inque capistratis tigribus alta sedet.* 'She – I don't begrudge it – is blessed with a better husband and rides high above Bacchus' team of harnessed tigers.' (tr. Kline). In fact, Phyllis blesses Ariadne for her good fortune – so much better than her own – because she became the wife of a god. In Ariadne's letter (*Her.* 10) there is no mention of her wedding with Dionysus, because the letter is supposedly written immediately after her abandonment by Theseus and while he is sailing away. Ovid, however, has made sure to insert in the letter – as he usually does in the *Heroides* – certain allusions to Dionysus' impending arrival [*Her.* 10.85 f.: *forsitan et fulvos tellus alat ista leones? / quis scit an et saevas tigridas insula habet* 'Perhaps this land breeds tawny lions? Who knows if this island harbours savage tigers?' (tr. Kline), 95: *caelum restabat; timeo simulacra deorum!* 'The sky remains: I fear visions from the gods' (tr. Kline)]. Ariadne's Ovidian letter is supposedly written in the age of the *Catalogue*, a time when gods mingle freely with mortals. In effect, Ariadne's Ovidian letter heralds the creation of yet another *ehoie* and the beginning of a new family line that could be inserted easily into the *Catalogue* retrospectively.[44] Indeed, a new genealogy is created: Hypsipyle, the writer of a letter to Jason (*Her.* 6), is the daughter of Thoas, the son of Dionysus and Ariadne, and she is very proud of her origin (6.113–116): *si te nobilitas generosaque nomina tangunt: / en ego Minoo nata Thoante feror. / Bacchus avus: Bacchi coniunx redimita corona / praeradiat stellis signa minora suis.* 'If high birth and a noble name move you: see, I was born the daughter of Thoas and of Ariadne. Bacchus was my grandfather: as Bacchus' wife she wears a crown, and her constellation outshines the lesser stars' (tr. Kline). Hypsipyle in turn is the mother of two

---

[44] Considering, of course, that it was not included in some lost part of the *Catalogue* in the first place.

children by Jason (*Her.* 6.119f.): *nunc etiam peperi. gratare ambobus, Iason – / dulce mihi gravidae fecerat auctor onus.* 'Now I have given birth, also. Rejoice for us both, Jason – sweetly its author had made a burden for my womb' (tr. Kline). All this perfectly fits the genealogic tradition of the *Catalogue*.[45]

The sexual unions of gods with mortal women and the consequent creation of a new family line occupies a key position in Phaedra's letter to Hippolytus (*Her.* 4), and, tellingly, in the form of a catalogue. Phaedra unfolds the troubled past of the women in her family in matters of love (Europa, Pasiphae, Ariadne) and includes herself in this line. Just like her sister, Ariadne, who was captivated by Theseus, she has now been captivated by Theseus' son, Hippolytus (*Her.* 4.53–62). Nevertheless, Phaedra claims that she is not to blame, because Venus has turned against the women of her family;[46] this is a hereditary issue. Ovid's Phaedra presents a list of loves of Cretan women starting with Zeus and Europa, continuing with Pasiphae and the bull, and then including Ariadne and Theseus. Once again, the list begins with the love union of a god with a mortal woman, which also features in the *Catalogue* (*Her.* 4.55f.): *Iuppiter Europen – prima est ea gentis origo – / dilexit, tauro dissimulante deum.* 'Jupiter loved Europa, as a bull, hiding his godhead, she was the first origin of our people' (tr. Kline). Cf. fr. 140: Εὐρώπην τὴν Φοίνικος Ζεὺς θεασάμενος ἔν τινι λειμῶνι μετὰ νυμφῶν ἄνθη ἀναλέγουσαν ἠράσθη, καὶ κατελθὼν ἤλλαξεν ἑαυτὸν εἰς ταῦρον καὶ ἀπὸ τοῦ στόματος κρόκον ἔπνει· οὕτως τε τὴν Εὐρώπην ἀπατήσας ἐβάστασε, καὶ διαπορθμεύσας εἰς Κρήτην ἐμίγη αὐτῆι. εἶθ' οὕτως συνώικισεν αὐτὴν Ἀστερίωνι τῶι Κρητῶν βασιλεῖ. γενομένη δὲ ἔγκυος ἐκείνη τρεῖς παῖδας ἐγέννησε Μίνωα, Σαρπηδόνα καὶ Ῥαράμανθυν. ἡ ἱστορία παρ' Ἡσιόδωι καὶ Βακχυλίδηι.[47] Phaedra's phrase *prima est ea gentis origo* (4.55) essentially plays the role of an Alexandrian footnote,[48] indicating that Ovid is drawing from an earlier source, Euripides' *Hippolytus*,[49] or another work which probably belongs to an established tradition of genealogic-catalogue poetry of the kind of the *Catalogue*. Pasiphae's unnatural union with the bull – second in Phaedra's list (57f.: *Pasi-*

---

[45] Cf. *Her.* 11.17f. where Canace claims that she is a descendant of Jupiter: *quid iuvat admotam per avorum nomina caelo / inter cognatos posse referre Iovem?*
[46] Venus punishes the Cretan princesses either because Pasiphae had failed to honour her or because she wanted to take revenge on the descendants of Helios, who had revealed her secret affair with Mars (Sen. *Phaed.* 112ff.).
[47] See also fr. 141.2f.: Διὸς δμηθεῖσα δόλοισι. / τῆι δὲ μίγη φιλότητι.
[48] The term was introduced by Ross (1975) 78. On the Alexandrian footnote, see Hinds (1987) 17–19; Harrison (1991) Verg. *Aen.* 10.189 with bibliography; Horsfall (1990); Thomas (1992); Miller (1993); Michalopoulos (2006) 34f. and on Ov. *Her.* 16.137–8 with bibliography.
[49] In Euripides' *Hippolytus* (337–343) Phaedra's recollection of her family's unfortunate past occurs just before the revelation of her love for Hippolytus.

phae mater, decepto subdita tauro, / enixa est utero crimen onusque suo) – also features in the *Catalogue* (fr. 145.13–17): τῆς δ' ἄρ' [ἐν ὀ]φθαλμοῖσιν ἰδὼν ἠράσ[σατο / †ταύρωι.[...]ριμενησκαμερμιδαοτα[† / ἢ δ' ὑποκ[υσα]μένη Μίνωι τέκε κα[ρτερὸν υἱόν, / θαῦμα ἰ[δεῖν·] σα μὲν γὰρ ἐπέκλιν[εν δέμας ἀνδρὶ / ἐς πόδα[ς], αὐτὰρ ὕπερθε κάρη τα[ύροιο πεφύκει.⁵⁰

Phaedra's listing habit resurfaces later in her letter, when she cites three mythological *exempla* in order to persuade Hippolytus that love can surely exist in the woods (*Her.* 4.93–102): Aurora-Cephalus, Venus-Adonis, Meleager-Atalanta.⁵¹ The first two of these examples are love affairs between divine beings and mortals, as is typically the case in the *Catalogue*, only now the gender roles are reversed: goddesses fall in love and mingle with mortal men (Aurora-Cephalus, Venus-Adonis). The third couple involves Meleager and Atalanta, who also feature in the *Catalogue*.⁵² Notice in particular Phaedra's words after these examples. She openly expresses her wish to be numbered together with Hippolytus in that company, essentially to become part of this c/*Catalogue* (4.101f.): *nos quoque quam primum turba numeremur⁵³ in ista! / si Venerem tollas, rustica silva tua est.* 'We too could soon be numbered in this throng! If you take Love away your woods are uncivilized' (tr. Kline) On a metaliterary level, a character from Ovid's poetry longs to be included in an already existing catalogue of couples in love. In this way the open-endedness of the catalogue form is highlighted: by definition a c/*Catalogue* may be expanded *ad infinitum*.

Zeus/Jupiter, the god responsible for the majority of new genealogical lines, could not be absent from a list of love affairs between gods and mortal women. After featuring in Hermione's letter to Orestes in a list of abductions of women in her family⁵⁴ (Leda-Jupiter, Hippodamia-Pelops, Helen-Paris, *Her.* 8.65–74),⁵⁵ Ju-

---

50 The patronymic *Aegides* used for Theseus in the third entry in Phaedra's list (*Her.* 4.59f.: *perfidus Aegides, ducentia fila secutus, / curva meae fugit tecta sororis ope*) belongs to the type of epithets which feature most frequently in genealogical lists. For the importance of heroes' patronymics, see Higbie (1995).

51 The mythological *exempla* used by Phaedra are ominous, since they all ended in tragedy. Cephalus returned to his beloved wife, Procris, but killed her by accident, Adonis was killed by a boar, and Meleager was killed by his own mother, Althaea. Phaedra's own story will end in disaster: Hippolytus will be dragged to his death by his own horses and Phaedra will kill herself. For a detailed examination of Phaedra's mythological catalogue, see C. N. Michalopoulos (2006) 77–95.

52 Meleager: fr. 25 / Atalanta: frr. 72, 73, 74, 75, 76.

53 For the use of the nouns *numerus, (e)numeratio* and the verbs *numero, dinumero, recenseo* to denote inclusion in a catalogue see Kyriakidis (2007) 72.

54 For an extensive discussion of Hermione's manipulation of genealogy in her letter, see C. N. Michalopoulos (2006) 98–111.

piter reappears as a lover of mortal women in Hypermestra's letter to Lynceus (*Her.* 14). Hypermestra recounts the adventures of Io, the daughter of Inachus, the river god and king of Argos. Io was pursued by Juno after she was raped by Jupiter (*Her.* 14.85–110). Hypermestra considers this rape as the ultimate cause of her own sufferings. This affair is closely associated with the Danaids both because Io was the princess of Argos and because, after her long wanderings in the form of a cow, Io ended up in Egypt and was transformed into the goddess Isis on the banks of the Nile.[56] In a way Hypermestra places herself within a catalogue of Argive women harassed and chased by Juno, who takes revenge on the royal house of Argos because of Jupiter's affair with Io. This is a classic case of a story with genealogical interest taken from the *Catalogue*; in fact, Hypermestra writes that she learned this story from some old man (*Her.* 14.109 f.): *ultima quid referam, quorum mihi cana senectus / auctor?* 'Why recall these earliest things, sung to me by old men?' (tr. Kline, with modifications). This may be taken as an Alexandrian footnote picking up a certain literary source. Indeed, both the internal (Hypermestra) and the external (Ovid) writer of the letter point to their source: Hypermestra points to stories from old men, Ovid points to texts of genealogic-erotic content, such as the *Catalogue* or some other work of this genealogic-catalogic tradition. The story of Io actually features in the narrative about the family of the Inachids in the *Catalogue* (fr. 124).[57]

1.3 The *Catalogue* and Deianira's letter to Hercules (*Her.* 9)

Deianira's letter to Hercules (*Her.* 9) displays numerous points of contact with the *Catalogue* and its tradition, perhaps more so than any other letter of the single *Heroides*. Deianira was the sister of Meleager[58] and Tydeus, daughter of Oeneus and Althaea, the royal couple of Calydon. Hercules married her after defeating the river god Achelous, an ardent contender. During this struggle the river god

---

[55] A few lines later (*Her.* 8.78) Hermione recalls Leda's pleas to Jupiter for help after Helen's abduction by Paris – which, let us not forget, is the final phase of the *Catalogue*: *orabat superos Leda suumque Iovem.* 'Leda prayed to the heavens and her Jupiter' (tr. Kline).

[56] The story of Io was very popular in both Greek and Latin literature. See esp. Aesch. *Suppl.* 40–57, 291–324, 531–589, *Prom.* 561–886. The neoteric poet Calvus Macer wrote an epyllion entitled *Io*, which, sadly, is lost. Ovid narrated Io's story in detail in the first book of the *Metamorphoses* (1.583–750).

[57] For Io in the *Catalogue*, see West (1985) 76 f. For Io in Ovid's *Metamorphoses* and her relationship with the *Catalogue*, see Ziogas (2013) 69 f., 75–81.

[58] For Meleager and Deianira in myth, see March (1987) 29–46, 49–77; Bremmer (1988); Grossardt (2001).

kept changing shapes, but Hercules managed to break one of his rival's two horns.[59]

The story of Deianira is preserved in an extensive fragment of the *Catalogue*. Sixteen lines narrate her marriage to Hercules, the four sons she bore, the story of Nessus' fatal cloak, Hercules' death, and his apotheosis (fr. 25.17–33):[60]

κ[αὶ ἐπί]φ[ρ]ονα Δηϊάνειραν,
ἣ τέχ' ὑποδμηθεῖ[σα βίηι Ἡρ]ακλη[ε]ίηι
Ὕλλον καὶ Γλῆνον καὶ [Κτή]σιππον καὶ Ὀνείτην·
τοὺς τέκε καὶ δείν' ἔρξ[', ἐπεὶ ἀάσατ]ο μέγα θυμῶι,
ὁππότε φάρμακον .[ἐπιχρί]σασα χιτῶνα
δῶκε Λίχηι κήρυ[κι] φ[έρειν· ὃ δὲ δῶ]κεν ἄνακτι
Ἀμφιτρυωνιά[δ]ηι Ἡ[ρακλῆϊ πτολιπό]ρθωι.
δ[εξ]αμένωι δέ ο[ἱ αἶψα τέλος θανάτοι]ο παρέστη·
καὶ] θάνε καί ῥ' Ἀΐδ[αο πολύστονον ἵκε]το δῶμα.
– νῦν δ' ἤδη θεός ἐστι, κακῶν δ' ἐξήλυθε πάντων,
– ζώει δ' ἔνθά περ ἄλλοι Ὀλύμπια δώματ' ἔχοντες
– ἀθάνατος καὶ ἄγηρος, ἔχων καλλ[ίσ]φυρον Ἥβην,
– παῖδα Διὸς μεγάλοιο καὶ Ἥρης χρυσοπεδίλου·
– τὸν πρὶν μέν ῥ' ἤχθηρε θεὰ λευκώλενος Ἥρη
– ἔκ τε θεῶν μακάρων ἔκ τε θνητῶν ἀνθρώ[πων,
– νῦν δ' ἤδη πεφίληκε, τίει δέ μιν ἔξοχον ἄλλ[ων
– ἀθανάτων μετά γ' αὐτὸν ἐρισθενέα Κρ[ο]νίωνα.

'[and] thoughtful Deianira, / who, overpowered by Heracles' [force], bore / Hyllus and Glenus and Ctesippus and Onites; / these she bore, and she committed terrible deeds, [for / she acted] very [foolishly] in spirit, / when, [smearing] the philter on the cloak, / she gave it to the herald Liches [to take; and he gave] it / to lord / [Heracles], Amphitryon's son, [the city-sacker]. / Once he received it, [the end of death was swiftly] at / hand for him; and] he died and [came to the much-groaning] house of / Hades. / Now he is already a god, and has escaped from all evils, / and he lives where the others do who have their / mansions on Olympus, / immortal and ageless, possessing beautiful-ankled Hebe, / daughter of great Zeus and of golden-sandaled Hera. / Previously the goddess, white-armed Hera, hated him / more than any of the blessed gods and any mortal / human beings, / but now she loves him, and honors him beyond the other / immortals, except for Cronus's mighty son himself.' (tr. Most)

In the *Heroides* Deianira is supposed to be writing her letter in Trachina, after she has been informed that Hercules has captured Oichalia and is coming back with Iole, the daughter of the king Eurytus. Deianira makes a flashback to her husband's great feats and blames him for his inclination to extra-marital

---

59 Ovid treats this story at *Met.* 9.1–88 too.
60 For Hercules in the *Catalogue*, see Davies (1992) 102; Haubold (2005).

affairs, especially for his shameful stay at the court of the Lydian queen Omphale. While Deianira is writing her letter, news arrives that Hercules is dying because of the poisonous cloak that she sent him as a gift.[61] Deianira, feeling remorseful and guilty, decides to kill herself, after making clear that she was deceived by Nessus and that she had no intention of killing Hercules.[62]

Ovid's main source for this letter is Sophocles' *Trachiniae*; however, as I hope to show here, he also borrowed certain themes and details from the *Catalogue*. Already from the beginning of her letter Deianira takes up her official role as queen of Hercules' house. She congratulates her husband on the addition of Oichalia to the long catalogue of their acquisitions, which thus grows longer.[63] Deianira's main concern is to defend her place as queen in Hercules' royal house against her rival, Iole, who has subdued Hercules with her love (*Her.* 9.6): *huic Iolen inposuisse iugum*. The sack of Oichalia by Hercules for the sake of Iole features in the *Catalogue* too (fr. 26.29–33): τοῦ δ' υἱεῖς ἐγένοντο Δηΐων <τε> Κλυτίος τε / Τοξεύς τ' ἀντίθεος ἠδ' Ἴφιτος ὄζος Ἄρηος. / τοὺς δὲ μέθ' ὁπλοτάτην τέκετο ξανθὴν Ἰόλειαν, / τ[ῆς ἕ]νεκ' Οἰχ[αλ]ί[η]ν / 'Αμφι]τρυωνιάδης 'From him were born sons, Deion and Clytius / and god-like Toxeus and Iphitus, scion of Ares. / After these, last of all he begot blonde Iolea, / for whose sake Oechalia [/ Amphitryon's son' (tr. Most). Deianira expresses the same dynastic concern for her place as queen and wife of Hercules[64] again at *Her.* 9.131–134: *forsitan et pulsa Aetolide Deianira / nomine deposito paelicis uxor erit, / Eurytidosque Ioles atque Aonii Alcidae / turpia famosus corpora iunget Hymen.*[65] 'and perhaps Aetolian Deianira will be beaten off, and Iole will be your

---

[61] Hercules had killed with his poisoned arrows the Centaur Nessus, who had tried to ravish Deianira, while she was crossing the flooded river Euenus on his back. Before dying, Nessus secretly told Deianira that with his blood she could win back Hercules' love, if she ever needed to (Ov. *Met.* 9.101–33). When Hercules fell in love with Iole and took her with him, Deianira sent him Nessus' cloak, hoping to restore Hercules' love for her. Hercules put on the cloak, which started devouring his flesh.

[62] The name Δηιάνειρα derives from the verb δηιόω 'cut down, slay' and the noun ἀνήρ, 'man, husband', hence Δηιάνειρα is the woman that kills her spouse, see LSJ s.v. Δηιάνειρα.

[63] Ov. *Her.* 9.1 f.: *gratulor Oechaliam titulis accedere nostris.* 'I give thanks that Oichalia is added to our titles' (tr. Kline).

[64] See Finkelberg in this volume for the paramount importance of women for both form and content of Greek genealogy.

[65] Deianira's words here about her possible, shameful replacement by Iole as Hercules' wife (*nomine deposito paelicis uxor erit* and *turpia corpora*) are distantly reminiscent of certain comments in the *Catalogue* on the adulterous affairs of Clytemnestra and Helen (fr. 176.5–8): ὣς δὲ Κλυταιμήστρη <προ>λιποῦσ' Ἀγαμέμνονα δῖον / Αἰγίσθωι παρέλεκτο καὶ εἵλετο χείρον' ἀκοίτην· / ὣς δ' Ἑλένη ἤισχυνε λέχος ξανθοῦ Μενελάου.

wife, dropping the label of mistress, and wicked Hymen will join the shameful bodies of Iole, Eurytus' daughter and Aonian Hercules' (tr. Kline). Deianira's interest in origins and genealogy shows in her use of patronymic and national epithets: <u>Aetolide</u> *Deianira* (131), <u>Eurytidosque</u> *Ioles atque* <u>Aonii</u> *Alcidae* (133).⁶⁶

Deianira raises many issues concerning Hercules and their relationship. She brings up Jupiter's paternity of Hercules, a theme totally in line with the tradition of the *Catalogue*, in an age when gods sleep with mortal women. Deianira touches on this matter when she refers to Hercules' erotic subjugation to Iole (*Her.* 9.9f.): *at non ille velit, cui nox (si creditur) una / non tanti, ut tantus conciperere, fuit.* 'But Jupiter would not, for whom (if it is to be believed) one night was not sufficient to father so great a child' (tr. Kline). Contrary to Hercules' enemies, his father, Jupiter, who was forced to upset the natural order and join two nights in a row so as to father him,⁶⁷ will be deeply disappointed at his son's downfall. Deianira picks up again Jupiter's union with Alcmene and her own marriage with Hercules at *Her.* 9.27f.: *at bene nupta feror,* <u>*quia nominer Herculis uxor,*</u> */ sitque socer, rapidis qui tonat altus equis.* 'But they say I married well, since I am called Hercules' wife, and my father-in-law is he who thunders through the heights' (tr. Kline). Her words are particularly important as regards the relationships of gods with mortal women. Although Deianira is proud to be Hercules' wife (cf. the beginning of her letter, 9.1f.) and Jupiter's daughter-in-law, she expresses her doubts about how happy a wedding can be when the two members of the couple are not equal. The phrase *quia nominer Herculis uxor* (*Her.* 9.27) may be taken as an Alexandrian footnote pointing to a source-text such as the *Catalogue*, in which Deianira becomes Hercules' wife. In effect, Ovid's Deianira criticizes the cardinal theme of the *Catalogue*, the ill-matched unions between gods and mortal women. She portrays her case as an example of an unfortunate wedding, despite its initial favorable prospects. Her advice to women is to marry their equals (*Her.* 9.32): *siqua voles apte nubere, nube pari.* 'if you wish to be well married, marry an equal' (tr. Kline). Deianira continues her criticism of the affairs of gods with mortal women and of their negative consequences for the women involved⁶⁸ when she refers to Hercules' mother,

---

66 As noted above, in the *Catalogue* such concern is not registered, since the women are not heard.
67 Hercules' birth features at *Cat.* fr. 195 = *Asp.* 1–56.
68 Cf. Arachne's negative commentary on the rapes of mortal women by transformed gods, which she depicts on her tapestry at Ov. *Met.* 6.103–128. See Obbink (2004) 194ff.; Fletcher (2005) 303–9. Rosati (2009, 364) rightly points out that Arachne 're-writes a profane, desecrating version of the *Catalogue*', since mortal women are victims of the gods' sexual violence and this

Alcmene (*Her.* 9.43f.): *mater abest queriturque deo placuisse potenti, / nec pater Amphitryon nec puer Hyllus adest.* 'Your mother Alcmena is absent, and grieves that she pleased the god, neither your father Amphitryon nor your son Hyllus are here' (tr. Kline). The elegiac Deianira empathizes with Alcmene and they both complain about the constant absence of Hercules and Jupiter respectively, as well as for the absence of Amphitryo and Hyllus. In the *Catalogue* such criticism has no place: Because the women do not speak, they do not voice their opinion; they are simply rings in genealogical chains, unable to change their fortunes.[69] The world of Ovid's *Heroides* is different because the voiceless heroines of myth express their views openly, even if they are still unable to change the course of things.

Ovid's Deianira does not refrain from attacking her husband, Hercules. At lines 47–118, the core of her letter, Deianira protests against Hercules' inclination to extra-marital affairs, which she actually considers even harder to bear than Hercules' sufferings and labours (9.47: *haec mihi ferre parum*). She lays out a long list of Hercules' affairs, either expanding on or drawing from the *Catalogue*. Deianira becomes an unwilling narrator of Hercules' affairs. Out of these love affairs Hercules fathered innumerable children, thus creating new genealogies in a *Catalogue*-like fashion (9.47f.): *peregrinos addis amores, / et mater de te quaelibet esse potest.* 'but you add foreign lovers, and whichever girl wishes to can become a mother by you' (tr. Kline). In effect, Deianira protests against an essential feature of men in the *Catalogue:* their erotic promiscuity. In her new, elegiac environment the Ovidian Deianira has the opportunity to complain about her husband's sexual freedom, which, of course, was totally acceptable in the world of the *Catalogue*, in which new family lines and genealogies were created thanks to such extra-marital affairs.

By means of a *praeteritio*[70] Deianira mentions some of Hercules' love affairs, although she claims she will not speak about them. First, she mentions Hercules' affairs with Auge and Astydameia (*Her.* 9.49f.): *non ego Partheniis temeratam*[71] *vallibus Augen / nec referam partus, Ormeni nympha, tuos.* 'I won't mention Auge, violated in the valleys of Parthenius, or your child by Ormenus' nymph'

---

does not bring them any honour, in contrast to the *Catalogue* where the sexual union with a god was regarded as a sign of a privilege.

69 Cf. Deianira's parallelism of an unequal couple with oxen unequally yoked (*Her.* 9.29f.): *quam male inaequales veniunt ad aratra iuvenci, / tam premitur magno coniuge nupta minor.*
70 For the rhetorical figure *praeteritio*, see von Albrecht (1964) 197; Usher (1965) 175ff.; Lausberg (1998) 393f.
71 The juxtaposition of the epithet *Partheniis* and the participle *temeratam* forms an exceptionally ironical pair, since the rape of Auge took place on Mount Παρθένιον.

(tr. Kline, with modifications). Hercules' mistresses are mentioned by the *Catalogue* poet in his invocation to the Muses (fr. 1.22]: ἠδ' ὅσσαισι] βίη Ἡ[ρακλῆος 'and all those with whom Heracles' force' (tr. Most). Auge and Astydameia, the first two lovers of Hercules mentioned by Deianira in her Ovidian letter, come directly from the *Catalogue*. Auge (*Her.* 9.49) was the daughter of the king of Arcadia, Aleus. She was Athena's priestess at Tegea. Hercules raped her and she gave birth to Telephus. Auge's sexual union with Hercules is recorded in the *Catalogue* (fr. 165.6–9): κούρη]ν δ' [ἐ]ν μεγάροισιν ἐὺ τρέφεν ἠδ' ἀτ[ίταλλε / δεξάμ]εν[ο]ς, ἶσον δὲ θυγατράσιν ᾗσιν ἐτίμ[α. / ἣ τέκε] Τήλεφον Ἀρκασίδην Μυσῶν βασιλῆ[α, / μιχθεῖσ' ἐν φιλότητι βίηι Ἡρακληείηι 'receiving the maiden] in his halls he raised and reared her up well, and he honored her equally with his daughters. She bore] Telephus, Arcas' descendant, king of the Mysians, mingling] in the desire of Heracles' force' (tr. Most).

Hercules' second lover, Astydameia (*Her.* 9.50), was the daughter of Amyntor and grand-daughter of Ormen(i)us. She is also mentioned in the *Catalogue* as Tlepolemus' mother by Hercules (fr. 232 = Σ Pind. *Ol.* 7.42): καὶ Ἡσίοδος δὲ Ἀστυδάμειαν αὐτήν φησι…ἣν δὲ Φύλαντος θυγάτηρ…ἐνταῦθα δὲ Ἀμύντορος αὐτήν φησιν ὁ Πίνδαρος, Ἡσίοδος δὲ καὶ Σιμωνίδης Ὀρμένου. 'and Hesiod too says that she was Astydamea…She was the daughter of Phylas…Pindar says there that she was Amyntor's daughter, but Hesiod and Simonides say she was Ormenus" (tr. Most). It is noteworthy that Ovid adopts the version of Hesiod and Simonides, and not Pindar's, as regards the paternity of Astydameia (*Her.* 9.50, quoted above).

Continuing her list[72] of Hercules' extra-marital affairs Deianira mentions the fifty daughters of Thespius, Teuthras' son (*Her.* 9.51f.): *non tibi crimen erunt, Teu-*

---

[72] The listing habit of the Ovidian Deianira, second to none other in the single *Heroides*, does not pertain only to her husband's love affairs, but also to his famous labours. Contrasting his unheroic downfall at Omphale's palace with his illustrious heroic past, Deianira/Ovid finds the opportunity to present a catalogue of Hercules' labours (9.61–72 and 85–100). Hercules is mythology's super-hero and his labours fit even in the narrow and humble frame of an elegiac letter. In her Ovidian letter Deianira claims that Hercules had not been crushed by his *series immensa laborum* (9.5), picking up Hercules' depiction in the Μεγάλαι Ἠοῖαι (fr. 248) as πονηρότατος. Cf. *Her.* 9.75f. where Deianira calls Hercules' hand *victricem mille laborum*. Hercules' labours were set by Eurystheus, Sthenelus' son, on Hera's advice (*Her.* 9.25): *Stheneleius hostis*. Cf. *Cat.* fr. 190.9–12: Νικίππην δ' ἄρ' ἔγημε βίη Σθε]νέλοι[ο ἄν]ακτο[ς / [ ].[..]..[.].... / [βίη. Ἡρακλ]ηείη[.] / [ἐπ]έτελλεν ἀέθλο[υς 'Lord Sthenelus' [force married Nicippe /] [[Heracles' force] /] he ordained labors [' (tr. Most). Hercules' labours also feature in the *Catalogue* (fr. 190) and were a very common theme in literature. Deianira's remark about Hera's wrath against Hercules (*Her.* 9.45: *irae Iunonis iniquae*) may be an echo of the *Catalogue* (fr. 25.30): τὸν πρὶν μέν ῥ' ἤχθηρε θεὰ λευκώλενος Ἥρη.

thrantia turba, sorores, / quarum de populo nulla relicta tibi est. 'it wasn't your fault, the sisters, Thespius' daughters, of whose company not one was left alone by you' (tr. Kline, with modifications). Hercules slept with them for fifty consecutive nights (or for seven nights or even on the same night according to other versions) and had fifty sons with them. Nevertheless, the core of Deianira's complaint against Hercules is Omphale, the queen of Lydia.[73] Leaving aside Iole for the moment, she dedicates the largest part of her letter (53–120) to Hercules' relationship with Omphale, with whom Hercules had one son, Lamus (*Her.* 9.54): *unde ego sum Lydo facta noverca Lamo.* 'by whom I am made a stepmother to your Lydian Lamus' (tr. Kline). The Ovidian Deianira constantly thinks in terms of family and dynasty, which is also a cardinal feature of the *Catalogue*. Hercules' extra-marital adventures make her stepmother to new children all the time. This would not be a problem in the *Catalogue* – besides, the opinion of the women on the matter is not heard – because, as mentioned above, it is thanks to such extra-marital affairs that genealogical trees grow bigger. On the contrary, in the *Heroides* things get personal; family and love relationships actually do matter. This is a different world altogether and this is a subjective genre. The habits and the values of the world of the *Catalogue* are now criticized.

Hercules was subdued both literally and metaphorically (*servitium amoris*)[74] by Omphale. They swapped gender roles and Omphale had every reason to boast that she enslaved the hero of heroes. She wore his emblematic lion skin and held his club, while he was wearing women's clothes, helping the other slaves with spinning the wool and with household labour.[75] A man (Hercules) – actually, *the* man – became the (erotic) slave of a woman (Omphale), and a woman (Omphale) became the *domina* of a man (Hercules). Hercules was completely stripped of his heroic stature, and adopted a new, feminine and elegiac identity. One of the women of the *Catalogue*, Deianira, in her new capacity as writer of an elegiac letter, inserts Hercules into a catalogue of women. In a sense, Hercules becomes one of the *Ehoie*.[76]

---

[73] In order to purify himself from the killing of Iphitus, the son of king Eurytus, Hercules was sold as a slave to the queen Omphale. Casanova (1970) suggests that Hercules' enslavement to Omphale appeared in the *Catalogue*.

[74] For the elegiac motif of the *servitium amoris*, see Michalopoulos (2014) on *Her.* 20.77–90 with bibliography.

[75] For Hercules' service to Omphale see also Prop. 4.9.47–50: *idem ego Sidonia feci servilia palla / officia et Lydo pensa diurna colo, / mollis et hirsutum cepit mihi fascia pectus, / et manibus duris apta puella fui.*

[76] The points of contact between Deianira's letter and the tradition of the *Catalogue* also include another standard feature of the *Catalogue*, female beauty and contests with a woman as a prize. Deianira reminds Hercules of his struggles against Achelous and Nessus, which he

As she is still writing her letter (*Her.* 9.143–150), Deianira is informed that Hercules is dying from Nessus' poisonous cloak, which she sent him as a gift, hoping – this was Nessus' treacherous promise⁷⁷ – that in this way she would win back Hercules' love. This is the only time in the *Heroides* that the writing of a letter is interrupted by an external incident, which changes the situation dramatically. This sudden twist gives Deianira/Ovid the opportunity to treat Hercules' death, thus covering the full span of Hercules' life, which was also the case in the *Catalogue*.⁷⁸ Deianira feels the need to apologize for her actions and to explain why she sent the fatal cloak to Hercules. She wants to make clear that she was deceived by Nessus and that her only intention was to win back Hercules' love. The words she uses to refer to Nessus' cloak and to his poisonous blood – <u>infecit</u> (9.142), <u>tunicae</u> tabe (9.144), and in particular the phrase <u>inlita</u> Nesseo misi tibi texta <u>veneno</u> (9.163) – pick up the *Catalogue*'s φάρμακον ἐπιχρίσασα χιτῶνα (fr. 25.21).

One of the arguments that Deianira uses to justify her actions is her family's troubled past, her *devota domus* (9.153). She mentions her brother, Meleager [9.151: *tu quoque cognosces in me, Meleagre, sororem!* 'You will recognise a sister of yours in me too, Meleager!' (tr. Kline), 9.156: *alter fatali vivus in igne fuit* 'the other was burned by the fatal flame' (tr. Kline)], her father, Oeneus [9.153 f.: *heu devota domus! solio sedet Agrios alto; / Oenea desertum nuda senecta premit* 'Alas for my accursed house! Agrius sits on Calydon's high throne: defenceless old age weighs on forsaken Oeneus' (tr. Kline)], her half-brother, Tydeus [9.155: *exulat ignotis Tydeus germanus in oris* 'Tydeus, my brother, is an exile on an unknown shore' (tr. Kline)] and her mother, Althaea who killed Meleager by burning the log that stood for his life and then killed herself [9.157: *exegit ferrum sua per praecordia mater* 'our mother, pierced her breast with a blade' (tr. Kline)]. Ge-

---

fought for her sake (*Her.* 9.137–142): *me quoque cum multis, sed me sine crimine amasti; / ne pigeat, pugnae bis tibi causa fui. / cornua flens legit ripis Achelous in udis / truncaque limosa tempora mersit aqua; / semivir occubuit in letifero Eveno / Nessus et infecit sanguis equinus aquas*. In his letter to Helen, Paris mentions Deianira in a catalogue of women whom their husbands earned in a contest (*Her.* 16.263–8). See Michalopoulos (2006) ad loc.; Ziogas (2013) 50 f. For Hercules' struggle with Achelous for Deianira, see Soph. *Trach.* 9–29, 507–525. Cf. Ov. *Am.* 3.6.35–38 (*cornua si tua nunc ubi sint, Acheloe, requiram, / Herculis irata fracta querere manu; / nec tanti Calydon nec tota Aetolia tanti, / una tamen tanti Deianira fuit*) and Ov. *Met.* 9.8–10 (*nomine siqua suo fando pervenit ad aures / Deïanira tuas, quondam pulcherrima virgo / multorumque fuit spes invidiosa procorum*).

77 For wedding gifts and gifts offered by suitors in the *Catalogue*, see Osborne (2005) 17 f.; Ziogas (2013) 142 n. 79. In a sense Nessus' cloak is his gift to Deianira for her wedding to Hercules.
78 As noted by Haubold (2005), Hercules lives his life backwards in the *Catalogue*.

nealogy and family relations, cardinal features of the tradition of the *ehoie*-poetry, once again invade the world of the *Heroides*.

Deianira closes her letter by bidding farewell to her sister, Gorge, and her son, Hyllus (*Her.* 9.165–168): *iamque vale, seniorque pater germanaque Gorge / et patria et patriae frater adempte tuae / et tu lux oculis hodierna novissima nostris / virque – sed o possis! – et puer Hylle, vale!* 'Now farewell my aged father, and you, my sister Gorge, and my land, and my brother wrenched from that land, and you the last day's light to meet my eyes: and my husband – but O can you still be – and Hyllus my son, farewell!' (tr. Kline, with modifications). Both figures are mentioned in the *Catalogue*. Gorge was another daughter of Oeneus and Althaea (fr. 25.17): Γόργην τ' ἠύκομον 'and beautiful-haired Gorge' (tr. Most), while Hyllus was one of the four sons Deianira had with Hercules (fr. 25.18–20: ἣ τέχ' ὑποδμηθεῖ[σα βίηι Ἡρ]ακλη[ε]ίηι / Ὕλλον καὶ Γλῆνον καὶ [Κτή]σιππον καὶ Ὀνείτην· / τοὺς τέκε 'who, overpowered by Heracles' [force], bore / Hyllus and Glenus and Ctesippus and Onites; these she bore'. Deianira closes her letter and dies, but her family line continues with Hyllus, whose daughters are mentioned at the Μεγάλαι Ἠοῖαι fr. 251a (= Paus. 4.2.1): πυθέσθαι δὲ σπουδῆι πάνυ ἐθελήσας, οἵ τινες παῖδες Πολυκάονι ἐγένοντο ἐκ Μεσσήνης, ἐπελεξάμην τάς τε Ἠοίας καλουμένας καὶ τὰ ἔπη τὰ Ναυπάκτια, πρὸς δὲ αὐτοῖς ὁπόσα Κιναίθων καὶ Ἄσιος ἐγενεαλόγησαν. οὐ μὴν ἔς γε ταῦτα ἦν σφισιν οὐδὲν πεποιημένον, ἀλλὰ Ὕλλου μὲν τοῦ Ἡρακλέους θυγατρὶ Εὐαίχμηι συνοικῆσαι Πολυκάονα υἱὸν Βούτου λεγούσας τὰς μεγάλας οἶδα Ἠοίας, τὰ δὲ ἐς τὸν Μεσσήνης ἄνδρα καὶ τὰ ἐς αὐτὴν Μεσσήνην παρεῖταί σφισι.

In the *Catalogue* Deianira is initially called ἐπίφρων 'thoughtful' (fr. 25.17), but soon loses her mind (ἀάσατο μέγα θυμῶι, fr. 25.20). The situation is similar in the *Heroides*. Ovid's Deianira too loses her mind (*mens fugit admonitu*, 9.135, cf. *Catalogue* fr. 25.17: ἀάσατο μέγα θυμῶι), carried away by her erotic *furor* (*quo me furor egit amanti?*, 9.145), and calls herself *inpia* four times (146, 151, 157, 164): *inpia quid dubitas Deianira mori?* The reason for Deianira's transformation from ἐπίφρων to ἄφρων is love (9.145). What's more, the answer to her emotional question at *Her.* 9.145 (*quid feci?*) has already been given in the *Catalogue* (fr. 25.20): δείν' ἔρξε, which also corresponds to the Ovidian Deianira's *sceleris tanti causa* (*Her.* 9.148). Such verbal similarities and parallels strengthen and confirm the links between the *Catalogue* and the *Heroides*, actually showing that Ovid had firsthand knowledge of this work.

Conclusions

I hope to have shown that numerous verbal, thematic, and structural parallels suggest that there is compelling connection between Ovid's *Heroides* and the Hesiodic *Catalogue*. The two works share a lot in common as regards certain generic features and, most importantly, their focus on women and love stories. Ovid had direct access to the *Catalogue* and integrated in his *Heroides* numerous themes and features of poetics from the genealogic-catalogic tradition. Most of the single *Heroides* deal with love stories that take place during the time span of the *Catalogue*. Lists of various content are a standard feature, while emphasis is laid on female beauty, genealogies, and contests with women as prizes. More than any other letter of the single *Heroides* Deianira's letter to Hercules (*Her.* 9) stands close to the *Catalogue* and shares cardinal features with it: concern for the *oikos*, a listing habit (Hercules' labours, his love affairs, her family tree), sexual unions of gods with mortal women, love affairs, struggles for the sake of a woman, interest in ancestors and genealogy, and, most importantly, Hercules, the most illustrious mythical hero whose whole life is narrated in the *Catalogue*. Nevertheless, the world of the *Catalogue* is different from the world of the *Heroides*. The elegiac voice of Ovid's Deianira criticizes certain cardinal principles and values of the world of the Hesiodic *Catalogue*, in particular the sexual affairs (or rather rapes) and the sexual freedom of men in the *Catalogue*, and questions the happiness of relationships between unequal partners.

Bibliography

Alfonsi, L. (1949). 'Ps.-Esiodo in Properzio?', *Revue de Philologie* 1: 17–26.
Arrighetti, G. (ed.) (1998). *Esiodo Opere*, Turin.
Arrighetti, G. (2008). 'Il *Catalogo* esiodeo: un genere letterario?', in: Bastianini and Casanova, 11–27.
Asquith, H. (2005). 'From Genealogy to *Catalogue:* The Hellenistic Adaptation of the Hesiodic *Catalogue* Form', in: Hunter, 266–286.
Barchiesi, A. (1992). Heroides *I, II, III. Introduzione, testo critico e commento*, Florence.
Barchiesi, A. (1996). 'Review of E. J. Kenney (ed.), *Ovid Heroides* xvi–xxi (Cambridge)', *Bryn Mawr Classical Review* 12.1.
Bastianini, A. and A. Casanova (eds.) (2008). *Esiodo. Cent'anni di papiri, Atti del Convegno internazionale di studi* (Florence, 7–8 June 2007), Florence.
Bilinski, B. (1959). 'Elementi Esiodei nelle "Metamorfosi" di Ovidio', in: *Atti del Convegno Internazionale Ovidiano*, II (Rome), 101–123.
Boyd, B.W. (ed.) (2002). *Brill's Companion to Ovid*, Leiden.

Bremmer, J. N. (1988). 'La plasticité du mythe: Méléagre dans la poésie homérique', in:
    C. Calame (ed.), *Métamorphoses du mythe en Grèce antique*, Geneva, 37–56.
Cairns, F. (2006). *Sextus Propertius. The Augustan Elegist*, Cambridge.
Cameron, A. (1995). *Callimachus and his Critics*, Princeton.
Casanova, A. (1970). 'Tre note al *Catalogo* esiodeo', *Studia Florentina Alexandro Ronconi Sexagenario Oblata*, Rome, 61–67.
Cingano, E. (2005). 'A Catalogue Within a Catalogue: Helen's Suitors in the Hesiodic *Catalogue of Women* (frr. 196–204)', in: Hunter, 118–152.
Cingano, E. (2009). 'The Hesiodic Corpus' in: Montanari, Rengakos, and Tsagalis, 91–130.
Clausen, W. (1994). *Virgil's* Eclogues, Oxford.
Clay, J. S. (2003). *Hesiod's Cosmos*, Cambridge.
Clay, J. S. (2005). 'The Beginning and End of the *Catalogue of Women* and its Relation to Hesiod', in: Hunter, 25–34.
Cohen, I. M. (1983). *The Hesiodic* Catalogue of Women, PhD Diss., University of Toronto.
Collins, D. (2004). *Master of the Game: Competition and Performance in Greek Poetry*, Cambridge, MA.
Davies, D. R. (1992). *Genealogy and Catalogue: Thematic Relevance and Narrative Elaboration in Homer and Hesiod*, PhD Diss., University of Michigan.
Dräger, P. (1997). *Untersuchungen zu den* Frauenkatalogen *Hesiods*, Stuttgart.
Farrell, J. (1991). *Vergil's* Georgics *and the Traditions of Ancient Epic. The Art of Allusion in Literary History*, New York and Oxford.
Fletcher, R. (2005). 'Or such as Ovid's *Metamorphoses*', in: Hunter, 299–319.
Gale, M. R. (1994). *Myth and Poetry in Lucretius*, Cambridge.
Gibson, R. K. (2003). *Ovid* Ars amatoria *Book 3*, Cambridge.
González, M. (2010). 'The *Catalogue of Women* and the End of the Heroic Age (Hesiod fr. 204.94–103 M-W)', *TAPA* 140: 375–422.
Graziosi, B. (2001). 'Competition in Wisdom', in: F. Budelmann and P. Michelakis (eds.), *Homer, Tragedy and Beyond: Essays in Honour of P. E. Easterling*, Cambridge, 54–74.
Grimal, P. (1962). 'Tibulle et Hésiode', in: *Hésiode et son influence*. Six exposés et discussions par K. von Fritz, G. S. Kirk, W. J. Verdenius, Fr. Solmsen, A. La Penna, P. Grimal, Vandoeuvres and Geneva, 271–287.
Grossardt, P. (2001). *Die Erzählung von Meleagros. Zur literarischen Entwicklung der kalydonischen Kultlegende*, Leiden.
Hardie, P. (2005). 'The Hesiodic *Catalogue of Women* and Latin poetry', in: Hunter, 287–298.
Harrison, S. J. (1991). *Virgil:* Aeneid *Book 10*, Oxford.
Haubold, J. (2000). *Homer's People: Epic Poetry and Social Formation*, Cambridge.
Haubold, J. (2005). 'Heracles in the Hesiodic *Catalogue of Women*', in: Hunter, 85–98.
Häussler, R. (1976). *Das historische Epos der Griechen und Römer bis Virgil*, Heidelberg.
Heldmann, K. (1982). *Die Niederlage Homers im Dichterwettstreit mit Hesiod*, Göttingen.
Henderson, J. (1986). 'Becoming a Heroine (1st): Penelope's Ovid...', *LCM* 11: 7–10, 21–24, 37–40, 67–70, 82–85, 114–120.
Hess, K. (1960). *Der Agon zwischen Homer und Hesiod, seine Entstehung und kulturgeschichtliche Stellung*, Meisenheim am Glan.
Higbie, C. (1995). *Heroes' Names, Homeric Identities*, New York.
Hinds, S. (1987). 'Generalizing about Ovid', *Ramus* 16: 4–31.
Hinds, S. (1985). 'Booking the return trip: Ovid and *Tristia* 1', *PCPS* 31: 13–32.

Hinds, S. (1999). 'First among Women: Ovid, *Tristia* 1.6 and the Traditions of the Exemplary *Catalogue*', in: S. M. Braund and R. Mayer (eds.), *Amor: Roma. Love and Latin Literature, Eleven Essays (and One Poem) by former Research Students presented to E. J. Kenney on his Seventy-fifth Birthday*, Cambridge, 123–142.

Hirschberger, M. (2004). *Gynaikōn Katalogos und Megalai Ēhoiai: Ein Kommentar zu den Fragmenten zweier hesiodeischer Epen*, Leipzig.

Holford-Stevens, L. (1998). *Aulus Gellius*, London.

Hollis, A. S. (1970). *Ovid:* Metamorphoses: *Book viii*, Oxford.

Horsfall, N.M. (1990). 'Virgil and the Illusory Footnote', *PLLS* 6: 49–63.

Hunter, R. (ed.) (2005a). *The Hesiodic* Catalogue of Women: *Constructions and Reconstructions*, Cambridge.

Hunter, R. (2005b). 'The Hesiodic *Catalogue* and Hellenistic Poetry', in: Hunter, 239–265.

Keith, A. (1992). *The Play of Fictions: Studies in Ovid's* Metamorphoses, Ann Arbor.

Keith, A. (2002). 'Sources and Genres in Ovid's *Metamorphoses* 1–5', in: Boyd, 235–269.

Kennedy, D. F. (1984). 'The Epistolary Mode and the First of Ovid's *Heroides*', *CQ* 34: 413–422.

Kenney, E. J. (1996). *Ovid:* Heroides *XVI-XXI*, Cambridge.

Knox, P. E. (1995). *Ovid* Heroides. *Select Epistles*, Cambridge.

Koning, H. H. (2010). *Hesiod: The Other Poet. Ancient Reception of a Cultural Icon*, Leiden and Boston.

Kyriakidis, S. (2007). *Catalogues of Proper Names in Latin Epic Poetry. Lucretius – Virgil – Ovid*, Newcastle.

La Penna, A. (1962). 'Esiodo nella cultura e nella poesia di Virgilio', in: K. von Fritz (ed.), *Hésiode et son influence*, Geneva 213–270.

Lafaye, G. [1904] (1971). *Les Métamorphoses d'Ovide et leurs modèles grecs*, Paris, new edition by M. von Albrecht with add. and intr., Hildesheim and New York.

Lausberg, H. (1998). *Handbook of Literary Rhetoric. A Foundation for Literary Study* (tr. D.F. Orton and R.D. Anderson), Leiden, Boston and Cologne.

Ludwig, W. (1965). *Struktur und Einheit der Metamorphosen Ovids*, Berlin.

March, J. (1987). *The Creative Poet: Studies on the Treatment of Myths in Greek Poetry*, London.

Mazzoli, G. (1970). *Seneca e la poesia*, Milan.

McKay, K. (1962). *Erysichthon. A Callimachean Comedy*, Leiden.

McKeown, J. C. (1989). *Ovid: Amores, vol. II: A Commentary on Book One*, Leeds.

Merkelbach, R. and M. L. West (eds.) (1967). *Fragmenta Hesiodea*, Oxford.

Michalopoulos, A. N. (2006). *Ovid* Heroides *16 and 17: Introduction, Text and Commentary*, Cambridge.

Michalopoulos, A. N. (2008). '*Sed mihi quid prodest?* (Ov. *Her.* 1.47): «γυναικεία» οπτική και ανδροκρατούμενος κόσμος στις *Ηρωίδες* του Οβιδίου', in: B. Κοντογιάννη (ed.), *Λόγος γυναικών*. Proceedings of an International Conference in Komotini (26–28 May 2006), Athens, 339–354.

Michalopoulos, A. N. (2014). *Οβίδιος. Ηρωίδες 20–21, Ακόντιος και Κυδίππη (εισαγωγή, κείμενο, μετάφραση, σχόλια)*, Athens.

Michalopoulos, C. N. (2006). *Ovid's* Heroides *4 and 8. A Commentary with introduction*, PhD Diss., University of Leeds.

Miller, F. J. (1993). 'Ovidian Allusion and the Vocabulary of Memory', *MD* 30: 153–164.

Montanari, F., A, Rengakos, and C. Tsagalis (eds.) (2009). *Brill's Companion to Hesiod*, Leiden.
Most, G. (2007). *Hesiod: The Shield, Catalogue of Women, Other Fragments*, Cambridge, MA and London.
Myers, K. S. (1994). *Ovid's Causes: Cosmogony and Aetiology in the Metamorphoses*, Ann Arbor.
Nasta, M. (2006). 'La typologie des Catalogues d'*Éhées:* un réseau généalogique thématisé', *Kernos* 19: 59–78.
Obbink, D. (2004). 'Vergil's *De pietate:* from *Ehoiae* to Allegory in Vergil, Philodemus, and Ovid', in: D. J. Armstrong-Fish, P. A. Johnston, and M. B. Skinner (eds.), *Vergil, Philodemus, and the Augustans*, Austin, 175–209.
Osborne, R. (2005). 'Ordering Women in Hesiod's *Catalogue*', in: Hunter, 5–24.
Palmer, A. (1898). *P. Ovidi Nasonis Heroides with the Greek translation of Planudes*, Oxford (= Hildesheim 1967) [= *Ovid: Heroides*, edited by Arthur Palmer, with a new introduction by Duncan F. Kennedy, Bristol 2005, vol. 1: Introduction and Latin Text, with Greek Translation by Maximus Planudes, vol. 2: Commentary, Exeter and Bristol.
Papaioannou, S. (forthcoming). 'When Catalogues are Middles and have Significant Closures: Revisiting the Composition of the Calydonian Catalogue in Ovid, *Met.* 8.298–328', in: A. N. Michalopoulos, S. Papaioannou, and A. Zissos (eds.), *From Middles to New Beginnings*, Newcastle.
Pontani, F. (2000). 'Catullus 64 and the Hesiodic *Catalogue:* a Suggestion', *Philologus* 144: 267–276.
Reinsch-Werner, H. (1976). *Callimachus hesiodicus*, Berlin.
Richardson, N. J. (1981). 'The Contest of Homer and Hesiod and Alcidamas' *Mouseion*', *CQ* 31: 1–10.
Rosati, G. (2009). 'The Latin reception of Hesiod', in: Montanari, Rengakos, and Tsagalis, 343–374.
Rosen, R. M. (1997). 'Homer and Hesiod', in: B. Powell and I. Morris (eds.), *A New Companion to Homer*, Leiden, 463–488.
Ross, D. O. Jr. (1975). *Backgrounds to Augustan Poetry: Gallus, Elegy and Rome*, Cambridge.
Rutherford, I. (2000). 'Formulas, Voice, and Death in *Ehoie-Poetry*, the Hesiodic *Gunaikon Katalogos*, and the Odysseian *Nekuia*, in: D. Obbink, (ed.) *Matrices of Genre: Authors, Canons, and Society*, Cambridge, MA and London, 81–96.
Rutherford, I. (2005). 'Mestra at Athens: Hesiod fr. 43 and the poetics of panhellenism', in: Hunter, 99–117.
Schroeder, Ch.-M. (2006). *Hesiod in the Hellenistic Imagination*, PhD Diss., University of Michigan.
Schwartz, J. (1960). *Pseudo-Hesiodeia. Recherches sur la composition, la diffusion et la disparition ancienne d'œuvres attribuées à Hésiode*, Leiden.
Setaioli, A. (1988). *Seneca e i Greci. Citazioni e traduzioni nelle opere filosofiche*, Bologna.
Sistakou, E. (2009). '*Callimachus Hesiodicus* revisited', in: Montanari, Rengakos, and Tsagalis, 219–252.
Skempis, M. (2011). 'Ironic genre demarcation: Bacchylides 17 and the Epic Tradition', *Trends in Classics* 3: 254–300.
Thomas, R. F. (1992). 'The old man revisited: Virg. *Georg.* 4.116–48', *MD* 29: 44–51.

Tsagalis, C. (2009). 'Poetry and Poetics in the Hesiodic Corpus', in: Montanari, Rengakos, and Tsagalis, 131–177.
Usher, S. (1965). '*Occultatio* in Cicero's speeches', *AJP* 86: 175–192.
von Albrecht, M. (1964). *Die Parenthese in Ovids* Metamorphosen *und ihre dichterische Funktion*, Hildesheim.
West, M. L. (1967). 'The Contest of Homer and Hesiod,' *CQ* 17: 433–450.
West, M. L. (1985). *The Hesiodic* Catalogue of Women. *Its Nature, Structure, and Origins*, Oxford.
Wimmel, W. (1960). *Kallimachos in Rom: Die Nachfolge seines apologetischen Dichtens in der Augusteerzeit*, Wiesbaden.
Ziogas, I. (2011). 'Ovid as a Hesiodic Poet: Atalanta in the *Catalogue of Women* (fr. 72–6 M-W) and the *Metamorphoses.* (10.560–707)', *Mnemosyne* 64: 249–270.
Ziogas, I. (2013). *Ovid and Hesiod: The Metamorphosis of the* Catalogue of Women, Cambridge.

Marta Cardin and Filippomaria Pontani
Hesiod's Fragments in Byzantium*

ἀλλ' οὐ μόνος ταῦτα σὺ οὐδὲ κατ' ἐμοῦ μόνου, ἀλλὰ πολλοὶ καὶ ἄλλοι τὰ τοῦ ὁμοτέχνου τοῦ ἐμοῦ Ὁμήρου κατακνίζουσι λεπτὰ οὕτω κομιδῆι καὶ μάλιστα μικρά ἄττα διεξιόντες.

(Luc. Hes. 5)[1]

1 Foreword: Hesiod in Byzantium

'Tell me, then... do you prefer Homer's poetry or Hesiod's? or that of any other poet beyond these both? "Homer's", I know you will reply, "and then Hesiod's", unless I totally misunderstand your nodding; and you are perfectly right to extol these two as the wisest of all poets. But would you then let the young study the language on their poetry? I see that you agree with that too'.

This is how Theodore Prodromos (ca. 1100–1158/70), a prolific and renowned writer of the Comnenian age (ca. 1081–1185), addresses the protagonist of the satire called *An ignorant, or a self-proclaimed professor* (no. 144 Horändner).[2] Through these and similar questions, he attempts to unmask the insufficient preparation and the unsatisfying dialectical skill of his silent interlocutor; in order to drive him into an embarrassing *impasse*, he casts doubts on the *communis opinio* that presents the study of the works of the two greatest poets as most useful: Plato, he argues, banned Homer's epic from education, and Hesiod is of no use even to sailors and peasants, who are not capable of understanding his teachings, clad as they are in meter and poetry.[3] The self-proclaimed teacher has no answer, whence Theodore invites him to go back and study grammar from

---

* While the authors have cooperated in writing this chapter, sections 1–2 are the work of Marta Cardin and 3–4 of Filippomaria Pontani.
1 Hesiod speaks: 'You are not alone in this, nor am I the only victim. Many others pick the poetry of my fellow-craftsman Homer utterly to pieces, pointing out similar niggling details, the merest trifles' (transl. Koning 2010, 94–95).
2 Ἀμαθὴς ἢ παρὰ ἑαυτῷ γραμματικός, ll. 95–101 Migliorini (2010, 29–51; formerly ed. Podestà [1945] 242–252, here 246.13–247.1, and *AO* III 222–27 Cramer, here 225.15–22; see also Romano 1999, 298–309): εἰπέ [ἐπεὶ Cramer Podestà] τοιγαροῦν...· Ὁμήρου ἀποδέχῃ ποίησιν ἢ Ἡσιόδου; ἢ παρ' ἄμφω τὼ ἄνδρε ἄλλου του; Ὁμήρου εὖ οἶδ' ὅτι λέγεις καὶ μετ' αὐτὸν Ἡσιόδου, εἰ μὴ παντάπασι καταψεύδομαί σου τῆς κεφαλῆς, καὶ εὖγε ποιεῖς τοὺς σοφωτάτους τῶν ἄλλων ὑπερτιθέμενος. ἆρα γοῦν καὶ τοῖς τούτων ποιήμασιν ἐγγυμνάσαις τοὺς νέους; καὶ τοῦτο μόγις κατένευσας.
3 Ll. 101–116 Migliorini (p. 247.1–14 Podestà = *AO* III 225.22–226.7). References are to Plat. *R.* 10.606e-8b and *Lg.* 7.801c-2c; Hesiod is considered here for his practical *opheleia* in the *Erga*.

the very beginning, evoking the famous Hesiodic *dictum* that the gods have placed sweat before virtue (*Op.* 289–290).⁴

With his penetrating irony, Theodore gives us a glimpse of the reception of Hesiod in 12th-century Byzantium, the 'Homeric century' that witnessed an important Renaissance of Classical studies. In this period, the comparison between Homer and Hesiod was still among the favourite topics for erudites: while Hesiod regularly came second – both in scholastic and in scribal practice – his works were nonetheless quite widespread.⁵ This can be appreciated by consulting the *apparatus comparandorum et testimoniorum* in the editions of Alois Rzach and Martin West, as well as the indices and the *apparatus fontium* of some of the main works of Comnenian literature.

An historian such as Niketas Choniates (ca. 1155/7–1217), for instance, did not hesitate to blend into the same *iunctura* a line from the *Works and Days* (442) with a verset of *Isaiah* (58.7), in order to indicate that Isaac Angelos was expected to give bread to his Norman prisoners.⁶ In the novel *The love story of Hysmine and Hysminias* by Eustathios Makrembolites (12th c.), we find several consecutive Hesiodic echoes in the *ekphrasis* of the paintings of the twelve months: a peasant bent on the grain-spikes wears on his head πῖλον ἀσκητὸν καθ' Ἡσίοδον, 'a well-made felt cap, as Hesiod says' (*Op.* 545–546); another one marks the time for ploughing ὃν καί τις σοφὸς ἐκ τῶν Πληιάδων ... ἠκριβώσατο, 'that a wise man determined exactly ... from the Pleiades' (see *Op.* 383–384); the winter is the old man ὁ τῆι ἱστίηι ἐμπελαδόν, 'near the hearth'

---

4 Ll. 116–136 Migliorini (pp. 247.14–248.15 Podestà = AO III 226.8–32). On the *Nachleben* of *Op.* 289–292 in an educative context see Koning (2010) 144–149 and Hunter (2014) 93–100. Basil of Caesarea describes these lines as τὰ ἔπη ἃ πάντες ᾄδουσιν (*Ad adul. de ut.* 5.8–15 Boulenger); Ioannes Tzetzes in his scholium *ad loc.* (p. 198.1–8 Gaisf.) gives as an example precisely the toil of whoever chooses to acquire ἀρετή in the art of grammar (the text is that of Cardin's forthcoming edition): τυχὸν γάρ τις ἐθέλει γραμματικὴν ἀρετὴν ἐπικτήσασθαι, καὶ οὐκ εὐθέως αὐτῆς γίνεται μέτοχος, ἀλλὰ ἡμέτερον αὐτὸν ἐκδίδωσι τοῖς στοιχειώδεσι γράμμασιν, εἶτα ταῖς συλλαβαῖς καὶ τῆι λοιπῆι προπαιδείαι, ἔπειτα τῆι Διονυσίου βίβλωι (cf. Uhlig 1883, vi, 3) προσέχει καὶ τοῖς Θεοδοσίου κανόσι (cf. Hilgard [1894] vii) καὶ ποιηταῖς, εἶτα σχεδογραφίας ἀπάρχεται· καὶ πολλὰ πολλοῖς μογήσας τοῖς χρόνοις, μόγις τὴν ἀρετὴν ἐπικτᾶται.
5 See Kaldellis (2007) 225–316 ('The twelfth was... a *Homeric* century', p. 243), and (2009); Flusin (2008) 390–395; Pontani (2015) 366–394. Homeric studies in the 12th century are investigated especially by Basilikopoulou-Ioannidou (1971); Browning (1975) and (1992a); Pontani (2005) 159–178; Cullhed (2014) 27–89. On Hesiod's role in the Byzantine scholastic curriculum (commentaries, editions, etc.), see Krumbacher (1897) 505; Browning (1992b) 134; Wilson (1996²) 24. Hesiod is particularly present in the work of Prodromos: *Op.* 158 and 737–738 are taken up in the tetrasticha on the Holy Scriptures (248b4 e 264b2): see Magnelli (2003) 193–194.
6 *Hist.* 12.3, p. 364.3 van Dieten (τρύφος ἄρτου διαθρύπτειν ὀκτάβλωμον), with the note *ad loc.* by Pontani (1999) 695–696.

(*Op.* 734), because ὁ ... χειμὼν διὰ κόρης ἁπαλόχροος οὐ διάησι, τροχαλὸν δὲ γέροντα τίθησι, 'the winterly wind "does not blow through the soft-skinned maiden", "but it makes the old man curved like a wheel" ' (*Op.* 518–519).[7] And more examples could be added.[8]

To the same period we owe the first instances of systematic commentaries to the Hesiodic poems, a clear sign of their being taught in schools and of the attention devoted by erudites to their text: Ioannes Tzetzes (born around the 1110s and died after the mid-1160s) is the author of an exegesis on the *Works and Days*, and probably also of a peculiar recension of the scholia to the *Aspis* – both preserved in the important collection of ancient poetry and erudite literature represented by ms. *Ambr.* C 222 inf. (end of the 12th c.) – as well as of a popular *vita Hesiodi* (contained in his *prolegomena* to the *Works*), and of a brand-new *Theogony* in political verse, overtly inspired by that of Hesiod.[9] To all this, one should

---

[7] (Translations of Hesiod's lines, here and elsewhere, are mostly by G. W. Most). References are to *Hysm. amor.* 4.9.2, 18.10, 12 and 13 (pp. 40.5–6, 45.4–6, 16 and 18–20 Marcovich). On authorship and date of this novel see Hunger (1978) II 137–142, and *ODB* II 1273 s.v. (A. Kaldellis); more parallels can be detected, e.g. *Op.* 24 in 9.2.3 (p. 110.1–2) Marcovich.

[8] The story of Hesiod's reception in Byzantium has yet to be analysed in a systematic study. Recent inquiries have been carried out on his reception in antiquity (Koning 2010), especially of the two main poems (Hunter 2014 for the *Works and Days*, Scully 2015 for the *Theogony* – the latter also alludes to Byzantine reception: pp. 162–163). Information on the abiding interest in Hesiod's work after Late Antiquity can be gathered from scattered hints in West (1966) 69–72 (*Th.*), and (1978) 69–71 (*Op.*); Russo (1965²) 52–57 (*Scut.*); Schwartz (1960) 47–62 (fragments); as well as from the reference works on Byzantine philology and literature, esp. Wilson (1996²) (p. 3 on the quotation of *Op.* 240 in a letter of Alexios III to the Republic of Genoa in 1199) and Pontani (2015) (p. 368 on the quotation of *Op.* 343 in a letter of Michael Italikos to Alexios Komnenos).

[9] On ms. *Ambr.* C 222 inf. and its dating, see Mazzucchi (2000, 2003 and 2004); on the scholia to the *Aspis*, and on Tzetzes' possible intervention, see Martano (2002), esp. 162–166. In the last years of the 12th c. (or in the early years of the 13th) was produced ms. *Messanensis* F.V. 11, a key witness of the early spreading of Tzetzes' commentary to the *Op.* in Southern Italy: see esp. Colonna (1953) 30–31; Mioni (1965) 139–141 no. 74; Lucà (1993) 85–86. On these mss. also Pontani (2015) 393–394, 396. On Hesiod's life and Tzetzes' *Theogony* see also below, § 2.1. Tzetzes' exegesis to the *Works and Days* – as the ms. witnesses indicate – circulated in the form of a commented edition; see for a comparable case the *Iliad* edition prepared by Isaac Porphyrogennetos ('Par. gr. 2862 is a unique manuscript, in that it preserves a true "edition" of the *Iliad* produced from the beginning to the end by a single identifiable Byzantine scholar... a neat and careful copy of the manuscript originally conceived and produced by Isaac Porphyrogennetos, including a preface, a text with copious scholia and an appendix designeted to "integrate" the Homeric account of the Trojan war': Pontani (2006) 556).

add a Neoplatonic commentary to the *Theogony* compiled by an obscure figure known by the name of Ioannes Diakonos Galenos.[10]

Finally, the 12th century is also the last moment when scholars deal with the conspicuous ancient erudite material (of both mythographical and lexicographic-grammatical nature) concerning the fragments of the minor works of the Hesiodic *corpus*.[11] Key figures in this process are the aforementioned Ioannes Tzetzes and Eustathios the archbishop of Thessalonike (ca. 1115–1195/96), who were also the most important Homerists of their time, and who will keep us busy in §§ 2 and 3:[12] to them we owe, *inter alia*, the transmission of several Hesiodic fragments (for some of which they are our only witnesses), coming from the *Catalogue of Women*, but also from the *Melampodia*, the *Astronomy*, the *Aigimios*, and many others *incertae sedis*. The erudite output of these two outstanding scholars, however inspired by very different, indeed sometimes almost opposite approaches to Hesiod's poetry, represents, together with the lexicographical and grammatical tradition (whose long roots may in fact tell us less about the culture of the age than about the ancient sources employed by the compilers), the most important source of information on the Hesiodic *corpus* in the entire Byzantine millennium.[13]

Of course, this lively presence of our poet in the 12th century would have been impossible without some continuity of transmission over the earlier ages. We still have important traces of the reception of Hesiod between the 9th and the 11th centuries in manuscript witnesses of both the three main poems and the related ancient exegesis, as well as in references and allusions in literary and sub-literary works. The second half of the 10th century is the age of an es-

---

[10] Ed. Flach (1876) 294–365. The dating of this Galenos is uncertain, but recent studies agree in placing him in the lively environment of the Comnenian age: see Cullhed (2014) 65–67; Roilos (2014); Pontani (2015) 376–377. On the novelty of Byzantine commentaries to the great classics of pagan literature, see Kaldellis (2009); Pontani (2015) 375–378.
[11] On the Hesiodic *corpus*, see now Cingano (2009).
[12] Morgan (1983) 165 terms Ioannes 'the leading interpreter of Homer' and Eustathios 'the leading commentator on Homer'.
[13] Admittedly, this interest is not widespread. Fr. 286 (= 221 Most: two lines from the *Megalai Ehoiai*) appears in an anonymous commentary on the *Nicomachean Ethics* (*CAG* XX, 222.22–26 Heylbut): the second line, relating Achilles' death, is mentioned without attribution by Aristotle (*EN* 5.8; later proverbial, see e.g. Suda αι 165 Adler), and is evoked in the 12th century by Isaac Porphyrogennetos in his short work on the Trojan stories not narrated by Homer: οὕτως δίκην ὁ Ἀχιλλεὺς προσήκουσαν ὤφλησε τῆι περὶ τὸν Ἕκτορα τούτου ἀπανθρώπωι καὶ ἀτεράμονι μήνιδι φιλοσόφως τοῦ ποιητοῦ φάσκοντος ὡς εἰ καὶ πάθηι τις ἅ κ' ἔρεξε, δίκη τ' ἰθεῖα γένοιτο (p. 70.19–24 Hinck). The Aristotelian commentator Michael of Ephesos clearly knew the Hesiodic authorship of the line (*CAG* XXII.3, p. 31.31–32 Hayduck: ἔστι δὲ τὸ ἔπος Ἡσιόδου).

sential codex for the transmission of the *Works and Days* and its scholia, namely *Par. gr.* 2771 (in which Hesiod is flanked by another pillar of didactic literature, namely Dionysius Periegetes' *Orbis descriptio*).[14] To the same turn of years should be dated a single parchment sheet containing 52 lines of the *Aspis* (now kept in ms. *Par. suppl. gr.* 663);[15] from the 11th c. (or early 12th) stem other sheets now gathered in the same *Par. suppl. gr.* 663, carrying passages from the *Theogony* and the *Aspis*, and copied by the same hand who wrote scholia to both *Theogony* and *Works and Days* in a bifolium of ms. *Par. suppl. gr.* 679;[16] finally, to the second half of the 11th c. should be dated ms. *Laur. Plut.* 31.39, containing both the *Works* and Oppian's *Halieutica*.[17]

Large excerpts from the text and the scholia of the three poems are inserted in the 9th-century lexicon known as *Etymologicum Genuinum*, where they have been accommodated (with slight adjustments) through a first-hand collection from one or more codices equipped with glosses and scholia (i.e., they were not inherited wholesale from the pre-existing lexicographical tradition): in the case of the *Works and Days*, this lost Hesiodic model represents a line of transmission that is clearly different from the one witnessed in the aforementioned *Par. gr.* 2771.[18] From the 10th c. onwards, erudite materials in the *Etymologica* preserve passages of lost works attributed to Hesiod: e.g. the words Χαρίτων ἀμαρύγματ' ἔχουσα, ascribed by *Etym. Genuinum* α 589 L.-L. to the *Catalogue of*

---

[14] On this ms., see Pertusi (1950) 528–544; Tsavari (1990) 55; Pontani (2015) 348. On the history of the medieval and humanist manuscript tradition of Hesiod's main works, see West (1964) and (1974); on the *Aspis*, see Corrales Pérez (1994). On the manuscripts with scholia to the three Hesiodic poems, see Schultz (1910) and (1913), as well as Pertusi (1950), (1951), (1952) (*Works and Days*), Di Gregorio (1971–1972) (*Theogony*), Martano (2002), (2005), (2006), (2008) (*Aspis*). There are approximately (see West 1974, 161 and the *Pinakes* database) 260/270 manuscripts of the *Works and Days*, 70/80 of the *Theogony* and just about 60 of the *Aspis*.
[15] This new dating (formerly: 11th or early 12th c.) is suggested on palaeographical grounds by Stefec (2014) 223 n. 41.
[16] On the relationship between these mss., see Corrales (1997) (already Corrales Pérez 1994, 66–67); Menchelli (2001); Ronconi (2007) (who has also suggested the idea that the various fragments should in fact belong to one and the same codex). *Par. suppl. gr.* 663 also contains the *Battle of Frogs and Mice*, and excerpts from the *Iliad:* see West (2001) 141–142. Both the dating to the 11th c. (rather than the 12th) and the exact geographical provenance (Mt. Athos? another province?) remain uncertain, but if the folia of the two mss. belonged to one and the same codex, this codex would constitute a complete Hesiodic collection, equipped with scholia (which were transcribed *à pleine page* separately from their respective poems).
[17] On this ms. we find hand B of the so-called 'circle of Ioannikios' (see Degni 2008, 184 and 233), although the ms. was certainly not produced in this milieu; a provincial, perhaps South Italian provenance, is quite possible (Wilson 1983, 164).
[18] See West (1974) 162–163, 183; Pertusi (1953) 180; Di Gregorio (1975) xvi-xvii; Martano (2006).

Women, are now attested in four papyrus fragments.[19] The lexicon of *Suda* (η 583 Adler = p. 1 Solmsen = T 1 Most) preserves the only existing biography of Hesiod if we except the one by Ioannes Tzetzes.

Furthermore, the writings of the intellectuals of this age also attest to the popularity and to the good degree of *auctoritas* attained by the Askran poet: in a speech held in front of emperor Leo VI the Wise (on July 20th, 902), archbishop Arethas (ca. 850 – *post* 932), discussing the possibility that his work might be left unfinished, juxtaposed τὴν Ἡσιόδου κορώνην – the crow screaming her bad omen from the roof of an unfinished house (*Op.* 746–747) – to the words of Christ in Luke 9.62.[20] In his *De thematibus*, Constantine Porphyrogennetos (905–959), quotes three lines of 'Hesiod the poet' on the genealogy of the eponymous hero of Macedonia (*Cat.* fr. 7 M.-W. = 3 H = 7 Most), which we do not know from any other source.[21] Poets such as John Geometres (ca. 935/940–1000) and Christopher of Mytilene (first half of the 11th c.) echo and reuse several expressions from the hexameters of the *Works and Days*.[22] A polygraph like Michael Psellos (1018–1092/3) refers to Hesiod as παιδευτικώτατος on the ground of the inimitable force of his myth of the Ages,[23] only later to contrast his misleading pagan teachings with the far more reliable Christian truths.[24]

This continuity in the study and reading of Hesiod made possible his 'rediscovery' in the 12th century: the conspicuous materials prepared in this age were then handed over to the other great season of Byzantine philology, namely the so-called early Palaeologan Renaissance[25]. In Palaeologan Byzantium, Hesiod is the poet – no less ancient than Homer – who has been initiated

---

[19] 'Hes.' *Cat.* frr. 43a.4; 70.38; 73.3; 196.6 M.-W. = 37.4; 31.38; *2.3; 104.6 H = 69.4; 41.38; 47.3; 154a.6 Most.

[20] *Or.* 61, II 24.16–20 Westerink, on which see Wilson (1996²) 131 (see also p. 126 for another quotation, this time of *Op.* 295). The same rhetorical use of Hes. *Op.* 746–747 about an unfinished work can be found already in Dexipp. *in Aristot. Cat., CAG* IV.2, 64.6–8 Busse, and in Tz. *in Herm., AO* IV 126.22 Cramer. Pertusi (1953, 181) suggests Arethas may have had a role in the preparation of the codex from which *Par. gr.* 2771 was copied: see Lemerle (1971) 226. In a scholium to Lucian's *Hesiod* (p. 240.13–15 Rabe), Arethas shares in a criticism to the Ascran poet: see Russo (2012) 49, 261.

[21] *De them.* 2.1–5, pp. 86–87 Pertusi.

[22] Compare Jo. Geom. *Carm.* 300.14 van Opstall (ῥεῖα δ' ἀρίζηλα καὶ εὔθετα πᾶσιν ἰδέσθαι) with *Op.* 14, and Christ. Mityl. *Carm.* 17.12 De Groote (τρεῖς θέρεος μῆνας καματώδεος εὕρετο ὥρη) with *Op.* 584 and 664.

[23] Psell. *or. paneg.* 11.62–76 Dennis.

[24] The typical pattern is: ὁ μὲν μῦθος... οἱ δὲ τῆς ἀληθείας λόγοι: see *or. hagiogr.* 4.14–17 Fisher (with the reference to Dike in Hes. *Op.* 256–260) and *or. funebr.* 2.3.44 Polemis (with the reference to the Giants in Hes. *Th.* 664–686).

[25] See e.g. Fryde (2000); Mergiali (1996); Pontani (2015) 403–434.

by the Muses: in one of his speeches, the great intellectual Nikephoros Choumnos (1250/5–1327) stumbles upon a reference to Hesiod in (Ps.-)Plato (*Epin.* 990a.5–6), and presents him as 'the one after Homer, the laurel-eating creature of the Muses, whose poetry did not proceed from human teaching, but was generated autodidactically by the intervention of the Muses'.[26]

Although this age 'non contemplò Omero fra i suoi autori principali',[27] we still come across a great number of manuscripts of pagan authors, including the epic poets; amongst them, the first fruits of philological activity on the text of the three Hesiodic poems, i.e. the famous manuscripts *Laur.* 32.16 (ca. 1280–1283), belonging to the circle of Maximos Planudes (1255–1304/5), and *Marc. gr.* 464 (a. 1316–1319), written by Demetrios Triklinios (early 14th c.).[28] Whether or not they were conceived for use in schools, one should not forget Planudes' scholia to the *Works and Days* and the commentary to the same poem by his pupil Manuel Moschopoulos (ca. 1265 – *post* 1316),[29] as well as the numerological commentary to the *Days* by John Protospatharios,[30] and the scholia of John Pediasimos Pothos (ca. 1250–1310/14) to the *Aspis*.[31] Still, the interest for Hesiodic lost works is now episodic, and such will it remain until well into the humanistic age. The last chapter (§ 4) of this essay will investigate an interesting case of ideological re-use and re-creation of a single fragment from the *Catalogue* (5 M.-W. = 2 H = 2 Most) in late 15th-century Italy.

---

[26] *AG* III 385.7–11 Boissonade: τὸν μετὰ τὸν Ὅμηρον, τὸ τῶν Μουσῶν δαφνοφάγον θρέμμα, καὶ οὗ γ' ἡ ποίησις οὐκ ἐξ ἀνθρώπου τινὸς διδάξαντος, ἀλλ' αὐταῖς ἦν ταῖς Μούσαις αὐτοδιδάκτως ἐξειργασμένη. See West (1966) 165; cf. Tz. *proll. in Hes. Op.* pp. 14.14–16.10 Gaisf. (Hesiod's δαφνηφαγία) and on the Muses' allegory *in Hes. Op.* 1, pp. 29.5–30.11, 32.14–34.2, 6–16 Gaisf., with Pontani (2015) 380–381.
[27] Pontani (2005) 266.
[28] *Laur.* 32.16, a famous collection of non-Homeric poetry born in Planudes' circle (Maximos' own hand is not to be discerned in the Hesiodic section) is the earliest known manuscript to contain the three poems together, and the earliest preserved complete witness of the *Theogony*: see Turyn (1972) 28–39; Speranzi (2014) 108–109 no. 25. Ms. *Marc. gr.* Z 464 (coll. 762) is a copy of Hesiod's poems with all the extant exegesis, compiled by Demetrios Triklinios, and equipped with his personal notes and additions: see esp. West (1978) 71; Turyn (1972) 123–127; Derenzini (1979); Mioni (1985) 248–251; Bianconi (2005) 96–100, 104, 248.
[29] Ed. Pertusi (1951); Grandolini (1991). See West (1978) 70; Wilson (1996²) 245–247; Pontani (2005) 267–269, and (2015) 413 and 417. Moschopoulos quotes the *Theogony* in his scholia to the *Works and Days*: see Hes. *Th.* 124, 927–928 in the *scholl.* 3 and 60, pp. 3–4 and 19 Grandolini.
[30] Ed. Gaisford (1823²) 448–459; see Krumbacher (1897) 558; West (1978) 70.
[31] Ed. Gaisford (1823²) 609–654; see Russo (1965²) 56; Bianconi (2005) 61–62; Pontani (2015) 406–407. Other anonymous commentaries or paraphrases to the three poems are attested from this turn of years: see Russo (1965²) 57 n. 45; West (1966) 71–72; West (1978) 71.

2 Hesiod's Fragments in Ioannes Tzetzes

2.1 Ioannes Tzetzes and Hesiod

Ioannes Tzetzes can well be regarded as the most Hesiodic among the 'professional Hellenists' of the Comnenian age.[32] He parades himself as the first commentator of the *Works and Days* after Proclus the Neoplatonist (whom he of course deems inferior), and as the best connoisseur of the genealogies of the heroes and gods as presented in the *Theogony*.[33] Like Homer (to whose *Iliad* Tzetzes produced a long preface and scholia to book 1), Hesiod becomes the object of a painstaking line-by-line analysis, as well as of an imitative and interpretative effort of a didactic kind: Tzetzes does not resort here to hexametrical re-creation, as in the isolated experiment of the *Carmina Iliaca*, nor to a pervasive exegesis in poetic fashion, as in the *Homeric Allegories*, but he attempts a fresh reading with exegetical thrust of the πᾶσα θεογονία ἐν βραχεῖ ('summary of the entire theogony').[34]

These works are very different in terms of the intended audience – pupils in the case of the *exegesis* devoted to the *Works and Days*, aristocratic circles for the versified *Theogony* – but beyond the well-known, idiosyncratic character of the author, we can discern a genuine interpretative effort that manages to combine a detailed reading of the text, categories of literary criticism, and an erudite

---

[32] See Kaldellis (2007) 301: Tzetzes and Eustathios 'were both what we call professional Hellenists, in that they made their living teaching the classics and commenting on ancient texts (thought their careers were quite different)'; cf. p. 240: 'We should, then, think more in terms of a spectrum ranging from creative sophists obsessed with Greek things (Prodromos and Tzetzes); bishop-scholars who combined Hellenic nobility with Christian ethics (Eustathios and Michael Choniates)'. On Tzetzes and Hesiod, see also Roilos (2014) 232 n. 8.
[33] See Tz. *proll. in Hes. Op.* pp. 10–12.11 Gaisf., with Wilson (1996²) 194; Budelmann (2002) 152; Pontani (2015) 380; and Tz. *Th.* 24–32 with Jeffreys (1974) 149.
[34] Tzetzes' *Theogony*, after a proem directed to the sponsor of the work (the sebastokratorissa Eirene, ll. 1–47), traces the genealogies of the gods down to the classical Olympian pantheon (ll. 48–377), and then crosses over to the genealogical catalogue of Greek and Trojan heroes (with their allies) and their deeds (ll. 378–723); in the epilogue, a text with an especially complicated editorial history (see Wendel 1940; Hunger 1953), Tzetzes shows off his knowledge of the various foreign languages spoken in Constantinople. The idea of writing a companion to the whole of Greek mythology (in the terms that were suitable for the skills of his audience) is the same presiding over the *Carmina Iliaca*, which retrace συνοπτικῶς τὴν πᾶσαν Ἰλιάδα (Σ *Carm. Il.* p. 101.2 Leone): see Braccini (2009–2010). On the exegesis to the *Erga* see Dahlén (1933); Ponzio (2003).

mythographical inquiry.³⁵ In the scholium to *Op.* 113–114, for example, Tzetzes proposes two readings of the passage οὐδέ τι δειλόν / γῆρας ἐπῆν (the golden race, immune from old age).³⁶ The discussion of the word-division of οὐδέτι into either οὐδέ τι (the prevailing reading in our mss.) or οὐδ' ἔτι (a reading attested in just a few codices) shows that the exegete pays attention to even the most detailed and minute textual variants.³⁷ But Tzetzes also tries his hand at broader literary interpretations, nourished by his own personal readings: When he comments on the famous Hesiodic apologue on the roads to virtue and vice (*Op.* 288–292), he points to a parallel with a passage in Quintus Smyrnaeus (*Posthom.* 5.49–56) in which Arete is personified as a woman sitting atop a palm-tree on a steep, almost inaccessible mountain.³⁸ In his own *Theogony*, when following Hesiod's text in tracing the offspring of Ouranos and Ge (ll. 48–108), he does not resist the temptation to add references to various mythographical variants: between the Erinyes and the Giants, born from Ouranos' blood (Hes. *Th.* 183–186), there come the Telchines, for whom Tzetzes offers two more alternative genealogies, one according to Bacchylides (fr. 52 Snell-Maehler, of which he is our only source) and one according to unknown τινές.³⁹ The opportunity to insert mythographical stories into a didactic context,

---

35 On Tzetzes' works on commission see Rhoby (2010); on the sebastokratorissa Eirene, patron of Tzetzes' *Theogony*, see now Jeffreys (2014). The commentaries on ancient poets are meant for pupils as well as for erudites: Kaldellis (2009) 29–31.
36 P. 115.3–7 Gaisf. 'οὐδὲ κατά τι δειλὸν ὑπῆρχεν αὐτοῖς τὸ γῆρας', ὡς νῦν ἡμῖν, ἢ οὕτω· 'οὐδὲ ἔτι, καὶ ἀκμήν, ἐπῆν γῆρας δειλόν, καὶ ἄθλιον ἢ δειλίας ἀνάμεστον'.
37 To the best of our knowledge, οὐδ' ἔτι is only attested in three mss. of the φ family (all 13th-14th c.: see West 1974, 176–181) that also carry Tzetzes' exegesis: hence it is more likely that this note (with no equivalent in what we possess of the ancient scholia) has influenced the main text than viceversa; in Hesiod's line, τι is 'hardly more than a metrical stopgap' (West 1978, 179 *ad loc.*). Tzetzes' painstaking attention to orthographical details brings to mind his special attention to the decipherment of 9th-century manuscripts, as witnessed in the case of Thucydides, where he took pains to add and correct accents and diacritical signs in order to make reading easier: see Luzzatto (1999) 21–30. Another comparable case in *in Hes. Op.* 438, p. 279.18–23 Gaisf.
38 Quintus numbers to Tzetzes' main sources for part III of the *Carmina Iliaca*: see Leone (1984). Homeric scholia and Eustathios refer to the poet by name, whereas Tzetzes dubs him Κόϊντος ὁ Σμυρναῖος (*proll. in Il.* p. 67.19 Papath.; *Hist.* 2.492): See Vian (1963) vii–viii, l.
39 Tz. *Th.* 82–85: καὶ σὺν αὐταῖς οἱ τέσσαρες ὀνομαστοὶ Τελχῖνες, / Ἀκταῖος Μεγαλήσιος Ὁρμενός τε καὶ Λύκος, / οὓς Βακχυλίδης μέν φησι Νεμέσεως Ταρτάρου, / ἄλλοι τινὲς δὲ λέγουσι τῆς Γῆς τε καὶ τοῦ Πόντου. Without any reference to their genealogy, the Telchines are presented by Tzetzes also in *Hist.* 7.119–28 and 12.829–34, where he adds two more names (cp. Zenob. 5.41; Suda τ 293 Adler) to the four listed here (all unattested elsewhere except for Lykos): See Harder (1886) 75 and H. Herter in *RE* VA.1 (1934), 199 and 211; Leone (2007) *ad locc.*

however unrelated, cannot be missed; in this case, we are faced with the conceptual leap from the Erinyes to other daemons, the Telchines (also in Tzetzes' *ep.* 94 and 102, pp. 136.10–11 and 148.7–8 Leone): for the latter, the erudite information is taken from one or more sources which – as in many other cases – remain unknown to us.

Tzetzes' approach to Hesiod (and to classical authors in general) goes well beyond self-celebration and a weary re-statement of ancient material.[40] For Tzetzes, Hesiod is a reference author; while he cannot equal Homer – even the bare thought that he may have defeated Homer in a contest is ridiculous –[41] he is still an *auctoritas* as a source of *dicta* and of mythographical doctrine. In the scholia to Lycophron, the *Theogony* provides Tzetzes with much material that helps explain the Alexandrian poet's cryptic allusions: e.g. the reason why Styx is the warrant of divine oaths (Lyc. 707), namely the help she gave to Zeus during his battle against the Titans (Hes. *Th.* 397–400);[42] or the etymology of Herakles' epithet βοαγίδης (Lyc. 652), which depends on the fact that the hero took Geryon's cattle away from the island of Erytheia (see Oppian, *Cyn.* 2.110–111 and Hesiod, *Th.* 289–294).[43] The ancient scholia to these passages contain no references to mythographical sources:[44] While it is certainly possible that Tzetzes may have embarked on a study of lost exegetical materials, it is more likely that, being such an attentive student of the Hesiodic text, so proud of his culture and his readings, Tzetzes should himself be credited with their adoption to exegetical ends.[45]

---

[40] The studies of Maria Jagoda Luzzatto (1998, 1999, 2000) have shed light on Tzetzes' working method. His importance in the history of Classical scholarship, after recent reassessments (see Grünbart [2005] 143; Pontani [2015] 378–385), still needs a comprehensive, in-depth reappraisal (see Cesaretti 2010).

[41] See *proll. in Hes. Op.* pp. 16.15–18.10 Gaisf.; *scholl.* 238, 253, 262, 270, 276, 282–285, 654–659, pp. 172.5–173.8, 181.33–182.3, 185.3–17, 188.26–28, 191.4–13, 195.6–11, 368.12–25 Gaisf.; *Hist.* 12.157–60, 185–204 (with the scholia *ad locc.*), 13.641–44; and Koning (2010) 247. In these passages of the exegesis to the *Works and Days*, Hesiod's inferiority is demonstrated on the grounds of his alleged rhetorical or metrical inadequacy.

[42] Tz. *in Lyc.* 707, p. 232.2–6 Scheer: ὁ δὲ Ἡσίοδος ἐν τῆι Θεογονίαι διὰ τοῦτό φησι τὸν Δία ὅρκον τῶν θεῶν ποιῆσαι τὴν Στύγα, ὅτι πρώτη κτλ.

[43] Tz. *in Lyc.* 651, p. 217.22–26 Scheer: βοαγίδα ὅτι τὰς βοῦς τοῦ Γηρυόνου ἤγεν ἐξ Ἐρυθείας τῆς περὶ τὸν Ὠκεανὸν νήσου ὥς φησι καὶ Ὀππιανὸς ἐν τοῖς Κυνηγετικοῖς 'αὐτῶι ἐπ' Ὠκεανῶι δηρίσατο Γηρυονῆι' καὶ Ἡσίοδος, οἶμαι, ἐν Θεογονίαι ''Ὄρθον – Εὐρυτίωνα'. The partial quotations refer to Opp. *Cyn.* 211 and Hes. *Th.* 293.

[44] See *scholl. vett.* Lyc. 652d, 706a-7b, pp. 133, 141–142 Leone.

[45] See οἶμαι in the second passage (n. 43). Tzetzes often boasts his sensational memory: As for the books he needs to consult in order to find information (*Hist.* 12.2–6), he is able to repeat by heart their contents as if he could hold them once again in his hands (1.278–279); he is liable to

On the other hand, Tzetzes' *Letters* offer a different kind of rhetorical use of quotations from the *Works and Days*; in *ep.* 79, he deftly modifies a well-known hexameter (*Op.* 101), and in the related *historia* he reveals the learned allusion: ὁ μὲν Ἡσίοδός φησι ἐν Ἔργοις καὶ Ἡμέραις, / 'πλείη μὲν γὰρ γαῖα κακῶν, πλείη δὲ θάλασσα'. / τοῦτο δὲ κατὰ ῥήτορας καλεῖται παρῳδία, / τὸ 'πλείη μὲν γὰρ γαῖα σοφῶν, πλείη δὲ θάλασσα'. / παραγραμματισμόν φασι δ' οἱ ποιηταὶ τὸ σχῆμα, / τὸ χρῆσθαι τοῖς τοιούτοις δε δεινότητος μεθόδωι.[46] Hesiod's line becomes – as is so often the case with Homer's hexameters – a rhetorical paradigm: This confirms that the author of the *Works and Days*, however inferior to Homer, still occupied a place of honour in Tzetzes' cultural horizon, and in the culture of his age.[47]

2.2 Tzetzes and the Lost Hesiod: *Heroogonia*, *Astronomia*, and Other Fragments

In Tzetzes, predictably, the confrontation between Homer and Hesiod mostly ends in favour of the former; there are, however, some passages in which the Askran poet is defended from the attacks of ancient critics.[48] For instance,

---

error, but his mind, working as a library (*All. Il.* 15.87–88), allows him to display a huge amount of data (*Hist.* 8.173–180). More relevant passages in Wendel (1948) 2008.

46 'Hesiod says in the *Works and Days* that "the earth is full of evils, and the sea is full". To say "the earth is full of wise men, the sea is full" is what rhetors call parody. Poets term this figure *paragrammatismos*, i.e. to use similar words for rhetorical effectiveness' Tz. *Hist.* 11.866–871. See Tz. *ep.* 79 (1150/54), p. 118.10 Leone: πλείη μὲν γὰρ γαῖα σοφῶν, πλείη δὲ θάλασσα. The modified quotation has an ironical sense: the world is full of wise men, so the *chartoularios* attending Tzetzes' classes *à contrecoeur* will find a teacher who suits him better. More Hesiodic quotations in the *Letters*, then explained in the *Histories* (remarkably, all from the *Works and Days*): *ep.* 8, p. 17.8–9 Leone with *Hist.* 6.739–42 (Hes. *Op.* 319); *ep.* 16, p. 30.16 Leone with *Hist.* 7.228–234 (*Op.* 40); *ep.* 31, p. 46.15–16 Leone with *Hist.* 8.41–3 (*Op.* 486); *ep.* 57, pp. 83.4–5, 84.6–9 Leone with *Hist.* 9.331–47 and 355–357 (*Op.* 86–88 e 270–272); *ep.* 60, p. 89.18–21 Leone with *Hist.* 9.719–726 (*Op.* 296–297); *ep.* 67, p. 96.17–18 Leone with *Hist.* 10.209–15 (*Op.* 373). As Rzach's apparatus (however incomplete) amply shows, many passages in Tzetzes' oeuvre quote or allude to Hesiodic passages, as in the case of Hes. *Th.* 123 (ἐκ Χάεος δ' Ἐρεβός τε), reworked by Tzetzes in *Carm. Il.* 1.67 (ἐκ Χάεος Ἐρέβους τε).

47 Ll. 101–103 of the *Works and Days* feature in Stobaeus' *Anthologium* (4.34.32). On the rhetorical use of Homeric quotations, see Nünlist (2012); Cullhed (2014) 39–49 (with the reference to Tzetzes' Homeric quotation in *ep.* 14, p. 25.5–6 Leone and *Hist.* 7.103–9, see esp. 108–109: ἐγὼ παρεγραμμάτισα ῥητορικῶι δὲ τρόπωι / πρὸς τὸ συμφέρον νῦν ἐμοί κτλ.).

48 In several cases the criticism to which Tzetzes responds is levelled by the ancient scholia: Tz. *in Hes. Op.* 58, p. 32.4–6 Gaisf. (Procl. *in Hes. Op.* 58 Pertusi = fr. *52 Marzillo); Tz. *in Hes. Op.* 152,

against a certain Poseidonius of Apollonia, who accused Hesiod of altering Homeric words such as Ὀιλεύς and νήδυμος into Ἰλεύς and ἤδυμος, Tzetzes attempts to justify the occurrences of both these terms, corresponding to fragments 235 M.-W. (= 112 H = 176 Most) and 330 M.-W. (= 280 Most).[49] In a scholium on his introduction to the *Iliad* (pp. 418.12–420.4 Papath.), Tzetzes scolds Poseidonius for plainly ignoring Hesiod's passage, where the name Ὀιλεύς simply undergoes an Ionic aphaeresis, to be explained in the light of a dialectal choice or of the name's etymology, as documented by the Hesiodic lines connecting it to the benevolence of Oileus' mother, the nymph whom Apollo ingravidated at the time when Poseidon built the walls of Troy (οὕνεκα νύμφην / εὐρόμενος ἵλεων μίχθη ἐρατῆι φιλότητι).[50] As for ἤδυμος, Tzetzes argues that it occurs in Orpheus, whom Homer imitates, and even in Homer himself.[51]

Beyond the specific content of these observations, which affect delicate (and hotly debated) philological problems in Homer's text, it is interesting to see that Tzetzes reacts to Poseidonius' criticism by gathering his knowledge of ancient epic poetry, and thus recovers an invaluable quotation of Hesiodic lines transmitted in the *Etymologica*.[52] The last two lines of fr. 235, dealing with the fortifi-

---

p. 134.6–10 Gaisf. (Σ Hes. *Op.* 2a); Tz. *in Hes. Op.* 383, p. 249.6–9 Gaisf. (Σ Hes. *Op.* 383f Pertusi). On the Homer/Hesiod comparison, see above n. 41.

49 *Proll. in Il.* p. 4.14–17 Papath. Tzetzes is the only witness of fr. 330. As suggested by the editors, this Poseidonius might be identified with the pupil of Aristarchus mentioned by some scholia to the *Iliad* (see *RE* XXII.1 [1953], 826 [C. Wendel]; Schwartz [1960] 51–52; *LGGA* s.v. 'Posidonius [1]'). Another, analogous reference to one Poseidonius (who argued for Homer's priority and for Hesiod's tampering with Homeric lines) is to be found in Tzetzes' *Prolegomena* (proll. in Il. pp. 27.13–28.7 Papath.): This is today fr. 459 Theiler of the philosopher Poseidonius of Apamea (= Hes. T 5 Most), but the comparison with the passage just discussed may rather suggest its identification with Aristarchus' pupil (*contra* F. Jacoby in *FGrHist* 279, IIIa Kommentar, pp. 362–363), or it might at least rule out its being identified with the philosopher from Apamea.

50 The issue of Hesiod's Ἰλεύς was ubiquitous in ancient philological discussions on Homeric Ὀιλεύς and Ὀιλιάδης: Aristarchus rejected the variant without initial omikron as belonging to the *neoteroi* (see Σ [A] A 264 and B 527–531, I 83 and II 299 Erbse), but it was supported by Zenodotus (see Σ [T] Ξ 336d, IV 83 Erbse, with Stesich. 291 Finglass); see also Pind. *Ol.* 9.112 with Σ *ad loc.* I 306.15–17 Dr. and other passages collected by M-W *ad loc.* (see also Eustathios below § 3).

51 The reference is here to frr. 741 and 855 Bernabé. Homer's textual transmission attests almost exclusively νήδυμος (*Il.* 2.2; 10.91, 187; 14.242, 253, 354; 16.454; 23.63; *Od.* 4.793; 12.311, 366; 13.79 see also *Il.* 12.311), and Tzetzes himself employs the clausula νήδυμον ὕπνον in *Carm. Il.* 3.229. The reading ἤδυμος (which in some cases could be legitimate by linking the ephelkystic *ny* with the foregoing word) was rejected by Aristarchus: See Σ (AbT) B 2b-c² (I 175.19–176.36 Erbse); Leaf *ad Il.* 2.2 (who adopts ἤδυμος in the text); Leumann (1950) 44–45.

52 *Etym. Gud.* s.v. Ἰλεύς (Reitzenstein (1897) 161 ll. 4–9 (ll. 1–5, from a commentary on Simonides: fr. 650 Page); *Etym.Gen.* A (vv. 1–4) and B (vv. 1–3), see M-W *ad loc.*; *Etym. Magn.* (s.v.

cations of Troy, are also quoted by Tzetzes in a scholium to Lycophron's *Alexandra*, where they serve as poetic evidence of the gods' support to Laomedon: they clearly belonged to a group of quotations that Tzetzes kept at hand so as to use them in different contexts, a common practice that emerges throughout his writings.[53]

Tzetzes ascribes the hexameters on the birth of Ileos to Hesiod ἐν τῆι ἡρωικῆι γενεαλογίαι. This peculiar indication reappears in other Tzetzian quotations of Hesiodic fragments of genealogical content, mostly attributed today to the *Catalogue of Women*: frr. 9 and 205 M.-W. (= 4 and 95 H = 9 and 145 Most). As for the former – two lines on Hellen's sons Xouthos and Aiolos – it is taken over from an ancient scholium to Lycophron,[54] but Tzetzes contributes two things: The indication of the work (the source speaks generically of 'Hesiod') and the comparison with three lines of similar content drawn from a scholium to Pindar (fr. 10a.25–27 M.-W. = 5.25–27 H = 10.25–27 Most).[55] Two further quotations of the same fr. 9 M.-W. in the *Exegesis* to the *Iliad* present a curious textual interference with these lines on the Aiolids: The second hemistich of l. 1 rings θεμιστοπόλου βασιλῆος in one case and θεμιστοπόλοι βασιλῆες in the other,[56] rather than φιλοπτολέμου βασιλῆος. Tzetzes' memory is clearly misled by the very analogy he is pointing out in his commentary to Lycophron.[57]

Another Hesiodic passage attributed by Tzetzes to the '*Heroic genealogy*' comes from the scholia to Pindar, and it is re-used both in his exegesis of Lyco-

---

Ἴλεως) p. 470.137–41 Gaisf. (ll. 1–3). Etymology is also the reason why the fragment is quoted by Eustathios (*in Il.* 650.46, see below § 3.2).

53 Tz. *in Lyc.* 393, p. 147.16–21 Scheer (with no mention of Hesiod), to be compared with Σ vet. 393e, p. 76 Leone. The fragment is thus quoted once for a linguistic issue (see also *Carm. Il.* 3.644 Ἰλέος ἄλκιμος Αἴας with Leone's apparatus) and once for a mythographical issue: It is more economical to think that the hexameters were deployed toward different goals in different contexts, rather than that he drew on different sources.

54 Tz. *in Lyc.* 286 (p. 121.30–35 Scheer) from Σ vet. *ad loc.* (p. 58.1–3 Leone). The lines read Ἕλληνος δ' ἐγένοντο φιλοπτολέμου βασιλῆος / Δῶρός τε Ξοῦθός τε καὶ Αἴολος ἱππιοχάρμης.

55 Σ Pind. *Pyth.* 4.253c, II 133.7–10 Dr. The three lines of fr. 10a, known today through papyrological finds (Αἰολίδαι δ' ἐγένοντο θεμιστοπόλοι βασιλῆες / Κρηθεύς ἠδ' Ἀθάμας καὶ Σίσυφος αἰολομήτης / Σαλμωνεύς τ' ἄδικος καὶ ὑπέρθυμος Περιήρης), are copied by Tzetzes right after those of fr. 9 with no introduction or mediation.

56 Respectively, Tz. *in Il.* 1.2, pp. 94.13–95.5 Papath. and Tz. Σ *proll. in Il.* p. 430.10–13 Papath., with attribution to the 'Heroic genealogy'.

57 This contamination may in theory go back to Plutarch, who quotes the first line of fr. 9 (with no attribution to Hesiod: Hunter (2014) 283–284) with θεμιστοπόλοι βασιλῆες (*Qu. Conv.* 9.15.2 [747 f]), but it may well be the fruit of Tzetzes' own confusion (θεμιστοπολ- βασιλ- is much more frequent, see *Hom. Hymn. to Demeter* 103, 215, 473; PSI VI 722.1; *Il.* 1.238–239 with D.H. *Ant.* 5.74; φιλοπτολέμωι βασιλῆι only in Q.S. 9.526).

phron and in that of *Iliad* book 1.⁵⁸ The lines concern the birth of Aiakos and the myth of the autochthony of the Myrmidons/Aiginetes, the first sailors, born through a metamorphosis from the ants by virtue of Aiakos' prayer to Zeus. Tzetzes inserts the quotation in two long, partly overlapping mythographic digressions, where the very sequence (illustration of myth / quotation of Hesiodic fragment / allegorical interpretation by Theogenes, *FGrHist* 300 F 1) points to a close adherence to Pindar's scholium.⁵⁹

The attribution of all these Hesiodic lines to an ἡρωικὴ γενεαλογία should be paralleled with the title Ἡρωογονία mentioned by Tzetzes in his introduction to the *Works and Days* in a partial list of Hesiod's works: οὕτω δὲ [i. e. Ἔργα καὶ Ἡμέραι τὸ βιβλίον] ἐπιγέγραπται πρὸς ἀντιδιαστολὴν τῶν ἑτέρων αὐτοῦ πεντεκαίδεκα βίβλων Ἀσπίδος, Θεογονίας, Ἡρωογονίας, Γυναικῶν καταλόγου, καὶ λοιπῶν ἁπασῶν.⁶⁰ The complex transmission of Tzetzes' *prolegomena* to the *Works and Days*, an abridged form of which was pasted with the *prolegomena vetera* under the heading Πρόκλου Διαδόχου in some humanistic manuscripts, has long obliterated Tzetzes' paternity of this label.⁶¹ A poem by Hesiod labelled *Heroogonia* is otherwise unknown, whereas there are various ancient references to the genealogies of heroes at the end of the *Theogony* and in the *Catalogue of Women*: In a scholium on the beginning of the *Works and Days* we read that Hesiod μετὰ τὴν ἡρωικὴν γενεαλογίαν καὶ τοὺς Καταλόγους ἐπεζήτησε καινουργῆ-

---

58 Tz. *in Lyc.* 176, pp. 85.20–86.11 Scheer; Tz. *in Il.* 1.180, pp. 233.15–235.13 Papath.: From Σ Pind. *Nem.* 3.21, III 45 Dr. = Hes. fr. 205.1–6 (a seventh line is quoted by Σ Pind. *Ol.* 8.26e, I 242.20–23 Drachmann).
59 In Tzetzes' exegesis of Homer the allegorical interpretation of the myth's 'true' meaning is followed by a different account of the origin of the Myrmidons (τὸ δ' ἀληθέστερον πάντων οὕτως ἔχον ἐστί κτλ.: Myrmidon's birth from Zeus and Eurymedusa, see e.g. Clem. Al. *Protr.* 2.39 and Σ *ad loc.* p. 309.4–6 Stählin). The myth of Aiakos and the ants, together with its allegoresis, is taken up once again by Tzetzes in *Hist.* 7.303–17 (περὶ Αἰακοῦ, οὗ χάριν ὁ Ζεὺς τοὺς μύρμηκας ἀνθρώπους ἐποίησεν).
60 'And it is entitled in this way to set it apart from his fifteen other books, *Aspis, Theogony, Heroogony, Catalogue of Women*, and all the others' (transl. Most), pp. 19.21–20.2 Gaisf. = Hes. *Cat. test.* p. 1 M.-W. = T 43 Most. On the number of works attributed by Tzetzes to Hesiod see Pertusi (1951) 269 n. 2; Cingano (2009) 93–94.
61 The humanistic manuscript transmission (most notably mss. *Par. gr.* 2736 and 2833; but see also *Par. gr.* 2777) determined the *facies* of these materials in Gaisford's edition, and thus the prevailing attribution of the catalogue of Hesiod's works to Proclus rather than Tzetzes (only exception: Casanova [1979a] 218–219). On the complex issue see Cardin (2009).

σαι πάλιν ἑτέραν ὑπόθεσιν;⁶² in an epigram of the *Greek Anthology*, we read that he wrote about μακάρων γένος, ἔργα, and γένος ἀρχαίων ἡμιθέων.⁶³

These witnesses, together with the rather foggy memory of the exact content of the *Catalogue of Women*, suggest that Tzetzes might have himself coined this new title, applying it to some lines on heroic genealogies that he found in his sources.⁶⁴ It is not by chance that, among the Hesiodic material transmitted by Tzetzes, the only genealogical fragment that does not carry a specific attribution is also the only one for which he had no exact wording (fr. 194 M.-W. = 137b–c Most), and thus could not suggest a more exact provenance.⁶⁵

Another attribution unmatched in ancient texts is that of ll. 7 and 10 of fr. 211 M.-W. (= 100 H = 152 Most), now known through papyrological evidence. In the excursus on poetical genres contained in the *prolegomena* to Lycophron's *Alexandra*, Tzetzes names among the writers of epithalamia a certain Agamestor

---

62 'After the heroic genealogy and the *Catalogues*, he wanted to begin anew with a different subject matter' (transl. Most), *prol.* B in Hes. *Op.* p. 3.9–10 Pertusi = Hes. *Cat. test.* p. 1 M.-W. = T 48 Most. Cf. Schwartz (1960) 50–51.

63 *AP* 9.64.7–8 (= Asclep. dub. 45 Gow-Page, Guichard) = Hes. T 44 Most. See also POxy 3537r (MP³ 1849.1 and 1857.32; LDAB 5556; III–IV c.) = Hes. T 95 Most, ll. 5–6: αὐτή μοι γένος εἰπ[ὲ θεῶν πτολ]έμους τε γιγάντων / πάντων θ' ἡρώ[ων γενεήν, φῦλ]όν τε γυναικῶν.

64 The only exact indication on the content of the *Catalogue of Women* (as opposed to *Theogony* and *Works and Days*) is in Max. Tyr. 26.4 = T 46 Most (ὁ Ἡσίοδος... τὰ γένη τῶν ἡρώων, ἀπὸ γυναικῶν ἀρχόμενος καταλέγει). Lucian (*Hes.* 1 = T 45 Most) speaks of γυναικῶν ἀρεταί, Pausanias (9.31.4–5 = T 42 Most) of ἐς γυναῖκας ἀιδόμενα; the list in *Suda* η 583 Adler reports the title Γυναικῶν ἡρωϊνῶν κατάλογος ἐν βιβλίοις ε'. See Hes. TT 56–65 Most and Eustathios, below § 3. None of Tzetzes' sources for *Cat.* frr. 9, 10a, 205 and 235 M.-W. quotes the title of the original Hesiodic work. Marckscheffel (1840) 104–5 already observed that both 'Heroogonia' and 'Heroic genealogy' were false titles to indicate the *Catalogue*, whereas Schwartz (1960) 24–25, and Cohen (1983) 131–133 (= [1986] 140–141) attached it to the end of the *Theogony* (ll. 963–1020), and Casanova (1979a) 218–219 to the end of the *Theogony* and to the *Catalogue*. This title (considered as ancient by Hirschberger 2004, 29–30), rather than a *trouvaille* in some lost ancient source, should be regarded as Tzetzes' own coinage on the *proll. vett.* B.

65 This is fr. 137a Most, an alternative genealogy for Agamemnon, found in Σ (AD) A 7, p. 21 van Thiel. Tzetzes deals with this issue (flanking Hesiod's witness with Aeschyl. *Ag.* 1601–1602) three times: Tz. *in Il.* 1.7 and 1.122, pp. 103.10–104.8 e 210.8–12 Papath.; Σ *All. Il.*, proem. 510, III 378.9–11 Cramer = 605.6–8 Matranga. See Papathomopoulos (1980) 11–26, and below § 3 on Eustathios' witness. Three more fragments are ascribed by Tzetzes generically to 'Hesiod': fr. 67b M.-W. (= 36 H = 68 Most), on Autolykos' ability as a thief (Tz. *in Lyc.* 344, p. 134.1–5 Scheer, from *Etym. Magn.* α 317, I 87.31–88.6 L.-L., where it is quoted for the occurrence of the adj. ἀείδηλος); fr. 270 M.-W. (= 206 Most), quoted for its metrical peculiarity by Tz. Σ *De metr.* 25, III 318 Cramer (from Σ Hephaest. p. 109.4 Consbruch; see also Σ [T] Ψ 644b); fr. 304 M.-W. (= 254 Most), a famous riddle on the lifetime of nymphs, partly quoted by Tz. *in Il.* 1.225, p. 263.12–15 Papath. and Σ *proll. in Il.* p. 415.10–14 Papath. from Plut. *De def. or.* 11 (415c-d).

of Pharsalos, who is then mentioned as the author of an epithalamium for Thetis,⁶⁶ and Ἡσίοδος αὐτὸς γράψας ἐπιθαλάμιον εἰς Πηλέα καὶ Θέτιν 'τρὶς μάκαρ, Αἰακίδη, καὶ τετράκις ὄλβιε Πηλεῦ, / ὃς τοῖσδ' ἐν μεγάροις ἱερὸν λέχος εἰσαναβαίνεις'.⁶⁷ Tzetzes' source is unknown, and scholars have supposed that he might have got the reference to both Agamestor's and Hesiod's epithalamia from the notoriously unreliable *New History* of Ptolemy the Quail.⁶⁸ But the papyrus seems to lend support to the authenticity of these lines, and so do various data pointing to the existence of a long section on the myth of the Aiakids in the *Catalogue of Women*.⁶⁹ Tzetzes' attribution of an 'epithalamium' is generally interpreted as referring to an ancient title for this particular section of the *Catalogue*,⁷⁰ but it might as well have been suggested to Tzetzes – who was interested in the history of this poetic genre – by the very content of the lines (e. g. the *makarismos* of the bridegroom).⁷¹ What is certain is that John's words do not explicitly link these hexameters either with the *Catalogue of Women* or with the *Heroogonia*.

One more fragment is ascribed by Tzetzes to a lost poem by Hesiod, once again in the wake of an unknown source. Three and a half lines carrying the catalogue of the Iades are preserved by a scholium to Aratus' *Phaenomena* (fr. 291 M.-W. = 227a Most),⁷² and they are quoted by Tzetzes in a long mythographical digression on the Pleiades in his exegesis to the *Works and Days* (Σ 383–384, pp. 246.23–247.2 Gaisf.) as well as, with some metrical adjustments, in a *historia* dealing with Meton and ancient astronomy (*Hist.* 12.161–65). In both passages,

---

66 Tz. *in Lyc.* 178, II 89.8–15 Scheer and *in Il.* 1.58, p. 162.1–8 Papath. = Agamest.Phar. *SH* 14, four lines reported as found ἐν τῶι τῆς Θέτιδος ἐπιθαλαμίωι / ἐν τῶι ἐπιθαλαμίωι τῶν Θέτιδος γάμων. The content of the lines matches what Phot. *Bibl.* 152b.29–32 gathers from Ptolemy the Quail.
67 'Hesiod who also wrote an epithalamium for Peleus and Thetis, "three times blessed, o Aiakides, and four times, o Peleus, you who in these halls go up into the holy marriage-bed" ': Tz. *proll. in Lyc.* p. 4.9–15 Scheer.
68 See Schwartz (1960) 52. The reliability of this Agamestor of Pharsalos, recently questioned by Cameron (2004) 152–153, is argued by the editors of the *Supplementum Hellenisticum*.
69 See the fragments of Aigina's *ehoie* (205–214 M.-W. = 145–153, 292 Most ~ 95, 97, 99–100, *26 H) discussed in Cardin (2010).
70 See M.-W. *ad loc.* and Hirschberger (2004) 30.
71 See Cardin (2009) 245–247; Cingano (2009) 94 n. 7.
72 Σ Arat. 172, p. 166.6–10 Martin. See Dahlén (1933) 58–63; Martin (1974) xxviii. Tzetzes' passage on the Pleiades myth was so complete and well-thought as to end up in some manuscripts of Aratus (see Martin 1956, 74–80 and 276–277; Martin 1974, xxiv and *exc. de Pleiadibus* pp. 547–8.16 Martin) and of Aeschylus (see Σ Aeschyl. *Prom.* 425b-d, p. 136 Herington; Allegrini 1971–1972, 232–233).

Hesiod's words are cited as belonging to a βίβλος ἀστρική.⁷³ Once again, our limited knowledge, as opposed to the multiplicity of the sources available to Tzetzes, does not allow us to take for granted that the attribution is Tzetzes' own invention; he certainly studied and quoted Aratus and the transmitted scholia to the *Phaenomena*;⁷⁴ he possibly also knew of the existence of an Hesiodic poem by the title Ἀστρονομία, quoted by Athenaeus in relation to some lines about the Pleiades;⁷⁵ and he could recognise in a passage of Plutarch a reference to the existence of a Hesiodic work on astronomy.⁷⁶

Albeit with great caution, we can outline Tzetzes' specific *modus operandi* in quoting the minor works of the Hesiodic *corpus*. First and foremost, he privileges the quotations of entire lines, which he memorised and reused in different contexts, with a bias for those of mythographical content. Even in the absence of clear clues in his direct source, he tends to indicate regularly the work to which the lines belonged, thus displaying on the one hand his deep knowledge of the ancient *testimonia* to Hesiod and his literary output, on the other hand his desire to show off his erudition by referring to poetical *auctoritates* in as clearly identifiable a way as possible.⁷⁷

The same holds true for other groups of hexameters from the Hesiodic *corpus* transmitted in Tzetzes' writings, albeit not written by Hesiod in Tzetzes' view. Two fragments of the *Melampodia* concerning Teiresias – the famous answer about the proportions of sexual pleasure in men and women (fr. 275 M.-W. = 211a – b Most) and a lament to Zeus for his long life, stretching over 7 generations (fr. 276 M.-W. = 212 Most) – are attributed by Tzetzes, following the scholia to Lycophron, to ὁ τῆς Μελαμποδίας ποιητής.⁷⁸ Finally, the eyes of Argo, the

---

73 *Hist.* 12.161–162: οὐ γράφει [*scil.* Ἡσίοδος] βίβλον ἀστρικήν; ἧς τὴν ἀρχὴν οὐκ οἶδα· / ἐν μέσωι τοῦ βιβλίου δὲ τὰ ἔπη κεῖνται ταῦτα. In *Hist.* 12.166 Tzetzes mentions the astrological content of the *Works and Days*: καὶ ἐν τῆι βίβλωι Ἡμερῶν ἀστρολογεῖ δὲ πόσα.
74 See p. 246.11–14 Gaisf., with (somewhat jumbled) quotations of ll. 257/261, 258, 262–263 of the *Phaenomena*.
75 Athen. 11.80 (491c-d) = Hes. *Cat.* frr. 288–290 M.-W. (= 223–225 Most) = T 75 Most, where the attribution to Hesiod is uncertain: ὁ τὴν εἰς Ἡσίοδον ἀναφερομένην ποιήσας Ἀστρονομίαν.
76 The list of authors of verse or prose astronomies in Plut. *De Pyth. orac.* 18 [402f] = Hes. *Astr. test.* p. 148 M.-W. = T 76 Most. Few other traces of this poem are extant: see Cingano (2009) 129–130.
77 The only non-mythographical fragments are frr. 235, 270 and 330. The only poetic quotation devoid of attribution is that of fr. 235.4–5 (see above n. 53), although one wonders if this depends on the poor editorial state of Tzetzes' commentary to the *Alexandra*. See also below (with n. 81) on frr. 61 and 170.
78 For the former fragment see Σ vet. Lyc. 683, p. 183.2–11 Leone and Tz. *in Lyc.* 683, p. 226b.19–22 Scheer. Both lines are evoked, without any attribution, in Apollod. 3.6.7 and in

guardian of Io, were four in number according to the author of the *Aigimios* (fr. 294 M.-W. = 254 Most).[79] Here too, Tzetzes patiently and subtly reconstructs from his sources the mythographical context and the attribution of the original work.[80]

When the sources do not mention the work or the author of the lines, and the subject does not help, the poetic words lend themselves to all sorts of attributions. This is the case of fr. 61 M.-W. (= *24 H = 240 Most) νήπιος, ὃς τὰ ἑτοῖμα λιπὼν ἀνέτοιμα διώκει ('fool, who rejects the available and pursues the unavailable', transl. Most): Tzetzes, when quoting this gnomic line in a learned letter (*ep.* 60, p. 89.25 Leone), omits the name of the source, but then, in his *Histories*, he feels obliged to compensate for this inexactitude and for the temporary blackout of his prodigious memory (*Hist.* 9.744–50):

> τίνος τυγχάνει τὸ ῥητὸν ἐκ λήθης παρεσύρην,
> εἴτ' οὖν ἐξ Ὀδυσσείας γε καθέστηκεν Ὁμήρου,
> εἴτ' οὖν ἑτέρου ποιητοῦ. βίβλους γὰρ ὡσεὶ δύο,
> εἴτε καὶ τρεῖς ἢ τέσσαρας στέρνοις ἐμοῖς συγκρύπτω,
> καὶ 'ἀργαλέον μοί ἐστιν θεὸν ὡς πάντα λέγειν'.
> εἰκός δε καὶ λανθάνεσθαι τίνων εἰσὶ τὰ ἔπη·
> Ἑρμῆς γὰρ ὁ χρυσόρραπις οὐ μάχεται τῆι λήθηι.[81]

'Out of forgetfulness I passed over the author of the saying, whether it is from Homer's *Odyssey*, or by another poet. I keep hidden inside me, as it were, two books, or even

---

various scholia to the *Odyssey* (ad 10.494, pp. 475 and 782 Dindorf and 218–219 Ernst): Tzetzes reports the first line in the correct form attested in the latter witnesses (more particularly the Homeric scholia, as is customary for him), not in the wrong one carried by the scholium to Lycophron. For fr. 276, Tzetzes is our only witness, again in his exegesis to Lycophron (*in Lyc.* 682, p. 255.14–26 Scheer) and to Homer (*proll. in Il.* pp. 33.12–34.16 Papath.): It is impossible to gauge whether the attribution derives from Tzetzes' lost source, or if it is simply the product of Tzetzes' extrapolation from the nearby Σ vet. 683.

79 See Σ Eur. *Ph.* 1116, pp. 365.21–366.8 Schwartz and Tz. *in Il.* 1.109 and Σ *proll. in Il.*, pp. 199.20–200.7 and 457.11–15 Papath.

80 In one of the two quotations of the *Aigimios*, Tzetzes even mentions the poet as an otherwise unknown Kleinias; but this indication may be the result of a simple blunder, or a forgery (see Papathomopoulos [1980] 27–28; Cingano [2009] 123–124). On Tzetzes' reliability as a witness of ancient fragments (Archilochus) see most lately Cannatà Fera (2012) (esp. pp. 705–706 with earlier bibliography).

81 The gnome is quoted by many authors (Σ Pind. *Pyth.* 3.38c, II 68.10–12 Dr.; Plut. *De garrul.* 7.505d, with no indication of author; Σ Theoc. 11.75, p. 248.14–17 Wendel, with Hesiod's name). Another fragment of the Hesiodic *corpus* (fr. *170 M.-W. = 74 H = 119 Most) is quoted anonymously by Tzetzes (*in Lyc.* 219, p. 102.7–26 Scheer, esp. 24–25), who clearly derives if from Σ Pind. *Nem.* 2.17c, III 34.5–36.10 Scheer (the same source we also have), where equally no attribution is mentioned. On Tzetzes' memory see above n. 45.

three or four, and "it is hard for me to tell everything like a god". It is easy that one should forget whose are the lines, for golden-wanded Hermes cannot compete with forgetfulness'.

3 Hesiod's Fragments in Eustathios*

3.1 Eustathios and Hesiod

Until 1840, the only existing collection of Hesiod's fragments was ordered by source, and it opened with a series of Hesiodic lines drawn 'ex Eustathio', i.e. those quoted by Eustathios of Thessalonike in his monumental commentaries to the *Iliad* and the *Odyssey*.[82] This prominent position, however, did not help: To the best of our knowledge, no proper inquiry into the topic *de Eustathii studiis Hesiodeis* has ever been carried out,[83] which might partly be explained by the fact that, though of course interested in archaic epic poetry, the learned archbishop nowhere displays a special favour for the Askran poet.[84] In his *Parekbolai* we do come across dozens of quotations from the *Works and Days* and (to a lesser extent) from the *Theogony* and the *Aspis*, and we also find references to the literary tradition about the *certamen Homeri et Hesiodi*,[85] as well as snapshots from both the ancient and the Byzantine exegesis to the poet.[86] However, there are relatively few traces of Eustathios' interest in Hesiod's peculiar literary

---

* My thanks to Baukje van den Berg for her comments on an earlier draft of this chapter.
82 We are referring to the collection of Hesiod's ἀποσπασμάτια first put together by Daniel Heinsius in the 1603 edition (*Hesiodi Ascraei quae extant*, ex off. Plantiniana Raphelengii), and later reproduced (e.g. in Graevius' 1667 Amsterdam Elzevier edition), augmented (most notably by Thomas Robinson, *Hesiodi Ascraei quae supersunt*, Oxford 1737, and by J.Fr. Boissonade, *Hesiodi Opera*, Paris 1824), and finally superseded by Marckscheffel, who in 1840 (Hesiodi, Eumeli etc. *Fragmenta*, Leipzig) opted for ordering the fragments according to Hesiod's lost works rather than to the ancient sources. But Marckscheffel had a predecessor: Henri Estienne's 1566 Geneva edition of the *Poëtae Graeci principes heroici carminis* was in fact the first to collect Hesiodic fragments (on pp. 134–135), and while it did not gather more than four (all from Athenaeus' *Deipnosophistae*) it did arrange them according to Hesiod's works (one from the *Catalogue* and three from the *Melampodia*).
83 Such as Benedetti (1976–1977), or van der Valk (1983), though both these essays are more narrowly focused on issues of textual criticism.
84 van der Valk (1971) xc-xci.
85 See *in Il.* 4.38–39 with van der Valk's apparatus.
86 See e.g. *in Il.* 194.31; where the ancient scholiasts (τινες τῶν παλαιῶν σχολιαστῶν τοῦ Ἡσιόδου) are overtly evoked as such; Tzetzes is never mentioned, but his exegesis (*in Hes. Op.* 32) probably stands behind the ἔνιοι who wrongly use ἀκτής in the masculine according to *in Il.* 868.31. More hidden cases of possible interaction can be detected.

quality and/or in the genre(s) or the style of his works; indeed, even the specifically genealogical information scattered throughout the *Theogony* is but rarely put to use in the explanation of Homer's tales.

Most of Eustathios' quotations from Hesiod's extant works have to do with lexical, morphological or syntactical issues, or else – and perhaps even more frequently – with ethical maxims to be gained from a close reading of the *Works and Days*. This conspicuous moral thrust also explains the good number of Hesiodic reminiscences in Eustathios' non-exegetical works, from his *Letters* down to his speeches and minor treatises: single passages of moral value could of course provide interesting material for the writer of Byzantine rhetoric, and proverbial or paradigmatic 'one-liners' could easily be evoked in speeches of various kinds.[87] The comparison with Homer does surface *hic illic* throughout the *Parekbolai*, often in the wake of suggestions in the ancient scholia,[88] but it often amounts to assigning the Askran poet a secondary role vis-à-vis his more illustrious contemporary, because of his pedantry (μικροπρέπεια),[89] the ambiguity of his vocabulary,[90] or his less effective style.[91] Eustathios, in other words, seems to

---

[87] Suffice it to consult the index of Eustathios' *opera minora* (ed. Wirth 2000) or that of his letters (ed. Kolovou 2006), where mostly proverbial *topoi* occur, in order to understand that Hesiod is the most frequently quoted ancient poet after Homer, on a par with the tragedians and Aristophanes. On the relationship between exegesis and rhetorical teaching in the case of Eustathios see Nünlist (2012).

[88] E.g. Eust. *in Il.* 263.6–12 (from Σ [b] B 494–877, quoting Plat. *Resp.* 393d-94d) on Hesiod's ἰδέα λόγου as being neither dramatic nor mimetic but mixed; Eust. *in Il.* 238.13–17 (from Σ [bT] B 360b) on the political skill of the men in power. But some of Eustathios' notes are in fact original, e.g. *in Od.* 1645.60–1646.3 with a comparison between Pandora's *pithos* of Elpis (Hes. *Op.* 94–104, also quoted in a Homeric context e.g. by Michael Psellos in *Philos. min.* 45.58 Duffy, probably in the wake of Σ [A and T] Ω 527–8ab) and the *askos* of the winds in *Od.* 10.9.

[89] See Eust. *in Il.* 613.5–10, where Hesiod's painstaking description of how to cut wood for carts (*Op.* 423–426) is deemed less effective than Homer's rapid and subtle hint in passing (ἐπιτρέχων καὶ ἐν παρέργωι) to such minutiae (the reference is to φήγινος ἄξων in *Il.* 5.838): Homer, Eustathios argues, pays more attention to the grander issues pertaining to heroes and heroic life. A similar stance appears in Eust. *in Il.* 501.37–38, where the swift comparison in *Il.* 4.482–87 is deemed more effective than the flat and boring prescriptions in Hes. *Op.* 455–457.

[90] Eust. *in Il.* 250.46–251.3 compares Homer's use of ἔργον as having a divine sanction (ὃ δὴ θεὸς ἐγγυαλίξει) in *Il.* 2.436 with Hesiod's potentially confusing use of the same word in the famous line ἔργον δ' οὐδὲν ὄνειδος, ἀεργίη δέ τ' ὄνειδος (Hes. *Op.* 311): Socrates, who repeated this motto again and again (Xen. *Mem.* 1.2.56–57), earned the fame of a relativist who praised activism regardless of its ethical purport, and this is because of the meaning of ἔργον. The same story, whose moral purport evidently appealed to Eustathios, is repeated in *Exeg. can. iamb.* 185.8–14 Cesaretti-Ronchey and, in a slightly different tone, in *De emend. vita monach.* 63.29–39 Metzler.

lack the deeply antagonistic dimension of the Hesiod-Homer confrontation that is so typical for Tzetzes (see above § 2).

Fragments of Hesiod's lost works do not play a major role in this context: Since they belong to works none of which had been preserved down to Eustathios' times, they could only be quoted at second hand, i.e. through the quotation of extant intermediary sources, and this process was more likely to happen in Eustathios' exegetical writings, rather than in his own creative prose.[92] However, there is at least one remarkable passage in which the archbishop not only shows an awareness of the existence and the nature of the *Catalogue of Women*, but also refers to it in order to back his idea of Homer's superiority: When commenting on Achilleus singing in his tent (the famous scene of *Il.* 9.189) in *in Il.* 745.47–50, he writes that the hero is singing κλέα ἀνδρῶν,

> οὐ μὴν γυναικῶν καταλόγου κλέα κατὰ τοὺς ἐν θηλυδρώδεσι κωμάζοντας μέλεσιν [ἢ καὶ κατὰ τὸν καλὸν Ἡσίοδον, ὅς Ὁμήρου, καθά τις παλαιὸς ἔφη, τὸν ἡρωϊκὸν ἀνδρῶνα σεμνύναντος, αὐτὸς ἐν τῶι τῶν ἡρωΐδων Καταλόγωι τῆς γυναικωνίτιδος γέγονε].

> Not the epic deeds of a catalogue of women, like the poets who revel in effeminate songs [or like good old Hesiod: according to an ancient author, while Homer had extolled the armory of the heroes, in his *Catalogue of Heroines* he became the master of the gynaeceum].

This is not an original observation: The first part of the sentence is taken wholesale from Σ (T) I 186, which tries to defend Achilleus from the charge of effeminacy; the rest, being a later addition penned by the author himself in the margins of his manuscript (the autograph *Laur.* 59.2–3), faithfully reports the argument made by Alexander the Great to his father Philip in Dio Chrysostom's account (*or.* 2.14 = Hes. T 57 Most).[93] This view of the *Catalogue*, however, ties in well with another passage where Eustathios insists on this poem as a foil for revealing Homer's superiority: In *in Od.* 1680.29 (on *Od.* 11.225; it is Hes. T 65 Most) we read that the *Nekyia* contains a catalogue of both male and female figures, not only of heroines as is the case with Hesiod. While this remark betrays an inevitable ignorance of the wider context and content of the lost epic poem, it also partially implies the archbishop's misogynist stance.

---

91 Hesiod's *Aspis*, for instance, originated from the 'envy for Homer', the ζῆλος Ὁμηρικός, but proved ultimately inadequate in comparison with its model: Eust. *in Il.* 1154.8–12 and 35–39; *in Il.* 1160.47.
92 A very short and selective survey of the quotations of Hesiod's fragments in Eustathios is offered by Schwartz (1960) 48–50.
93 On Alexander's judgment, see Scully (2015), chap. 4 n. 1; on Dio and Hesiod, see Hunter (2014) 1–20.

Most of the occurrences of Hesiodic fragments in Eustathios depend directly on the Homeric scholia. There are, however, a number of cases in which the Byzantine commentator decides to drop the reference to (or quotation from) Hesiod in the scholia, whether the latter concerns mythographical, genealogical or grammatical issues.[94] This phenomenon need not surprise us: It is clear that Eustathios adopts an utilitarian approach, lending Hesiod no peculiar *auctoritas*,

---

[94] Eust. *in Il.* 340.20–27 follows Σ (A) B 764 (Herodian) on the accent of ποδώκης, but does not quote the hemistich ποδώκης δῖ' Ἀταλάντῃ (fr. 73.2 and 76.5, 20 M-W. = *2.2 and *3.5,20 H = 47.2 and 48.5,20 Most). Eust. *in Il.* 661.47 is silent about the Hesiodic identification of Arne as a Boiotian city (Σ [T] H 9d1, with Hes. fr. 218 M.-W. = 166 Most). Eust. *in Il.* 750.44 refrains from evoking Hesiod (fr. 189 M.-W. = 132 Most) as the first to use the name "Argos" for the entire Peloponnese, as does the Σ (A) I 246. Eust. *in Il.* 816.37 disregards the hint in Σ (A) K 431a to Hesiod's and Homer's relative chronology on the basis of the name Μῄονες instead of Λυδοί (fr. 334 M.-W.). Eust. *in Il.* 837.55 does not invoke Hesiod's authority (fr. 314 M.-W. = 265 Most) on the meaning of ἄξυλος and ἀξυλίη (as does Σ [A] Λ 155b). Eust. *in Il.* 905.45 ignores the Hesiodic genealogy of Europa (fr. 140 M.-W. = 89 Most) contained in Σ (T) M 292–93. Eust. *in Il.* 971.47 tackles the issue of ἱππηλάτα / ἱππότα = φυγάς, but he does not follow Σ (A) Ξ 119a in quoting Hes. fr. 228 M.-W. (= *18 H = 173 Most) on the topic. Eust. *in Il.* 1053.21–22 on the name Polydore omits the reference to its occurrence in Hesiod (fr. 213 M.-W. = 153 Most, from Σ [T] Π 175c1). Eust. *in Il.* 1175.37 does not report that Hesiod (fr. 191 M.-W. = 134 Most) identified the wife of Sthenelus as Nikippe, daughter of Pelops (Σ [AT] T 116a). Eust. *in Il.* 1182.27 does not specify the Cretan origin of Lykomedes, which is known as Hesiod's version (fr. 202 M.-W. = 156 Most) from Σ [T] T 240. Eust. *in Il.* 1250.8 disregards Hes. fr. 328 M.-W. (= 278 Most) on the use of ἄφυζα as 'lion', quoted in Σ (AT) Φ 528b1. Eust. *in Il.* 1323.47–49 on the venue of Oedipus' death follows Σ (A) Ψ 679a, but not Σ (T) Ψ 679b (the latter has a reference to Hes. fr. 192 M.-W. = 135 Most). Eust. *in Il.* 1368.57 drops a Hesiodic line (fr. 316 M.-W. = 267 Most) on ὀπτάω and the action of cooking (quoted as a parallel in Σ [A] Ω 624). Eust. *in Od.* 1393.31, while dealing with Ogygia, does not mention Hes. fr. 204.60 M.-W. (= 155.60 Most) which appears in Σ α 85a. Eust. *in Od.* 1571.32 disregards the occurrence of Hes. fr. 337 M.-W. (= 285 Most; a line on the production of wheat) in Σ (EX) η 104. Eust. *in Od.* 1644.1 does not pick up the genealogy of Deukalion in Σ (H) κ 2 (Hes. frr. 4 and 9 M.-W. = 5 and 9 Most). Eust. *in Od.* 1713.40 does not dwell on the genealogy of Tyro (Jason from Aison and Polymela) in Σ (V) μ 69 (fr. 38 M.-W. = 37 Most). Eust. *in Od.* 1854.51 reports from Σ (HV) τ 34 that heroes did not make use of λύχνοι, but omits the reference to Hesiod fr. 341 M.-W. = 288 Most. Eustathios also disregards the Hesiodic lines on Demodoke (fr. 22.5–7 M.-W. = 14.5–7 H = 18.5–7 Most) transmitted by Porph. *Qu. Il.* 189.23 Schrader. We shall not consider here Hesiodic fragments that are not identified as such in the scholiastic source (frr. 60 and 240 M.-W. = 71 and 115 H = 239 and 181 Most), nor more problematic cases on the textual niveau (frr. 270 and 304.1 M.-W. = 206 and 254.1 Most). Eust. *in Il.* 882.16 omits a reference to fr. 17 M.-W. = 13 Most (Σ [A] Λ 750) on the genealogy of the Molionids, but fr. 18 M.-W. = 15 Most on the same topic is quoted immediately afterwards (see below).

and obviously not sharing in our modern enthusiasm for collecting fragments of lost ancient poems.⁹⁵

This said, there are quite a few instances in which Eustathios does pick up from his sources explicit references to passages of the *Catalogue*. In a minority of cases, he is our only extant source. Setting aside the so-called 'spurious fragments', i.e. false attributions to Hesiod that originated in mistakes of Eustathios' memory,⁹⁶ the true cases of one-source fragments are all to be explained by his having access to an intermediate source (most likely a scholium), now lost. The most useful distinction one can make among these quotations is thus less one of sources than one of typology: In order to exemplify Eustathios' preferences, we shall distinguish between fragments of grammatical/lexicographical and fragments of genealogical/mythographical content; for neither of these categories shall we offer a detailed discussion of all the relevant instances.

3.2 Hesiodic Fragments: Grammar and Vocabulary

According to Hesiod's *Catalogue*, Ileus, the father of the Lokrian Ajax, one of the protagonists of the war against Troy, was the offspring of Apollo (fr. 235 M.-W. = 112 H = 176 Most): This rare piece of information, delivered in five hexameters preserved by the Byzantine etymologica,⁹⁷ aroused the interest of Ioannes Tzetzes (see above § 2.2), but not that of Eustathios, who in *in Il.* 650.46 limited himself to a brief quotation of one and half lines out of the five (ll. 2–3), in order to establish the correct spelling of Ileus' name (vs. 'Oileus') and to link it etymologically with the adj. ἵλεως 'benign'.

---

95 On the development of this fashion, see e.g. Dionisotti (1997). For the case of Hesiod's fragments in particular, see below § 4.4.
96 When he assigns to Hesiod a 'Doric' form τέττορες (*in Od.* 1398.23 = Hes. fr. spur. 411), he is probably thinking of *Op.* 698 τέτορ' (see West [1966] 87; Eustathios believed, mostly in the wake of the ancient scholiasts, that Hesiod used Dorisms, see e.g. *in Il.* 558.21; *in Od.* 1759.32). When he credits Hesiod with the hemistich ὑπερβασίαι δ' ἀλεγειναί (*in Il.* 1318.7 = Hes. fr. spur. 386) he is probably confusing with the famous ending of the *Works and Days* (828) ὑπερβασίας ἀλεείνων. When he quotes (*in Il.* 124.37; see 447.26) the hemistich παῦροι δέ τε πατρὸς ἀρείους as being by Hesiod (fr. spur. 384), he certainly has in mind *Od.* 2.277. When he evokes Hesiod's authority for the role of springs as 'beginnings' (*in Il.* 1293.26 = fr. spur. 385), he is probably alluding to the role of πηγαί in *Th.* 736–38, whether or not this *rapprochement* was once contained in a lost scholium to *Il.* 23.148. When he attributes to Hesiod the story of Klymene's marriage with Helios (*in Od.* 1689.2 = fr. spur. 387), he is probably reflecting a wrong indication in Σ (V) λ 326.
97 *Etym. Gen.* s.v. Ἰλεύς (*Etym. Magn.* *470, 136–42); *Etym. Gud.* 276.41 Sturz (with Reitzenstein 1897, 161.4): the fragment once pertained to a commentary on Simonides (ἐν δ' Σιμωνίδου).

Who would not like to have some information on the infidelity of Tyndareos' daughters, amongst whom figure such prominent women as Helen and Clytaemestra? A scholium on Euripides' *Orestes* (249 = fr. 176 M.-W. = *8 H = 247 Most) preserves seven lines on this topic from Hesiod's *Catalogue* (or from the *Megalai Ehoiai*, as Hirschberger suggests), but of all this Eustathios (*in Il.* 125.3; 126.11; 797.46) appreciates only the paronomastic word-play (Φυλῆα φίλον) in line 4. Indeed, one might wonder whether the archbishop is drawing here on a repertoire of examples of the rhetorical figure of παρήχησις, rather than on the Euripides-scholium itself.

The fate of Proitos' daughters numbers among the cruellest punishments inflicted on characters of Greek myth: Eustathios (*in Od.* 1746.7) is our only witness for the three lines describing their leprosy and hair-loss (fr. 133.3–5 M.-W. = 49.3–5 H = 82.3–5 Most: ll. 1–2 are very fragmentarily preserved in POxy 2488 A), but following his declared (and lost) source, namely the grammarian Herodian,[98] he employs this quotation only to observe that the rare neuter noun κνῦος 'itch' in l. 3 is a verbal noun deriving from κνύω / κνύζω 'to scratch'. The archbishop states here explicitly that he is quoting from Hesiod's *Catalogue* (παρὰ Ἡσιόδωι ἐν Καταλόγωι περὶ τῶν Προιτίδων), and this is one of the very few times when he does so.

By contrast, Eustathios' only hint to the *Melampodia*, briskly described as a ποιημάτιον by Hesiod, is the reference to the peculiar spelling σκύπφος for σκύφος in fr. 271 M.-W. (= 207 Most; quoted by Athenaeus 11.498a-b), which provides a useful *comparandum* for Homer's famously irregular prosody of the word ὄφις in *Il.* 12.208 (see *in Il.* 900.16 and *in Od.* 1775.18).

These instances, as well as several other ones involving single words or expressions allegedly attested in Hesiod,[99] show that grammatical and lexical interests were often prominent over any other concern in Eustathios' consideration

---

[98] Hrd. *Cath. pros.* 1.445.15 Lentz: This passage, as Lentz's entire edition of the lost Καθολικὴ προσωιδία, is a mere modern reconstruction from fragments scattered in extant sources, in this case from Eustathios himself (Hirschberger's edition is misleading in this respect).

[99] See e.g. Eust. *in Il.* 265.4 on the orthography of the toponym Ὑρίη (from Σ [A] B 496: Hes. fr. 181 M.-W. = 87 H = 124 Most); *in Il.* 295.3 on the apocope in βρῖ (fr. 329 M.-W. = 279 Most, from Strabo 8.5.3, p. 364 C.); *in Il.* 631.4 and *in Od.* 1555.8 on the meaning of φυλλοχόος μήν (fr. 333 M.-W. = *31 H = 283 Most, from Pollux 1.231: but Eustathios omits Hesiod's name); *in Il.* 875.52 on the meaning of καλλιγύναιξ (fr. 277 M.-W. = 213 Most, from Athen. 13.609E; it is interesting to remark that Eustathios' comment starts from the variant reading καλλιγύναικα for πουλυβότειραν in *Il.* 11.770, see Σ [A] Λ 770b); *in Il.* 1337.32–34 on the Hesiodic attestation of μαχλοσύνη (fr. 132 M.-W. = 47 H = 81 Most, from Σ [A] Ω 25–30); *in Od.* 1424.6 on Megara being called σκιόεντα (fr. 204.48 M.-W. = 110.48 H = 155.48 Most, from Porph. *Qu. Od.* p. 22.9 Schrader, on *Od.* 1.365).

of our poet's fragments. It should be highlighted, however, that on the very first page of his commentary to the *Iliad* (*in Il.* 6.14) we find three lines of Hesiod illustrating the etymology of ῥαψῳδός from the verb ῥάπτειν, 'to weave' (fr. dub. 357 M.-W. = 297 Most): This fragment, no matter if evoked for mere grammatical purposes, and no matter if deemed spurious by most modern scholars today, is in fact a conspicuous autobiographical witness of Hesiod's *agon* with Homer in Delos, and thus a remarkable document of literary history in its own right.[100]

Finally, another linguistic observation – on the creation of patronymic forms such as Βουτάδης from the proper name Βούτης – leads Eustathios (*in Il.* 13.44) to a brief mention of Boutes as being the son of Poseidon (not of Pandion, as elsewhere in mythography, e.g. Apollod. *Bibl.* 3.14.8): This piece of information (Hes. fr. 223 M.-W. = 169 Most) is peculiar to the archbishop, and it is probably indebted to a lost grammatical source which is also the source of *Etym. Magnum* 210.7.[101] Here, once again, Eustathios, despite his primarily grammatical interest, insists that the genealogy of Boutes was stated by Hesiod ἐν Καταλόγωι: This leads us to consider now more closely the fragments quoted because of Eustathios' interest in genealogy.

3.3 Hesiodic Fragments: Genealogy and Mythography

That the *Catalogue of Women* should be invoked by later writers chiefly when the discussion of a genealogy is at stake is hardly surprising. The scholia present several such occurrences, and in many of them – including one where Tzetzes amplifies the exegesis in a display of all his erudition[102] – Eustathios simply summarizes the data he finds in earlier exegesis.[103] There are, however, some peculiar instances of Eustathios' *Vorgehensweise* with Hesiodic fragments.

---

[100] It has aroused multiple interpretations in modern scholarship: See the updated overview in Bassino (2013) 14–18.
[101] In Eustathios' passage, the part on the Eteoboutadai appears to have some connection with Harpocr. 75.13 Dind.; see also Schwartz (1960) 49–50.
[102] Eust. *in Il.* 21.14 on Agamemnon's genealogy from Pleisthenes rather than Atreus (Hes. fr. 194 M.-W. = 137 Most) is a simple transcription from Σ (D) Α 7, whereas Tzetzes, *in Il.* pp. 130.10–104.8, 210.8–12 Papath. (see Hes. fr. 137b-c, and above § 2.2) gives a much more detailed and fantastic genealogy for the generations in-between.
[103] See e.g. Eust. *in Il.* 882.27 and 1321.20 on the Molionians (from Σ [T] Λ 710 and Σ [A] Ψ 638–42: fr. 18 M.-W. = 15 Most, a fragment and a topic the archbishop will evoke again in *de emend. vita monach.* 25.5–6 Metzler); *in Il.* 1324.18 on Orsippos running naked at Olympia (from Σ [D] and [bT] Ψ 683b: fr. 74 M.-W. = 50 Most); *in Od.* 1494.12 on Apollo and Paeon as heal-

That Achilleus and Patroklos were cousins is common knowledge; but that Hesiod already endorsed this kinship is known only from fr. 212a M.-W. (= 147 Most), a passage of Eustathios' commentary on the *Iliad* (*in Il.* 112.45–113.1; on Patroklos' first appearance in the poem, *Il.* 1. 337) drawn from what the author calls a παλαιὰ ἱστορία. This formula is used in the *Parekbolai* for various pieces of ancient evidence, particularly mythographical tales:[104] In this case the genealogy of Menoitios' family (for which see e.g. Σ Pind. *Ol.* 9.104a and 106a-b) must derive, as van der Valk argued, from a scholium *ad locum* which has since been lost.

Maron is one of the descendants of Dionysos, but the details of his genealogy are rather confused in the extant scholia to the *Odyssey:* Σ (H) ι 197 Dind. presents him as the son of Dionysos' son Euanthes, whereas Σ (H) ι 198 Dind. (before Sittl's conjecture) reports that in Hesiod (fr. 238 M.-W. = 180 Most) he was the son of Dionysus' son Oinopion. Eustathios (*in Od.* 1623.44), who repeatedly shows a special interest for Maron (see *in Il.* 359.13), seems to choose yet another option, namely Maron as the son of Euanthes, who in his turn is the son of Dionysos' son Oinopion. It may well be that this is what Eustathios actually read in the Σ ι 198, if Sittl's integration of Euanthes' name in the scholium (p. 422.3 Dind.) hits the mark.

That Eustathios had a genuine interest in genealogy and mythography, even beyond the mere transcription of Homeric scholia, is proved by the way in which he dealt with the myth of Nestor's childhood in Gerenon / Gerena (*in Il.* 231.29): Not only did the Byzantine scholar draw on the D-scholium to *Il.* 2.336,[105] but he also resorted to Stephanus of Byzantium's *Ethnika* (γ 60 Bill.) in order to give some more precise geographical information about this mysterious city (fr. 34 M.-W. = 26c H = 34 Most) and to append three lines about the sad fate of Neleus' offspring (fr. 35.6–8 M.-W. = 26a.6–8 H = 33.6–8 Most, now in the middle of the fragment attested by POxy 2481, fr. 3).

Again in book 2 of the *Iliad*, the *Catalogue of ships* clearly opens up endless opportunities for a wide array of geographical, genealogical and mythographical explanations. The occurrence of the Kephisos river in *Il.* 2. 522 elicits the mention

---

ers (from Σ [V] δ 232a: fr. 307 M.-W. = 257 Most); Eust. *in Od.* 1567.64 on Arete being Alkinoos' sister (from Σ [V] η 54: fr. 222 M.-W. = 144 Most); Eust. *in Od.* 1685.62 (from Σ [V] λ 286) with the allusion to Neleus' children in fr. 33a, 12–19 M.-W. (= 25.12–19 H = 31.12–19 Most; now in the middle of POxy 2481, and attested in Σ Ap. Rhod. 1.156–60a); *in Od.* 1710.39 on the Sirens charming the winds (from Σ [V] μ 168: fr. 28 M.-W. = 25 Most).

104 E.g. Ptolemy the Quail in *in Il.* 78.45; Σ (D) B 581 in *in Il.* 293.37; Hellanicus (Σ [A] O 651) in *in Il.* 1036.1 (see van der Valk *ad loc.*) etc. See also Schwartz (1960) 49.

105 See on the topic the Σ γ 68d Pont. with the *apparatus testimoniorum*.

of its origin from Lilaia ('Hes.' fr. 70.18 M.-W. = 31.18 H = 41.18 Most) both in the D-scholium *ad loc.* and (hence) in Eustathios *in Il.* 275.16.[106] Stephanos of Byzantium (α 486 Bill.) is also Eustathios' sole source when he comments on the children of Orchomenos in *Il.* 2.511 (*in Il.* 272.18 = fr. 77* M.-W. = *17 H = 44 Most). In *Il.* 2.695 we find the mention of Phylake, one of the ancestors of Protesilaus, the first hero to die in the Trojan expedition: Eustathios (*in Il.* 323.44–324.1) quotes three lines from 'Hesiod's' *Catalogue* (fr. 62 M.-W. = 33a H = 62 Most) in order to illustrate the legendary speed in running of Phylakos' son Iphiklos. Here, too, it is likely that the archbishop is drawing on a lost source, a *scholium uberius* as Erbse puts it, because the extant scholia to the *Iliad* (and not even to that passage: Σ [bT] Y 227) only report l. 2 of the fragment, and in a different form.[107] Finally, *Il.* 2.608 contains a reference to Lykaon, whose παραιβασία against Zeus (fr. 164 M.-W. = 114 Most) is evoked by Eust. *in Il.* 302.19; however, one should not discard van der Valk's suggestion that we may be dealing here not with the myth of Lykaon, but with a simple quotation of the word παραιβασία, which also occurs in *Th.* 220.

The 'Geographer' *par excellence*, namely Strabo (1.2.34, p. 42.19 C.), provides crucial information on the antiquity of the name of Arabia and on the genealogy of Arabos and Thronia according to 'Hesiod' (fr. 137 M.-W. = 54 H = 88 Most; see Eust. *in Od.* 1464.83 on *Od.* 4. 84; see also Eust. *in Dion. per.* 927: the archbishop follows here his source in stressing that this information derives from the *Catalogue of Women*). And Strabo is implied in what is perhaps the most intriguing case of an Hesiodic fragment transmitted by Eustathios, namely that on the Danaids and the drought in Argos, quoted in his note on *Il.* 4.171 πολυδίψιον Ἄργος (*in Il.* 461.6). The line describing the miraculous intervention of the Danaids (fr. 128 M.-W. = 45a-b H = 76a-b Most) is preserved by Strabo (8.6.8, p. 371.15–17 C.) as Ἄργος ἄνυδρον ἐὸν Δανααὶ θέσαν Ἄργος ἔνυδρον, but in Eustathios the same line occurs with two diverging features: First and foremost, the attribution to Hesiod;[108] secondly, the wording Ἄργος ἄνυδρον ἐὸν Δαναὸς ποί-

---

[106] Here too, Eustathios provides an interesting variant: Λιλαίηθε(ν) προχέει (adopted in the text by M.-W. and Most) for Λιλαίῃσι προΐει of the D-scholium.
[107] The problematic issue is dealt with by Hirschberger (2004) 267, who prefers to detect here two different lines; see on the other hand Casadio (1977). At any rate, Eustathios' respect for his poetical source is shown by the fact that in his autograph ms. he left a blank space before the final hemistich of l. 3 καὶ οὐ σινέσκετο καρπόν, whether this reflected a lacuna in his antigraphon or his own deduction, on metrical grounds, that the first hemistich of l. 3 had gone lost at some stage of the textual transmission.
[108] This attribution also appears in an interlinear note on the Vatican palimpsest of Strabo, but it certainly did not belong to Strabo's original text: see Radt (2007) 461–462.

ησεν εὔυδρον, which changes both the subject and the entire structure of the line. These differences prevent us from believing (*pace* Erbse) that Eustathios may have used Strabo as his only source, and force us to conclude that he actually resorted to a different *Mittelquelle*, most probably a fuller version of the Σ (D) Δ 171, which in its present form contains what looks like a paraphrase of the Hesiodic line in the version attested by Eustathios, i.e. with Danaos as the subject.

The longest fragment of Hesiod's *Catalogue* to be found in the *Parekbolai* is fr. 305 M.-W. (= *11 H = 255 Most) on the genealogy of the mythical poet Linos, the son of Ourania and the grandson of Poseidon. The four hexameters constituting this fragment occur in *in Il.* 1163.62, and they derive *recta via* from the Σ (T) Σ 570c1; but, strikingly enough, the last of these lines (ἀρχόμενοι δὲ Λίνον καὶ λήγοντες καλέουσιν) receives a special intertextual exegesis in *in Il.* 1164.23, where Eustathios argues that the line

> Ὁμηρικοῦ μὲν ῥητοῦ ἤρτηται τοῦ 'ἐν σοὶ μὲν λήξω, σέο δ' ἄρξομαι' [I 97], σύμφωνον δὲ ἔχει καὶ τὸ 'τί κάλλιον ἀρχομένοις ἢ καταπαυομένοις ἢ τὸ ποθεινότατον;'[109]
>
> harks back to Homer's sentence 'I shall end with you, and with you I shall begin' [*Il.* 9.97], and has the same sense as the distich 'what is better than the most desired thing, for those who begin or for those who end?' [Dion. Chalc. fr. 6 West]

By any standard, a subtle stylistic remark.

3.4 Conclusions

Albeit anything but systematic, Eustathios' interest for catalogic poetry and its relationship with the Homeric masterworks does occasionally surface in his writings.[110] One might wonder, however, if the archbishop felt somewhat uneasy when dealing with fragments of a poem such as the *Catalogue of women*, structured around stories of sexual intercourse between mortal women and pagan gods.

A hint in this direction comes from what is perhaps the most spectacular genealogical doxography in the whole of the *Parekbolai*, namely the one concerning Arkeisios, Laertes, Odysseus, and finally Telemachos' marriage with Pol-

---

[109] See on this kind of formulas e.g. the commentary of Griffin (1995) 86.
[110] It might be argued that Hesiod is implied among οἱ μεθ' Ὅμηρον who proved inferior to Homer in the genre of catalogues according to *in Il.* 369.39–43 (the concluding lines of the exegesis on the *Catalogue of ships*).

ykaste and the birth of their son Persepolis: This lineage of descendance is secured for 'Hesiod' (fr. 221 M.-W. = *10 H = 168 Most) by Eustathios *in Od.* 1796.38 (on *Od.* 16.117–20), who heaps this piece of information about the *Catalogue* on top of other, partially quite diverse genealogies of the same family in the epic cycle (*Nostoi* and *Telegony*), in Sophocles, Aristotle and Hellanicus:[111] Eustathios' (probably mythographical) source remains unknown down to the present day.

However, at the end of this long catalogue of *Stammbäume*, the archbishop abruptly puts an end to this display of erudition, and rounds off the passage by a distich of dodecasyllables which almost attempts to disavow and obliterate his persisting interest in this kind of lurid pagan stories:

περιττὰ ταῦτα καὶ κενὴ μοχθηρία. / εἰ δ' οὖν στενῶς φράζοιντο, μικρὸν τὸ βλάβος.

'all this is superfluous, and vain evil; / if it is laid out in short, little will be the drawback'.[112]

4 Fr. 5 M.-W. and Greek Humanists in Italy

4.1 Generalities

As was mentioned above (§ 1), the popularity of Hesiod in the late Byzantine era was largely confined to his role in schools and to the editorial work performed on his poems: Planudes' scholia (and his important ms. *Laur.* 32.16, the first one to include the *Theogony* as well), Moschopoulos' commentary (and his curricular readings that also embraced the *Works and Days*), Triklinios' comprehensive edition, etc. In this context, there are virtually no traces of a specific attention paid to Hesiodic fragments, and this holds through to the mature age of Italian humanism.[113]

More work needs to be done in order to reconstruct the exact developments of this reception. For the time being, we shall point to a single instance in which

---

[111] See Hellan. fr. 156 Fowler (with Fowler's commentary).
[112] Maas (1952) 1, insisting on the unusual character of this *a parte*. For the *incipit* see e.g. Gal. *Diff. puls.* 8.497.6 K. περιττὰ γὰρ ταῦτα καὶ ἔξω τῆς ἡμετέρας τέχνης, but see also Basil. *Rebus mund. non adh.*, PG 31.548d, and often in John Chrysostom. For a similar idea see Eust. *in Dion. Per.* 205.7–8 Müller (about non-pertinent digressions in the exegesis to Dionysius) φιλοτιμία κενὴ καὶ φαύλη δοξοσοφία.
[113] Botley (2010) 100–102. See also the references in Wilson (1992) *ad indicem*.

the Byzantine and humanistic transmission of an important Hesiodic fragment has a bearing both on its editorial *facies* and on its ideological meaning.

4.2 Hes. fr. 5 M.-W. in John Lydos

This is *Cat*. fr. 5 in Merkelbach-West's edition (= 2 H = 2 Most), transmitted by John Lydos, *De mens*. 1.13, p. 7.22 Wünsch:

> τοσούτων οὖν ἐπιξενωθέντων τῆς Ἰταλίας, ὥσπερ ἐδείχθη, Λατίνους μὲν τοὺς ἐπιχωριάζοντας, Γραικοὺς δὲ τοὺς ἑλληνίζοντας ἐκάλουν, ἀπὸ Λατίνου τοῦ ἄρτι ἡμῖν ῥηθέντος καὶ Γραικοῦ τῶν ἀδελφῶν, ὥς φησιν Ἡσίοδος ἐν Καταλόγοις
>
> Ἄγριον ἠδὲ Λατῖνον (*Th*. 1013)
> <καὶ πάλιν>
> κούρη δ' ἐν μεγάροισιν ἀγαυοῦ Δευκαλίωνος
> Πανδώρη Διὶ πατρὶ θεῶν σημάντορι πάντων
> μιχθεῖσ' ἐν φιλότητι τέκε Γραικὸν μενεχάρμην.

> since so many people – as has just been shown – had wandered to Italy, they called the locals 'Latins', and the Greek-speaking people 'Graikoi', respectively from Latinus, whom we spoke of a little earlier, and Graikos, brothers, as Hesiod says in the *Catalogues*,
>
> 'Agrios and Latinos' (*Th*. 1013),
> and again,
> 'and a maiden in the halls of illustrious Deukalion,
> Pandora, who with Zeus the father, the commander of all the gods,
> having mingled in love, bore Graikos who delighted in remaining steadfast in battle'.

Due to their conspicuous place at the beginning of the genealogies, these lines have attracted a large body of scholarship. Modern critics disagree on a number of issues, above all their authenticity,[114] the nature and relevance of the hemistich Ἄγριον ἠδὲ Λατῖνον (a quotation of *Th*. 1013, as Merkelbach and later editors suppose, in the wake of Wilamowitz? the occasional note of an anonymous reader, as G. Hermann believed? the first words of the *Catalogue* fragment?), the identity of Pandora (the well-known Pandora sent to Epimetheus, or, as West and Hirschberger assume, a namesake character?), her relationship to Deukalion mentioned in the foregoing line (her husband? her father? her son-in-law?),[115]

---

114 Challenged by Niese, and defended by Wilamowitz, whose discussion (1962, 80–82) remains very helpful.
115 It is worth remarking that Eust. *in Il*. 23.41 τοὺς δὲ [scil. stones thrown by Deukalion's after the flood] τὴν γυναῖκα Πύρραν καὶ τὴν θυγατέρα Πανδώραν, ἣν Ἡσίοδος πρώτην γυναῖκά φησι has often been invoked as a witness to the genealogy of Pandora as Deukalion's daughter, pos-

and finally the role of Graikos, a character otherwise unknown to Greek mythology but taken here to be no less than the forefather of the Greeks (a role otherwise pertaining to Deukalion's other son, Hellen).

While not dwelling on these delicate and probably insoluble questions,[116] we shall try to draw attention to the transmission of the fragment's source, and then focus on its mysterious 'fourth line' as transmitted – per scholars and editions since Schultz[117] – by a marginal note in ms. *Matr.* 4607: καὶ Γραικὸς τὸν ἀδελφὸν ἐς Ἄγριον ἠδὲ Λατῖνον.

First of all, Lydos' text. The first book of the *de mensibus*, a treatise devoted to issues of comparative chronology and chronography, has come down to us not in its entirety, but only through numerous excerpts preserved in several manuscripts. As it happens, our fragment is known from a single independent witness, namely *Vat. Barb. gr.* 194 (Wünsch's A), a manuscript that watermarks and historical considerations help date safely within the 1480s:[118] This is the text of the *Barberinianus*, the sole basis for every speculation on the transmission of our fragment:

τοσούτων οὖν ἐπιξενωθέντων τῆς Ἰταλίας, ὥσπερ ἐδείχθη αὐτοῖς, Λατίνους μὲν τοὺς ἐπιχωριάζοντας, Γραικοὺς δὲ τοὺς ἑλληνίζοντας ἐκάλουν, ἀπὸ Λατίνου τοῦ ἄρτι ἡμῖν ῥηθέντος καὶ Γραικὸς τῶν ἀδελφῶν, ὥς φησιν Ἡσίοδος ἐν Καταλόγοις

ἄγριον εἶδε Λατῖνον
κούρη δ'ἐν μεγάροισιν ἀγαυοῦ Δευκαλίωνος
Πανδώρη Διὶ πατρὶ θεῶν σημάντορι πάντων
μιχθεῖσα ἐν φιλότητι τέκε Γραικὸν μενεχάρμην.[119]

John Lydos, the antiquarian and historian of Roman culture of the Justinianic age,[120] is clearly trying to show here that East and West belonged together:

---

sibly implied by this fragment, although this is far from certain: See Hirschberger (2004) 174–175 and the perplexity uttered by Casanova (1979b) 181–182.
116 A nice overview of the different solutions proposed by scholars is provided by Casanova (1975), and (more succinctly) by Hirschberger (2004) 171–172.
117 Schultz (1910) 11 and 132.
118 Amongst A's apographs the only interesting codex is *Par. gr.* 3094, a 17th-century book written by Emery Bigot, for which, *pace* Wünsch, there is no need to believe that it had access to a different witness: See Ferreri (2002) 205 and note 63, with many integrations to the textual history of the *De mensibus*.
119 Accents and spirits are misplaced in the first hemistich, which may in fact read something like ἀγριοῖειδε. The reading Γραικός for Γραικοῦ in l. 3 of Lydos' prose introduction should be remarked.
120 See Maas (1992) esp. 53–66 for the 'antiquarian' dimension of the *De mensibus*.

His reference to Hesiod therefore carries an ideological bias, for the brother-relationship between Latinos and Graikos is paramount to the construction of a shared identity between the Greek and the Roman world in an age when the political unity of the empire had been severed by history, and Justinian was attempting to revive it in some form.[121]

We shall not discuss here whether this genealogical link between Greeks and Latins was in fact already present in the *Catalogue of Women*, at least in the version Lydos was reading;[122] what is certain is that in the form reconstructed by Hesiod's editors, the link between Graikos and Latinos is conspicuously missing from the text. Precisely this *crux* – aggravated by the conflict with the *Theogony* tradition according to which Latinos is Kirke's son, and Graikos is Pandora's[123] – has pushed scholars of the last two centuries to attempt bold reconstructions of Lydos' wording, starting from the collocation of the first three words Ἄγριον ἠδὲ Λατῖνον. If we simply disregard and expunge this hemistich, we lose the mention of the forefather of the Latins; if we consider it a quotation from Hes. *Th.* 1013 (the offspring of Odysseus and Kirke: Agrios would thus become a proper name, to be written with capital alpha), we do get a glimpse of the Greek genealogy of Latinos, but we miss a clear connection with Graikos, or with the Deukalionids in general; if we consider the hemistich as belonging to the line immediately preceding κούρη δ' ἐν μεγάροισι, the textual proximity does not satisfactorily explain the syntactical and conceptual link between the two accusatives and Pandora's genealogy; alternatively, we might follow West, who proposed to transpose the hemistich (or parts of it) after l. 3.[124]

In what follows, we shall argue that the embarassment caused by the lack of a clear connection between Latinos and Graikos was not new when felt by modern scholars. Indeed, it was this very embarassment that gave rise to the 'fourth

---

121 See Hirschberger (2004) *ad loc.*, also concerning the choice of Graikos (whence the Latin term *Graecus* derives) instead of Hellen. The attempt of Dräger (1997) 27–41 (esp. 31–32) to read Lydos' passage in a different way (i.e. as not implying that Graikos and Latinos were brothers) rests on an utterly impossible syntactical interpretation, and on an inadequate knowledge of the ms. transmission.
122 As it happens, few scholars seem to have taken into account the interesting arguments in support of an early contact between East and West put forth by Jameson – Malkin (1998).
123 Casanova (1975) 128, who then resorts to the hypothesis that the lines were inserted in the text by an anonymous annotator wishing to contradict (rather than to support) Lydos' argument: This is far-fetched, and has found little support among scholars.
124 West believes that Lydos misunderstood ἄγριος in l. 4 as a proper name, and thus arbitrarily connected these lines with *Th.* 1013, where Latinos is also mentioned. A more straightforward alteration had been proposed by Mützell, who re-wrote l. 4 as ἄγριον, ἠδὲ Λατῖνον ἀμύμονά τε κρατερόν τε: See Casanova (1975) 126–127.

line' mentioned above, which has so far been dismissed by editors as *"sensu carens"*.¹²⁵

4.3 Ianos Laskaris

Thanks to the pioneering research of Luigi Ferreri,¹²⁶ we now know that ms. *Barb. gr.* 194 was first used in Florence in May 1491 by Angelo Poliziano as a source for the excerpts from John Lydos penned in his 'zibaldone', now ms. *Par. gr.* 3069:¹²⁷ unsurprisingly, Poliziano did not miss the opportunity to transcribe Hesiod's fragment, exactly in the same form as in the *Barb.*¹²⁸ More important, from Poliziano's notes we learn that in 1491 the owner of the *Barberinianus* was the celebrated Greek humanist Ianos Laskaris, who might have acquired it during his first book hunt in Greece (fall 1490-early 1491), or else in Italy, perhaps during his wanderings in Ferrara, Padua and Venice in the late 1480s.¹²⁹

Ianos Laskaris himself made use of Lydos' *de mensibus* in his public oration in support of Greek studies held in Florence in October or November 1493.¹³⁰ As in other speeches of the same genre, in this remarkable Latin text Laskaris wished to highlight the antiquity of Greek culture, and – this is something that will not feature e. g. in Pietro Bembo's or Scipione Forteguerri's later orations – its superiority vis-à-vis Roman culture.¹³¹ When it comes to stressing the original kinship between Greeks and Latins, Laskaris exclaims (ll. 141–151):

> 'Quid quod Italus et ipse Oenotrius, quid quod Latinus Graecus genere et Graeci frater ipsius, si credis Hesiodo, ut a duobus fratribus fraterna sint denominata genera? Haec auctores vestri ab Hesiodo referunt:
>
> κούρη δ' ἐν μεγάροισιν ἀγαυοῦ Δευκαλίωνος
> Πανδώρη Διὶ πατρί, θεῶν σημάντορι πάντων,
> μιχθεῖσ' ἐν φιλότητι τέκε Γραικὸν μενεχάρμην
> καὶ Γραικὸς τὸν ἀδελφὸν ἐς ἄγριον εἶδε Λατῖνον.

---

125 'Quite meaningless... and should be ignored' (West 1966, 434). Hirschberger and Most barely mention it.
126 Ferreri (2002) esp. 204–211.
127 On this manuscript see most recently Silvano (2010).
128 Save for εἶδε not εἴδε, and τέκεν not τέκε. Poliziano's 'zibaldone' was neither accessible to nor consulted by scholars for a long time after his death.
129 Ferreri (2002) 207–212. Laskaris was later to lend the manuscript to the Calabrian humanist Aulo Giano Parrasio: See particularly Formentin (2010).
130 Meschini (1983). This reference has escaped so far all editors of Hesiod.
131 See Gastgeber (2014); Lamers (2015) 167–195.

> Illustris virgo sub tectis Deucalionis
> Pandore divum patri commixta tonanti
> atque hominum domino Graecum produxerat acrem,
> et fratrem durum inspexisti, Graece, Latinum'.

Hesiod's *auctoritas* is crucial for Ianos Laskaris in order to show that Greeks and Romans share a common origin since the earliest times: This is why he must overcome the aforementioned problem concerning the lack of a clear statement of kinship between Graikos and Latinos in Hesiod's fragment as transmitted by Lydos. The fourth line of the fragment is thus fashioned by Laskaris *suo Marte* through a small intervention on the wording of Lydos' sentence as it appears in the *Barberinianus*:[132] καὶ Γραικὸς τῶν ἀδελφῶν ἄγριον εἶδε Λατῖνον becomes καὶ Γραικὸς τὸν ἀδελφὸν <ἐς> ἄγριον εἶδε Λατῖνον (indeed, in his first attempt he had chosen the preposition ἐπ' rather than ἐς: in either case, we have a highly unusual tmesis of the verb ἐσεῖδε - or ἐπεῖδε -, "*inspexisti*" as the Latin goes).[133]

This is not the place to speculate on the reference to Graikos rather than Hellen as the forefather of the Greeks: It should be kept in mind that Γραικός was often (if not always) perceived by the Byzantines as a slightly pejorative ethnonym vis-à-vis Ἕλλην (or, in political terms, Ῥωμαῖος); in humanistic times, attitudes toward this name were rather ambivalent and mainly still negative.[134] Be that as it may, Ianos Laskaris' adoption of Hesiod's genealogy bolstered his argument and prepared the ground for his overt exaltation of Greek culture as essential in all fields of knowledge.[135]

---

[132] This had already been seen by West (1966) 434 (followed by Hirschberger 2004, 172), although he only knew Wünsch's text (not the *Barberinianus*) and only Konstantinos Laskaris' version of the line (for which see below § 3.4). Dräger (1997) 27–40, who takes the line seriously, also believes it originated from some misunderstanding of Lydos' words, but his interpretation of the textual evidence is misleading.

[133] See Meschini's apparatus criticus *ad loc.*, registering the variants of Laskaris' earlier (autograph) draft in ms. *Vat. gr.* 1414 (ff. 1r-40v: here, f. 9r), which also had a different wording for the Latin rendering of l. 4: '*Et Graecus* [then corrected into *durum*] *fratrem vidit mox deinde Latinum*'. Meschini's text (with a faulty Γραῖκος for Γραικός) is based on the "clean" copy from *Vat. gr.* 1414 contained in ms. *Riccard.* 3022 (ff. 36r–63v: here, f. 42r).

[134] See on the topic Kaldellis (2007) *passim* (esp. 115 note 224), and for the humanistic period Lamers (2015) 64–72.

[135] See the penetrating analysis by Lamers (2015) 173–180 (on p. 175 n. 43 some partly correct comments on our fragment).

4.4 Konstantinos Laskaris

Having shown that the creation of l. 4 of our fragment was far from a senseless initiative by some uneducated scribe, and rather proceeded from a clear ideological choice of one of the most prominent Greek scholars of Western humanism, I now turn to the other witness of Hesiod's fragment containing this line, which is also the only one hitherto known to scholars and editors. Ms. *Matritensis* 4607 is a book that belonged to the Greek humanist Konstantinos Laskaris (no family relationship with Ianos can be established, nor did the two entertain any contact during their long stays in Italy),[136] and it contains above all Hesiod (with Tzetzes' and Proclus' exegesis) and Theocritus.[137] Except for an older core belonging to the early 15th century (ff. 54–66), all the rest of the manuscript was written by Konstantinos Laskaris himself, partly (ff. 1–131) in Milan in the early 1460s, and partly (the bucolic section in ff. 133–53) during his later years in Messina.[138]

Now, on f. 113r of the *Matritensis* we find the end of Hesiod's *Theogony*, in Konstantinos Laskaris' hand: the text once closed with l. 1020, then Laskaris himself added, in red ink, the two final lines 1021–1022, which notoriously introduce the *Catalogue of Women* (they correspond to fr. 1.1–2 M.-W., as attested also by POxy 2354),[139] and then the conclusive note τέλος τῆς Θεογονίας Ἡσιόδου. Below this note we find another addition, this time in K. Laskaris' later hand (i.e. the same handwriting we find in the Theocritus section of ms. 4607 in ff. 133–153).[140] The note is introduced by the indication Ἡσιόδου καὶ ταῦτα,

---

136 See Martinez Manzano (1994) 162–163 (= 1998, 170), against the idea that the two should be brothers.
137 See the descriptions by De Andrés (1974) 108–111 (to be integrated with Martinez Manzano [1994] 319, 181 and 134 [= (1998) 78 n. 5 and 132] esp. for the Nicander excerpts on ff. 85–88); Corrales Pérez (1994) 41 (and 209–19 on the philological value of the *Scutum* section); Schultz (1910) 11. The subscription on f. 153v reads Κωνσταντίνου τοῦ Λασκάρεως καὶ ὁ κόπος καὶ τὸ κτῆμα. On the scholia of the *Matritensis* see di Gregorio (1971).
138 That the final quires belong to the later years of Laskaris' stay in Messina (1465–1501) is confirmed by the watermarks (*fleur de lys* type 7312 Briquet, dated to 1479–82, but not identical), and by the handwriting: See De Andrés (1974) 110; Martinez Manzano (1994) 260 n. 21 and 319. Galán Vioque (2006) 42; Botley (2010) 219 n. 420.
139 On these two lines and their fate in manuscripts (they figure at the end of the *Theogony* in Vat. gr. 915, the second-oldest of our mss., and are sometimes added *après coup* in other codices) see West (1966) 437, as well as the apparatus of Solmsen *ad loc*. A proper inquiry on their presence in manuscripts still has to be carried out.
140 Examples in Martinez Manzano (1994) plates xxxiii–xxxv (= 1998, plates 9–10). Gallavotti (1999) 70–72 tentatively assumes on philological grounds that this section should in fact go back to the 1460s. But the Messina years were a time when K. Laskaris displayed a strong interest in archaic epic: See also Montanari (1979) 46 and 65–71 on ms. *Matritensis* 4629.

and it transmits precisely fr. 5 M.-W. of Hesiod's *Catalogue*, equipped with the fourth line in the form καὶ Γραικὸς τὸν ἀδελφὸν ἐς ἄγριον ἠδὲ Λατῖνον.

It is impossible that this textual *facies*, which mirrors so closely the one adopted by Ianos Laskaris in his 1493 oration,[141] should have been conceived independently by Konstantinos Laskaris in Messina (to cast away any doubt, there is no evidence that he was acquainted first-hand with the very rare text of John Lydos' *de mensibus*). Furthermore, we have seen that Ianos' source was the *Barberinianus* itself, so it is impossible to postulate a common source. We are thus left with the certainty that Ianos created the line and that Konstantinos simply received and propagated this innovation in his manuscript. Unfortunately, we are not in a position to reconstruct the channel by which Konstantinos came to know of this fragment. The idea of his trip to Florence in the 1490s, once envisaged by A. Diller on other grounds, is now mostly discarded by scholars.[142] And neither of the two extant manuscripts of Ianos Laskaris' oration ever arrived so far south (the *Riccardianus* never left Florence, and *Vat. gr.* 1414 followed Laskaris in his adventurous life). We might surmise that a role was played by Konstantinos' pupil Pietro Bembo, who must have been interested in this kind of orations *de studiis Graecis* (he delivered one in Venice in 1494–95),[143] and might therefore have had Ianos Laskaris' text sent to him in Messina, where he spent no less than two years (1492–1494) at Konstantinos' school.[144]

Be that as it may, as a humanist who had made such significant contributions to the learning of Greek in Europe (the Greek grammar known as *Erotemata* was the first Greek book to be published in the West in 1476), Konstantinos Laskaris must have been very sensitive to a fragment uniting Greeks and Latins at such a high mythographical level. His only preserved erudite works, two historical overviews on the writers of Sicily and Calabria, also attest to a sense of continuity between the Greek and the Roman taditions,[145] and so does his attention to the penetration of Latin vocabulary in Greek speech since the age of Constan-

---

[141] The only difference, ἠδέ for εἶδε, may have been prompted by the confusion with *Th.* 1013 which is to be found a few lines above on the same page.

[142] See Diller (1957) 179, contradicted by Martinez Manzano (1994) 16 note 51 (= 1998, 12 note 35). But see also *ibid.* 272 (= 1998, 194–195) on the issue of the manuscript of Gorgias' works allegedly seen by Laskaris in Florence. What K. Laskaris writes in his letter to Bembo of June 1494 (Martinez Manzano 1994, 29–30 = 1998, 24–25) basically rules out any journey of his in that period.

[143] See Wilson (2003).

[144] We know from Bembo's correspondence that Laskaris was on friendly terms with the Florentine Angelo Poliziano: Martinez Manzano (1994) 27–28 (= 1998, 26). Or one might suspect another one of his many pupils, listed by Martinez Manzano (1994) 25 (= 1998, 21).

[145] See Cohen-Skalli (2014), with updated bibliography on Laskaris.

tine the Great;[146] in the preface to his grammar, he boasts having taught in various Italian cities πολλοὺς ὠφελήσας Γραικοὺς καὶ Λατίνους.[147]

If Konstantinos Laskaris was thus deriving his knowledge from Ianos, he was not doing so in a passive way. And we might still credit him with a special, original merit: he was the first known scholar to unite on the same page what is now fr. 1 M.-W. = H = Most (of course limited to ll. 1–2; the rest is known to us today only through papyrological evidence) and what is now fr. 2 H = Most (= 5 M.-W.) of Hesiod's *Catalogue*. Whether this choice was made with some philological awareness or not, is impossible to tell. To the best of our knowledge, that the last two lines of the *Theogony* (1021–1022) should in fact introduce to the *Catalogue of Women* (the work to which Lydos openly ascribes the fragment he is quoting – a fragment whose position towards the beginning of the poem is ensured beyond doubt by the mention of Pandora), was first explicitly stated by Friedrich August Wolf (*Theogonia Hesiodea*, Halae Saxonum 1783), then more clearly by C. Göttling (*Hesiodi Carmina*, Lipsiae 1831).[148]

But perhaps the first to understand this continuity was the first Latin translator of the *Theogony*, namely the Italian scholar Bonino Mombrizio, who concluded his Ferrara 1474 Latin version of the poem (printed 21 years before the *princeps* of the Greek text) by adding 10 lines of his own invention where he complained about the loss of such an exciting text as the *Catalogue of Women*: 'O modo tam digno cur me fortuna fefellit / Codice, materia cur me privavit honesta? / An quo iam merito vatem fraudaret honore / neve suum decus esse suo furiata labori / ferret, et Ascraeas ea nollet vivere musas?/ Nos ea Romanis an quod convertere verbis / noluit? ah si sic quanti puto conscia diva es, / aemula Mombritium nolis emergere nomen. / Quae te causa movet? sunt quae nos multa valemus / scribere, sunt studiis accommoda plurima nostris'.[149]

Bibliography

Allegrini, S. (1971–1972). 'Note di Giovanni Tzetzes ad Eschilo', in: *Annali della Facoltà di Lettere e Filosofia dell'Università degli studi di Perugia* 9, 221–223.
Basilikopoulou-Ioannidou, A. (1971). Ἡ ἀναγέννησις τῶν γραμμάτων κατὰ τὸν ΙΒ′ αἰῶνα εἰς τὸ Βυζάντιον καὶ ὁ Ὅμηρος, Athens.
Bassino, P. (2013). *Certamen Homeri et Hesiodi*, Ph.D. Diss., University of Durham.

---

146 See Lamers (2015) 95–98, and Martinez Manzano (1994) 171.7–11.
147 'Being useful to many Greeks and Latins': See Martinez Manzano (1994) 199.71–72.
148 Göttling attributed the two lines to an interpolator. See also Fabricius – Harles (1790) 589.
149 On Mombrizio see most recently Raschieri (2011).

Benedetti, F. (1976–1977). 'De Eustathii grammatici studiis Oppianeis', in: *Annali della Facoltà di Lettere e Filosofia dell'Università degli studi di Perugia* 14, 431–441.

Bianconi, D. (2005). *Tessalonica nell'età dei Paleologi. Le pratiche intellettuali nel riflesso della cultura scritta*, Paris.

Botley, P. (2010). *Learning Greek in Western Europe*, Philadelphia.

Braccini, T. (2009–2010). 'Erudita invenzione: riflessioni sulla *Piccola grande Iliade* di Giovanni Tzetzes', in: *Incontri triestini di filologia classica* 9: 153–173.

Browning, R. (1975). 'Homer in Byzantium', in: *Viator* 6: 15–33 (= *Studies on Byzantine History, Literature and Education*, London 1977, no. XVII).

Browning, R. (1992a). 'The Byzantines and Homer', in R. Lamberton and J. J. Keaney (eds.), *Homer's Ancient Readers. The Hermeneutics of Greek Epic's Earliest Exegetes*, Princeton, 134–148.

Browning, R. (1992b). 'L'insegnante', in: G. Cavallo (ed.), *L'uomo bizantino*, Rome and Bari, 132–169.

Budelmann, F. (2002). 'Classical Commentary in Byzantium: John Tzetzes on Ancient Greek Literature', in: R. G. Gibson and C. Shuttleworth Kraus (eds.), *The Classical Commentary: Histories, Practices, Theory*, Leiden, 141–169.

Cameron, A. (2004). *Greek Mythography in the Roman World*, Oxford.

Cannatà Fera, M. (2012). 'Giovanni Tzetzes e i "giambi" di Archiloco (fr. 215 W. = 20 T.)', in: D. Castaldo, F. G. Giannachi, and A. Manieri (eds.), *Poesia, musica e agoni nella grecia antica*, Atti del IV Convegno internazionale ΜΟΙΣΑ (Lecce, 28–30 October 2010), Galatina, 694–710.

Cardin, M. (2009). 'Heroogonia. Il *Catalogo delle donne* di Giovanni Tzetzes', in: *Philologus* 153: 237–249.

Cardin, M. (2010). 'L'*ehoia* di Egina e le Asopidi nel *Catalogo delle donne* esiodeo', in: E. Cingano (ed.), *Tra panellenismo e tradizioni locali: generi poetici e storiografia*, Alessandria, 151–210.

Casadio, V. (1977). 'Hes. fr. 62 M.-W.', *Museum Criticum* 10–12: 7–9.

Casanova, A. (1975). 'Un'aporia in Giovanni Lido (de mens. I 13)', *Maia* 27: 125–131.

Casanova, A. (1979a). '*Catalogo, Eèe* e *Grandi Eèe* nella tradizione ellenistica', *Prometheus* 5: 217–240.

Casanova, A. (1979b). *La famiglia di Pandora*, Florence.

Cesaretti, P. (2010). 'Tzetzes, John', in: A. Grafton, G. W. Most, and S. Settis (eds.), *The Classical Tradition*, Cambridge MA, and London, 957.

Cingano, E. (2009). 'The Hesiodic Corpus', in: F. Montanari, A. Rengakos, and C. Tsagalis (eds.), *Brill's Companion to Hesiod*, Leiden and Boston, 91–130.

Cohen, I. M. (1983). *The Hesiodic Catalogue of Women. Studies on the Fragments of an Early Greek Epic*, Ph.D. Diss., University of Toronto.

Cohen, I. M. (1986). 'The Hesiodic *Catalogue of Women* and the *Megalai Ehoiai*', *Phoenix* 40: 127–142.

Cohen-Skalli, A. (2014). 'De Byzance à Messine: les *Vitae Siculorum* de Constantin Lascaris, leur genèse et leur tradition', *Revue d'Histoire des Textes*, 9: 79–116.

Colonna, A. (1953). 'I *Prolegomeni* ad Esiodo e la *Vita esiodea* di Giovanni Tzetzes', *Bollettino del comitato per la preparazione della edizione nazionale dei classici greci e latini* 2: 27–39.

Corrales, Y. (1997). 'La actividad en los centros de copia de los monasterios del Atos (siglos XI-XII): algunas consideraciones a la luz de los fragmentos del *Par. suppl. gr.* 663', in: P. Bádenas – A. Bravo – I. Pérez Martín (eds.), Ἐπίγειος οὐρανός. *El cielo en la tierra. Estudios sobre el monasterio bizantino*, Madrid: 171–181.
Corrales Pérez, Y. (1994). *Die Überlieferungsgeschichte des pseudohesiodeischen* Scutum Herculis, Ph.D. Diss., University of Hamburg.
Cullhed, E. (2014). *Eustathios of Thessalonike. Parekbolai on Homer's* Odyssey *1–2*, Ph.D. Diss., University of Uppsala.
De Andrés, G. (1974). *Catálogo de los códices griegos de la Biblioteca Nacional*, Madrid.
Dahlén, C. (1933). *Zu Johannes Tzetzes' Exegesis des hesiodeischen* Erga, Uppsala.
Degni, P. (2008). 'I manoscritti dello "scriptorium" di Gioannicio', *Segno e testo* 6: 179–248.
Derenzini, G. (1979). 'Demetrio Triclinio e il Codice Marciano Greco 464', *Scrittura e civiltà* 3: 223–241.
Di Gregorio, L. (1971). 'Sulla tradizione manoscritta degli *scholia vetera* alla *Teogonia* di Esiodo I. Le copie del Marc. gr. 464 (= 762), II. La famiglia del Vat. gr. 1332, III. I codici contaminati', *Aevum* 45: 1–24, 187–207, 383–408.
Di Gregorio, L. (1972). 'Sulla tradizione manoscritta degli *scholia vetera* alla *Teogonia* di Esiodo IV. Conclusioni', *Aevum* 46: 1–15.
Diller, A. (1957). 'The Manuscripts of Pausanias', *Transactions and Proceedings of the American Philological Association* 88: 169–188.
Dionisotti, A. C. (1997). 'On Fragments in Classical Scholarship', in: G. W. Most (ed.), *Collecting fragments / Fragmente sammeln*, Göttingen: 1–33.
Dräger, P. (1997). *Untersuchungen zu den* Frauenkatalogen *Hesiods*, Wiesbaden.
Fabricius, J. A. – G. Chr. Harles (1790[4]), *Bibliotheca Graeca*, I, Hamburg.
Ferreri, L. (2002). 'I codici parrasiani della Biblioteca Vaticana, con particolare riguardo al *Barberiniano greco* 194, appartenuto a Giano Lascaris', in: G. Abbamonte, L. Gualdo Rosa, and L. Munzi (eds.), *Parrhasiana* II, Atti del II Seminario di studi su Manoscritti medievali e umanistici della Biblioteca Nazionale di Napoli (Naples, 20–21 October 2000), Naples, 189–223.
Flach, H. (ed.) (1876). *Glossen und Scholien zur hesiodischen* Theogonie *mit Prolegomena*, Leipzig.
Flusin, B. (2008). 'L'insegnamento e la cultura scritta', in: J.-C. Cheynet (ed.), *Il mondo bizantino*, II, Turin: 363–395.
Formentin, M. R. (2010). 'Un nuovo codice di Giovanni Lido, autografo di Aulo Giano Parrasio', in: M. d'Agostino and P. Degni (eds.), *Alethes philia. Studi in onore di G. Prato*, II, Spoleto: 401–408.
Fryde, E. B. (2000). *The Early Palaeologan Renaissance (1261–c. 1360)*, Leiden and Boston.
Galán Vioque, G. (2006). 'Un nuevo testimonio de Nicandro, *Theriaca*, vv. 933–958', *Emerita* 74: 41–46.
Gastgeber, Chr. (2014). 'Griechischstudium im italienischen Humanismus. Eröffnungsvorträge des Demetrios Chalkondyles zum Griechischlehrgang in Padua 1463 und 1464', *Jahrbuch der Österreichischen Byzantinistik* 64: 67–104.
Gallavotti, C. (1999). *Theocritea*, Rome.
Grandolini, S. (ed.) (1991). *Manuelis Moschopuli Commentarium in Hesiodi Opera et dies*, Rome.
Griffin, J. (1995). *Homer. Iliad Book 9*, Oxford.

Grünbart, M. (2005). 'Byzantinisches Gelehrtenelend – oder: Wie meistert man seinen Alltag?', in: L. M. Hoffmann (ed.), *Zwischen Polis, Provinz und Peripherie. Beiträge zur byzantinischen Geschichte und Kultur*, Wiesbaden, 413–426.
Harder, Ch. (1886). *De Ioannis Tzetzae Historiarum fontibus quaestiones selectae*, Kiel.
Hilgard, A. (ed.) (1894). *Theodosii Alexandrini Canones. Georgi Choerobosci scholia. Sophronii Patriarchae Alexandrini excerpta, Grammatici Graeci* IV.1–2, *Prolegomena*, Leipzig.
Hirschberger, M. (2004). *Gynaikōn Katalogos und Megalai Ēhoiai. Ein Kommentar zu den Fragmenten zweier hesiodeischer Epen*, Munich and Leipzig.
Hunger, H. (1953). 'Zum Epilog der Theogonie des Johannes Tzetzes', *Byzantinische Zeitschrift* 46: 302–7 (= *Byzantinische Grundlagenforschung*, London 1973, no. XVIII).
Hunter, R. (2014). *Hesiodic Voices. Studies in the Ancient Reception of Hesiod's Works and Days*, Cambridge and New York.
Jameson, M. H. – Malkin, I. (1998). 'Latinos and the Greeks', *Athenaeum* 86: 475–485.
Jeffreys, E. (2014). 'The sebastokratorissa Irene as Patron', in: L. Theis, M. Mullett, and M. Grünbart (eds.), *Female Founders in Byzantium and Beyond*, Vienna, 177–194.
Jeffreys, M. J. (1974). 'The Nature and Origins of the Political Verse', *Dumbarton Oaks Papers* 28: 143–195 (= E. M. Jeffreys and M. Jeffreys, *Popular Literature in Late Byzantium*, London 1983, no. IV).
Kaldellis, A. (2007). *Hellenism in Byzantium. The Transformation of Greek Identity and the Reception of the Classical Tradition*, Cambridge and New York.
Kaldellis, A. (2009). 'Classical Scholarship in Twelfth-Century Byzantium', in: Ch. Barber and D. Jenkins (eds.), *Medieval Greek Commentaries on the Nicomachean Ethics*, Leiden and Boston, 1–43.
Kolovou, F. (ed.) (2006). *Die Briefe des Eustathios von Thessalonike*, Munich and Leipzig.
Koning, H. H. (2010). *Hesiod: The Other Poet. Ancient Reception of a Cultural Icon*, Leiden and Boston.
Krumbacher, K. (1897). *Geschichte der byzantinischen Literatur*, Berlin.
Lamers, H. (2015). *Greece Reinvented*, Leiden-Boston.
Lemerle, P. (1971). *Le premier humanisme byzantin. Notes et remarques sur enseignement et culture à Byzance des origines au Xe siècle*, Paris.
Leumann, M. (1950). *Homerische Wörter*, Basel.
Leone, P. L. M. (1984). 'I *Carmina Iliaca* di Giovanni Tzetzes', *Quaderni catanesi di studi classici e medievali* 6: 377–405.
Leone, P. L. M. (ed.) (2007). *Ioannis Tzetzae Historiae*, Galatina (LE).
Lucà, S. (1993). 'I Normanni e la rinascita del XII secolo', *Archivio storico per la Calabria e la Lucania* 60: 1–91.
Luzzatto, M. J. (1998). 'Leggere i classici nella biblioteca imperiale: note tzetziane su antichi codici', *Quaderni di storia* 48: 69–86.
Luzzatto, M. J. (1999). *Tzetzes lettore di Tucidide. Note autografe sul Codice Heidelberg Palatino Greco 252*, Bari.
Luzzatto, M. J. (2000). 'Note inedite di Giovanni Tzetzes e restauro di antichi codici alla fine del XIII secolo: il problema del Laur. 70, 3 di Erodoto', in: G. Prato (ed.), *I manoscritti greci*, Atti del V Colloquio Internazionale di Paleografia greca (Cremona, 4–10 October 1998), Florence, 633–654.
Maas, M. (1992). *John Lydus and the Roman Past*, London and New York.

Maas, P. (1952). 'Verschiedenes zu Eustathios', *Byzantinische Zeitschrift* 45: 1–3.
Magnelli, E. (2003). 'Reminiscenze classiche e cristiane nei tetrastici di Teodoro Prodromo sulle Scritture', *Medioevo Greco* 3: 181–194.
Martano, A. (2002). 'Scolii e glosse allo *Scudo di Eracle* del manoscritto Ambrosiano C 222 inf.', *Aevum* 76: 151–200.
Martano, A. (2005). 'La tradizione manoscritta dell'esegesi antica allo *Scudo di Eracle* esiodeo: la famiglia del Vat. Gr. 1332 (sec. XIII-XIV)', *Aevum* 79: 461–490.
Martano, A. (2006). 'L'esegesi antica allo *Scudo di Eracle* nell'*Etymologicum Genuinum* e *Gudianum*', *Memorie dell'Accademia Roveretana degli Agiati* 256: 85–119.
Martano, A. (2008). 'La tradizione manoscritta dell'esegesi antica allo *Scudo di Eracle* esiodeo: due gruppi di codici (sec. XIV–XVI)', *Aevum* 82: 543–580.
Martin, J. (1956). *Histoire du texte des Phénomènes d'Aratos*, Paris.
Martin, J. (ed.) (1974). *Scholia in Aratum vetera*, Stuttgart.
Martinez Manzano, T. (1990). *Konstantinos Laskaris*, Hamburg.
Martinez Manzano, T. (1998). *Constantino Láscaris*, Madrid.
Mazzucchi, C. M. (2000). 'Una curiosa legatura epsilon-iota nel codice Ambrosiano C 222 inf.', in: S. Lucà (ed.), *Omaggio a Enrica Follieri*, Grottaferrata, 203–207.
Mazzucchi, C. M. (2003). 'Ambrosianus C 222 inf. (Graecus 886): il codice e il suo autore. Parte prima: il codice', *Aevum:* 263–275.
Mazzucchi, C. M. (2004). 'Ambrosianus C 222 inf. (Graecus 886): il codice e il suo autore. Parte seconda: l'autore', *Aevum* 78: 411–440.
Menchelli, M. (2001). 'Nota paleografica a un Platone medio-bizantino: un copista "indoctus" e due codici di Minoïde Mynas (Par. suppl. gr. 663 e 668)', *Scrittura e civiltà* 25: 145–165.
Mergiali, S. (1996). *L'enseignement et les lettrés pendant l'époque des Paléologues (1261–1453)*, Athens.
Meschini, A. (1983). 'La prolusione fiorentina di Giano Làskaris', in: *Umanesimo e Rinascimento a Firenze e Venezia*, III, Florence, 69–113.
Migliorini, T. (ed.) (2010). *Gli scritti satirici in greco letterario di Teodoro Prodromo: introduzione, edizione, traduzione e commento*, Ph.D. Diss., University of Pisa.
Mioni, E. (1965). *Catalogo di Manoscritti Greci esistenti nelle biblioteche italiane* I, Rome.
Mioni, E. (1985). *Codices Graeci manuscripti Bibliothecae Divi Marci Venetiarum. Thesaurus antiquus II. Codices 300–625*, Rome.
Montanari, F. (1975). *Studi di filologia omerica antica I*, Pisa.
Morgan, G. (1983). 'Homer in Byzantium: John Tzetzes', in: C. A. Rubino and C. W. Shelmerdine (eds.), *Approaches to Homer*, Austin, 165–188.
Nünlist, R. (2012). 'Homer as a Blueprint for Speechwriters', *Greek, Roman and Byzantine Studies* 52: 493–509.
Pertusi, A. (1950). 'Intorno alla tradizione manoscritta degli scolii di Proclo ad Esiodo I. II Cod. Vat. gr. 38 ed il Cod. Marc. gr. IX 6, II. Il Cod. Paris. gr. 2771 (A)', *Aevum:* 10–26, 528–544.
Pertusi, A. (1951). 'Intorno alla tradizione manoscritta degli scolii di Proclo ad Esiodo III. Il Cod. Vat. gr. 904 (Q), IV. Proclo e non Proclo, V. Scolii planudei e bizantini inediti alle *Opere*', in: *Aevum* 25: 20–8, 145–59, 267–78, 342–52.

Pertusi, A. (1952). 'Intorno alla tradizione manoscritta degli scolii di Proclo ad Esiodo VI. Il Cod. Genav. 45 (Γ) e la classe b, VII. Il contributo degli scolî di Proclo al testo de "Le opere e i giorni"', *Aevum* 26: 131–146, 197–227.
Pertusi, A. (1953). 'La tradizione manoscritta degli scoli alle Opere e i Giorni e le note inedite attribuite a Massimo Planude', in: *Atti dello VIII Congresso internazionale di Studi Bizantini* (Palermo, 3–10 aprile 1951), Rome, 177–182.
Podestà, G. (1945). 'Le satire lucianesche di Teodoro Prodromo, I', *Aevum* 19: 239–252.
Pontani, A. (ed.) (1999). *Niceta Coniata. Grandezza e catastrofe a Bisanzio*, II, Milan.
Pontani, F. (2005). *Sguardi su Ulisse. La tradizione esegetica greca all'Odissea*, Rome.
Pontani, F. (2006). 'The First Byzantine Commentary on the *Iliad*: Isaac Porphyrogenitus and his Scholia', *Byzantinische Zeitschrift* 99: 551–596.
Pontani, F. (2015). 'Scholarship in the Byzantine Empire (529–1453)', in: F. Montanari, S. Matthaios, and A. Rengakos (eds.), *Brill's Companion to Ancient Greek Scholarship* I. *History. Disciplinary Profiles*, Leiden and Boston, 297–455.
Ponzio, A. (2003). 'Gli scolî di Tzetze agli *Erga* di Esiodo. Elementi per la costituzione del testo e rapporto con il commentario plutarcheo', in: P. Volpe Cacciatore (ed.), *L'erudizione scolastico-grammaticale a Bisanzio*, Atti della VII Giornata di studi bizantini (Salerno, aprile 2001), Naples, 129–147.
Radt, S. (ed.) (2007). *Strabons Geographika*, VI, Göttingen.
Raschieri, A. A. (2011). 'Bonino Mombrizio traduttore dell'*Epitome* grammaticale di Costantino Lascaris', in: A. Balbo, F. Bessone, and E. Malaspina (eds.), *Tanti affetti in tal momento*, Alessandria, 741–753.
Reitzenstein, R. (1897). *Geschichte der griechischen Etymologika*, Leipzig.
Rhoby, A. (2010). 'Ioannes Tzetzes als Auftragsdichter', *Graeco-Latina Brunensia* 15: 155–170.
Roilos, P. (2014). '"Unshapely Bodies and Beautifying Embellishments": The Ancient Epics in Byzantium, Allegorical Hermeneutics, and the Case of Ioannes Diakonos Galenos', *Jahrbuch der Österreichischen Byzantinistik* 64: 231–246.
Romano, R. (ed.) (1999). *La satira bizantina dei secoli XI-XV*, Turin.
Ronconi, F. (2007). *I manoscritti greci miscellanei. Ricerche su esemplari dei secoli IX-XII*, Spoleto.
Russo, C. F. (ed.) (1965²). *Hesiodi Scutum*, Florence.
Russo, G. (1992). *Contestazione e conservazione: Luciano nell'esegesi di Areta*, Berlin and Boston.
Schultz, H. (1910). *Die handschriftliche Überlieferung der Hesiod-scholien*, Berlin.
Schultz, H. (1913). 'Zur Nebenüberlieferung der Hesiodscholien', *Nachrichten von der königlichen Gesellschaft der Wissenschaften zu Göttingen* 2: 252–263.
Schwartz, J. (1960). *Pseudo-Hesiodeia. Recherches sur la composition, la diffusion et la disparition ancienne d'oeuvres attribuées à Hésiode*, Leiden.
Scully, S. (2015). *Hesiod's* Theogony. *From Near Eastern Creation Myths to* Paradise Lost, Oxford and New York.
Silvano, L. (2010). *Angelo Poliziano. Appunti per un corso sull'Odissea*, Alessandria.
Speranzi, D. (2014). 'Silloge di poeti greci esametrici', in: D. Lippi (ed.), *Animalia. Gli uomini e la cura degli animali nei manoscritti della Biblioteca Medicea Laurenziana*, Florence, 108–109.
Stefec, R. S. (2014). 'Aspekte griechischer Buchproduktion in der Schwarzmeerregion', *Scripta* 7, 205–234.

Turyn, A. (1972). *Dated Greek Manuscripts of the Thirteenth and Fourteenth Centuries in the Libraries of Italy*, Urbana.
Uhlig, G. (1883). *Dionysii Thracis Ars grammatica, Grammatici Graeci* I.1, Leipzig.
van der Valk, M. (ed.) (1971). *Eustathii Archiepiscopi Thessalonicensis Commentarii ad Homeri Iliadem pertinentes*, I, Leiden.
van der Valk, M. (1983). 'Eustathius and Callimachus', *Greek, Roman and Byzantine Studies* 24: 367–373.
Vian, F. (ed.) (1963). *Quintus de Smyrne. La suite d'Homère*, I, Paris.
Wendel, C. (1940). 'Das unbekannte Schluszstück der *Theogonie* des Tzetzes', *Byzantinische Zeitschrift* 40: 23–26.
Wendel, C. (1948). 'Tzetzes. Johannes', *RE* VII A.2: 1959–2010.
West, M. L. (1964). 'The Medieval and Renaissance Manuscripts of Hesiod's *Theogony*', *The Classical Quarterly* 14: 165–189.
West, M. L. (ed.) (1966). *Hesiod. Theogony*, Oxford.
West, M. L. (1974). 'The Medieval Manuscripts of the *Works and Days*', *The Classical Quarterly* 24: 161–185.
West, M. L. (ed.) (1978). *Hesiod: Works and Days*, Oxford.
West, M. L. (2001). *Studies in the Text and Transmission of the Iliad*, Munich and Leipzig.
von Wilamowitz-Moellendorff, U. (1962). *Kleine Schriften*, IV, Berlin.
Wilson, N. G. (1983). 'A Mysterious Byzantine Scriptorium: Ioannikios and his Colleagues', *Scrittura e civiltà* 7: 161–176.
Wilson, N. G. (1992). *From Byzantium to Italy*, London.
Wilson, N. G. (1996[2]). *Scholars of Byzantium. Revised Edition*, London.
Wilson, N. G. (ed.) (2003). *Pietro Bembo. Oratio pro litteris Graecis*, Messina.
Wirth, P. (ed.) (2000). *Eustathii Thessalonicensis Opera minora*, Berlin and New York.

List of Contributors

Antonio Aloni (24 Jan. 1947–5 Jan. 2016) was Professor Emeritus of Greek Literature at the University of Turin. The themes of his publications were performance, especially its relation to genre, and its social and political contexts. He took a particular interest in the sixth century and Athens' impact on the history of Greek verse. He was also a scholar of lyric and an expert on elegy. Among his numerous publications are: *L'aedo e i tiranni. Ricerche sull'inno omerico a Apollo* (1989); *L'elegia greca e l'epigramma: dalle origini al V secolo* (2007, with A. Iannucci); an article on elegy in *The Cambridge Companion to Greek Lyric* (2009).

Marta Cardin was trained in Greek Philology at Ca' Foscari University (Venice) and at the Scuola Normale Superiore (Pisa). She has held research grants from Ca' Foscari and from the Fondazione Giorgio Pasquali (Pisa), and has been a researcher in the national research program 'Homer, Hesiod, Pindar, Aeschylus: forms and transmission of the ancient exegesis' ('FIRB', 2014–2016). She has published papers on fragmentary Hesiodic poetry and its transmission, and is currently working on a new critical edition of Ioannes Tzetzes' commentary to Hesiod's *Works and Days*.

Malcolm Davies has been Professor of Greek and Latin Literature at Oxford since 2014 and a Fellow of St John's College, Oxford since 1978. He has published on early Greek epic, early Greek lyric, Greek tragedy and comedy, and Greek insects, and has recently branched out into epigraphy. His most recent book (2016) is on the *Aethiopis*. He has just finished a new text with full English commentary on the lesser and anonymous Greek lyric fragments, to be published with OUP.

Andrea Ercolani is Research Fellow at the Istituto di Studi sul Mediterraneo Antico (ISMA) of the Consiglio Nazionale delle Ricerche (CNR). He has published several essays on ancient Greek literature (on lyric poetry, tragedy, comedy, and archaic epic). His most recent works are the monograph *Omero. Introduzione allo studio dell'epica greca arcaica* (2006) and the edition, with commentary, of Hesiod's *Works and Days* (2010).

Hugo Koning is teaching Greek and Latin at Leiden University. His main interests are Hesiod, mythology, early philosophy and early epic. In 2010, he published a book on the ancient reception of Hesiod (*Hesiod: The Other Poet*). He is currently working, with Glenn Most, on an edition with translation of all the ancient exegetical texts on the *Theogony*.

Irini Kyriakou teaches Ancient Greek at the University of Cyprus. She is a member of the research center AnHiMA. She recently completed her PhD, *Naming the Female Ancestors. The Function of Genealogies in Greek Epic Poetry*, at the École des Hautes Études en Sciences Sociales (Paris).

Andreas N. Michalopoulos is Professor of Latin at the National and Kapodistrian University of Athens. He is the author of: *Ancient Etymologies in Ovid's* Metamorphoses: *A Commented Lexicon* (Leeds, 2001), *Ovid,* Heroides *16 and 17: Introduction, Text and Commentary* (Cambridge, 2006), *Οβίδιος. Ηρωίδες 20–21, Ακόντιος και Κυδίππη (εισαγωγή, κείμενο, μετάφραση, σχόλια*

(Athens, 2014). His research interests include: Augustan poetry, ancient etymology, Roman drama, and Roman novel.

Kirk Ormand is the Nathan A. Greenberg Professor of Classics at Oberlin College. He is the author of *Exchange and the Maiden: Marriage in Sophoclean Tragedy* (1999), *Controlling Desires: Sexuality in Ancient Greece and Rome* (2009), and *The Hesiodic* Catalogue of Women *and Archaic Greece* (2014), editor of *A Companion to Sophocles* (2012) and co-editor (with Ruby Blondell) of *Ancient Sex: New Essays* (2015). He has published articles on Homer, Hesiod, Hipponax, Sophocles, Euripides, Ovid, Lucan, the Greek novel, Clint Eastwood's *Unforgiven*, and Michel Foucault.

Filippomaria Pontani teaches Classical Philology at the University of Venice Ca' Foscari. He has published widely on Classical, Byzantine, and modern Greek literature, focusing on issues of manuscript transmission as well as on the history of philology, grammar, rhetoric, geography, and astronomy, writing on authors ranging from Aeschylus to Callimachus, from Sappho to Catullus, from Demosthenes to Eustathios of Thessalonike, from Planudes to Cavafy. His main ongoing project is a new edition of the Greek scholia to Homer's *Odyssey* (vols. 1–3, Rome 2007–2015).

Benjamin Sammons holds a Ph.D. in Classics from New York University. He is the author of *The Art and Rhetoric of the Homeric Catalogue* (Oxford, 2010) and various articles on Greek epic, tragedy and historiography. A new book on lost Greek epics, entitled *Device & Composition in the Greek Epic Cycle*, will be published by Oxford in 2017. He teaches in the Classics program at Queens College, City University of New York.

Deborah Steiner is the John Jay Professor of Greek at Columbia University. Her publications include books and articles on Homer (most recently a commentary on books 17 and 18 of the *Odyssey* in the Cambridge Greek and Latin Classics series), choral lyric ('Harmonic Divergence: Pindar's fr. 140b and early fifth-century choral polemics', *JHS* 2016), iambic poetry ('Making Monkeys: Archilochus frr. 185–187 W. in Performance', 2016), and intersections between the literary and visual tradition in archaic and early classical Greece ('The Priority of Pots: Pandora's *pithos* re-viewed', *Mètis* 2013). She is completing a book entitled *Constructing the Greek Chorus: choral performances in the art, texts, technology and social practices of archaic and early classical Greece*, to appear with CUP.

Christos Tsagalis is Professor of Greek at the Aristotle University of Thessaloniki and co-editor (with Jonathan Ready) of the journal *Yearbook of Ancient Greek Epic*. His research interests include Homer, Hesiod, the Greek Epic Cycle, fragmentary Greek epic, and Greek epigram. He is the author of the following monographs: *Epic Grief: Personal Laments in Homer's* Iliad (2004); *Inscribing Sorrow: Fourth-Century Attic Funerary Epitaphs* (2008); *The Oral Palimpsest: Exploring Intertextuality in the Homeric Epics* (2008); *From Listeners to Viewers: Space in the* Iliad (2012); *Ομηρικές μελέτες: προφορικότητα, διακειμενικότητα, νεοανάλυση* (2016); *Early Greek Epic Fragments: Genealogical and Antiquarian Epic* (2017).

General Index

Aigina 55, 58, 63–64, 66–71, 74–77, 83, 92
Aiolos (Aiolids) 20 n. 61, 85, 104 n. 21, 138, 147, 158–159, 163 167–171, 174–176, 178, 181–183, 185–186, 188–189, 257
ancestor 55, 84–85, 135, 138, 143 n. 35, 145–147, 149–150, 153, 155–159, 168, 226, 239, 271
Asopids 47–48, 55, 62, 64–65, 68–69, 71–78
assonance 60, 192–213
– alliteration (word-initial rhyme) 60, 192–195, 197, 206, 208–209, 211, 213
– complex cases 193, 202, 204
  – formula-bounded aural elements interacting with other features 213
  – long-range aural association 210–212
  – middle-range aural association 208–210
  – progressively-developed aural associations 204–205
  – short-range aural association 205–208
– syllabic repetition or near-repetition of final syllables 193, 203
– syllabic repetition or near-repetition of stem syllables 192, 199–203
– vocalic repetition 192, 194–199, 210 n. 46
Astronomia 42, 46, 255

birth 21, 23–24, 57, 61, 91, 93, 101, 104, 108, 112, 115, 136, 143–145, 147, 149–159, 168, 170–172, 176–178, 183, 185–186, 210, 222, 224, 227–228, 233, 235, 257–258, 273
Byzantine philology 247, 250

catalogue(s) / *Catalogue of Women* 4, 6, 19–25, 33, 47–62, 71, 73–79, 83–84, 86, 92–93, 99–109, 111, 113, 115–116, 118, 120–123, 126–133, 135–153, 156–159, 163–167, 169–178, 181–183, 185, 187–189, 191–193, 197, 201, 206–208, 210, 213, 219–239, 251–252, 257–260, 263, 265, 267–274, 280–281
catalogue poetry 55, 191–192, 213, 228
Cheironos Hypothekai 4, 37, 40–41, 46.
chorus 47–57, 59–69, 72–74, 77–78.
Comnenian age 245, 248, 252

Deianeira 109, 179, 182

ehoia/ehoiai/ ἠ' οἵη expression 165, 167, 171 n. 27, 175, 182–183, 188–189
eidolon 122–133
etymology 86–88, 91, 151 n. 57, 196 n. 18, 202–203, 254, 256–257, 267, 269
Eustathios 263–272

folklore 85
folktale 11

gender 33, 61, 77, 113, 135–136, 138, 142–143, 229, 236
genealogy 8, 20, 75, 136–137, 163–165, 170, 173, 187, 189, 226–227, 229 n. 54, 232–234, 236, 239, 250, 253, 257, 259, 266, 269–272, 274, 276, 278
grammar 128, 212, 245–246, 267–269, 280–281

Helen 20, 50–53, 57, 68, 77, 93, 99–100, 105–108, 112–113, 115–116, 119–123, 125, 127–132, 146–147, 150–151, 153, 176–177, 180–182, 194, 196, 206, 209, 221, 224, 229–230, 232 n. 65, 237 n. 76, 268
Herakles 21–22, 24 n. 71, 78, 88, 99–100, 103, 108–113, 159, 166, 179–182, 193, 196, 199, 201, 206, 212, 254
heroes 22, 24–25, 50–51, 57, 69, 75–77, 86, 99–102, 104–113, 136, 139–140, 142, 145, 147, 152, 158, 163–164, 169, 173, 180, 185, 189, 220, 222, 224, 227, 229, 236, 252, 258, 264–266
Humanism (in the West) 273, 279

indirect tradition 156
intertextuality 116–118, 120, 131

Keykos gamos 30–33, 46
kinship 48, 55, 135
Klytaimestra 149–152, 156, 175, 177–178, 181–182, 194

Laskaris
– Ianos 277–279
– Konstantinos 279–281
Lydos (John) 274–277

Megala Erga 35, 38–41, 46
Melampodia 4, 33–37, 46, 248, 261, 263, 268
Mestra 101, 106, 138, 140, 157–158, 185–189, 193, 197, 201
myth 8–9, 72, 77, 100, 104–105, 112, 117, 120, 122, 126, 132, 154, 165–166, 173, 180–181, 219, 222, 230, 234, 250, 258, 260, 268, 270–271
mythography 248, 253–254, 257–258, 260–262, 266–267, 269–270, 273, 280

Ovid 88–89, 91–92, 133, 171, 181–182, 187, 219–225, 227–235, 237–239
– *Heroides* 133, 171 n. 26, 219–227, 230–231, 234–239

paradigm/paradigmatic 10, 15, 31, 60, 62, 65, 73, 165–167, 172–177, 180–182, 185, 187–189, 222 n. 26, 255, 264

quotation 87, 117 n. 8, 122, 247 n. 8, 250 n. 20, 254–258, 261–268, 271, 274, 276

reception 116, 219, 246–248, 273
reuse 16, 24

sacrifice 3, 37, 39–41, 83–84, 100, 121, 125–127, 131, 150–151, 178
Stesichorus 88, 93, 115–116, 119–127, 129–133

traditional wisdom 29, 33, 37, 43
Troy 49, 54, 85, 88, 110–111, 115, 119, 123, 127, 150, 224, 256–257, 267
Tzetzes 252–263

Zeus 3, 6, 8, 20–21, 23–24, 36, 49, 56, 65–68, 70, 75, 77, 83–85, 87–88, 90–92, 100–111, 113, 138–139, 150, 153–156, 164, 166, 170, 172–174, 176, 178, 180–184, 186, 196–197, 199–200, 205–207, 209–212, 224, 226, 228–229, 231, 254, 258, 261, 271, 274

www.ingramcontent.com/pod-product-compliance
Lightning Source LLC
Chambersburg PA
CBHW031723230426
43669CB00007B/221